The Transformers Generation One

More than meets the eye!

V. 2

War and Peace

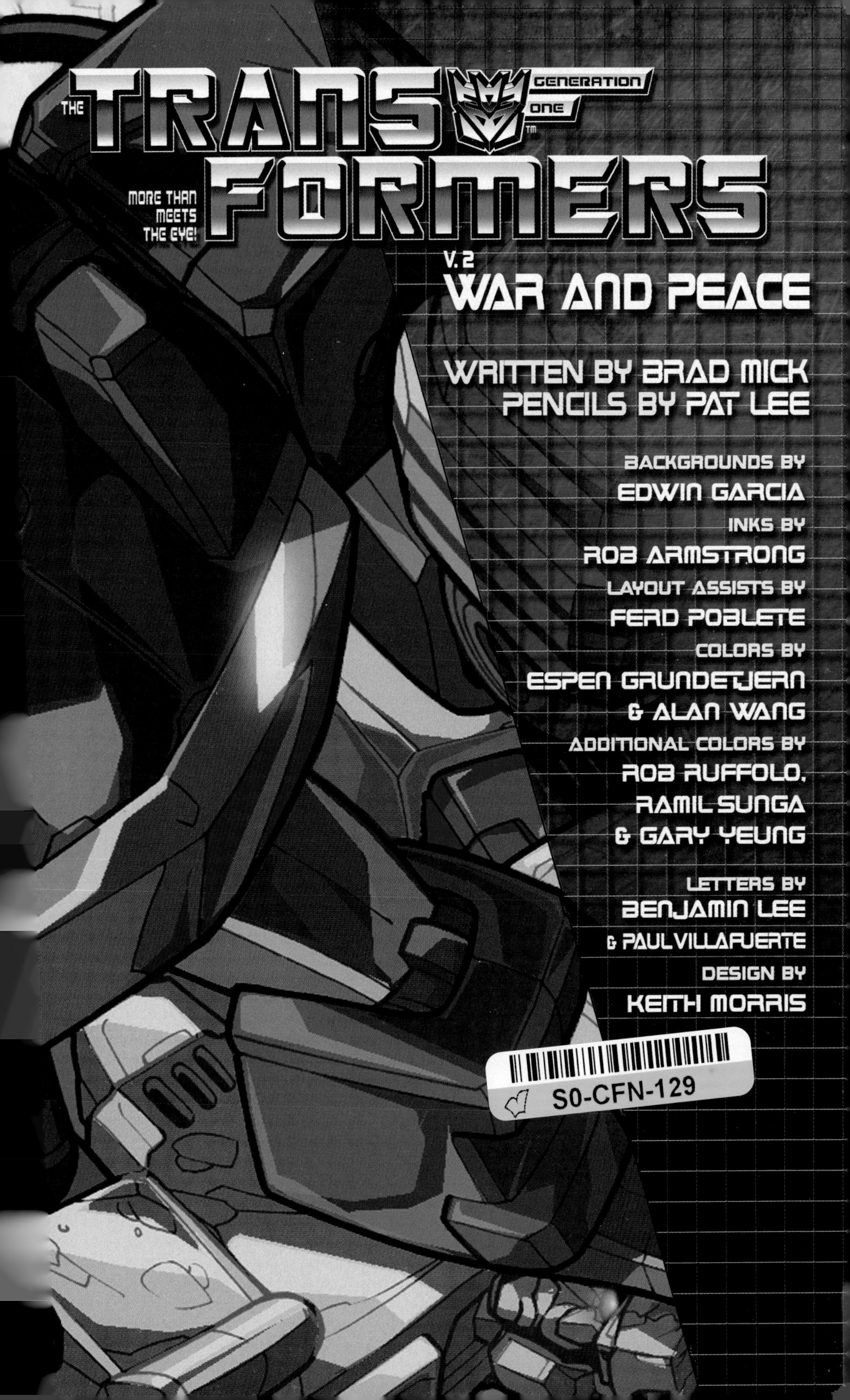

Written by Brad Mick

Pencils by Pat Lee

Backgrounds by
Edwin Garcia

Inks by
Rob Armstrong

Layout assists by
Ferd Poblete

Colors by
Espen Grundetjern
& Alan Wang

Additional colors by
Rob Ruffolo,
Ramil Sunga
& Gary Yeung

Letters by
Benjamin Lee
& Paul Villafuerte

Design by
Keith Morris

FOREWORD BY
SIMON FURMAN

Writer of *TRANSFORMERS ENERGON*
and *TRANSFORMERS: WAR WITHIN*

Who the $@&% is Brad Mick?

I'm sorry, but that was my initial reaction to the news item about Dreamwave's second *G1* volume, *"War and Peace"*. Drawn by Pat Lee... well, good. Great, in fact! Safe hands, if ever there were. But written by Brad Mick?!

I guess the problem, really, is throughout its 20-year history, there have (Chris Sarracini aside for the moment) really only been two *TRANSFORMERS* (comics) scriptwriters. Myself and Bob Budiansky (with, initially, Jim Salicrup and Ralph Macchio). So I'm always deeply suspicious of new writing talent. It's almost as if someone's intruding on my own private playground. It's a really bad attitude, and I'm working on it.

Of course, with such a limited pool of writing talent it's kind of inevitable (desirable even…healthy certainly) that things open up a bit. I was pleasantly surprised by Chris Sarracini's work on the f rst Dreamwave *G1* series, so perhaps Brad Mick would also shine. But…Brad Mick! Who's he? What's he ever done? All the old fears and prejudices started to bubble up again.

Along came the f rst issue. Mm, okay…pretty damn interesting 'high concept', I'll give him that. What if the war (on Cybertron) was over and the *TRANSFORMERS* on Earth never knew? What if the architect of this newfound peace was none other than the ultra-logical Decepticon, Shockwave? Hmm. I read on. Scourge—interesting! Grimlock—nicely in-character! Prime—suitably heroic and conf icted! Subsequent issues followed (not nearly fast enough for my liking), and suddenly we're on Cybertron (cool!), and he's back…and oh, it's him…and look it's…!!!!

I was hooked. Whoever Brad Mick was, he knew his stuff. The issues were teeming with revisionist continuity, well thought out back-story and downright, double take-inducing shocks. And what was more incredible (and pleasing to me) was that the guy could write, could tell a story, could characterize well (across a big cast!). So many can't. *"War and Peace"* is packed to the rafters with great action, crowd-pleasing moments, and essential *TRANSFORMERS* mythology, and—I'm delighted to say—supports and mirrors what I'm doing on *"The War Within"*. Having since met and chatted to Brad at length, I can see now we're on the same page, *TRANSFORMERS*-wise, and he knows enough to know exactly what the fans out there want to see. So, enjoy…and roll on the *G1* ongoing series.

So, who the $@&% is Brad Mick? He's the third *TRANSFORMERS* scriptwriter!

~SIMON FURMAN

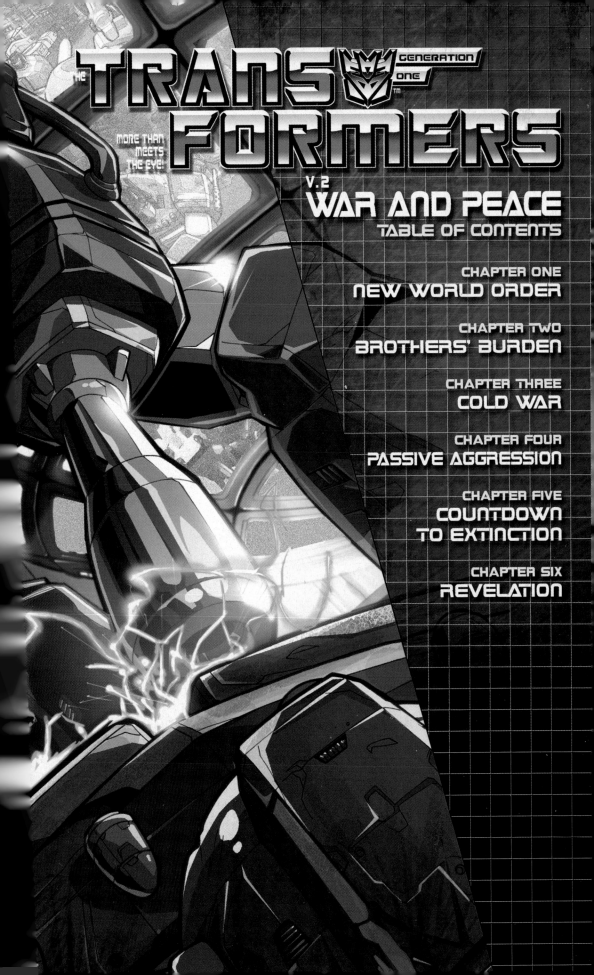

THE TRANSFORMERS
GENERATION ONE ™
MORE THAN MEETS THE EYE!

V.2
WAR AND PEACE
TABLE OF CONTENTS

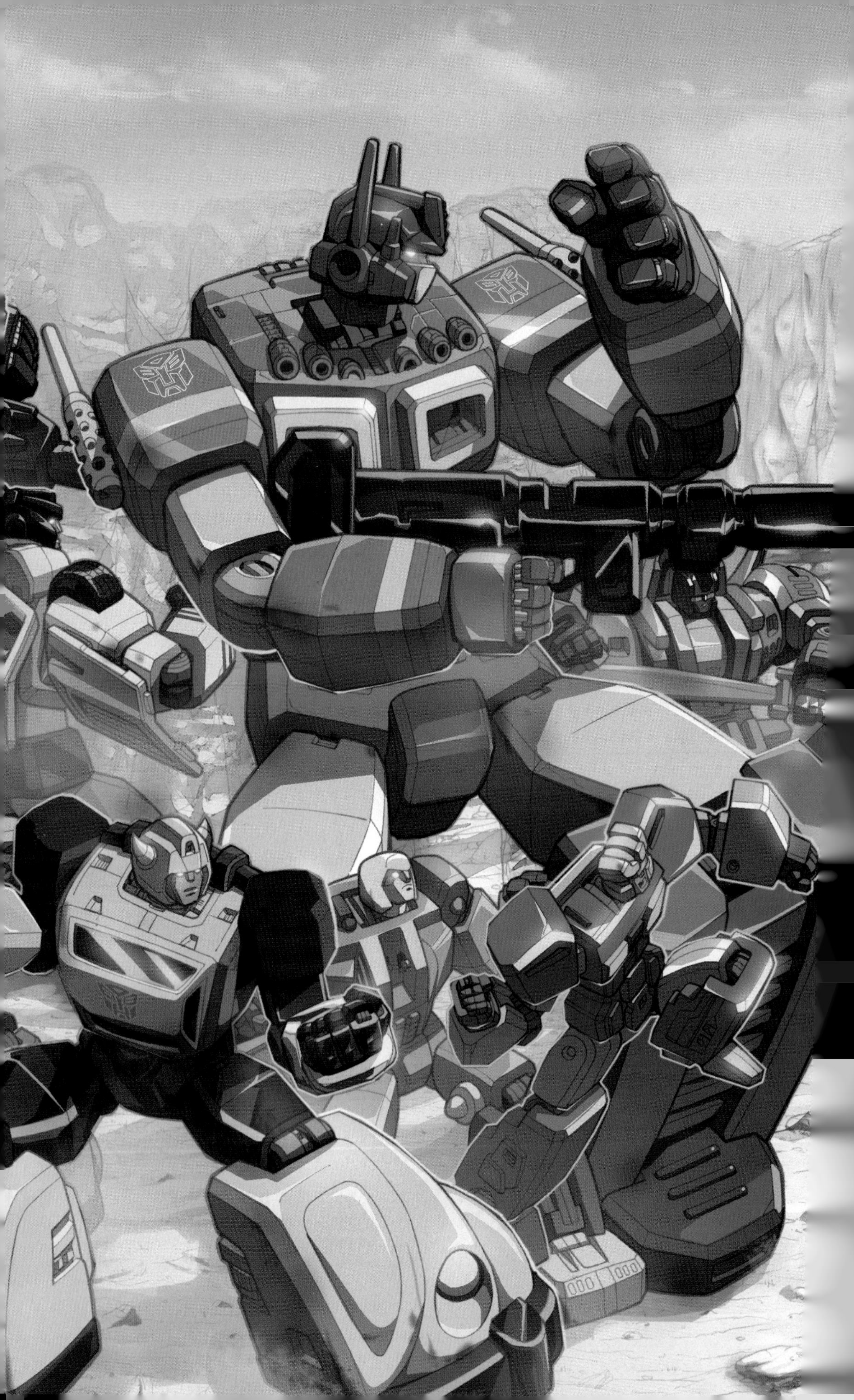

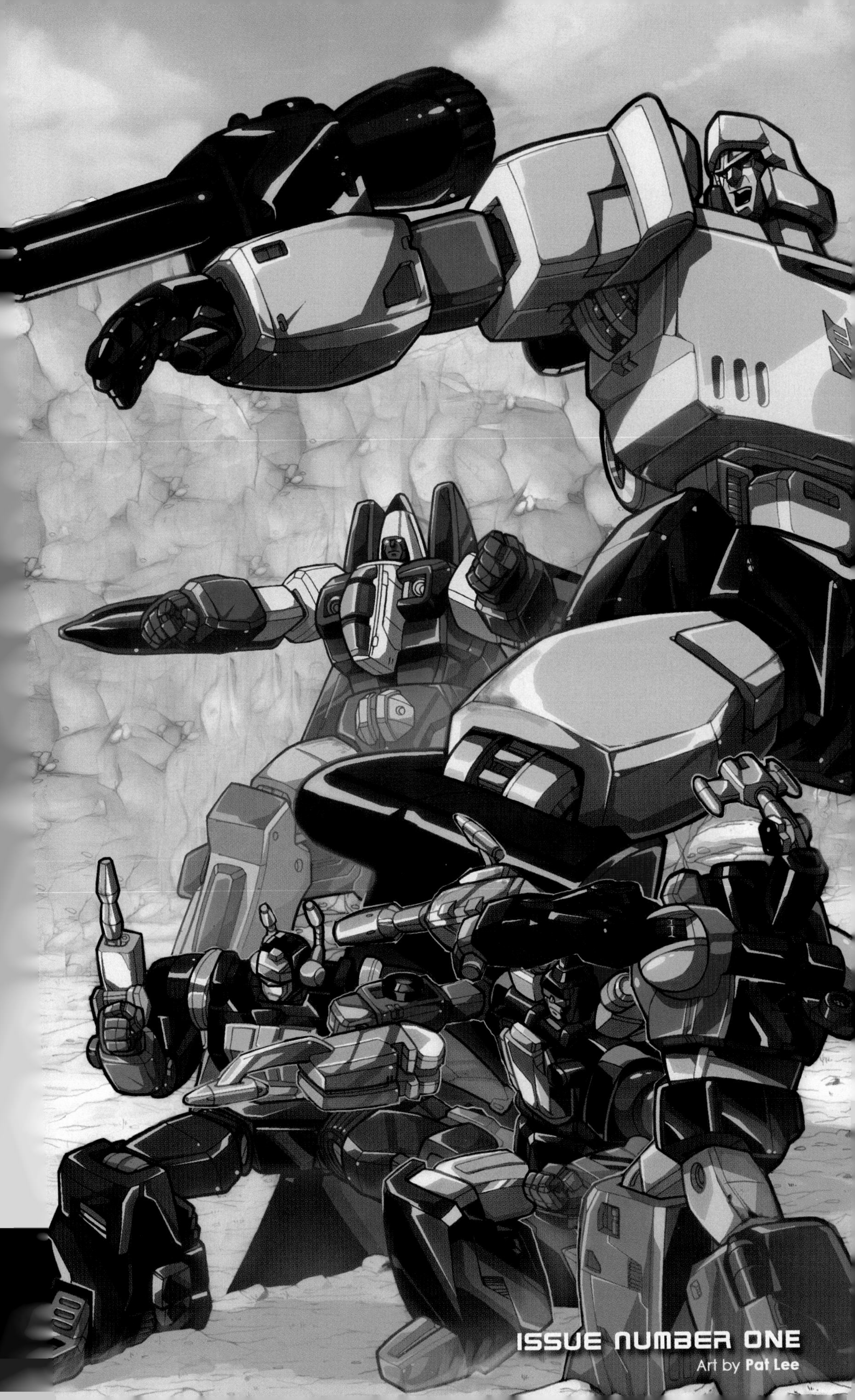

ISSUE NUMBER ONE

Art by **Pat Lee**

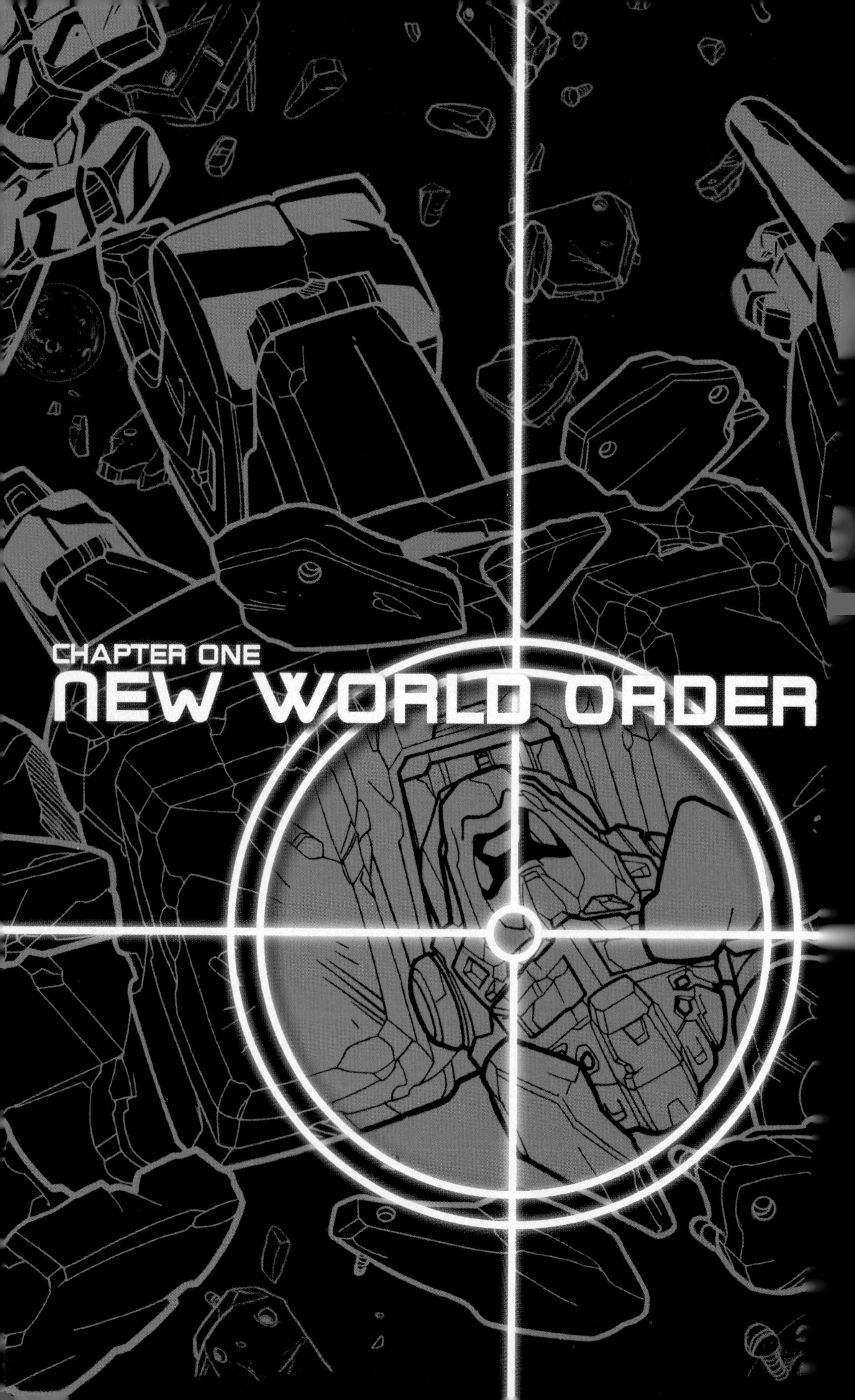
CHAPTER ONE
NEW WORLD ORDER

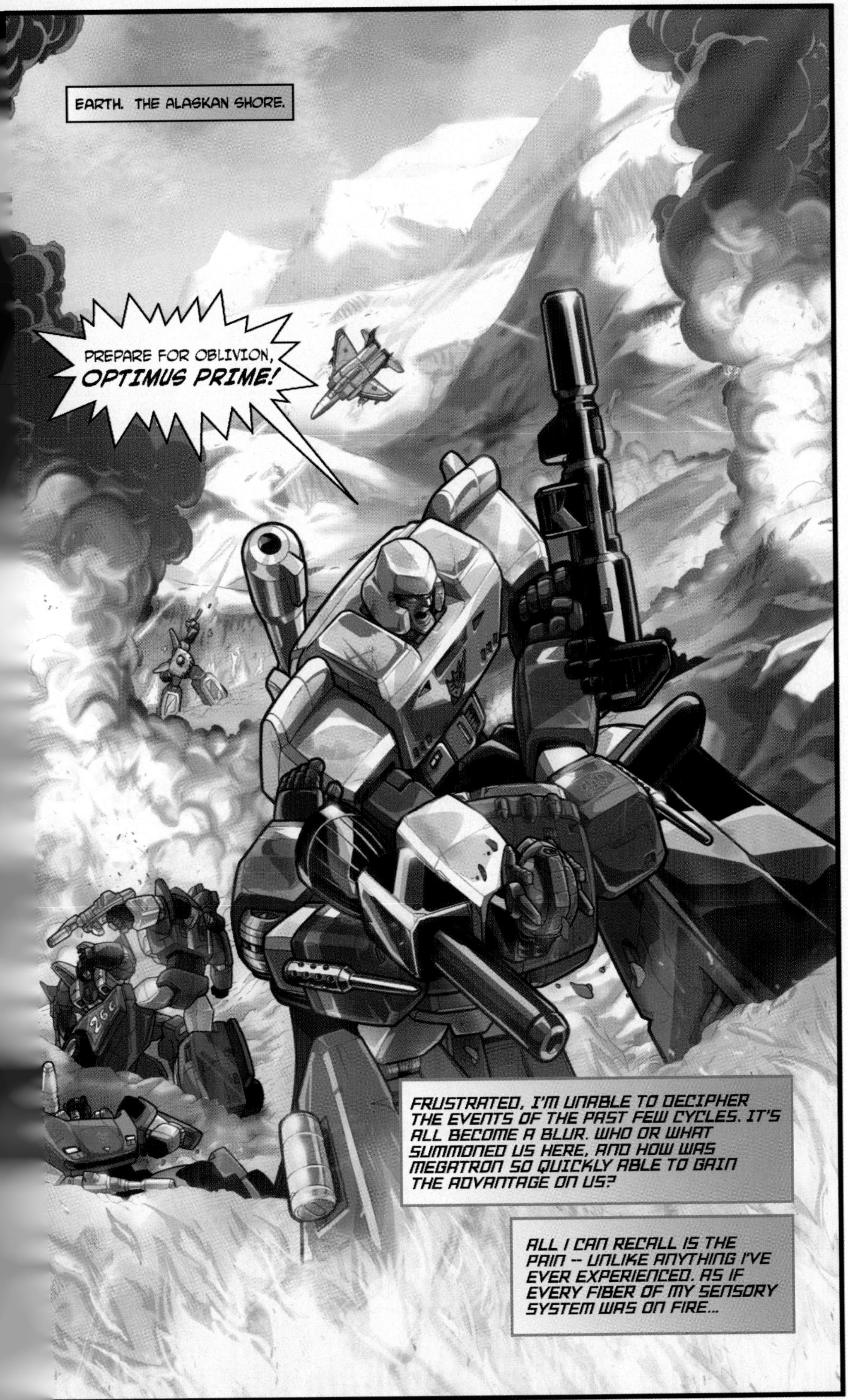
EARTH. THE ALASKAN SHORE.
PREPARE FOR OBLIVION, OPTIMUS PRIME!
FRUSTRATED, I'M UNABLE TO DECIPHER THE EVENTS OF THE PAST FEW CYCLES. IT'S ALL BECOME A BLUR. WHO OR WHAT SUMMONED US HERE, AND HOW WAS MEGATRON SO QUICKLY ABLE TO GAIN THE ADVANTAGE ON US?
ALL I CAN RECALL IS THE PAIN -- UNLIKE ANYTHING I'VE EVER EXPERIENCED. AS IF EVERY FIBER OF MY SENSORY SYSTEM WAS ON FIRE...

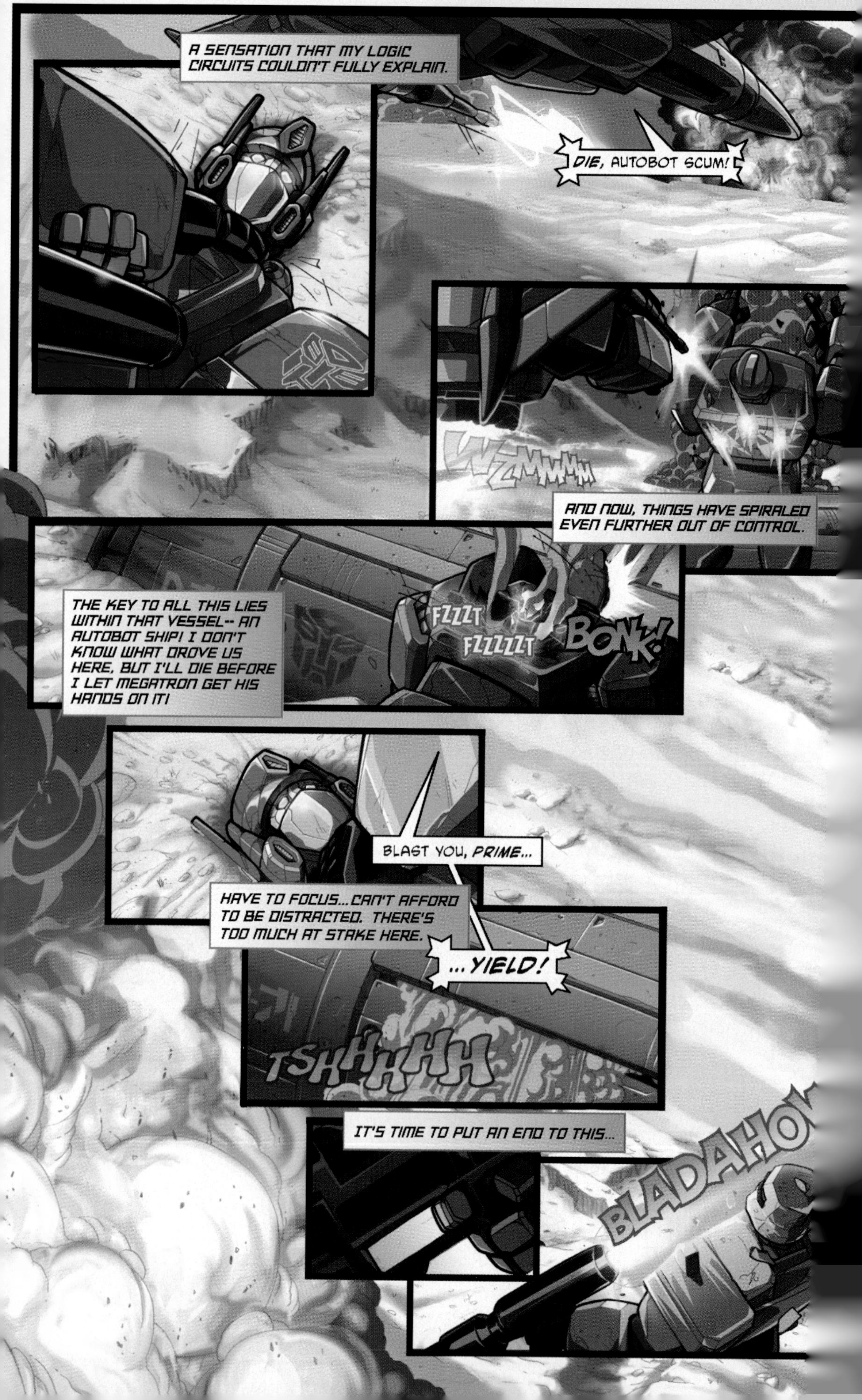
A SENSATION THAT MY LOGIC CIRCUITS COULDN'T FULLY EXPLAIN.
DIE, AUTOBOT SCUM!
WZMMMM
AND NOW, THINGS HAVE SPIRALED EVEN FURTHER OUT OF CONTROL.
THE KEY TO ALL THIS LIES WITHIN THAT VESSEL-- AN AUTOBOT SHIP! I DON'T KNOW WHAT DROVE US HERE, BUT I'LL DIE BEFORE I LET MEGATRON GET HIS HANDS ON IT!
FZZZT
FZZZZZT
BONK!
BLAST YOU, PRIME...
HAVE TO FOCUS... CAN'T AFFORD TO BE DISTRACTED. THERE'S TOO MUCH AT STAKE HERE.
...YIELD!
TSHHHHH
IT'S TIME TO PUT AN END TO THIS...
BLADAHO

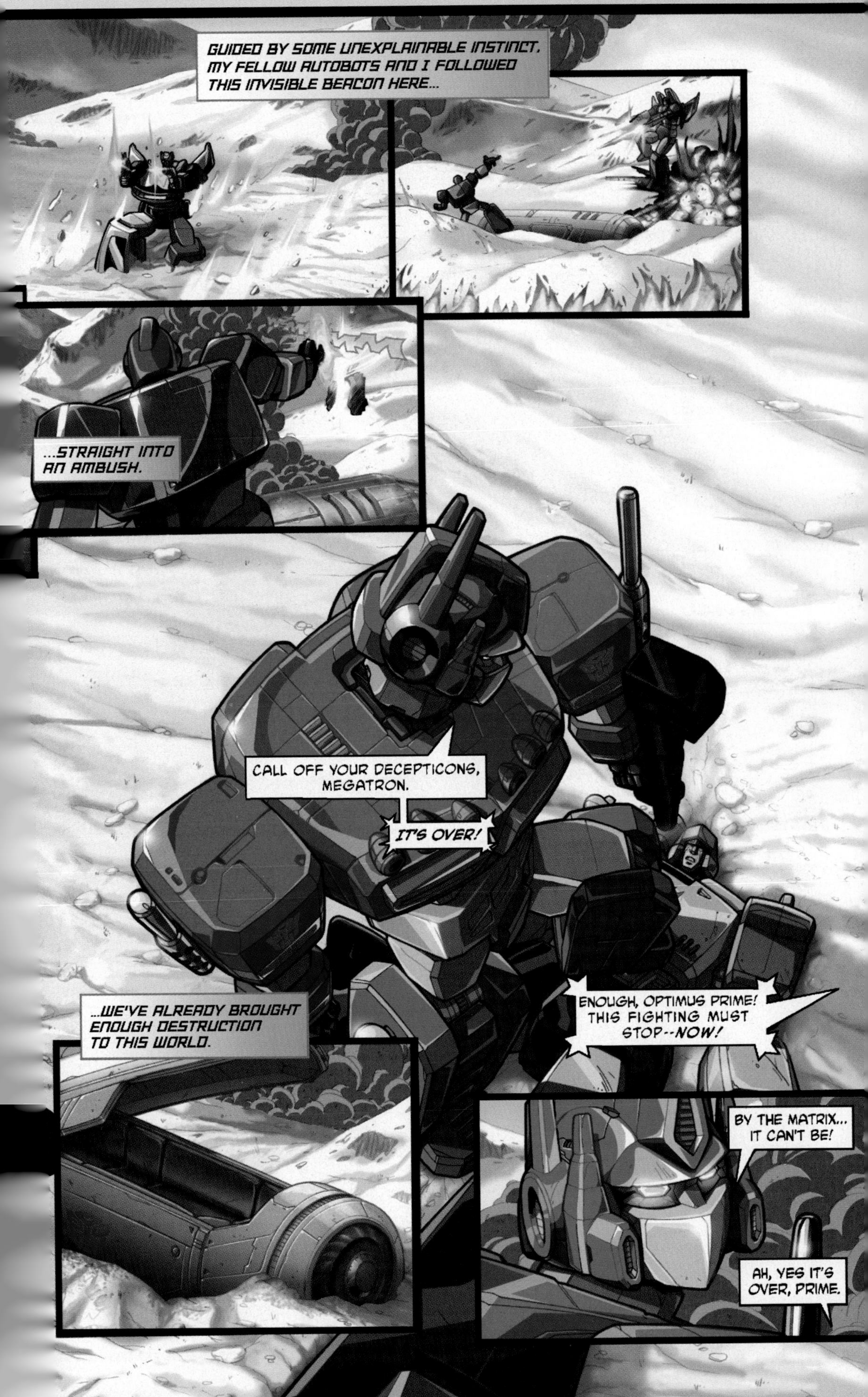
GUIDED BY SOME UNEXPLAINABLE INSTINCT, MY FELLOW AUTOBOTS AND I FOLLOWED THIS INVISIBLE BEACON HERE...
...STRAIGHT INTO AN AMBUSH.
CALL OFF YOUR DECEPTICONS, MEGATRON.
IT'S OVER!
...WE'VE ALREADY BROUGHT ENOUGH DESTRUCTION TO THIS WORLD.
ENOUGH, OPTIMUS PRIME! THIS FIGHTING MUST STOP--NOW!
BY THE MATRIX... IT CAN'T BE!
AH, YES IT'S OVER, PRIME.

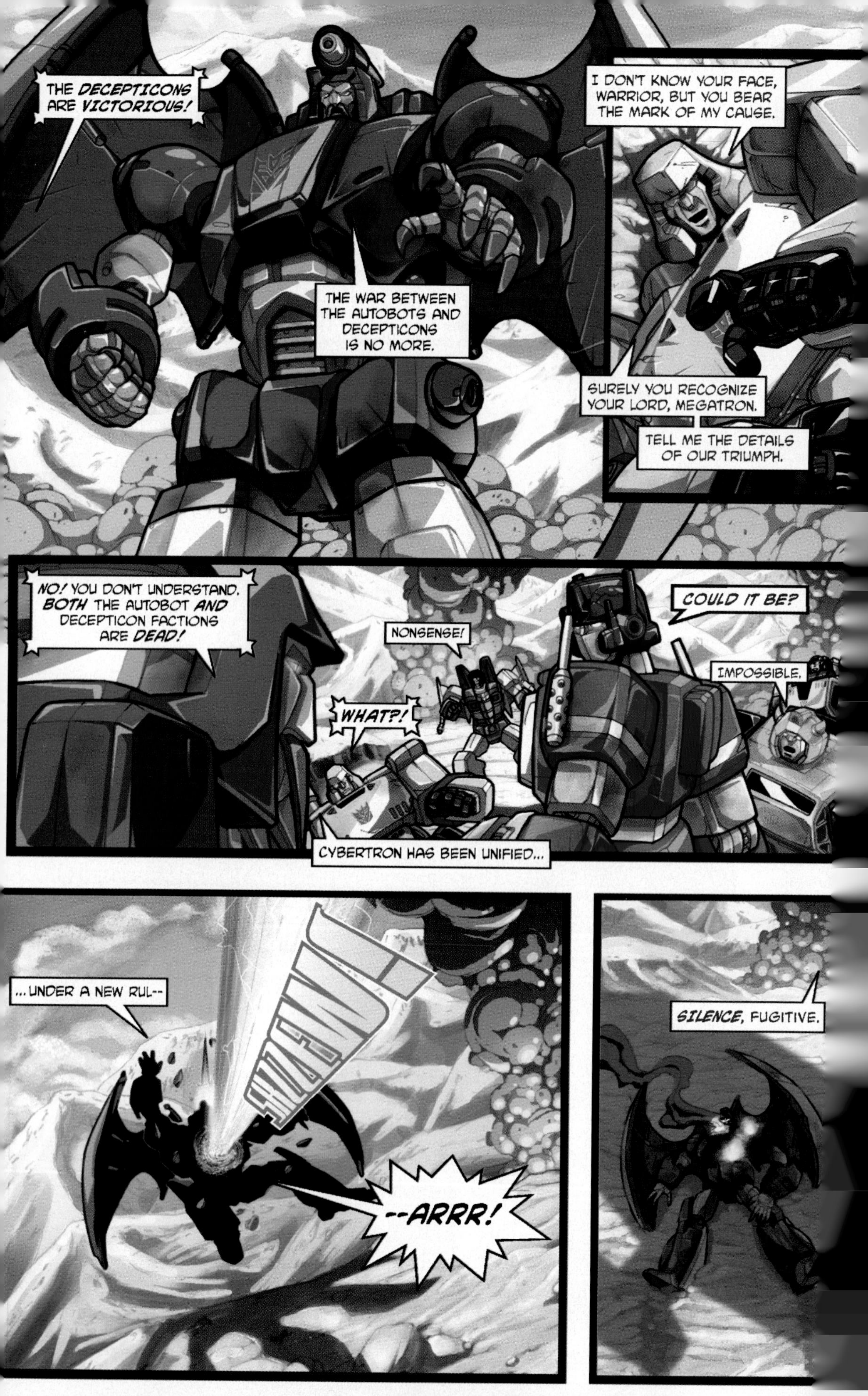

THE *DECEPTICONS* ARE *VICTORIOUS!*
THE WAR BETWEEN THE AUTOBOTS AND DECEPTICONS IS NO MORE.
I DON'T KNOW YOUR FACE, WARRIOR, BUT YOU BEAR THE MARK OF MY CAUSE.
SURELY YOU RECOGNIZE YOUR LORD, MEGATRON.
TELL ME THE DETAILS OF OUR TRIUMPH.
NO! YOU DON'T UNDERSTAND. ***BOTH*** THE AUTOBOT ***AND*** DECEPTICON FACTIONS ARE *DEAD!*
NONSENSE!
WHAT?!
COULD IT BE?
IMPOSSIBLE.
CYBERTRON HAS BEEN UNIFIED...
...UNDER A NEW RUL--
--ARRR!
SILENCE, FUGITIVE.

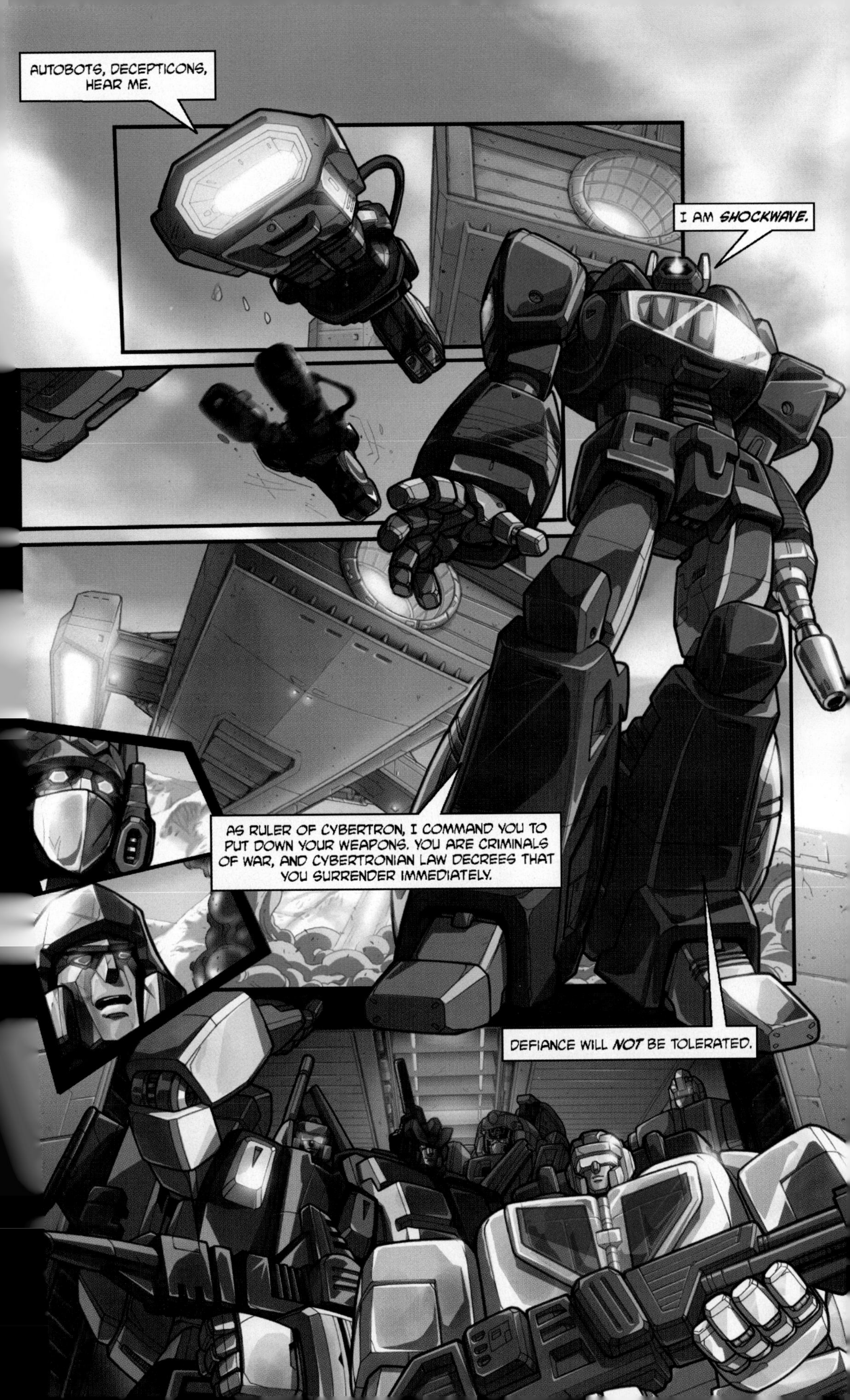
AUTOBOTS, DECEPTICONS, HEAR ME.
I AM *SHOCKWAVE.*
AS RULER OF CYBERTRON, I COMMAND YOU TO PUT DOWN YOUR WEAPONS. YOU ARE CRIMINALS OF WAR, AND CYBERTRONIAN LAW DECREES THAT YOU SURRENDER IMMEDIATELY.
DEFIANCE WILL *NOT* BE TOLERATED.

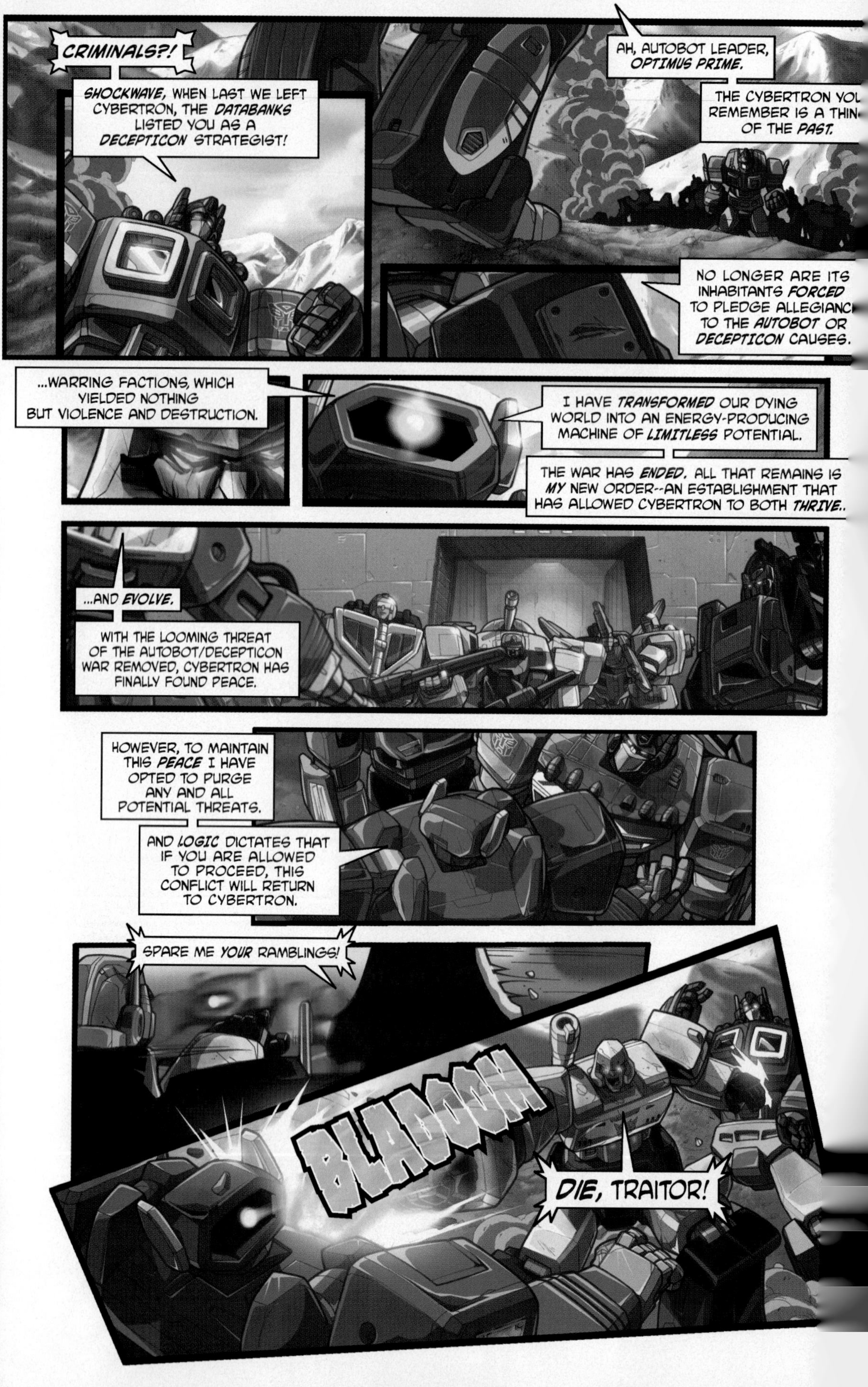
CRIMINALS?!
SHOCKWAVE, WHEN LAST WE LEFT CYBERTRON, THE DATABANKS LISTED YOU AS A DECEPTICON STRATEGIST!
AH, AUTOBOT LEADER, OPTIMUS PRIME.
THE CYBERTRON YOU REMEMBER IS A THIN OF THE PAST.
NO LONGER ARE ITS INHABITANTS FORCED TO PLEDGE ALLEGIANC TO THE AUTOBOT OR DECEPTICON CAUSES.
...WARRING FACTIONS, WHICH YIELDED NOTHING BUT VIOLENCE AND DESTRUCTION.
I HAVE TRANSFORMED OUR DYING WORLD INTO AN ENERGY-PRODUCING MACHINE OF LIMITLESS POTENTIAL.
THE WAR HAS ENDED. ALL THAT REMAINS IS MY NEW ORDER--AN ESTABLISHMENT THAT HAS ALLOWED CYBERTRON TO BOTH THRIVE..
...AND EVOLVE.
WITH THE LOOMING THREAT OF THE AUTOBOT/DECEPTICON WAR REMOVED, CYBERTRON HAS FINALLY FOUND PEACE.
HOWEVER, TO MAINTAIN THIS PEACE I HAVE OPTED TO PURGE ANY AND ALL POTENTIAL THREATS.
AND LOGIC DICTATES THAT IF YOU ARE ALLOWED TO PROCEED, THIS CONFLICT WILL RETURN TO CYBERTRON.
SPARE ME YOUR RAMBLINGS!
BLADOOM
DIE, TRAITOR!

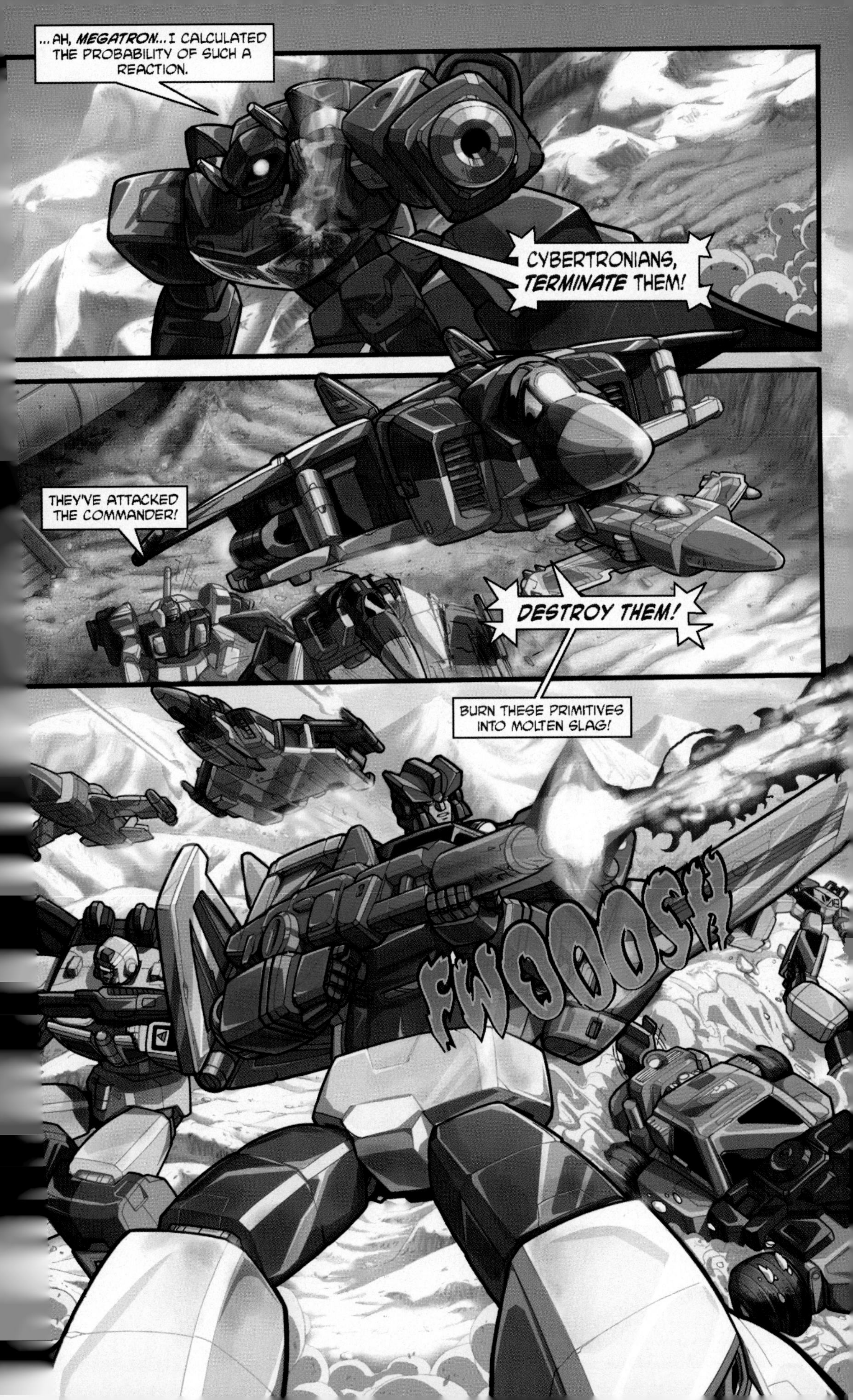
...AH, *MEGATRON*...I CALCULATED THE PROBABILITY OF SUCH A REACTION.
CYBERTRONIANS, *TERMINATE* THEM!
THEY'VE ATTACKED THE COMMANDER!
DESTROY THEM!
BURN THESE PRIMITIVES INTO MOLTEN SLAG!
FWOOOOSH

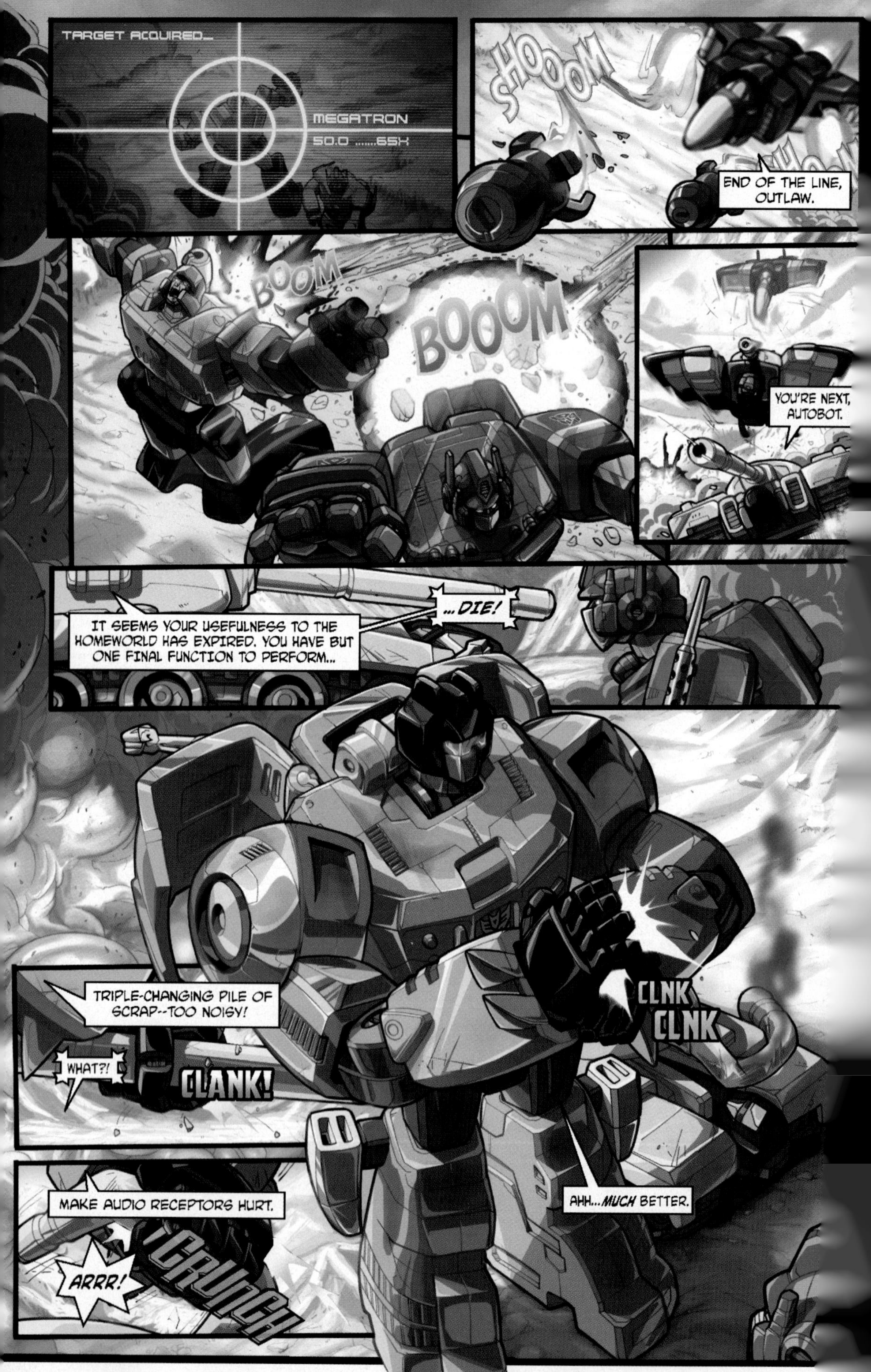
TARGET ACQUIRED...
MEGATRON
50.0 ....65X
SHOOOM
END OF THE LINE, OUTLAW.
BOOM
BOOOM
YOU'RE NEXT, AUTOBOT.
IT SEEMS YOUR USEFULNESS TO THE HOMEWORLD HAS EXPIRED. YOU HAVE BUT ONE FINAL FUNCTION TO PERFORM...
...DIE!
TRIPLE-CHANGING PILE OF SCRAP--TOO NOISY!
CLNK
CLNK
WHAT?!
CLANK!
MAKE AUDIO RECEPTORS HURT.
AHH...MUCH BETTER.
ARRR!
CRUNCH

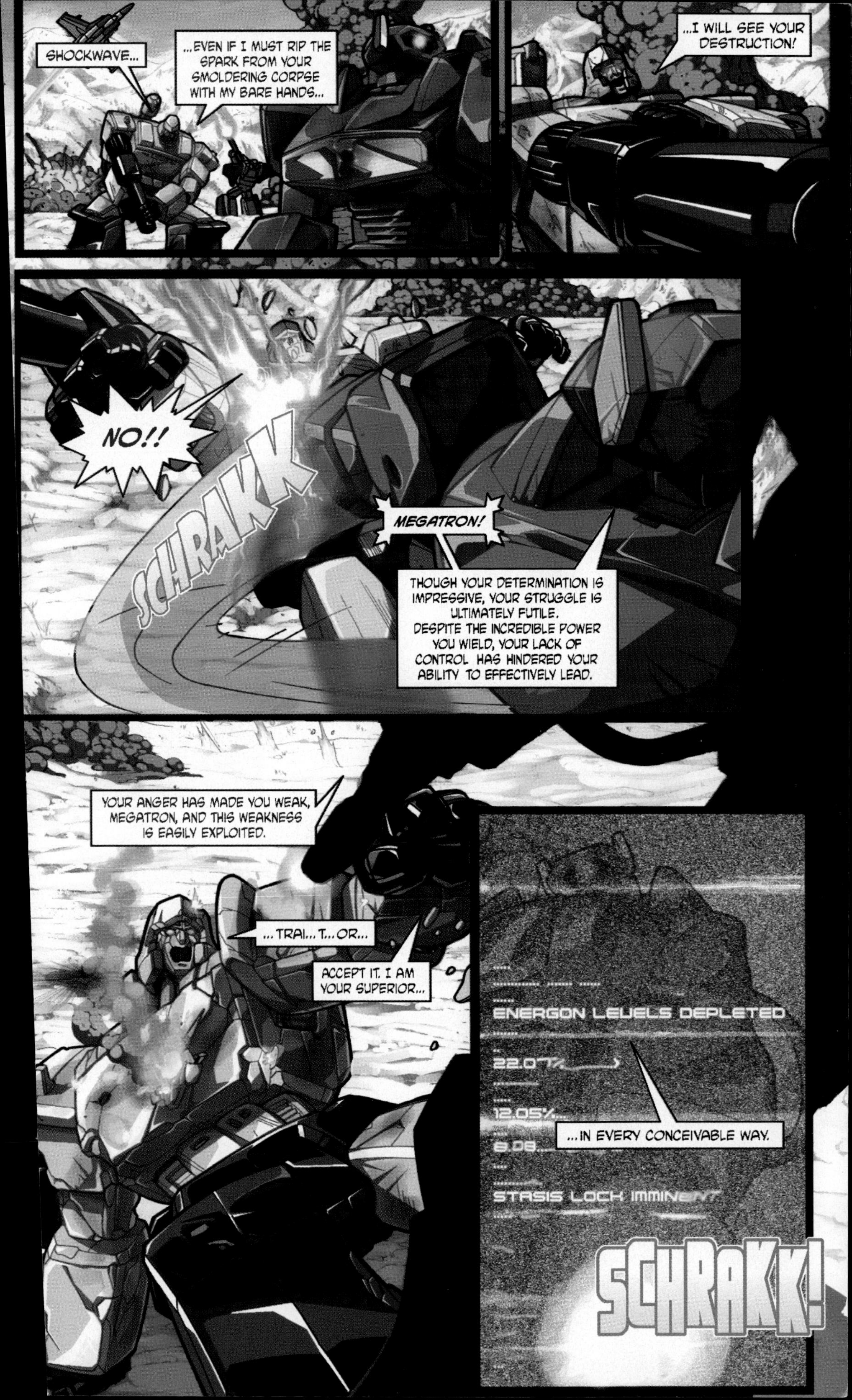
SHOCKWAVE...
...EVEN IF I MUST RIP THE SPARK FROM YOUR SMOLDERING CORPSE WITH MY BARE HANDS...
...I WILL SEE YOUR DESTRUCTION!
NO!!
SCHRAKK
MEGATRON!
THOUGH YOUR DETERMINATION IS IMPRESSIVE, YOUR STRUGGLE IS ULTIMATELY FUTILE.
DESPITE THE INCREDIBLE POWER YOU WIELD, YOUR LACK OF CONTROL HAS HINDERED YOUR ABILITY TO EFFECTIVELY LEAD.
YOUR ANGER HAS MADE YOU WEAK, MEGATRON, AND THIS WEAKNESS IS EASILY EXPLOITED.
...TRAI... T...OR...
ACCEPT IT. I AM YOUR SUPERIOR...
ENERGON LEVELS DEPLETED
22.07%
12.05%...
...IN EVERY CONCEIVABLE WAY.
8.08...
STASIS LOCK IMMINENT
SCHRAKK!

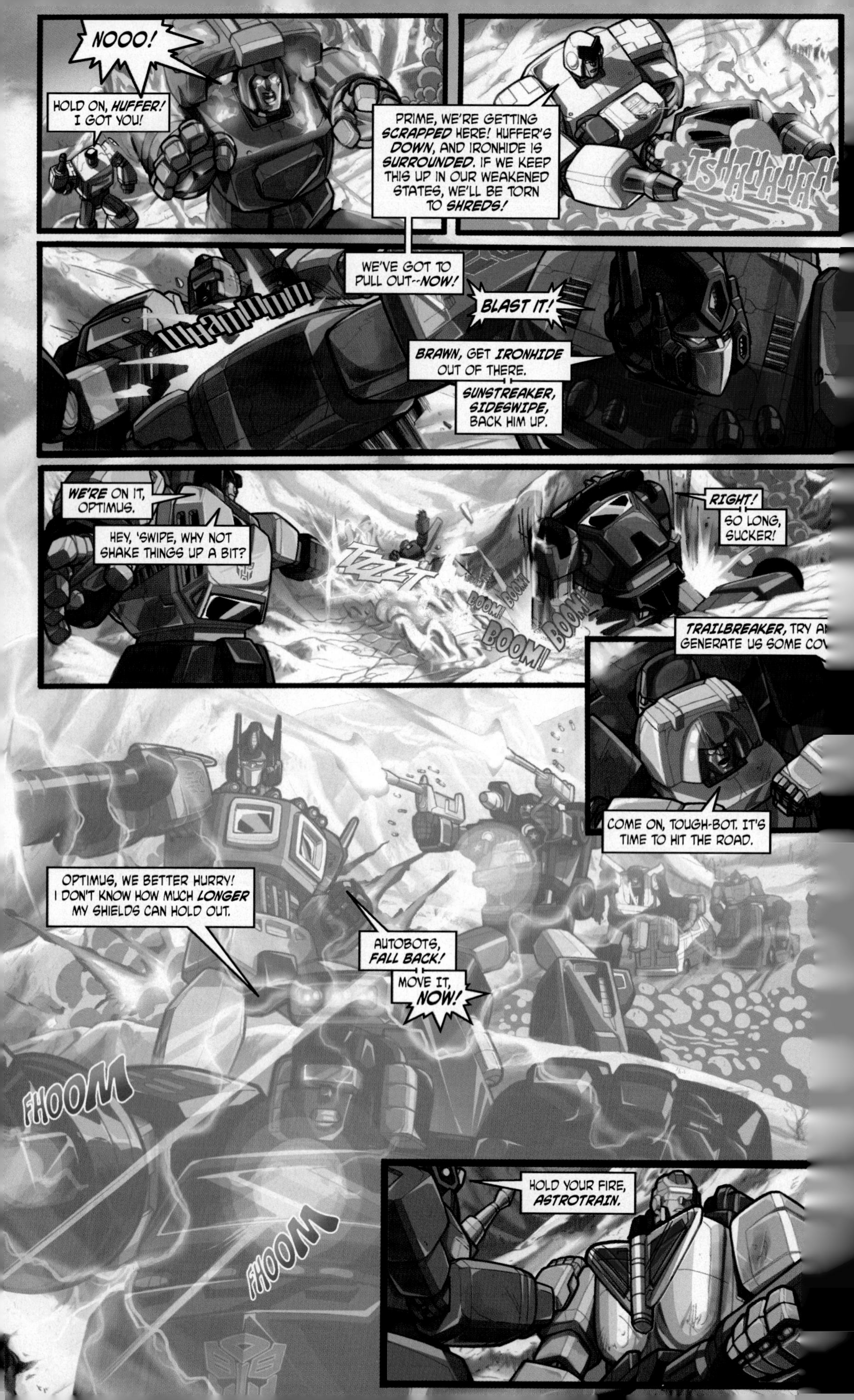
NOOO!
HOLD ON, HUFFER! I GOT YOU!
PRIME, WE'RE GETTING SCRAPPED HERE! HUFFER'S DOWN, AND IRONHIDE IS SURROUNDED. IF WE KEEP THIS UP IN OUR WEAKENED STATES, WE'LL BE TORN TO SHREDS!
TSHHHHHHH
WE'VE GOT TO PULL OUT--NOW!
BLAST IT!
BRAWN, GET IRONHIDE OUT OF THERE.
SUNSTREAKER, SIDESWIPE, BACK HIM UP.
WE'RE ON IT, OPTIMUS.
HEY, 'SWIPE, WHY NOT SHAKE THINGS UP A BIT?
RIGHT!
SO LONG, SUCKER!
TZZZT
BOOM! BOOM! BOOM! BOOM! BOOM!
TRAILBREAKER, TRY AN
GENERATE US SOME COV
COME ON, TOUGH-BOT. IT'S TIME TO HIT THE ROAD.
OPTIMUS, WE BETTER HURRY! I DON'T KNOW HOW MUCH LONGER MY SHIELDS CAN HOLD OUT.
AUTOBOTS, FALL BACK!
MOVE IT, NOW!
FHOOM
FHOOM
HOLD YOUR FIRE, ASTROTRAIN.

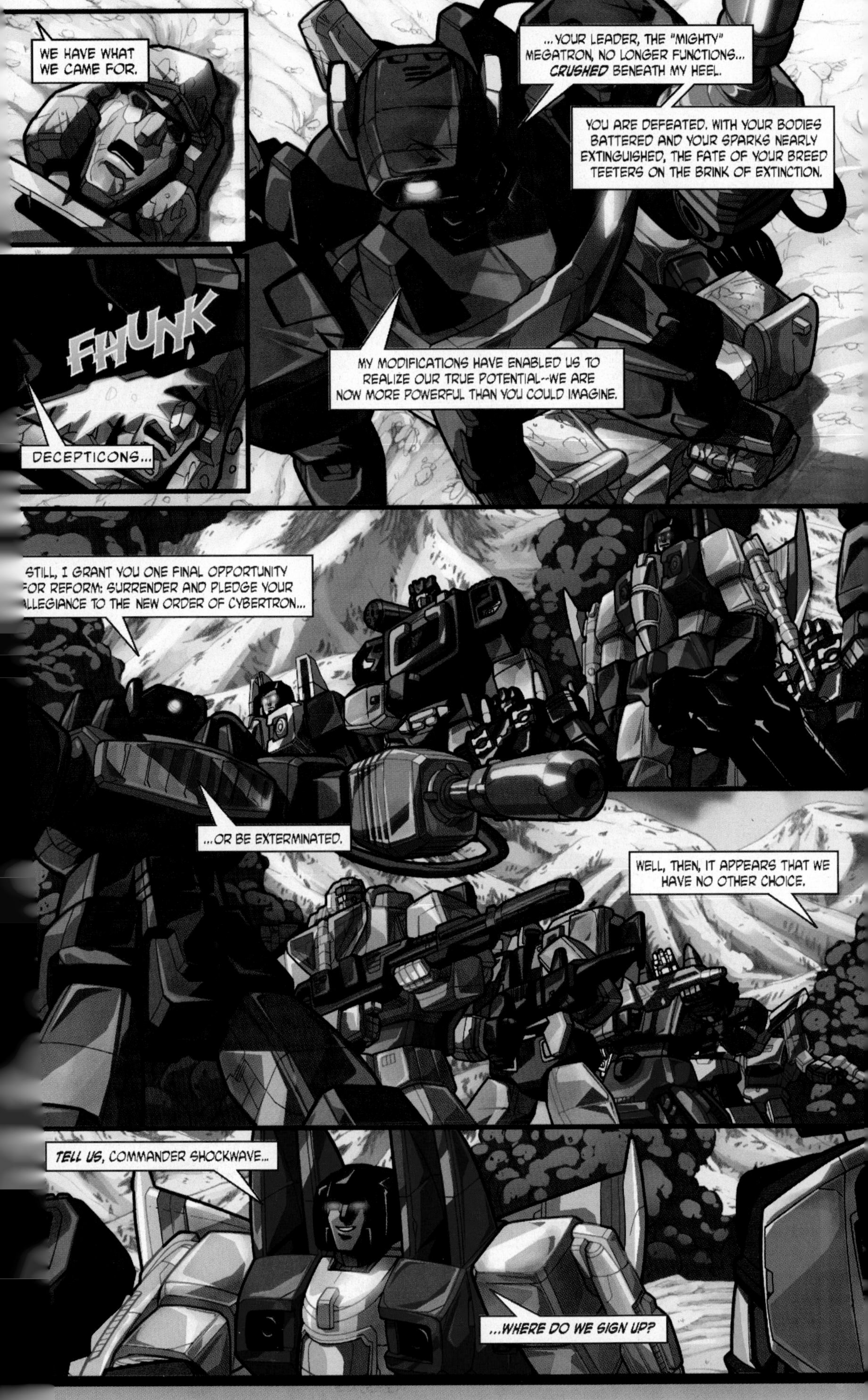
WE HAVE WHAT WE CAME FOR.
...YOUR LEADER, THE "MIGHTY" MEGATRON, NO LONGER FUNCTIONS... CRUSHED BENEATH MY HEEL.
YOU ARE DEFEATED. WITH YOUR BODIES BATTERED AND YOUR SPARKS NEARLY EXTINGUISHED, THE FATE OF YOUR BREED TEETERS ON THE BRINK OF EXTINCTION.
FHUNK
MY MODIFICATIONS HAVE ENABLED US TO REALIZE OUR TRUE POTENTIAL--WE ARE NOW MORE POWERFUL THAN YOU COULD IMAGINE.
DECEPTICONS...
STILL, I GRANT YOU ONE FINAL OPPORTUNITY FOR REFORM: SURRENDER AND PLEDGE YOUR ALLEGIANCE TO THE NEW ORDER OF CYBERTRON...
...OR BE EXTERMINATED.
WELL, THEN, IT APPEARS THAT WE HAVE NO OTHER CHOICE.
TELL US, COMMANDER SHOCKWAVE...
...WHERE DO WE SIGN UP?

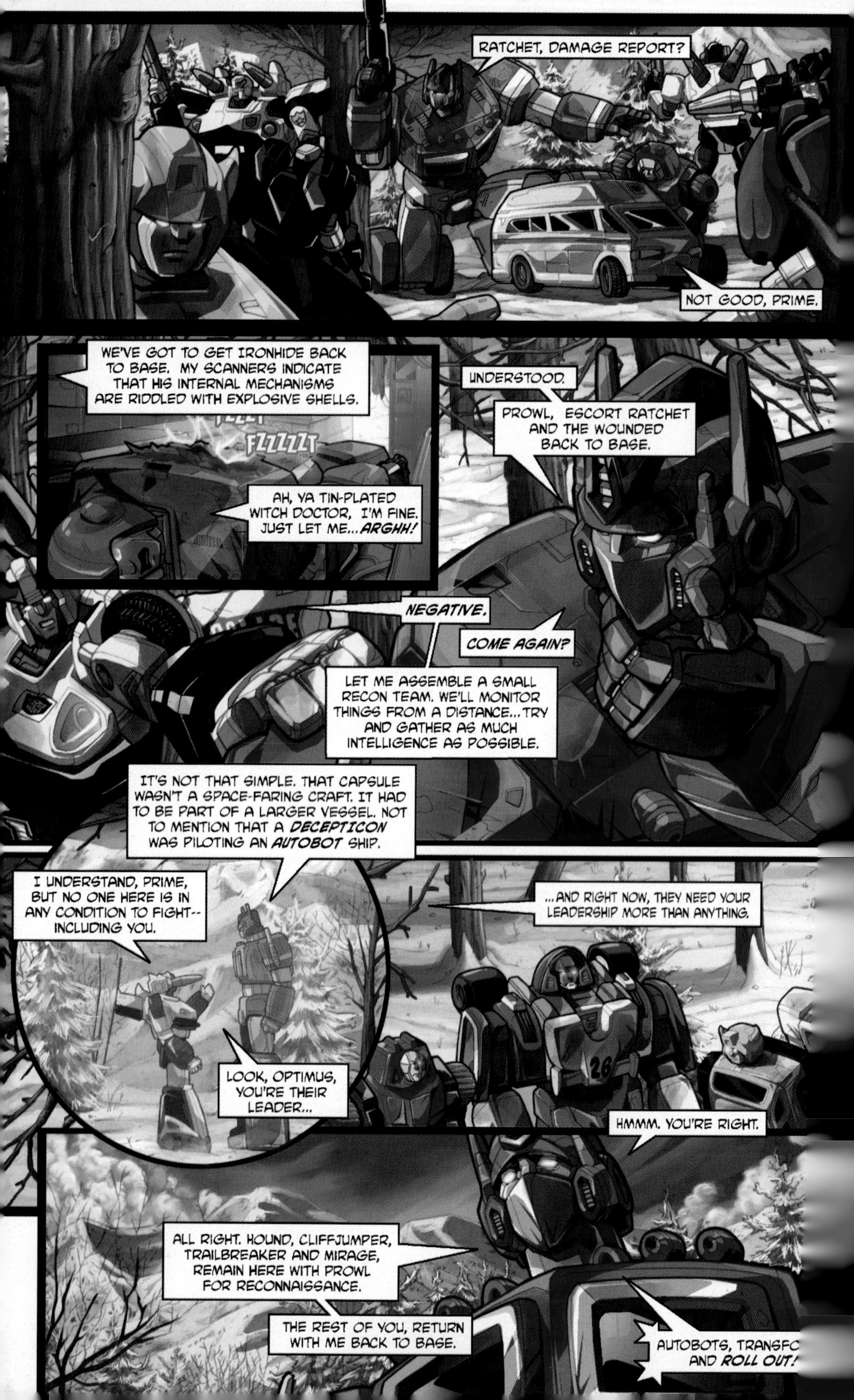
RATCHET, DAMAGE REPORT?
NOT GOOD, PRIME.
WE'VE GOT TO GET IRONHIDE BACK TO BASE. MY SCANNERS INDICATE THAT HIS INTERNAL MECHANISMS ARE RIDDLED WITH EXPLOSIVE SHELLS.
FZZZZZT
AH, YA TIN-PLATED WITCH DOCTOR, I'M FINE. JUST LET ME...*ARGHH!*
UNDERSTOOD.
PROWL, ESCORT RATCHET AND THE WOUNDED BACK TO BASE.
NEGATIVE.
COME AGAIN?
LET ME ASSEMBLE A SMALL RECON TEAM. WE'LL MONITOR THINGS FROM A DISTANCE...TRY AND GATHER AS MUCH INTELLIGENCE AS POSSIBLE.
IT'S NOT THAT SIMPLE. THAT CAPSULE WASN'T A SPACE-FARING CRAFT. IT HAD TO BE PART OF A LARGER VESSEL. NOT TO MENTION THAT A *DECEPTICON* WAS PILOTING AN *AUTOBOT* SHIP.
I UNDERSTAND, PRIME, BUT NO ONE HERE IS IN ANY CONDITION TO FIGHT-- INCLUDING YOU.
LOOK, OPTIMUS, YOU'RE THEIR LEADER...
...AND RIGHT NOW, THEY NEED YOUR LEADERSHIP MORE THAN ANYTHING.
HMMM. YOU'RE RIGHT.
ALL RIGHT. HOUND, CLIFFJUMPER, TRAILBREAKER AND MIRAGE, REMAIN HERE WITH PROWL FOR RECONNAISSANCE.
THE REST OF YOU, RETURN WITH ME BACK TO BASE.
AUTOBOTS, TRANSFO
AND *ROLL OUT!*

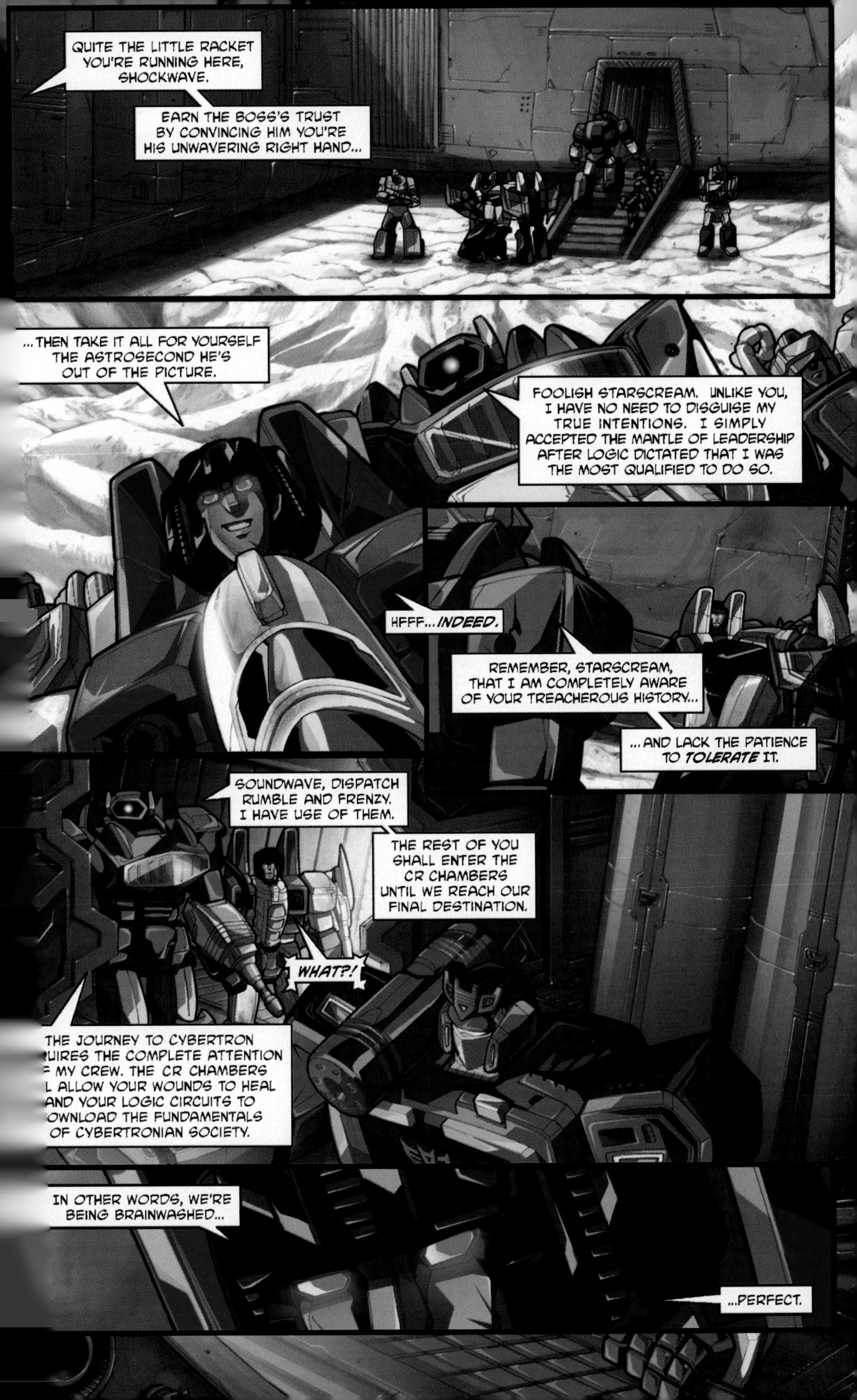
QUITE THE LITTLE RACKET YOU'RE RUNNING HERE, SHOCKWAVE.
EARN THE BOSS'S TRUST BY CONVINCING HIM YOU'RE HIS UNWAVERING RIGHT HAND...
...THEN TAKE IT ALL FOR YOURSELF THE ASTROSECOND HE'S OUT OF THE PICTURE.
FOOLISH STARSCREAM. UNLIKE YOU, I HAVE NO NEED TO DISGUISE MY TRUE INTENTIONS. I SIMPLY ACCEPTED THE MANTLE OF LEADERSHIP AFTER LOGIC DICTATED THAT I WAS THE MOST QUALIFIED TO DO SO.
HFFF... *INDEED.*
REMEMBER, STARSCREAM, THAT I AM COMPLETELY AWARE OF YOUR TREACHEROUS HISTORY...
...AND LACK THE PATIENCE TO *TOLERATE* IT.
SOUNDWAVE, DISPATCH RUMBLE AND FRENZY. I HAVE USE OF THEM.
THE REST OF YOU SHALL ENTER THE CR CHAMBERS UNTIL WE REACH OUR FINAL DESTINATION.
WHAT?!
THE JOURNEY TO CYBERTRON
QUIRES THE COMPLETE ATTENTION
F MY CREW. THE CR CHAMBERS
L ALLOW YOUR WOUNDS TO HEAL
AND YOUR LOGIC CIRCUITS TO
OWNLOAD THE FUNDAMENTALS
OF CYBERTRONIAN SOCIETY.
IN OTHER WORDS, WE'RE BEING BRAINWASHED...
...PERFECT.

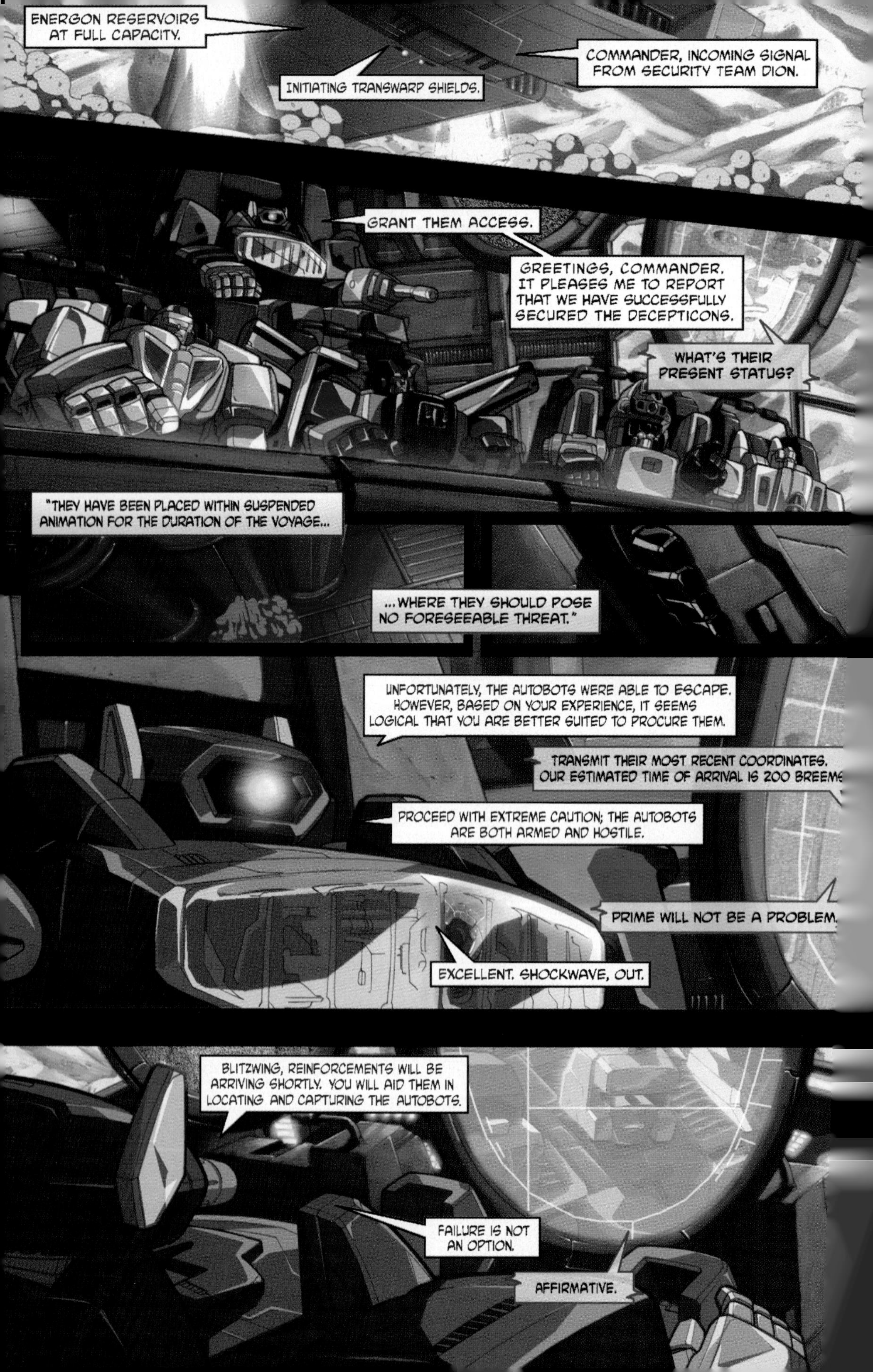
ENERGON RESERVOIRS AT FULL CAPACITY.
INITIATING TRANSWARP SHIELDS.
COMMANDER, INCOMING SIGNAL FROM SECURITY TEAM DION.
GRANT THEM ACCESS.
GREETINGS, COMMANDER. IT PLEASES ME TO REPORT THAT WE HAVE SUCCESSFULLY SECURED THE DECEPTICONS.
WHAT'S THEIR PRESENT STATUS?
"THEY HAVE BEEN PLACED WITHIN SUSPENDED ANIMATION FOR THE DURATION OF THE VOYAGE...
...WHERE THEY SHOULD POSE NO FORESEEABLE THREAT."
UNFORTUNATELY, THE AUTOBOTS WERE ABLE TO ESCAPE. HOWEVER, BASED ON YOUR EXPERIENCE, IT SEEMS LOGICAL THAT YOU ARE BETTER SUITED TO PROCURE THEM.
TRANSMIT THEIR MOST RECENT COORDINATES. OUR ESTIMATED TIME OF ARRIVAL IS 200 BREEMS
PROCEED WITH EXTREME CAUTION; THE AUTOBOTS ARE BOTH ARMED AND HOSTILE.
PRIME WILL NOT BE A PROBLEM.
EXCELLENT. SHOCKWAVE, OUT.
BLITZWING, REINFORCEMENTS WILL BE ARRIVING SHORTLY. YOU WILL AID THEM IN LOCATING AND CAPTURING THE AUTOBOTS.
FAILURE IS NOT AN OPTION.
AFFIRMATIVE.

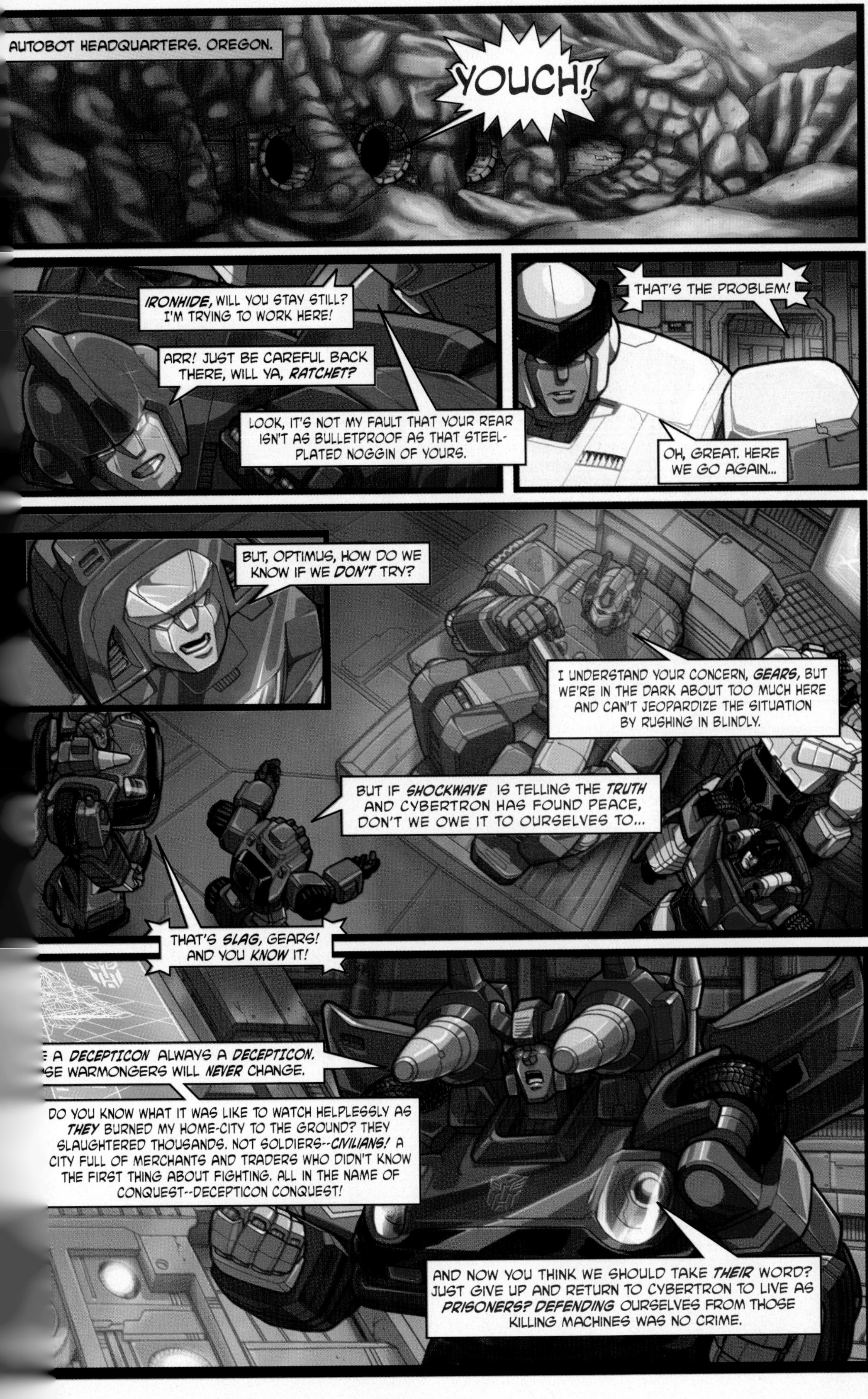
AUTOBOT HEADQUARTERS. OREGON.
YOUCH!
IRONHIDE, WILL YOU STAY STILL? I'M TRYING TO WORK HERE!
ARR! JUST BE CAREFUL BACK THERE, WILL YA, RATCHET?
LOOK, IT'S NOT MY FAULT THAT YOUR REAR ISN'T AS BULLETPROOF AS THAT STEEL-PLATED NOGGIN OF YOURS.
THAT'S THE PROBLEM!
OH, GREAT. HERE WE GO AGAIN...
BUT, OPTIMUS, HOW DO WE KNOW IF WE DON'T TRY?
I UNDERSTAND YOUR CONCERN, GEARS, BUT WE'RE IN THE DARK ABOUT TOO MUCH HERE AND CAN'T JEOPARDIZE THE SITUATION BY RUSHING IN BLINDLY.
BUT IF SHOCKWAVE IS TELLING THE TRUTH AND CYBERTRON HAS FOUND PEACE, DON'T WE OWE IT TO OURSELVES TO...
THAT'S SLAG, GEARS! AND YOU KNOW IT!
A DECEPTICON ALWAYS A DECEPTICON. WARMONGERS WILL NEVER CHANGE.
DO YOU KNOW WHAT IT WAS LIKE TO WATCH HELPLESSLY AS THEY BURNED MY HOME-CITY TO THE GROUND? THEY SLAUGHTERED THOUSANDS. NOT SOLDIERS--CIVILIANS! A CITY FULL OF MERCHANTS AND TRADERS WHO DIDN'T KNOW THE FIRST THING ABOUT FIGHTING. ALL IN THE NAME OF CONQUEST--DECEPTICON CONQUEST!
AND NOW YOU THINK WE SHOULD TAKE THEIR WORD? JUST GIVE UP AND RETURN TO CYBERTRON TO LIVE AS PRISONERS? DEFENDING OURSELVES FROM THOSE KILLING MACHINES WAS NO CRIME.

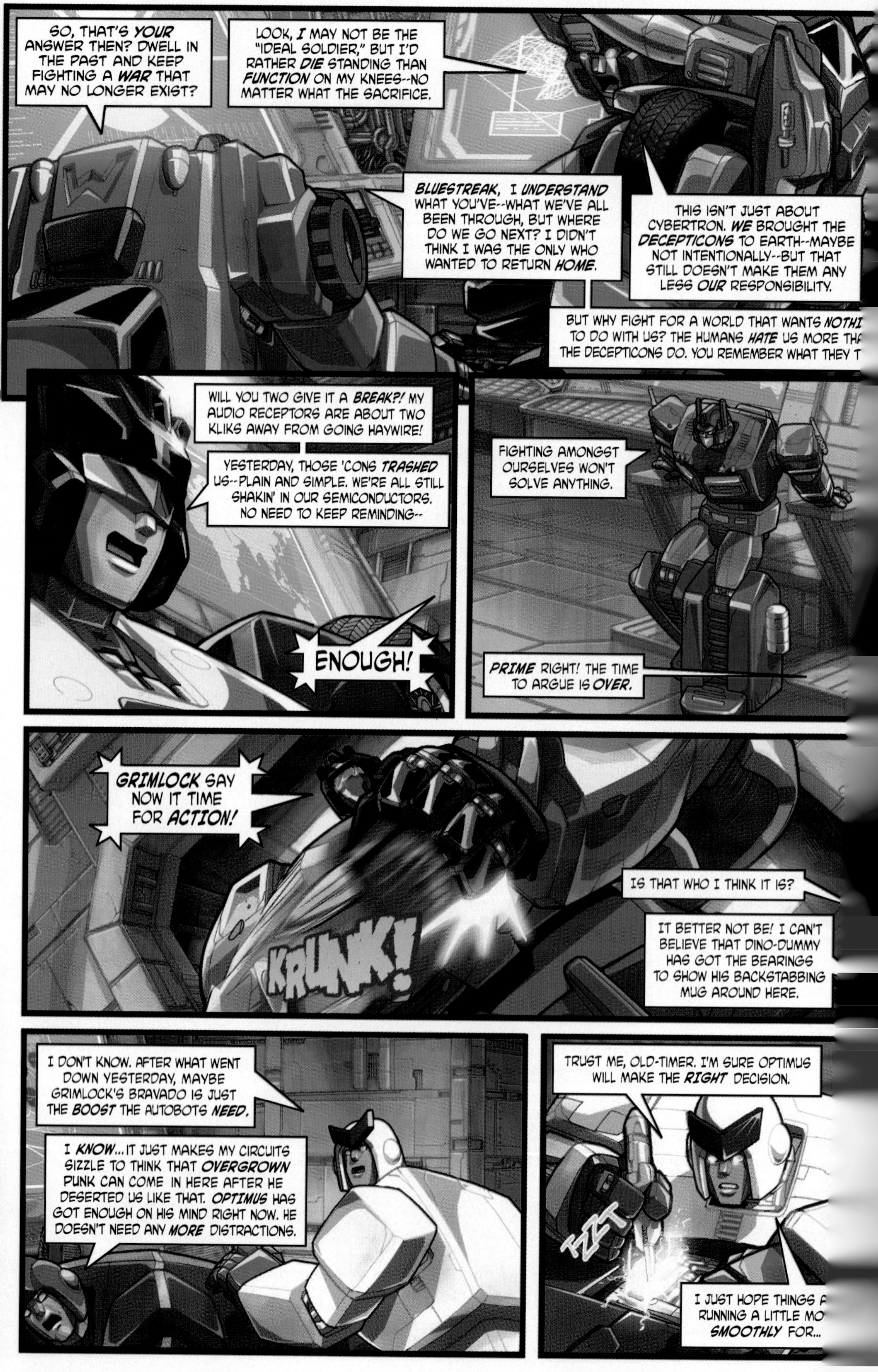

SO, THAT'S *YOUR* ANSWER THEN? DWELL IN THE PAST AND KEEP FIGHTING A *WAR* THAT MAY NO LONGER EXIST?
LOOK, *I* MAY NOT BE THE "IDEAL SOLDIER," BUT I'D RATHER *DIE* STANDING THAN *FUNCTION* ON MY KNEES--NO MATTER WHAT THE SACRIFICE.
BLUESTREAK, I *UNDERSTAND* WHAT YOU'VE--WHAT WE'VE ALL BEEN THROUGH, BUT WHERE DO WE GO NEXT? I DIDN'T THINK I WAS THE ONLY WHO WANTED TO RETURN *HOME*.
THIS ISN'T JUST ABOUT CYBERTRON. *WE* BROUGHT THE *DECEPTICONS* TO EARTH--MAYBE NOT INTENTIONALLY--BUT THAT STILL DOESN'T MAKE THEM ANY LESS *OUR* RESPONSIBILITY.
BUT WHY FIGHT FOR A WORLD THAT WANTS *NOTHI* TO DO WITH US? THE HUMANS *HATE* US MORE THA THE DECEPTICONS DO. YOU REMEMBER WHAT THEY T
WILL YOU TWO GIVE IT A *BREAK?!* MY AUDIO RECEPTORS ARE ABOUT TWO KLIKS AWAY FROM GOING HAYWIRE!
YESTERDAY, THOSE 'CONS *TRASHED* US--PLAIN AND SIMPLE. WE'RE ALL STILL SHAKIN' IN OUR SEMICONDUCTORS. NO NEED TO KEEP REMINDING--
ENOUGH!
FIGHTING AMONGST OURSELVES WON'T SOLVE ANYTHING.
PRIME RIGHT! THE TIME TO ARGUE IS *OVER.*
GRIMLOCK SAY NOW IT TIME FOR *ACTION!*
KRUNK!
IS THAT WHO I THINK IT IS?
IT BETTER NOT BE! I CAN'T BELIEVE THAT DINO-DUMMY HAS GOT THE BEARINGS TO SHOW HIS BACKSTABBING MUG AROUND HERE.
I DON'T KNOW. AFTER WHAT WENT DOWN YESTERDAY, MAYBE GRIMLOCK'S BRAVADO IS JUST THE *BOOST* THE AUTOBOTS *NEED.*
I *KNOW*... IT JUST MAKES MY CIRCUITS SIZZLE TO THINK THAT *OVERGROWN* PUNK CAN COME IN HERE AFTER HE DESERTED US LIKE THAT. *OPTIMUS* HAS GOT ENOUGH ON HIS MIND RIGHT NOW. HE DOESN'T NEED ANY *MORE* DISTRACTIONS.
TRUST ME, OLD-TIMER. I'M SURE OPTIMUS WILL MAKE THE *RIGHT* DECISION.
TZZT
I JUST HOPE THINGS A RUNNING A LITTLE MO *SMOOTHLY* FOR...

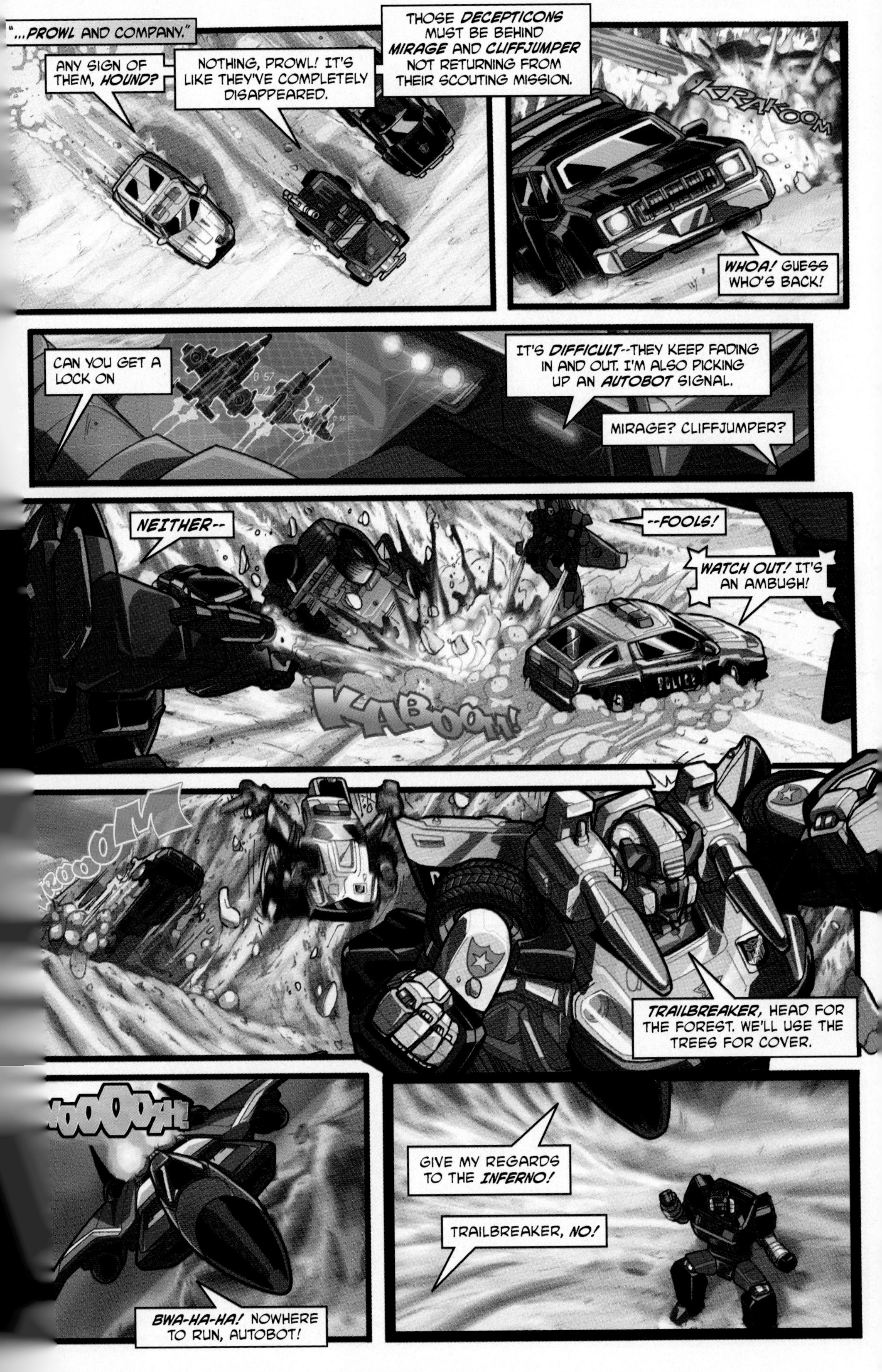
"...PROWL AND COMPANY."
ANY SIGN OF THEM, HOUND?
NOTHING, PROWL! IT'S LIKE THEY'VE COMPLETELY DISAPPEARED.
THOSE DECEPTICONS MUST BE BEHIND MIRAGE AND CLIFFJUMPER NOT RETURNING FROM THEIR SCOUTING MISSION.
KRAKOOM
WHOA! GUESS WHO'S BACK!
CAN YOU GET A LOCK ON
IT'S DIFFICULT--THEY KEEP FADING IN AND OUT. I'M ALSO PICKING UP AN AUTOBOT SIGNAL.
MIRAGE? CLIFFJUMPER?
NEITHER--
--FOOLS!
WATCH OUT! IT'S AN AMBUSH!
POLICE
KABOOM!
KROOOOM
TRAILBREAKER, HEAD FOR THE FOREST. WE'LL USE THE TREES FOR COVER.
WOOOOOSH!
BWA-HA-HA! NOWHERE TO RUN, AUTOBOT!
GIVE MY REGARDS TO THE INFERNO!
TRAILBREAKER, NO!

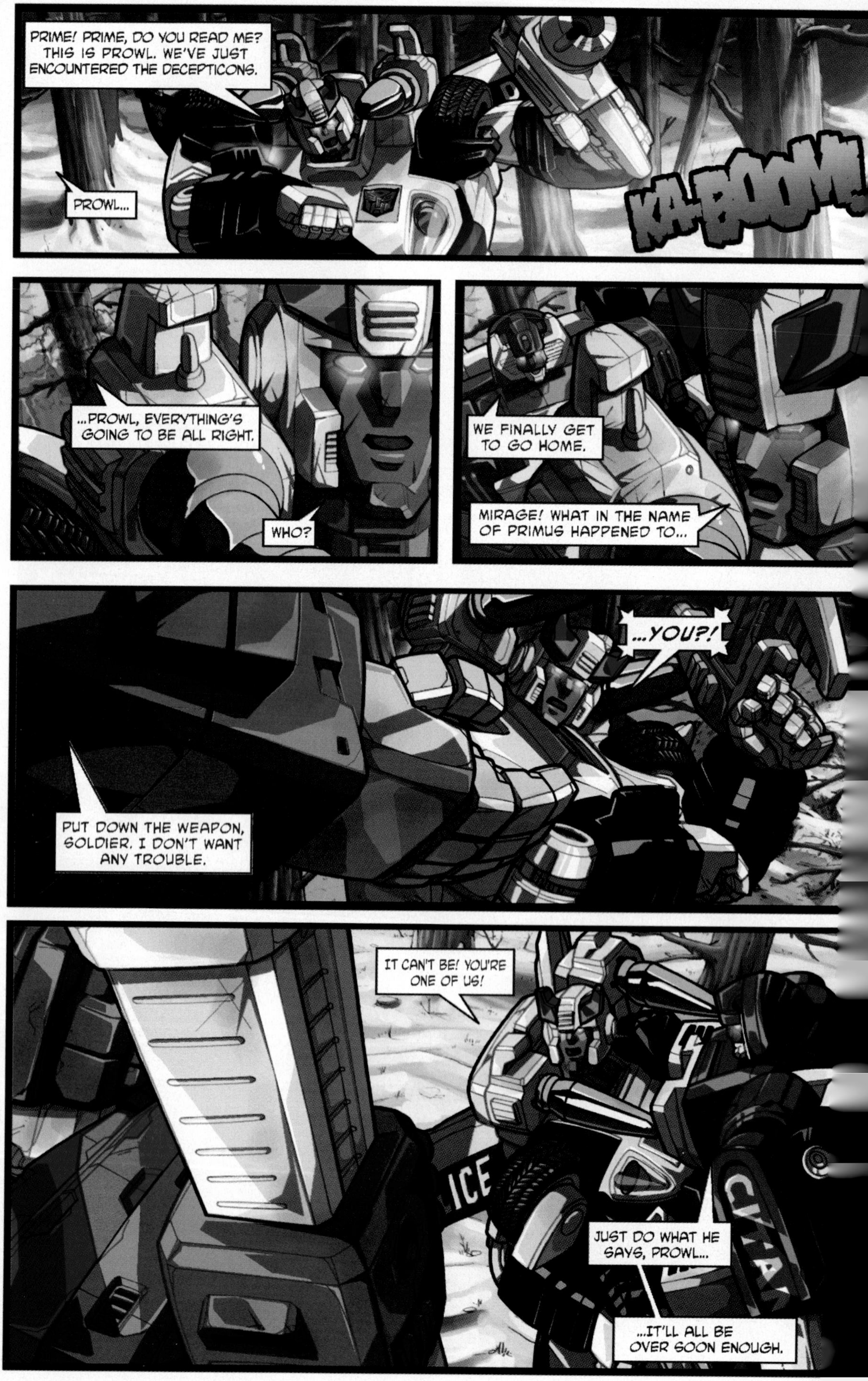
PRIME! PRIME, DO YOU READ ME? THIS IS PROWL. WE'VE JUST ENCOUNTERED THE DECEPTICONS.
PROWL...
KA-BOOM!
...PROWL, EVERYTHING'S GOING TO BE ALL RIGHT.
WHO?
WE FINALLY GET TO GO HOME.
MIRAGE! WHAT IN THE NAME OF PRIMUS HAPPENED TO...
...YOU?!
PUT DOWN THE WEAPON, SOLDIER. I DON'T WANT ANY TROUBLE.
IT CAN'T BE! YOU'RE ONE OF US!
JUST DO WHAT HE SAYS, PROWL...
...IT'LL ALL BE OVER SOON ENOUGH.

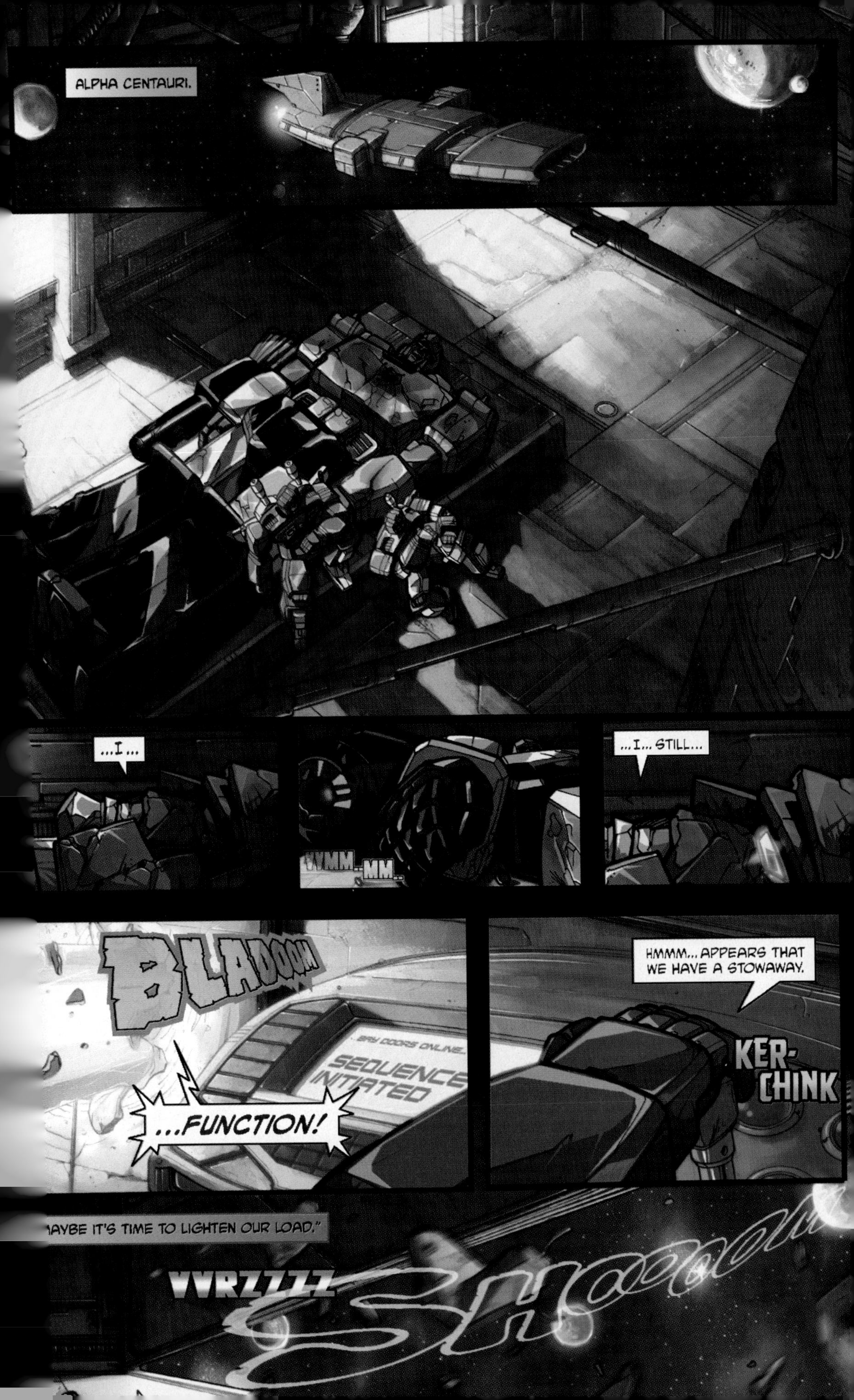
ALPHA CENTAURI.
...I...
VMM..MM..
...I... STILL...
BLADOOM
BAY DOORS ONLINE.
SEQUENCE INITIATED
...FUNCTION!
HMMM... APPEARS THAT WE HAVE A STOWAWAY.
KER-CHINK
"MAYBE IT'S TIME TO LIGHTEN OUR LOAD."
VVRZZZZ

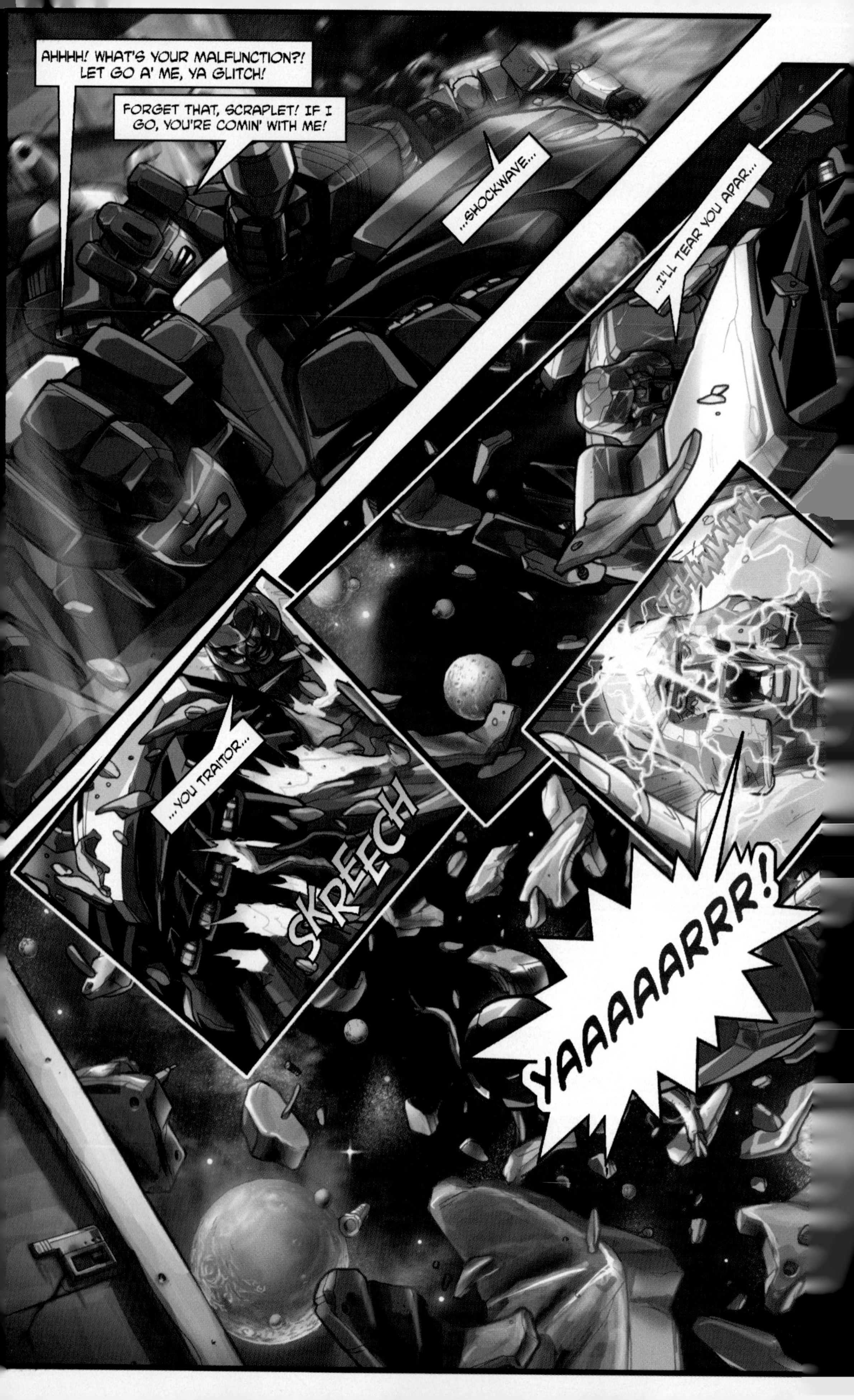
AHHHH! WHAT'S YOUR MALFUNCTION?! LET GO A' ME, YA GLITCH!
FORGET THAT, SCRAPLET! IF I GO, YOU'RE COMIN' WITH ME!
...SHOCKWAVE...
...I'LL TEAR YOU APAR...
...YOU TRAITOR...
SKREECH
YAAAAARRR!

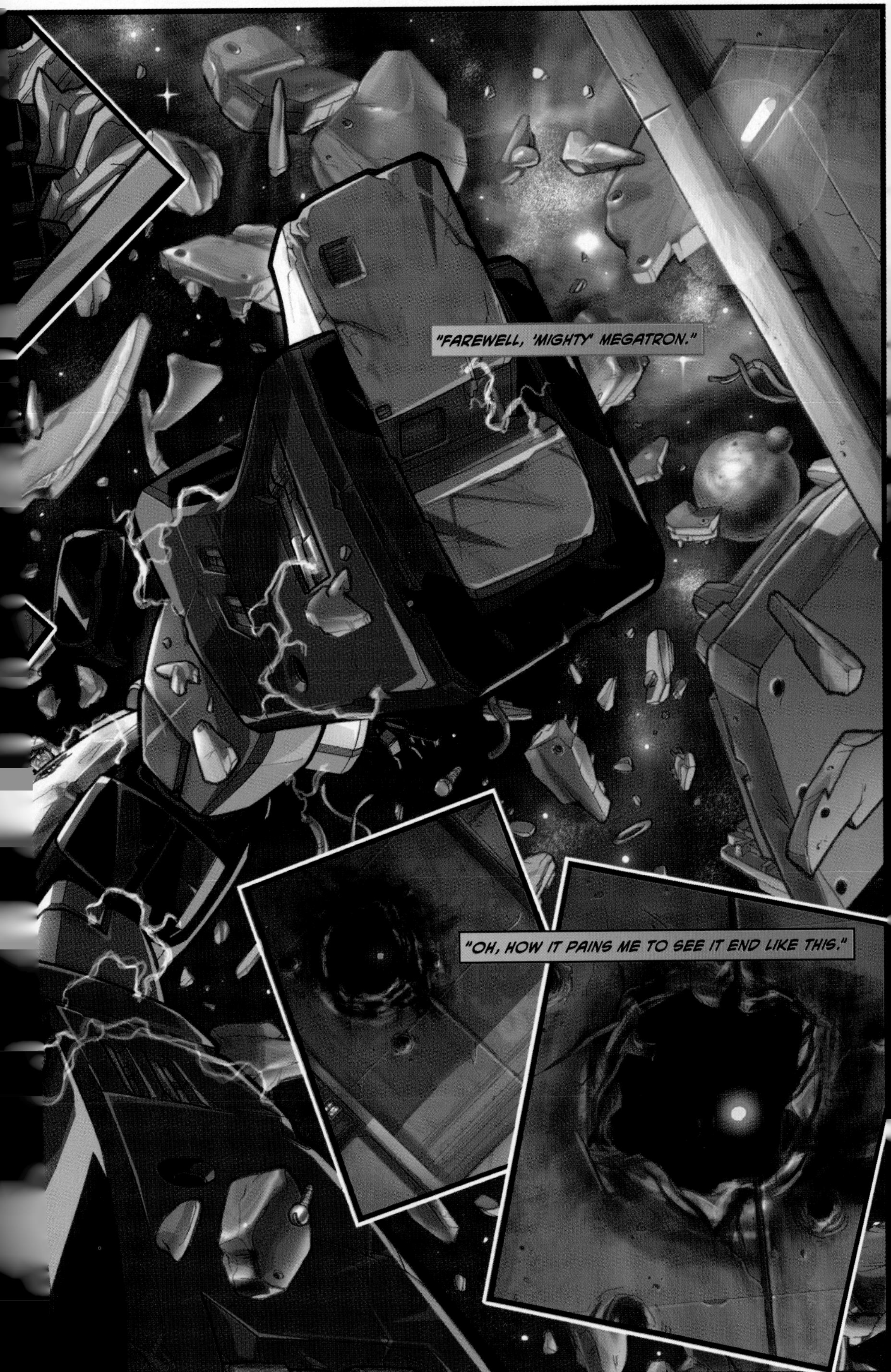
"FAREWELL, 'MIGHTY' MEGATRON."
"OH, HOW IT PAINS ME TO SEE IT END LIKE THIS."

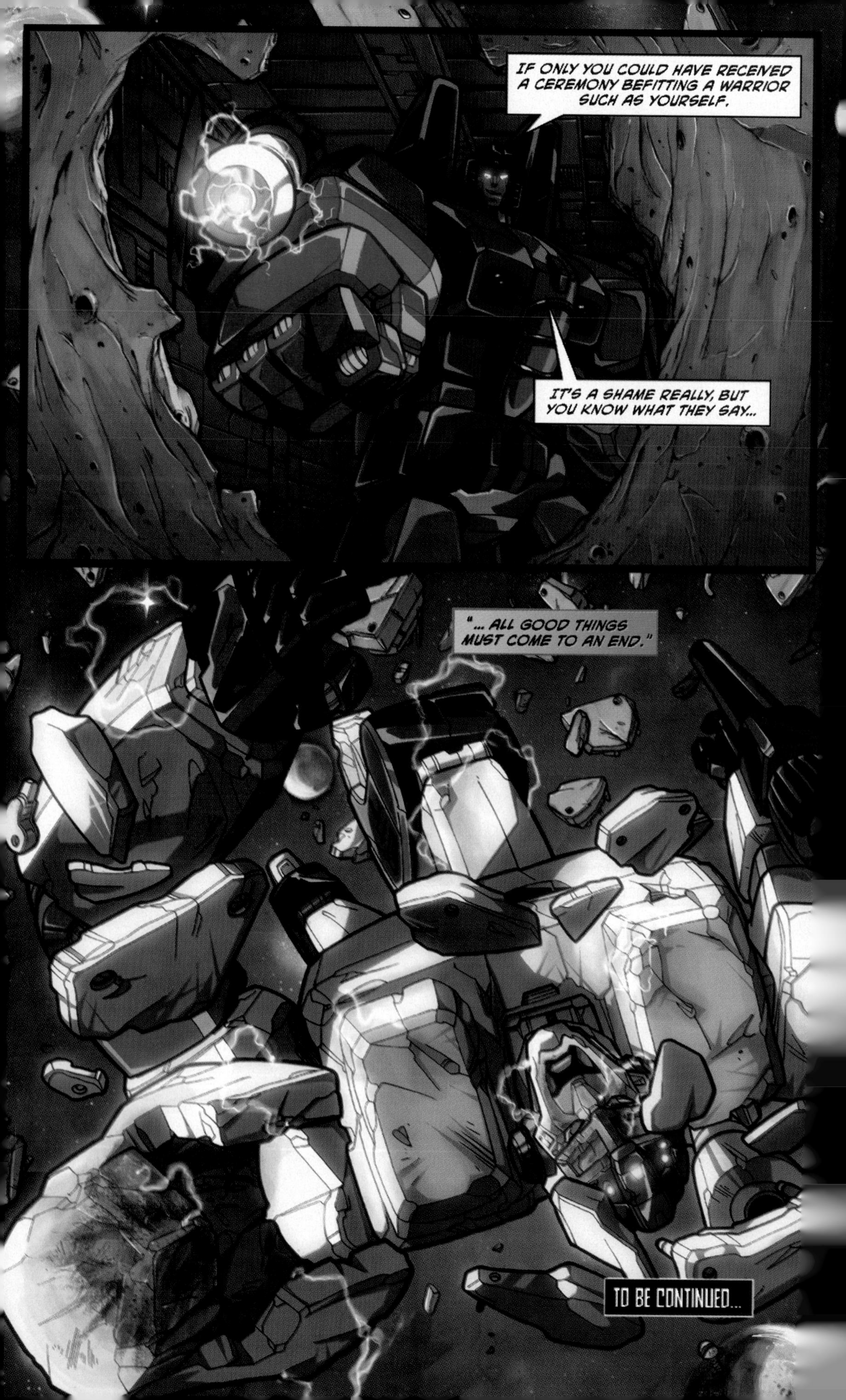
IF ONLY YOU COULD HAVE RECEIVED A CEREMONY BEFITTING A WARRIOR SUCH AS YOURSELF.
IT'S A SHAME REALLY, BUT YOU KNOW WHAT THEY SAY...
"... ALL GOOD THINGS MUST COME TO AN END."
TO BE CONTINUED...

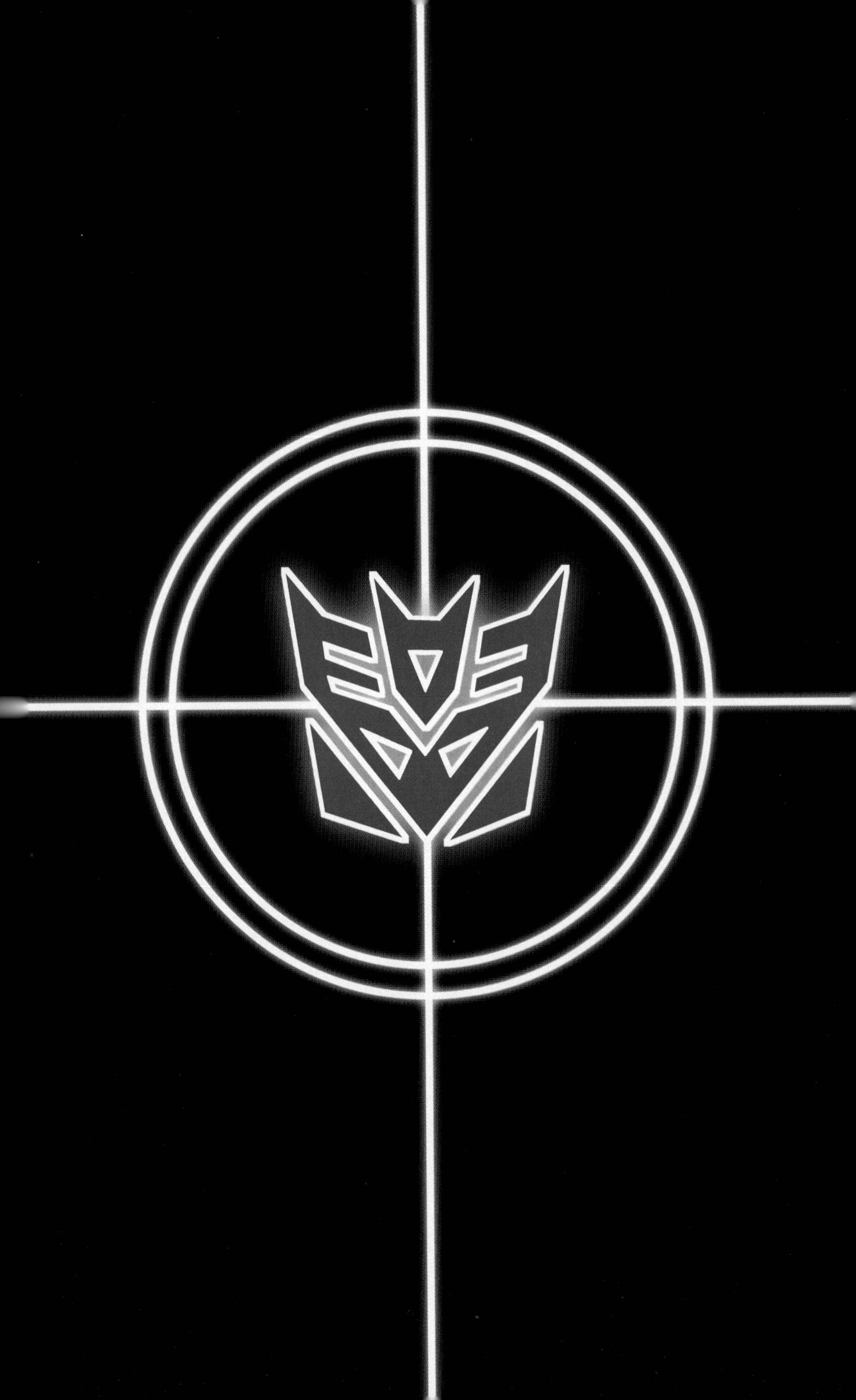

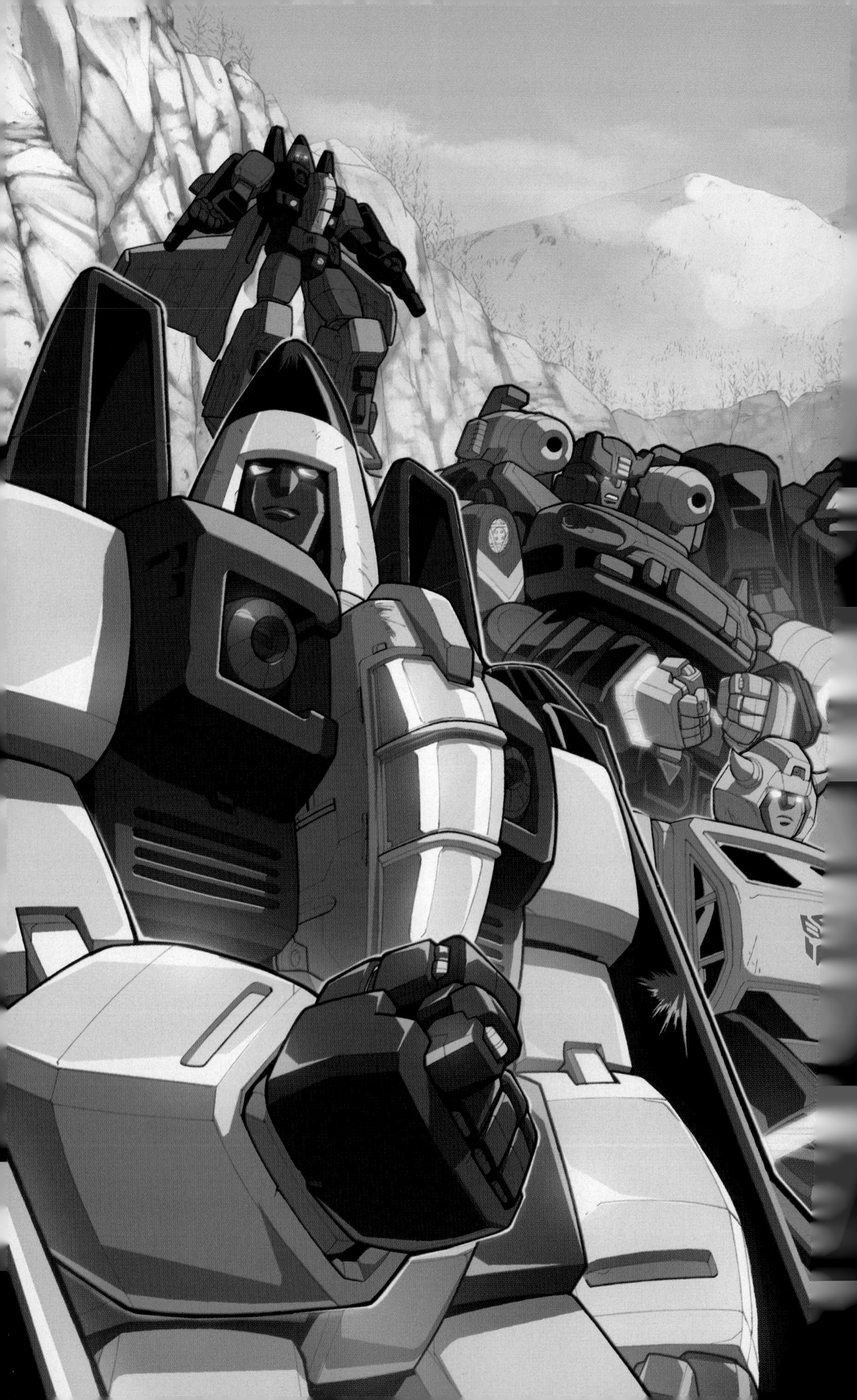

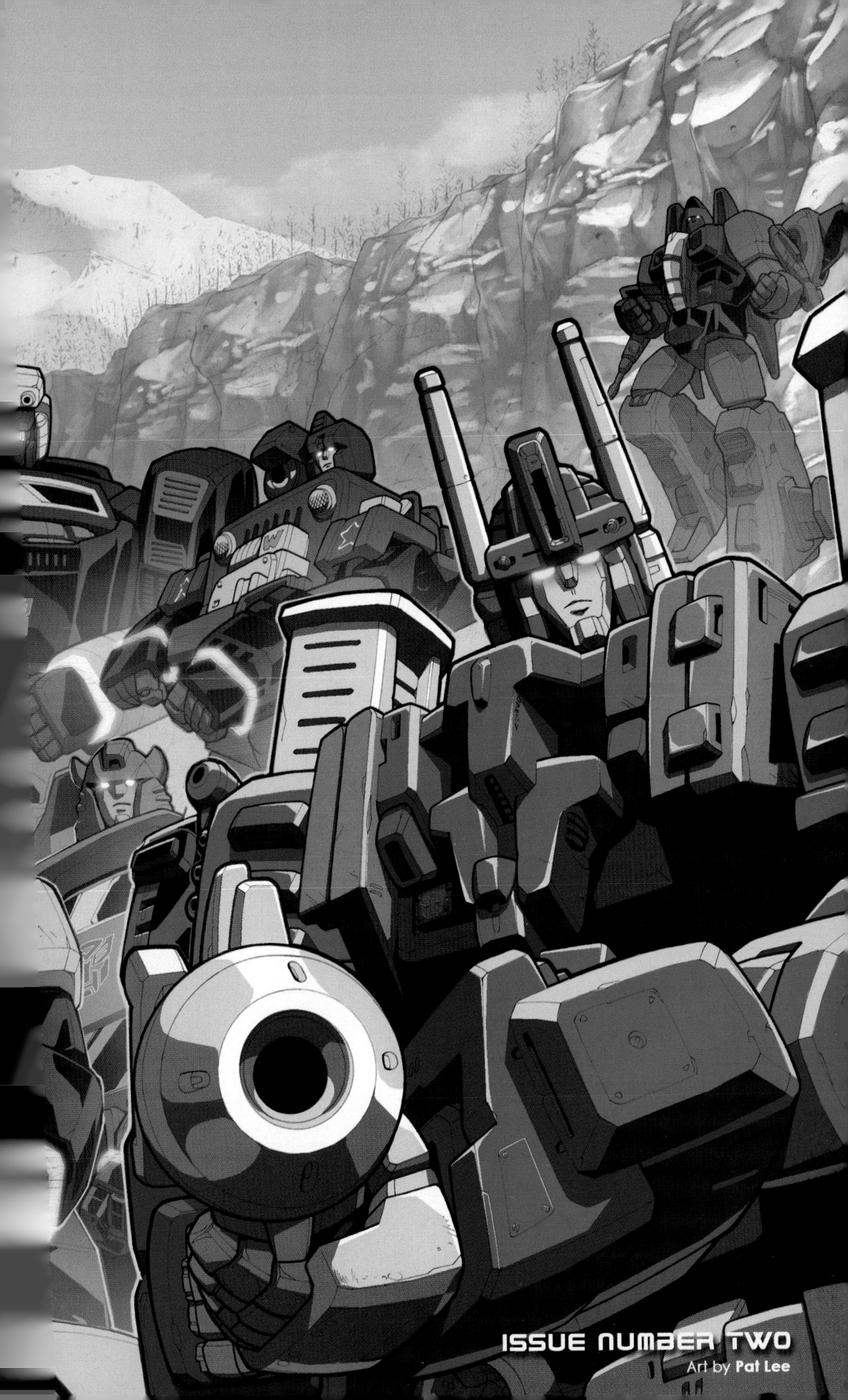

ISSUE NUMBER TWO

Art by **Pat Lee**

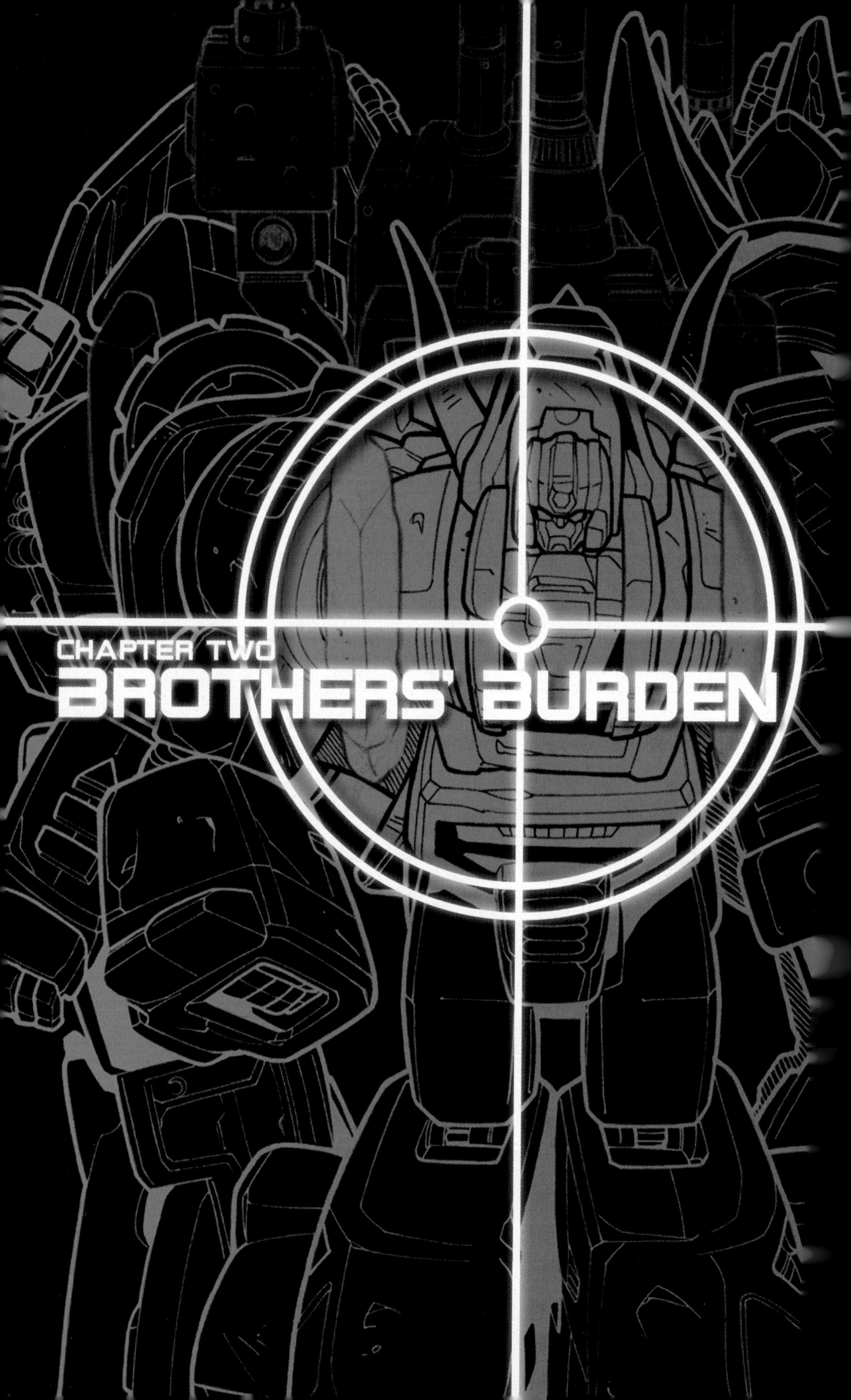
CHAPTER TWO
BROTHERS' BURDEN

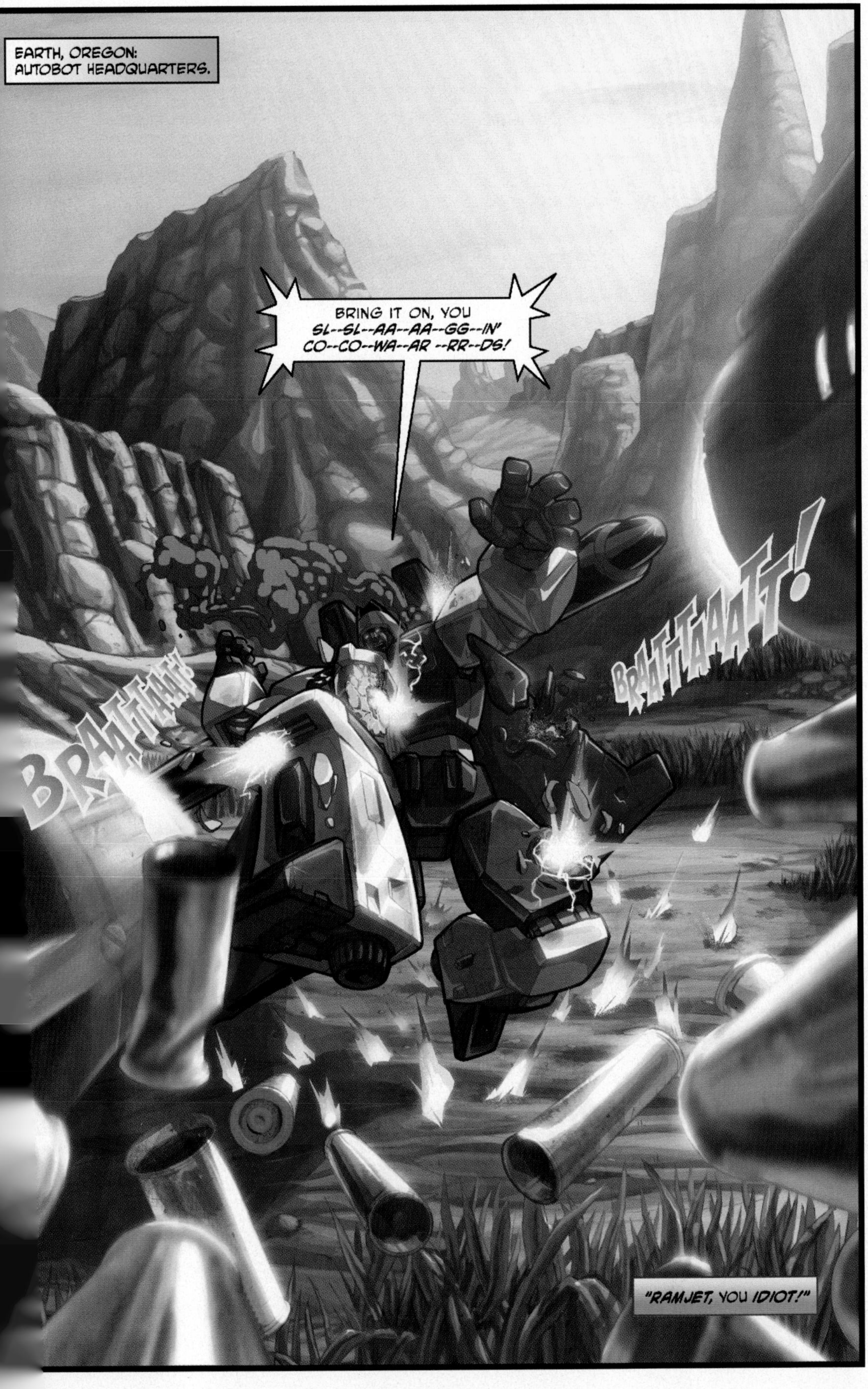
EARTH, OREGON:
AUTOBOT HEADQUARTERS.
BRING IT ON, YOU SL--SL--AA--AA--GG--IN' CO--CO--WA--AR --RR--DS!
BRAATTAAAT!
BRAATTAAATT!
"RAMJET, YOU IDIOT!"

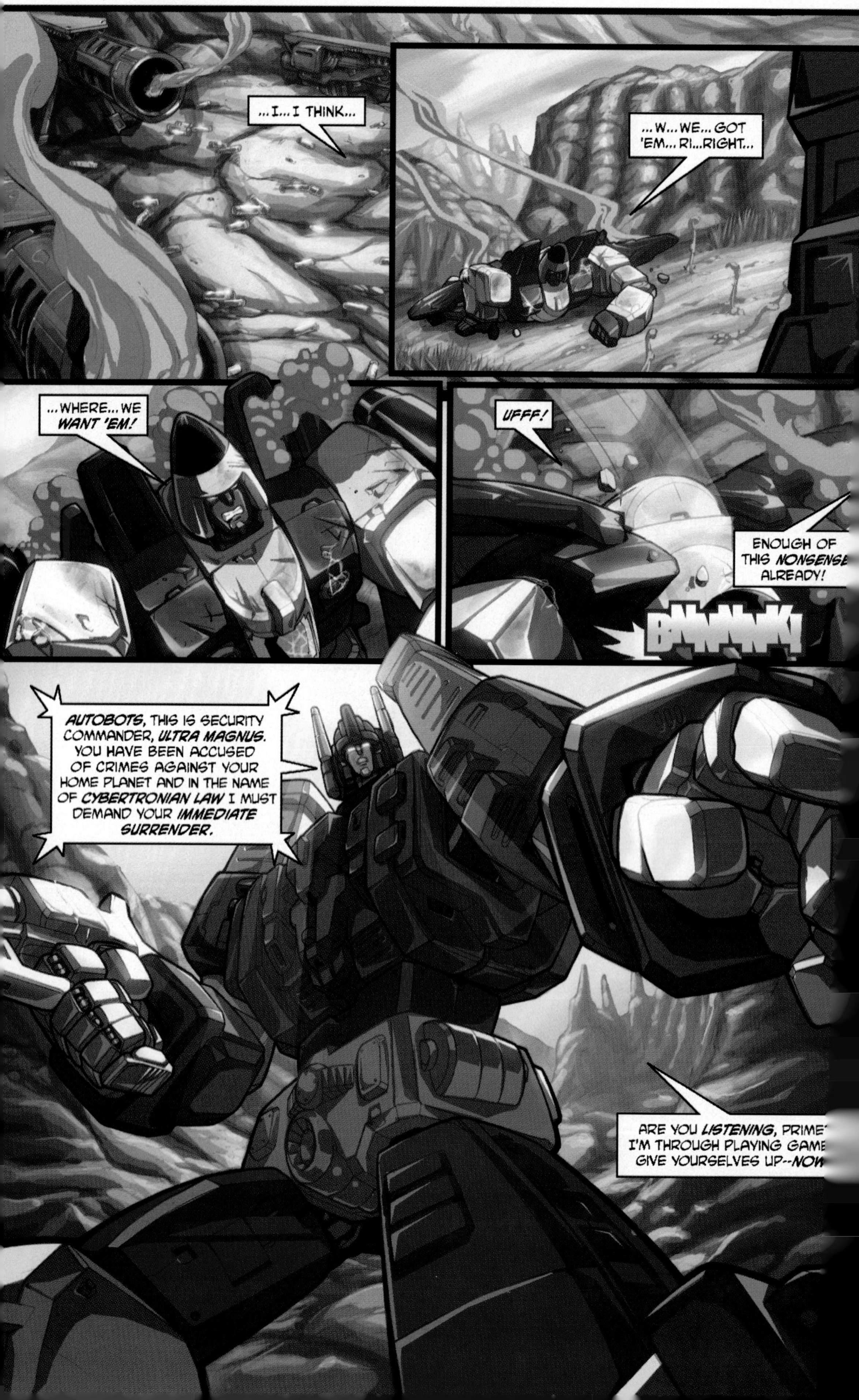
...I...I THINK...
...W...WE...GOT 'EM...RI...RIGHT...
...WHERE...WE WANT 'EM!
UFFF!
ENOUGH OF THIS NONSENSE ALREADY!
BAMMMK!
AUTOBOTS, THIS IS SECURITY COMMANDER, ULTRA MAGNUS. YOU HAVE BEEN ACCUSED OF CRIMES AGAINST YOUR HOME PLANET AND IN THE NAME OF CYBERTRONIAN LAW I MUST DEMAND YOUR IMMEDIATE SURRENDER.
ARE YOU LISTENING, PRIME? I'M THROUGH PLAYING GAMES. GIVE YOURSELVES UP--NOW!

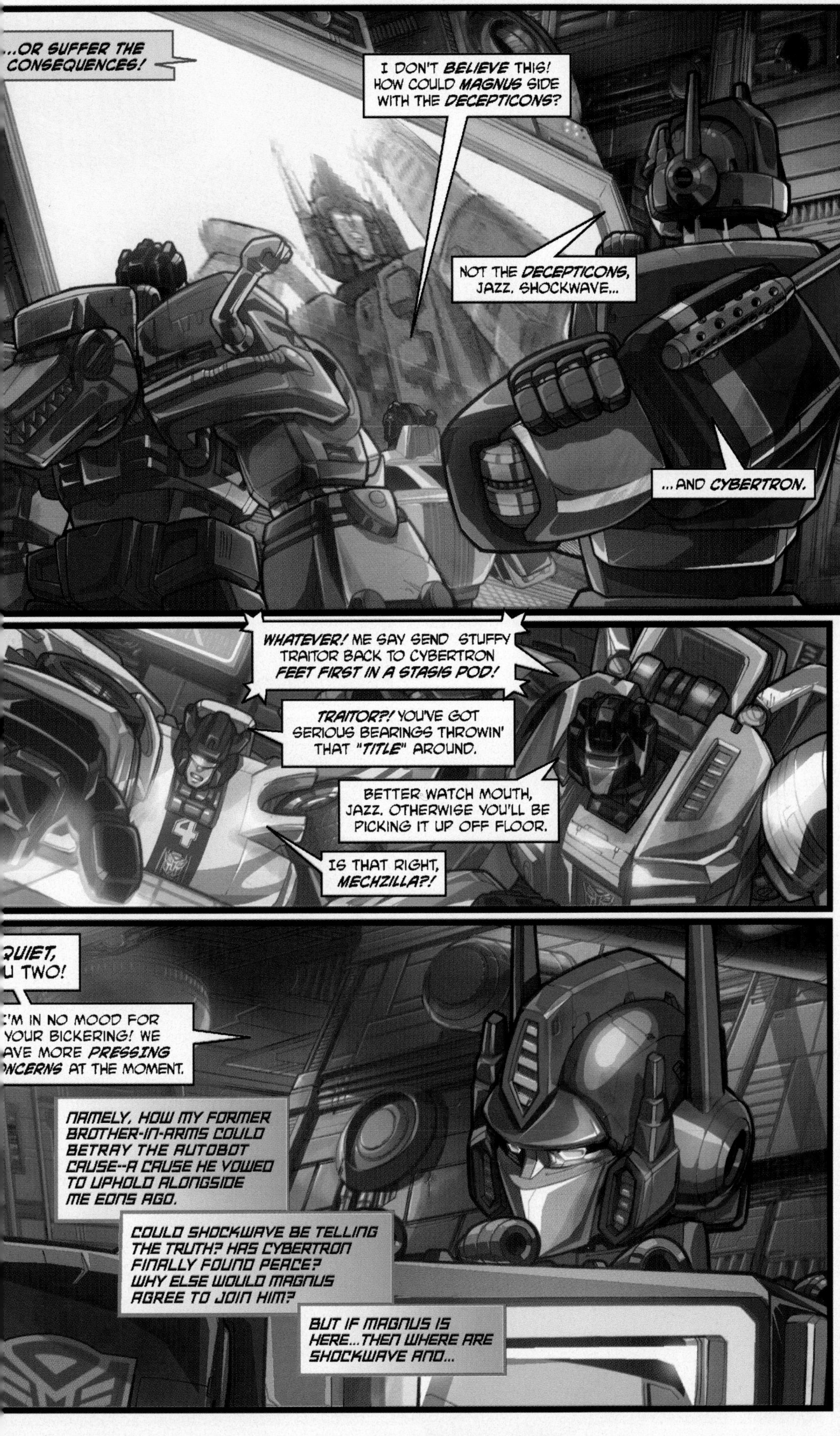
...OR SUFFER THE CONSEQUENCES!
I DON'T BELIEVE THIS! HOW COULD MAGNUS SIDE WITH THE DECEPTICONS?
NOT THE DECEPTICONS, JAZZ. SHOCKWAVE...
...AND CYBERTRON.
WHATEVER! ME SAY SEND STUFFY TRAITOR BACK TO CYBERTRON FEET FIRST IN A STASIS POD!
TRAITOR?! YOU'VE GOT SERIOUS BEARINGS THROWIN' THAT "TITLE" AROUND.
BETTER WATCH MOUTH, JAZZ. OTHERWISE YOU'LL BE PICKING IT UP OFF FLOOR.
IS THAT RIGHT, MECHZILLA?!
QUIET, U TWO!
I'M IN NO MOOD FOR YOUR BICKERING! WE AVE MORE PRESSING ONCERNS AT THE MOMENT.
NAMELY, HOW MY FORMER BROTHER-IN-ARMS COULD BETRAY THE AUTOBOT CAUSE--A CAUSE HE VOWED TO UPHOLD ALONGSIDE ME EONS AGO.
COULD SHOCKWAVE BE TELLING THE TRUTH? HAS CYBERTRON FINALLY FOUND PEACE? WHY ELSE WOULD MAGNUS AGREE TO JOIN HIM?
BUT IF MAGNUS IS HERE...THEN WHERE ARE SHOCKWAVE AND...

"...THE DECEPTICONS?"

AAARRRR! NO! NO... MORE! *YOU WIN...*

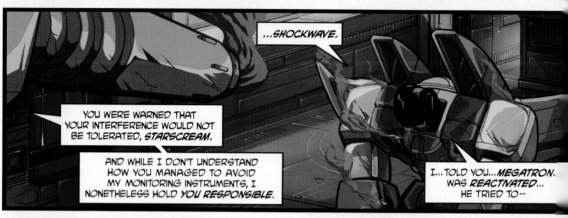

...SHOCKWAVE.

YOU WERE WARNED THAT YOUR INTERFERENCE WOULD NOT BE TOLERATED, *STARSCREAM.*

AND WHILE I DON'T UNDERSTAND HOW YOU MANAGED TO AVOID MY MONITORING INSTRUMENTS, I NONETHELESS HOLD *YOU RESPONSIBLE.*

I...TOLD YOU...*MEGATRON.* WAS *REACTIVATED...* HE TRIED TO--

SILENCE! HEED THIS FINAL WARNING, STARSCREAM. A SECOND INCIDENT...

...WILL RESULT IN YOUR *DESTRUCTION.*

COMMANDER SHOCKWAVE, PLEASE REPORT TO THE BRIDGE. WE ARE INITIATING RE-ENTRY INTO CYBERTRON'S ATMOSPHERE.

HAVE I MADE MY POSITION CLEAR, STARSCREAM?

Y...YES... COMMANDER...

...PERFECTLY...CLEAR.

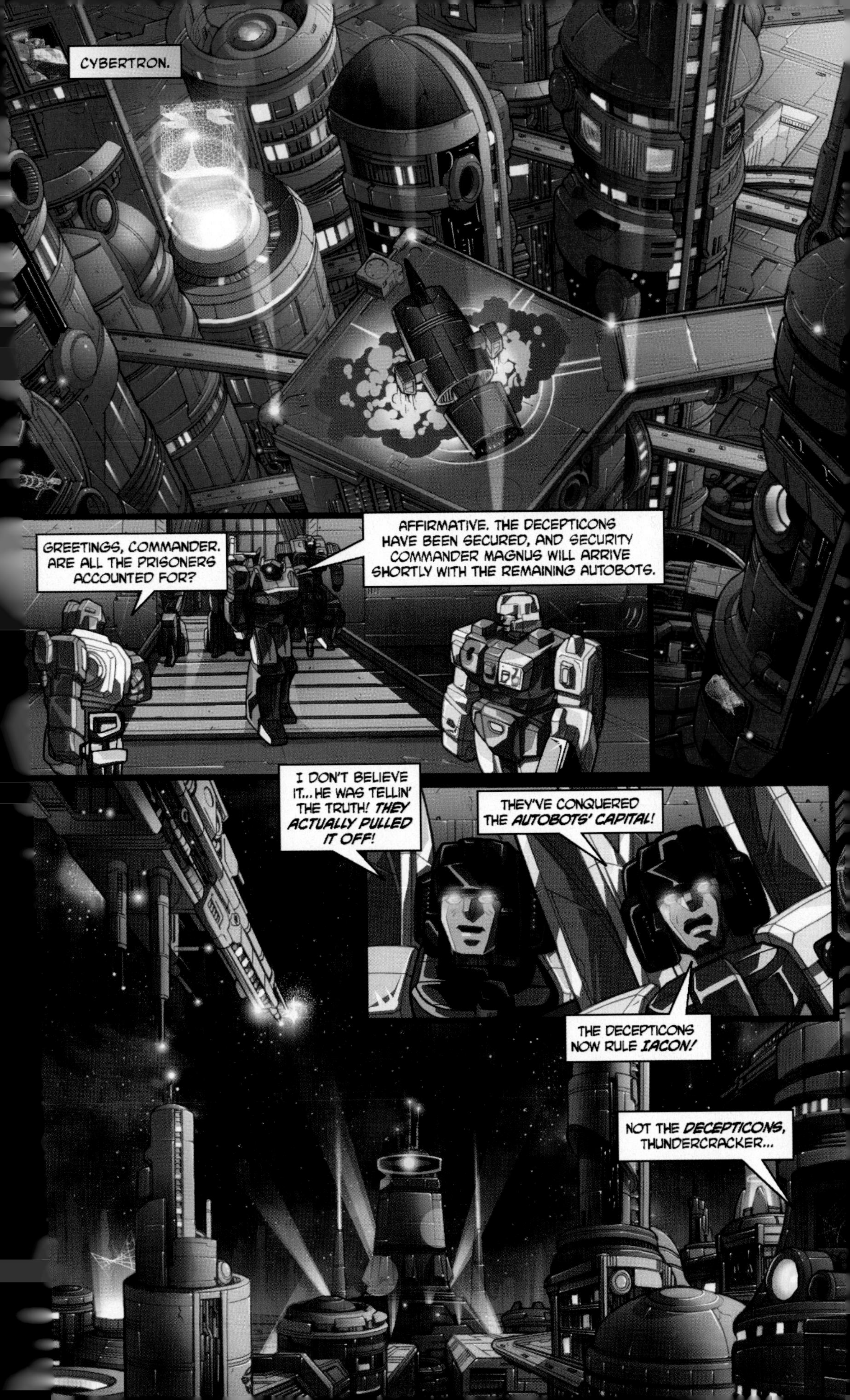
CYBERTRON.
GREETINGS, COMMANDER. ARE ALL THE PRISONERS ACCOUNTED FOR?
AFFIRMATIVE. THE DECEPTICONS HAVE BEEN SECURED, AND SECURITY COMMANDER MAGNUS WILL ARRIVE SHORTLY WITH THE REMAINING AUTOBOTS.
I DON'T BELIEVE IT... HE WAS TELLIN' THE TRUTH! THEY ACTUALLY PULLED IT OFF!
THEY'VE CONQUERED THE AUTOBOTS' CAPITAL!
THE DECEPTICONS NOW RULE IACON!
NOT THE DECEPTICONS, THUNDERCRACKER...

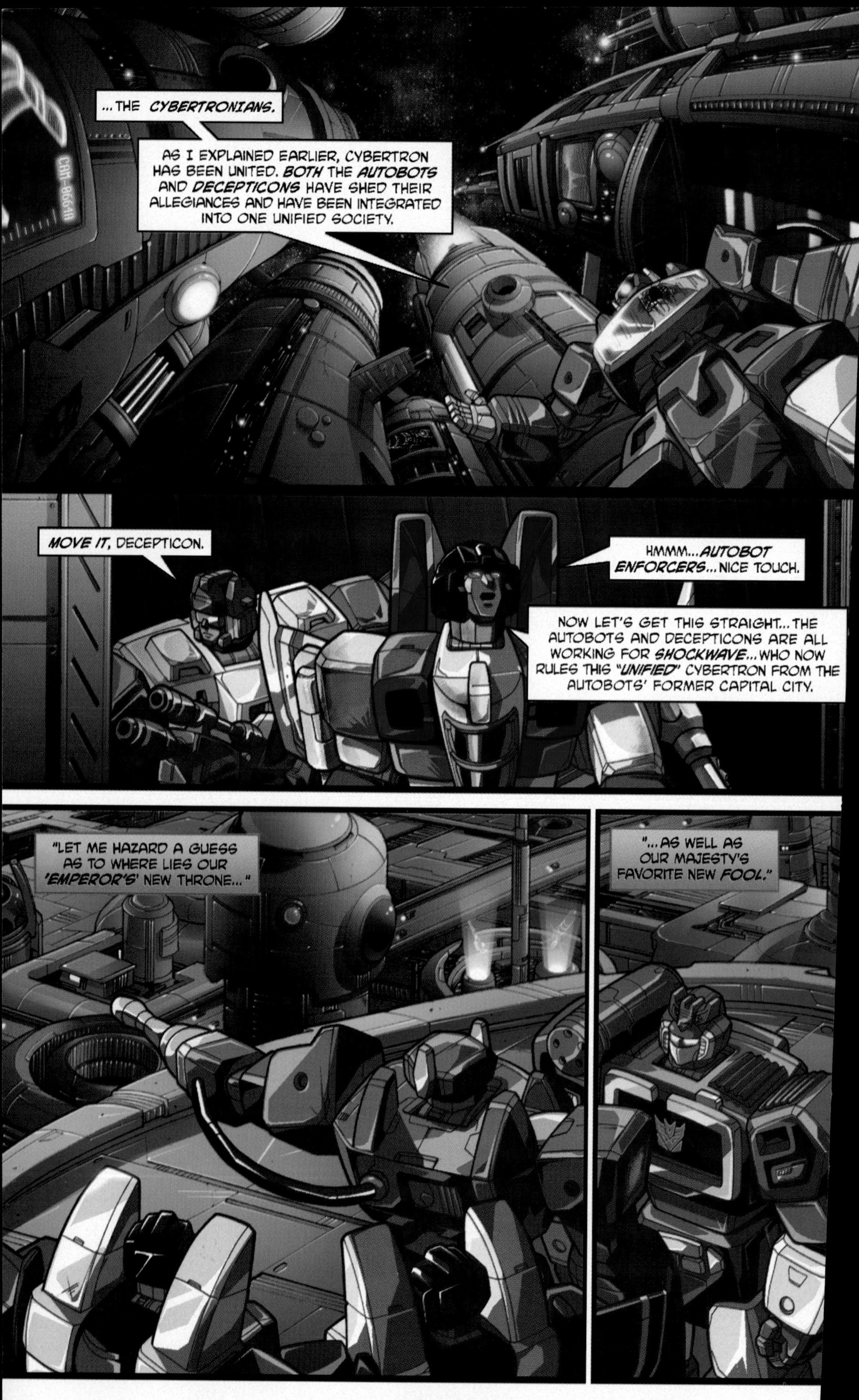
...THE CYBERTRONIANS.
AS I EXPLAINED EARLIER, CYBERTRON HAS BEEN UNITED. BOTH THE AUTOBOTS AND DECEPTICONS HAVE SHED THEIR ALLEGIANCES AND HAVE BEEN INTEGRATED INTO ONE UNIFIED SOCIETY.
MOVE IT, DECEPTICON.
HMMM...AUTOBOT ENFORCERS...NICE TOUCH.
NOW LET'S GET THIS STRAIGHT...THE AUTOBOTS AND DECEPTICONS ARE ALL WORKING FOR SHOCKWAVE...WHO NOW RULES THIS "UNIFIED" CYBERTRON FROM THE AUTOBOTS' FORMER CAPITAL CITY.
"LET ME HAZARD A GUESS AS TO WHERE LIES OUR 'EMPEROR'S' NEW THRONE..."
"...AS WELL AS OUR MAJESTY'S FAVORITE NEW FOOL."

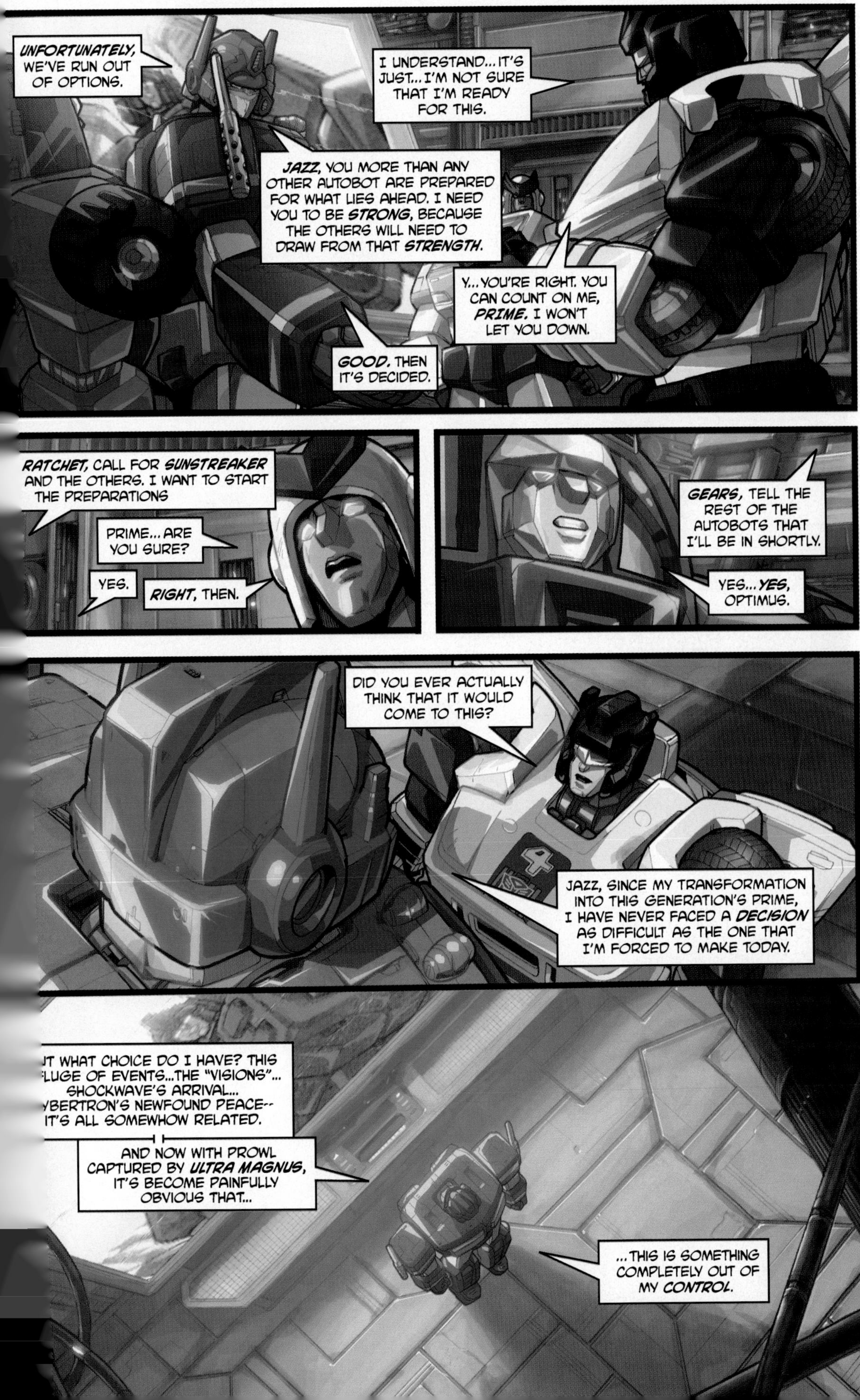
UNFORTUNATELY, WE'VE RUN OUT OF OPTIONS.
I UNDERSTAND... IT'S JUST... I'M NOT SURE THAT I'M READY FOR THIS.
JAZZ, YOU MORE THAN ANY OTHER AUTOBOT ARE PREPARED FOR WHAT LIES AHEAD. I NEED YOU TO BE STRONG, BECAUSE THE OTHERS WILL NEED TO DRAW FROM THAT STRENGTH.
Y... YOU'RE RIGHT. YOU CAN COUNT ON ME, PRIME. I WON'T LET YOU DOWN.
GOOD. THEN IT'S DECIDED.
RATCHET, CALL FOR SUNSTREAKER AND THE OTHERS. I WANT TO START THE PREPARATIONS
PRIME... ARE YOU SURE?
YES.
RIGHT, THEN.
GEARS, TELL THE REST OF THE AUTOBOTS THAT I'LL BE IN SHORTLY.
YES... YES, OPTIMUS.
DID YOU EVER ACTUALLY THINK THAT IT WOULD COME TO THIS?
JAZZ, SINCE MY TRANSFORMATION INTO THIS GENERATION'S PRIME, I HAVE NEVER FACED A DECISION AS DIFFICULT AS THE ONE THAT I'M FORCED TO MAKE TODAY.
UT WHAT CHOICE DO I HAVE? THIS LUGE OF EVENTS...THE "VISIONS"... SHOCKWAVE'S ARRIVAL... YBERTRON'S NEWFOUND PEACE-- IT'S ALL SOMEWHOW RELATED.
AND NOW WITH PROWL CAPTURED BY ULTRA MAGNUS, IT'S BECOME PAINFULLY OBVIOUS THAT...
...THIS IS SOMETHING COMPLETELY OUT OF MY CONTROL.

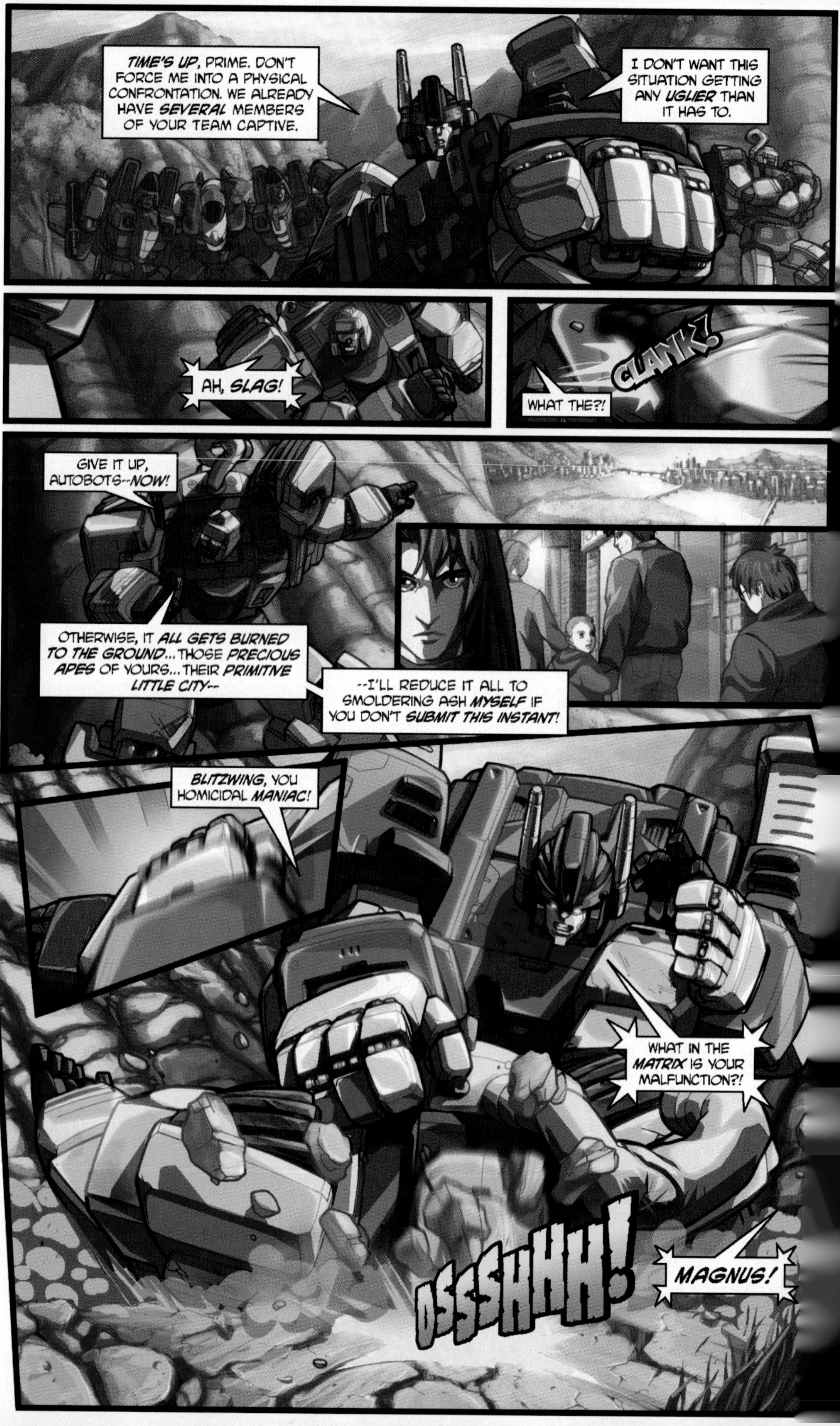

TIME'S UP, PRIME. DON'T FORCE ME INTO A PHYSICAL CONFRONTATION. WE ALREADY HAVE SEVERAL MEMBERS OF YOUR TEAM CAPTIVE.
I DON'T WANT THIS SITUATION GETTING ANY UGLIER THAN IT HAS TO.
AH, SLAG!
CLANK!
WHAT THE?!
GIVE IT UP, AUTOBOTS--NOW!
OTHERWISE, IT ALL GETS BURNED TO THE GROUND... THOSE PRECIOUS APES OF YOURS... THEIR PRIMITIVE LITTLE CITY--
--I'LL REDUCE IT ALL TO SMOLDERING ASH MYSELF IF YOU DON'T SUBMIT THIS INSTANT!
BLITZWING, YOU HOMICIDAL MANIAC!
WHAT IN THE MATRIX IS YOUR MALFUNCTION?!
OSSSHHH!
MAGNUS!

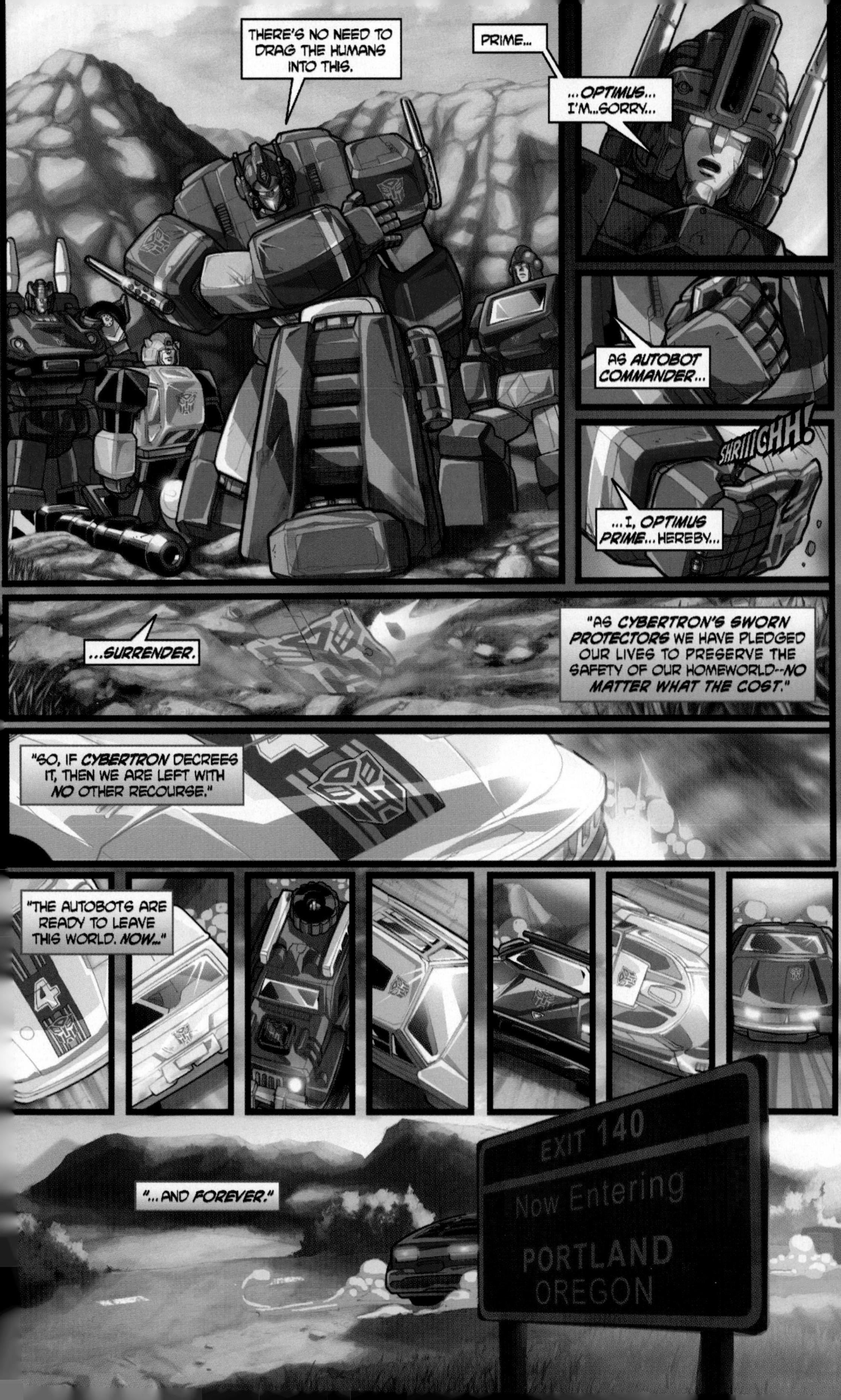
THERE'S NO NEED TO DRAG THE HUMANS INTO THIS.
PRIME...
...OPTIMUS... I'M...SORRY...
AS AUTOBOT COMMANDER...
SHRIIICHH!
...I, OPTIMUS PRIME... HEREBY...
...SURRENDER.
"AS CYBERTRON'S SWORN PROTECTORS WE HAVE PLEDGED OUR LIVES TO PRESERVE THE SAFETY OF OUR HOMEWORLD--NO MATTER WHAT THE COST."
"SO, IF CYBERTRON DECREES IT, THEN WE ARE LEFT WITH NO OTHER RECOURSE."
"THE AUTOBOTS ARE READY TO LEAVE THIS WORLD. NOW..."
EXIT 140
Now Entering
PORTLAND
OREGON
"...AND FOREVER."

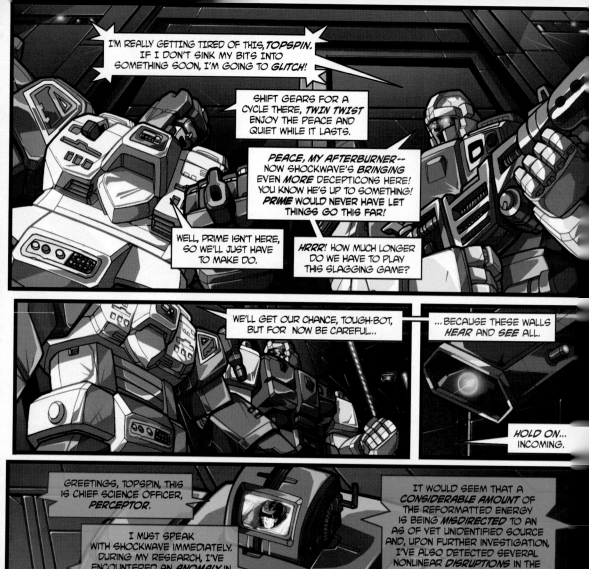

I'M REALLY GETTING TIRED OF THIS, *TOPSPIN.* IF I DON'T SINK MY BITS INTO SOMETHING SOON, I'M GOING TO *GLITCH!*

SHIFT GEARS FOR A CYCLE THERE, *TWIN TWIST* ENJOY THE PEACE AND QUIET WHILE IT LASTS.

PEACE, MY AFTERBURNER-- NOW SHOCKWAVE'S *BRINGING* EVEN *MORE* DECEPTICONS HERE! YOU KNOW HE'S UP TO SOMETHING! *PRIME* WOULD NEVER HAVE LET THINGS GO THIS FAR!

WELL, PRIME ISN'T HERE, SO WE'LL JUST HAVE TO MAKE DO.

HRRR! HOW MUCH LONGER DO WE HAVE TO PLAY THIS SLAGGING GAME?

WE'LL GET OUR CHANCE, TOUGH-BOT, BUT FOR NOW BE CAREFUL...

...BECAUSE THESE WALLS *HEAR* AND *SEE* ALL.

HOLD ON... INCOMING.

GREETINGS, TOPSPIN, THIS IS CHIEF SCIENCE OFFICER, *PERCEPTOR.*

I MUST SPEAK WITH SHOCKWAVE IMMEDIATELY. DURING MY RESEARCH, I'VE ENCOUNTERED AN *ANOMALY* IN CYBERTRON'S POWER CONVERSION PROCESS.

IT WOULD SEEM THAT A *CONSIDERABLE AMOUNT* OF THE REFORMATTED ENERGY IS BEING *MISDIRECTED* TO AN AS OF YET UNIDENTIFIED SOURCE AND, UPON FURTHER INVESTIGATION, I'VE ALSO DETECTED SEVERAL NONLINEAR *DISRUPTIONS* IN THE PLANET'S ORBITAL SEQUEN--

--WHOA!

TRY THAT AGAIN IN WORDS *WE CAN ALL UNDERSTAND.*

OH...AHEM...WELL, IT APPEARS THAT SHOCKWAVE'S MODIFICATIONS MAY HAVE RESULTED IN SOME SORT OF TRANSW--

PERCEPTOR...

CYBERTRON-- IT'S *MOVING!*

WELL, I'M SURE WE'VE GOT A FEW MORE KLIKS BEFORE THE SKY FALLS. BESIDES, OUR *"FEARLESS LEADER"* IS BUSY AT THE MOMENT AND DOESN'T WISH TO BE DISTURBED.

SHOCKWAVE'S OCCUPIED? *DOING WHAT?*

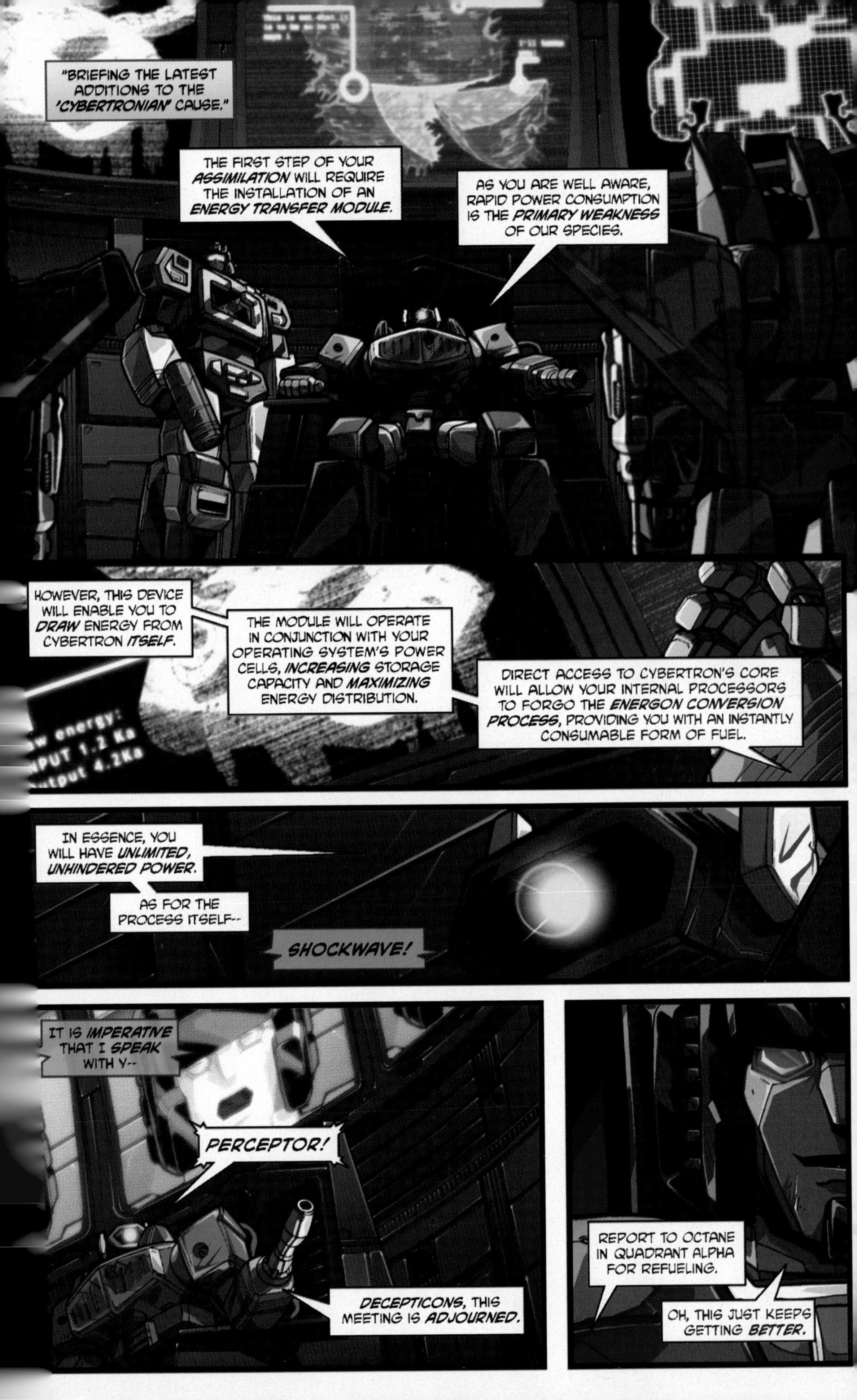
"BRIEFING THE LATEST ADDITIONS TO THE 'CYBERTRONIAN' CAUSE."
THE FIRST STEP OF YOUR ASSIMILATION WILL REQUIRE THE INSTALLATION OF AN ENERGY TRANSFER MODULE.
AS YOU ARE WELL AWARE, RAPID POWER CONSUMPTION IS THE PRIMARY WEAKNESS OF OUR SPECIES.
HOWEVER, THIS DEVICE WILL ENABLE YOU TO DRAW ENERGY FROM CYBERTRON ITSELF.
THE MODULE WILL OPERATE IN CONJUNCTION WITH YOUR OPERATING SYSTEM'S POWER CELLS, INCREASING STORAGE CAPACITY AND MAXIMIZING ENERGY DISTRIBUTION.
DIRECT ACCESS TO CYBERTRON'S CORE WILL ALLOW YOUR INTERNAL PROCESSORS TO FORGO THE ENERGON CONVERSION PROCESS, PROVIDING YOU WITH AN INSTANTLY CONSUMABLE FORM OF FUEL.
IN ESSENCE, YOU WILL HAVE UNLIMITED, UNHINDERED POWER.
AS FOR THE PROCESS ITSELF--
SHOCKWAVE!
IT IS IMPERATIVE THAT I SPEAK WITH Y--
PERCEPTOR!
DECEPTICONS, THIS MEETING IS ADJOURNED.
REPORT TO OCTANE IN QUADRANT ALPHA FOR REFUELING.
OH, THIS JUST KEEPS GETTING BETTER.

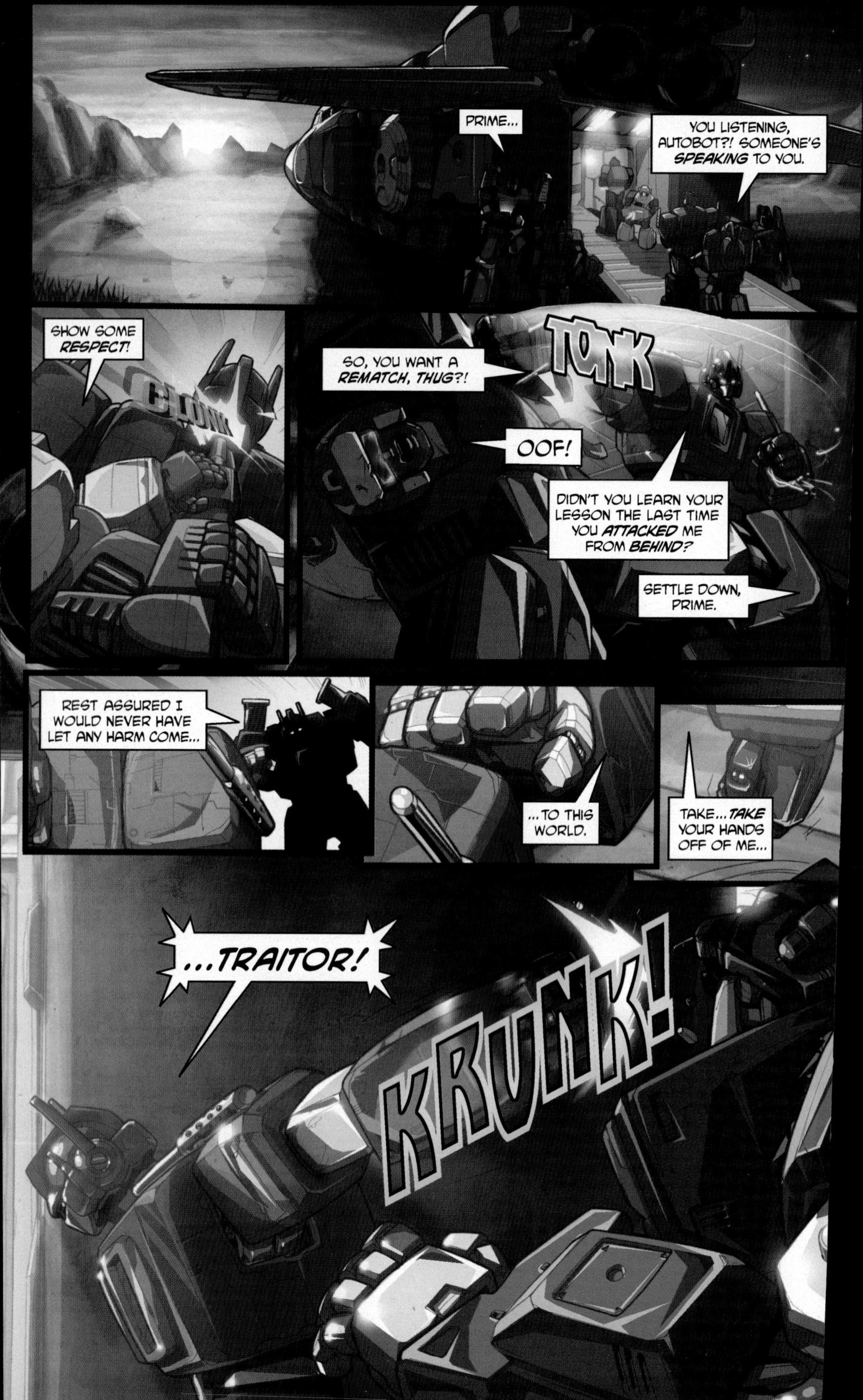
PRIME...
YOU LISTENING, AUTOBOT?! SOMEONE'S SPEAKING TO YOU.
SHOW SOME RESPECT!
CLONK
SO, YOU WANT A REMATCH, THUG?!
TONK
OOF!
DIDN'T YOU LEARN YOUR LESSON THE LAST TIME YOU ATTACKED ME FROM BEHIND?
SETTLE DOWN, PRIME.
REST ASSURED I WOULD NEVER HAVE LET ANY HARM COME...
...TO THIS WORLD.
TAKE... TAKE YOUR HANDS OFF OF ME...
...TRAITOR!
KRUNK!

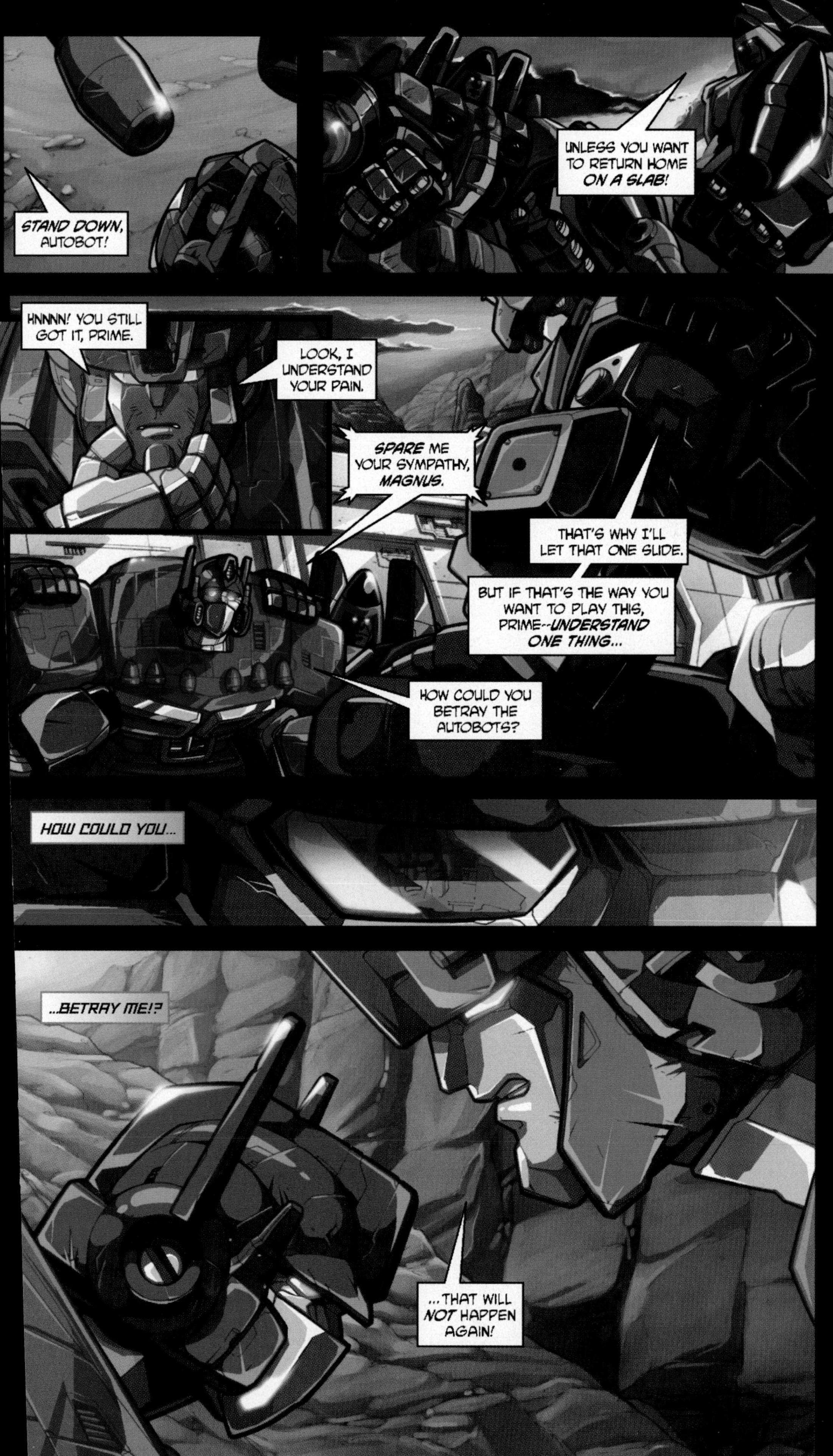
STAND DOWN, AUTOBOT!
UNLESS YOU WANT TO RETURN HOME ON A SLAB!
HNNNN! YOU STILL GOT IT, PRIME.
LOOK, I UNDERSTAND YOUR PAIN.
SPARE ME YOUR SYMPATHY, MAGNUS.
THAT'S WHY I'LL LET THAT ONE SLIDE.
BUT IF THAT'S THE WAY YOU WANT TO PLAY THIS, PRIME--UNDERSTAND ONE THING...
HOW COULD YOU BETRAY THE AUTOBOTS?
HOW COULD YOU...
...BETRAY ME!?
...THAT WILL NOT HAPPEN AGAIN!

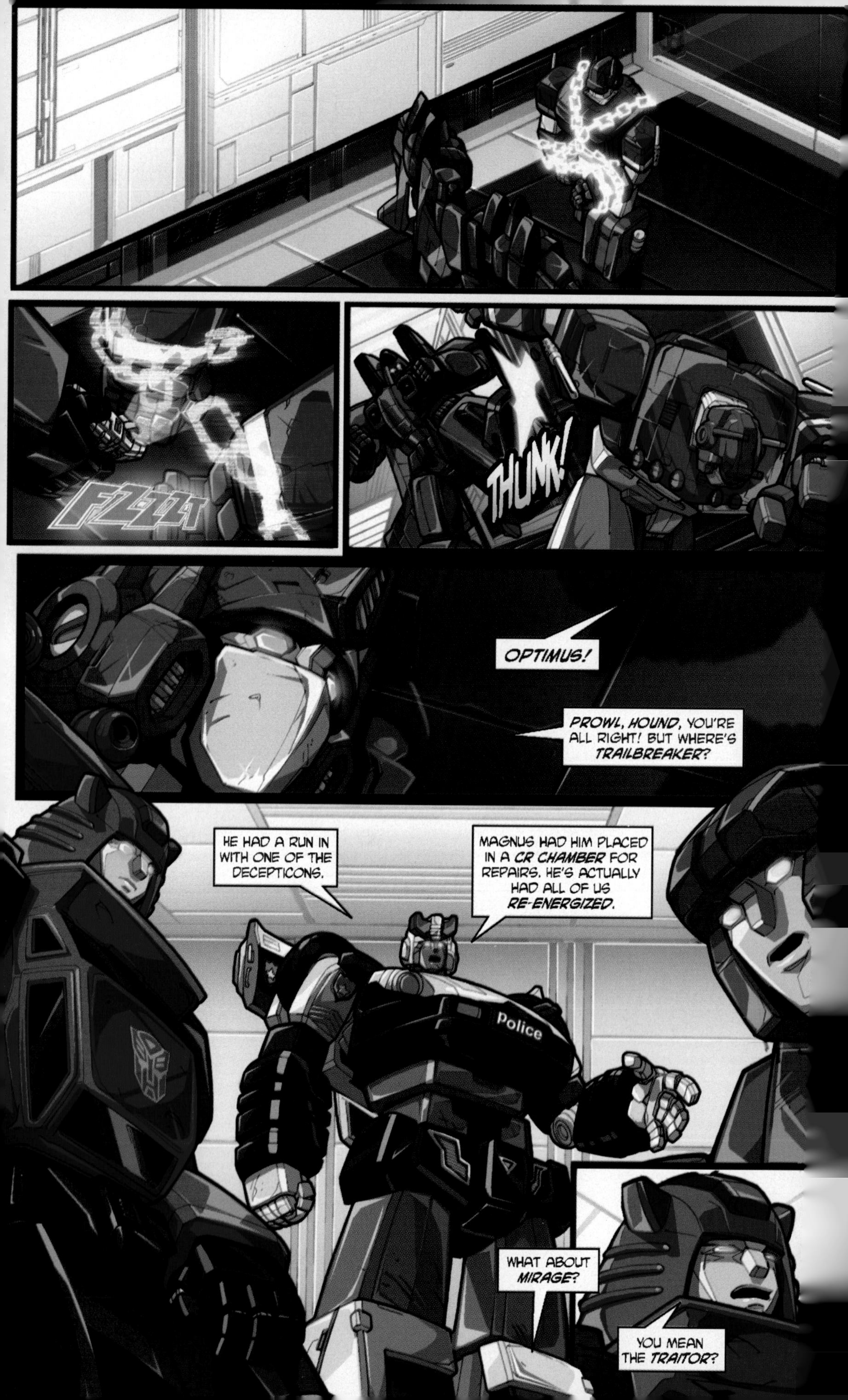
FZZZT
THUNK!
OPTIMUS!
PROWL, HOUND, YOU'RE ALL RIGHT! BUT WHERE'S TRAILBREAKER?
HE HAD A RUN IN WITH ONE OF THE DECEPTICONS.
MAGNUS HAD HIM PLACED IN A CR CHAMBER FOR REPAIRS. HE'S ACTUALLY HAD ALL OF US RE-ENERGIZED.
Police
WHAT ABOUT MIRAGE?
YOU MEAN THE TRAITOR?

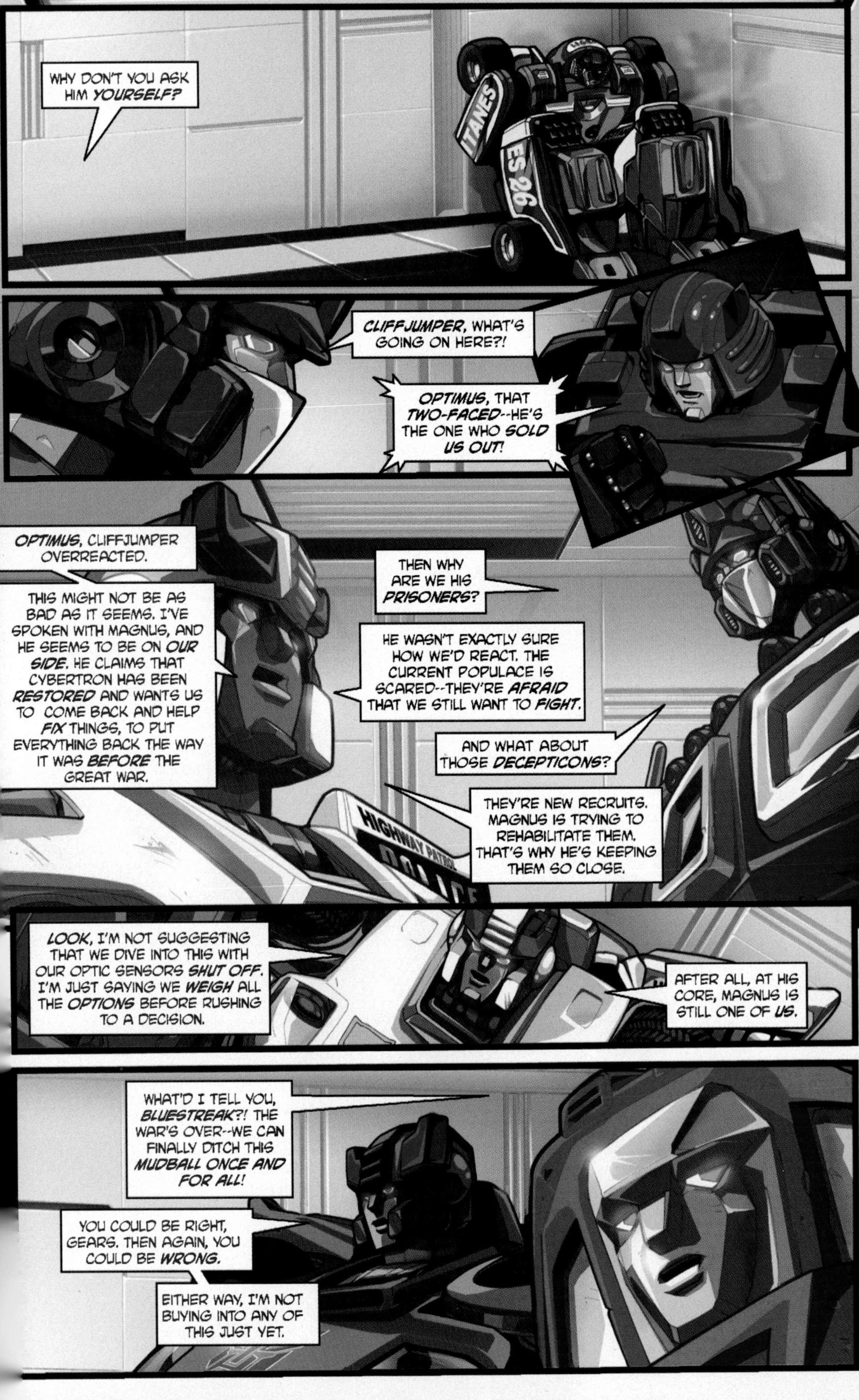
WHY DON'T YOU ASK HIM YOURSELF?
ITANES
ES 26
CLIFFJUMPER, WHAT'S GOING ON HERE?!
OPTIMUS, THAT TWO-FACED--HE'S THE ONE WHO SOLD US OUT!
OPTIMUS, CLIFFJUMPER OVERREACTED.
THIS MIGHT NOT BE AS BAD AS IT SEEMS. I'VE SPOKEN WITH MAGNUS, AND HE SEEMS TO BE ON OUR SIDE. HE CLAIMS THAT CYBERTRON HAS BEEN RESTORED AND WANTS US TO COME BACK AND HELP FIX THINGS, TO PUT EVERYTHING BACK THE WAY IT WAS BEFORE THE GREAT WAR.
THEN WHY ARE WE HIS PRISONERS?
HE WASN'T EXACTLY SURE HOW WE'D REACT. THE CURRENT POPULACE IS SCARED--THEY'RE AFRAID THAT WE STILL WANT TO FIGHT.
AND WHAT ABOUT THOSE DECEPTICONS?
THEY'RE NEW RECRUITS. MAGNUS IS TRYING TO REHABILITATE THEM. THAT'S WHY HE'S KEEPING THEM SO CLOSE.
HIGHWAY PATROL
LOOK, I'M NOT SUGGESTING THAT WE DIVE INTO THIS WITH OUR OPTIC SENSORS SHUT OFF. I'M JUST SAYING WE WEIGH ALL THE OPTIONS BEFORE RUSHING TO A DECISION.
AFTER ALL, AT HIS CORE, MAGNUS IS STILL ONE OF US.
WHAT'D I TELL YOU, BLUESTREAK?! THE WAR'S OVER--WE CAN FINALLY DITCH THIS MUDBALL ONCE AND FOR ALL!
YOU COULD BE RIGHT, GEARS. THEN AGAIN, YOU COULD BE WRONG.
EITHER WAY, I'M NOT BUYING INTO ANY OF THIS JUST YET.

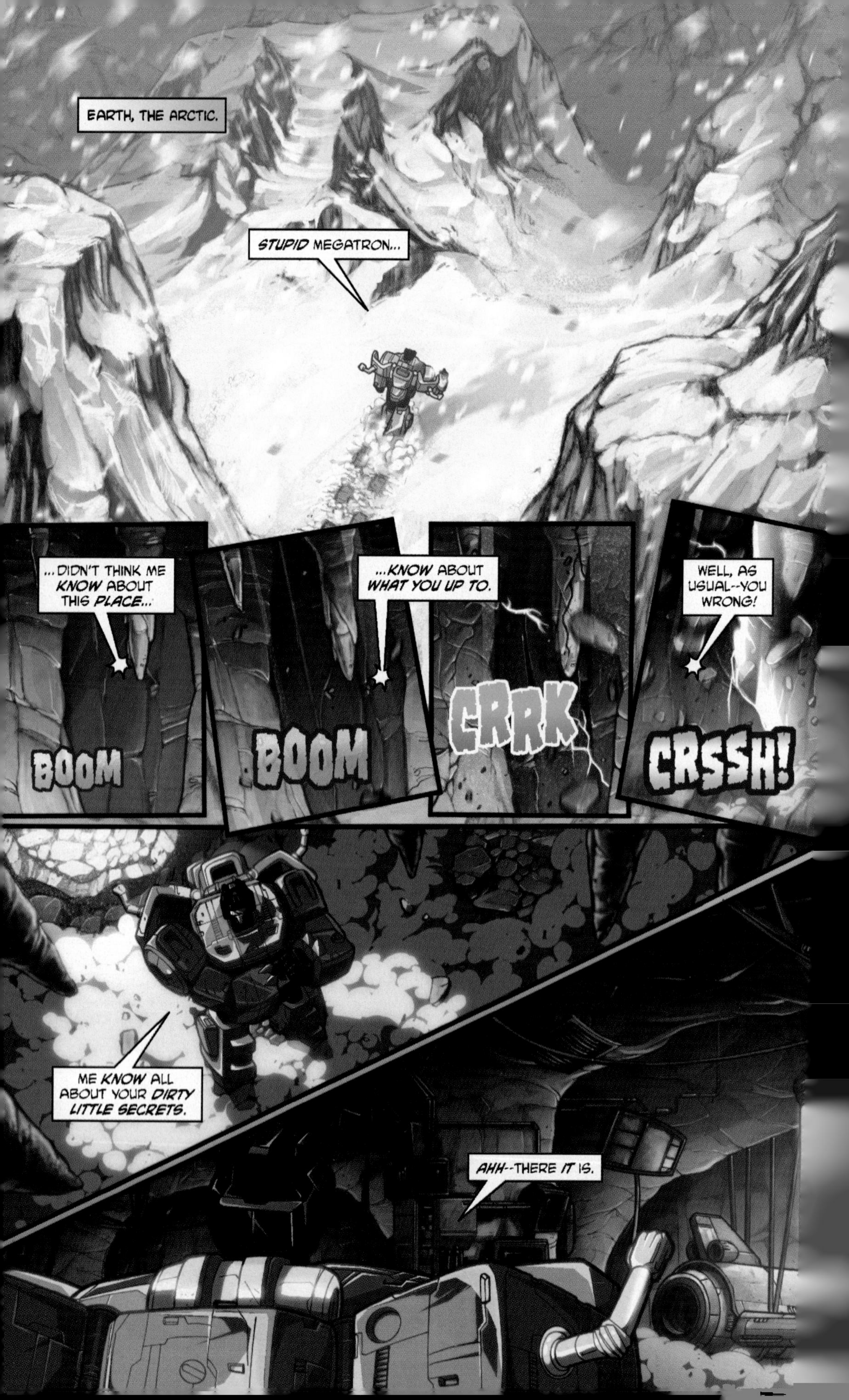
EARTH, THE ARCTIC.
STUPID MEGATRON...
...DIDN'T THINK ME KNOW ABOUT THIS PLACE...
BOOM
...KNOW ABOUT WHAT YOU UP TO.
BOOM
CRRK
WELL, AS USUAL--YOU WRONG!
CRSSH!
ME KNOW ALL ABOUT YOUR DIRTY LITTLE SECRETS.
AHH--THERE IT IS.

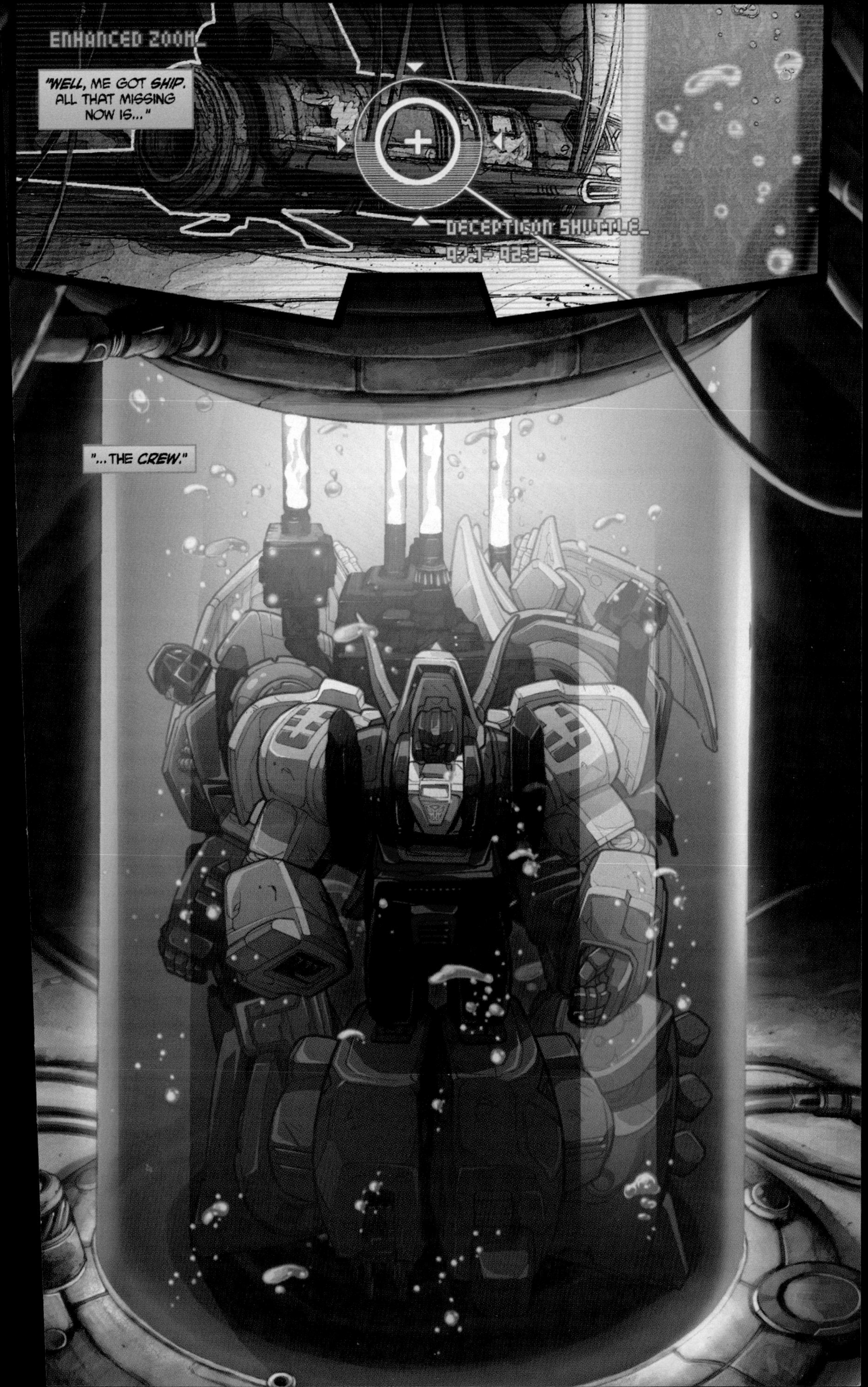

ENHANCED ZOOM_
"WELL, ME GOT SHIP. ALL THAT MISSING NOW IS..."
DECEPTICON SHUTTLE_
"...THE CREW."

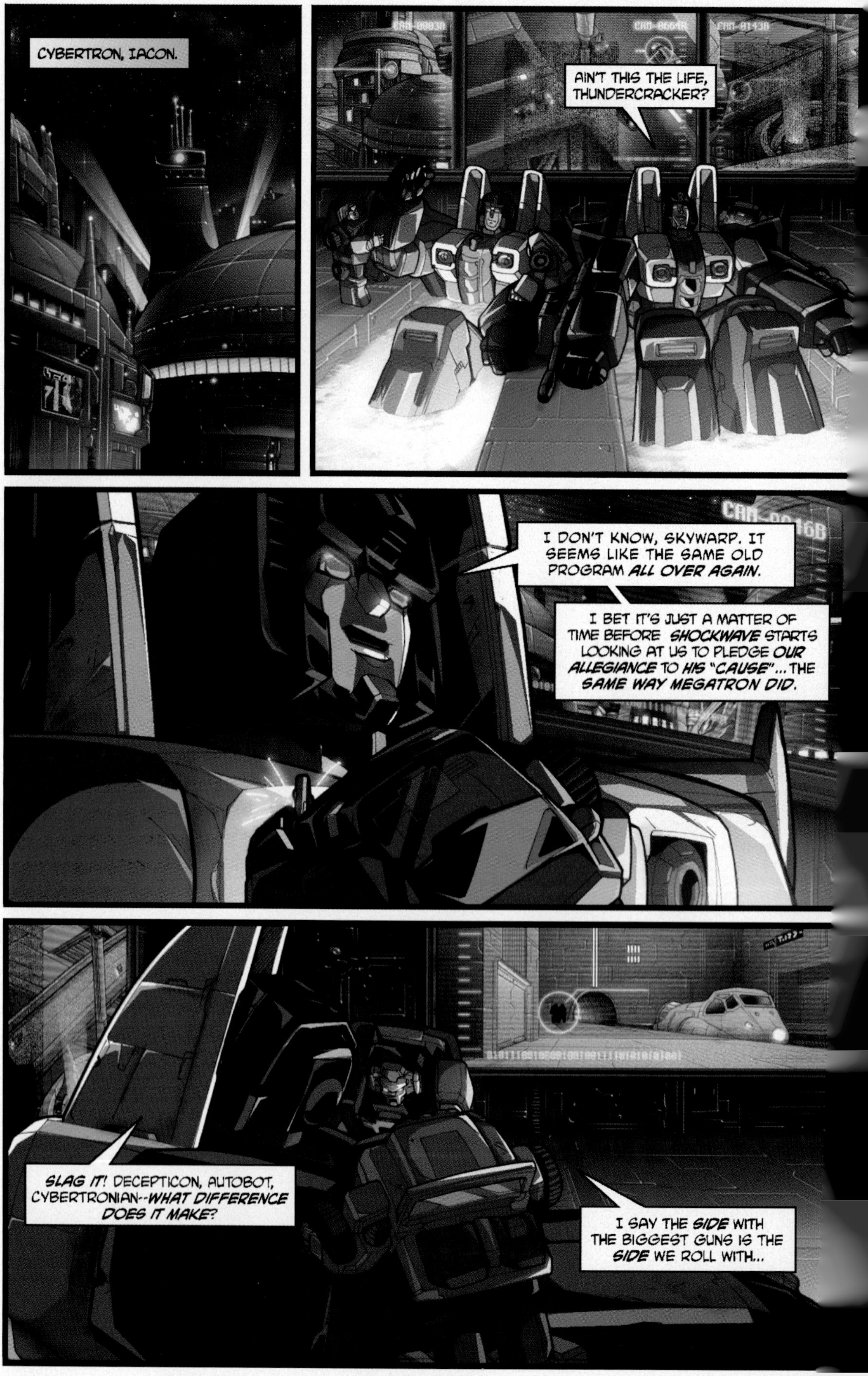
CYBERTRON, IACON.
AIN'T THIS THE LIFE, THUNDERCRACKER?
I DON'T KNOW, SKYWARP. IT SEEMS LIKE THE SAME OLD PROGRAM *ALL OVER AGAIN*.
I BET IT'S JUST A MATTER OF TIME BEFORE *SHOCKWAVE* STARTS LOOKING AT US TO PLEDGE *OUR ALLEGIANCE* TO *HIS "CAUSE"*... THE *SAME WAY MEGATRON DID*.
SLAG IT! DECEPTICON, AUTOBOT, CYBERTRONIAN--*WHAT DIFFERENCE DOES IT MAKE?*
I SAY THE *SIDE* WITH THE BIGGEST GUNS IS THE *SIDE* WE ROLL WITH...

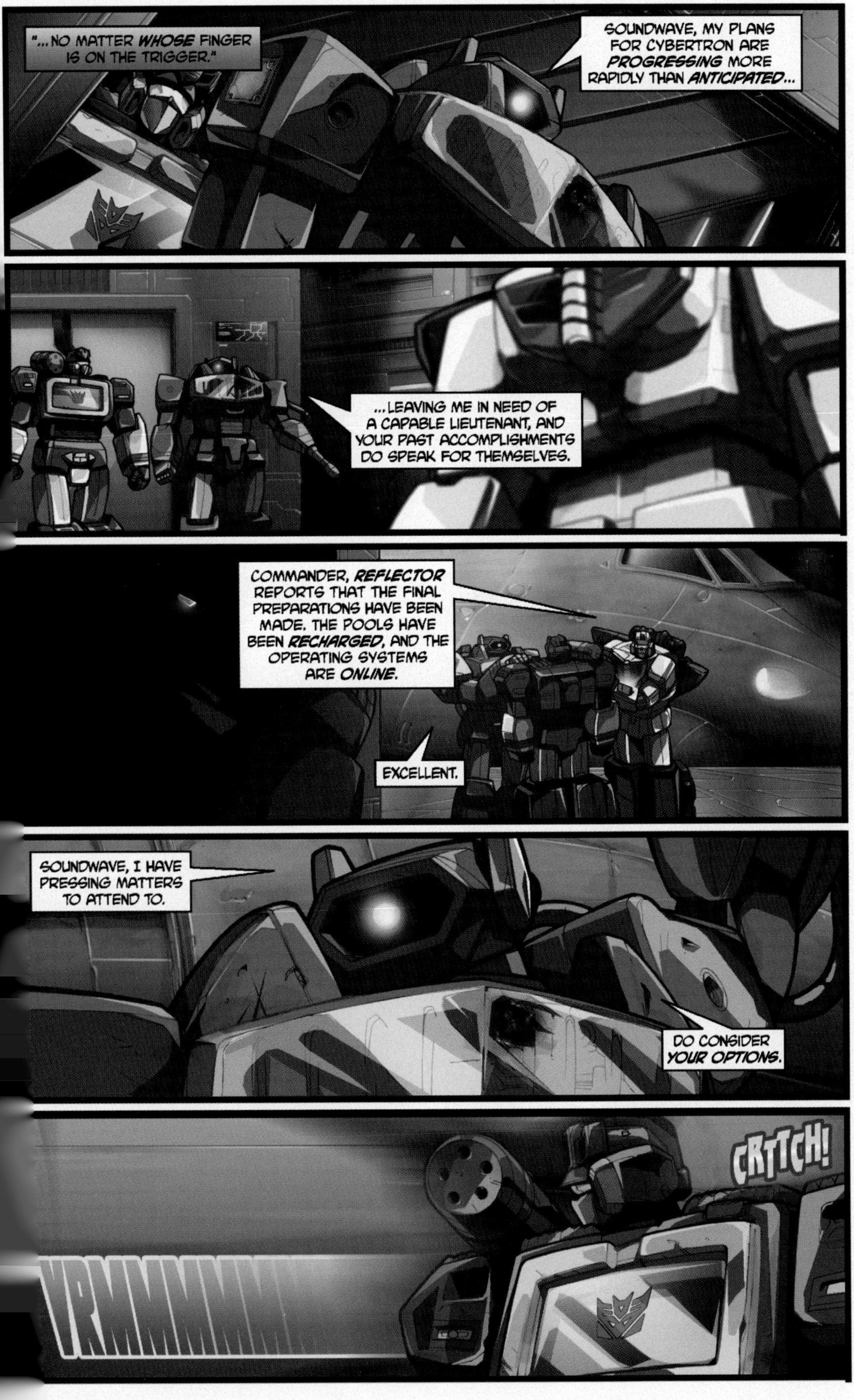
"...NO MATTER WHOSE FINGER IS ON THE TRIGGER."
SOUNDWAVE, MY PLANS FOR CYBERTRON ARE PROGRESSING MORE RAPIDLY THAN ANTICIPATED...
...LEAVING ME IN NEED OF A CAPABLE LIEUTENANT, AND YOUR PAST ACCOMPLISHMENTS DO SPEAK FOR THEMSELVES.
COMMANDER, REFLECTOR REPORTS THAT THE FINAL PREPARATIONS HAVE BEEN MADE. THE POOLS HAVE BEEN RECHARGED, AND THE OPERATING SYSTEMS ARE ONLINE.
EXCELLENT.
SOUNDWAVE, I HAVE PRESSING MATTERS TO ATTEND TO.
DO CONSIDER YOUR OPTIONS.
CRTTCH!
VRMMMMMMM

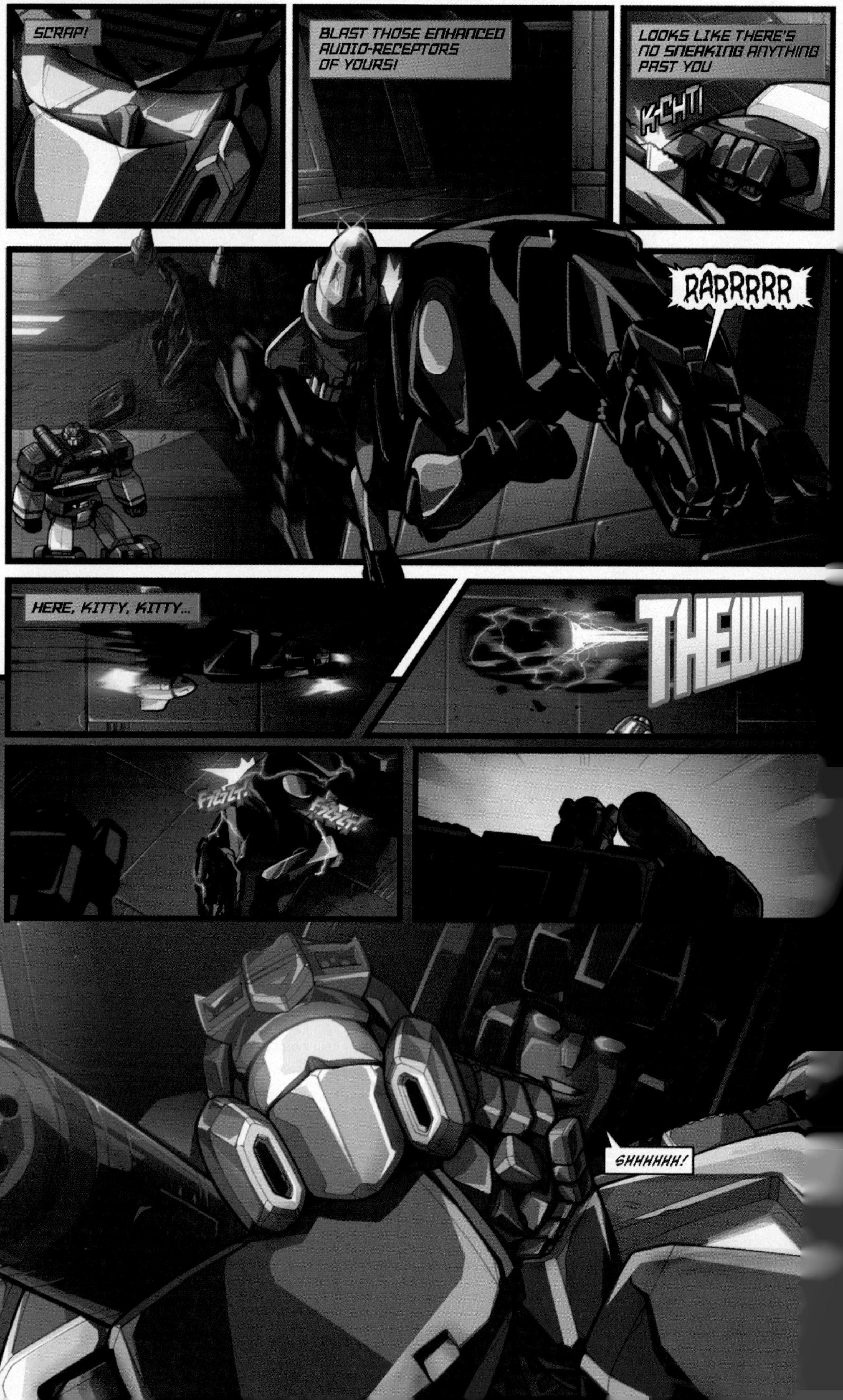
SCRAP!
BLAST THOSE ENHANCED AUDIO-RECEPTORS OF YOURS!
LOOKS LIKE THERE'S NO SNEAKING ANYTHING PAST YOU
K-CHT!
RARRRRR
HERE, KITTY, KITTY...
THEWMM
SHHHHHH!

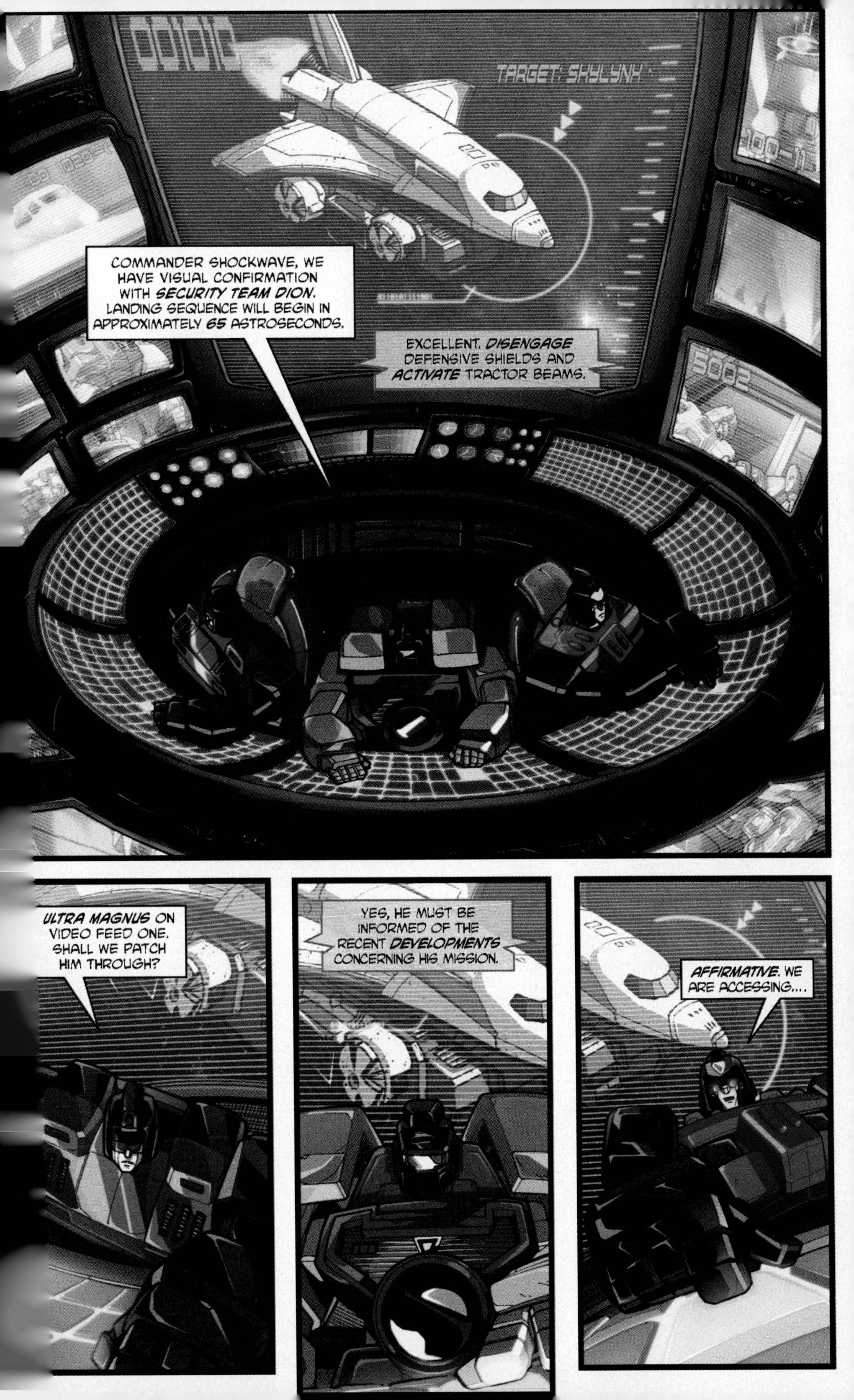
TARGET: SKYLYNX
COMMANDER SHOCKWAVE, WE HAVE VISUAL CONFIRMATION WITH *SECURITY TEAM DION.* LANDING SEQUENCE WILL BEGIN IN APPROXIMATELY *65* ASTROSECONDS.
EXCELLENT. *DISENGAGE* DEFENSIVE SHIELDS AND *ACTIVATE* TRACTOR BEAMS.
ULTRA MAGNUS ON VIDEO FEED ONE. SHALL WE PATCH HIM THROUGH?
YES, HE MUST BE INFORMED OF THE RECENT *DEVELOPMENTS* CONCERNING HIS MISSION.
AFFIRMATIVE. WE ARE ACCESSING....

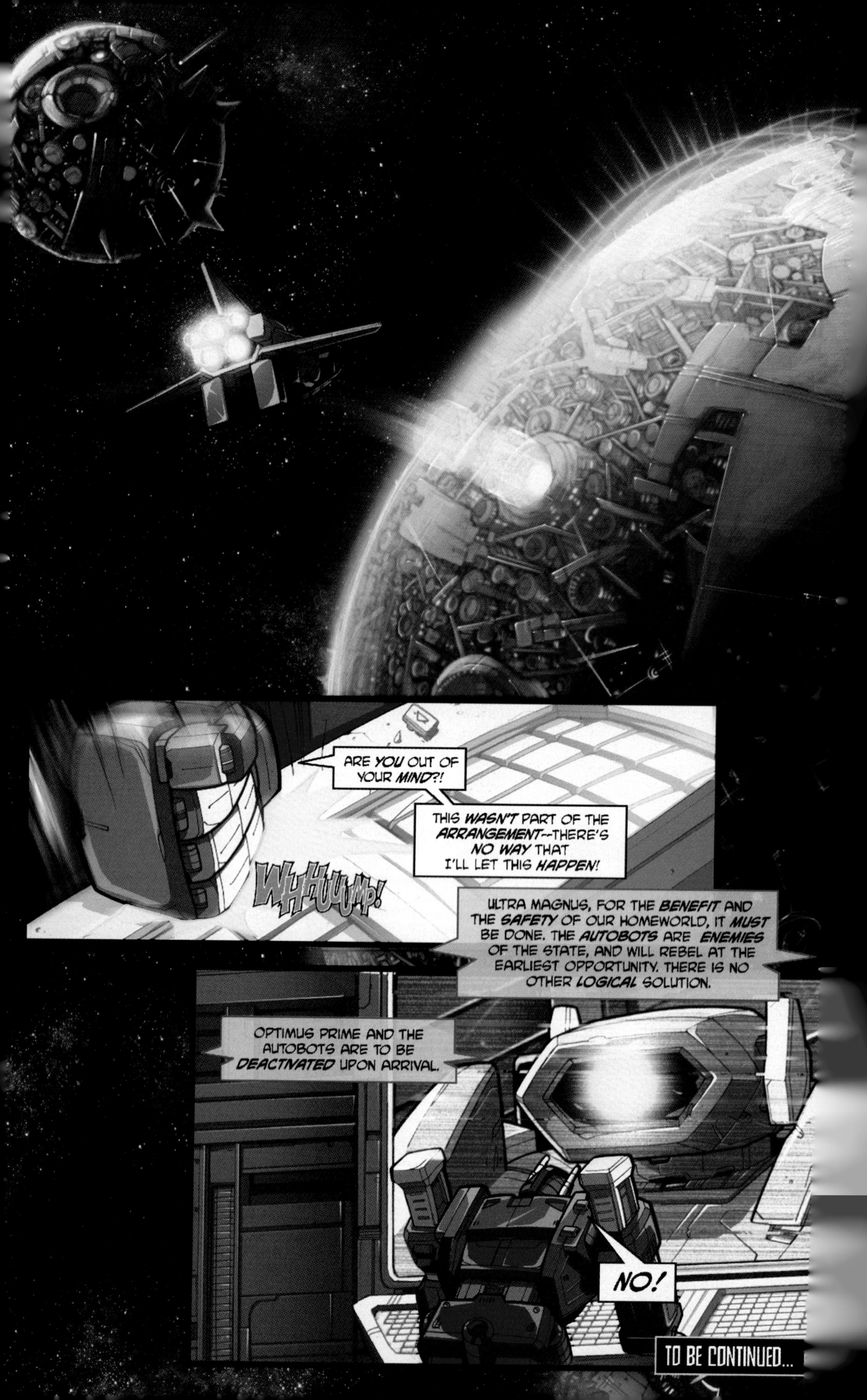
ARE YOU OUT OF YOUR MIND?!
THIS WASN'T PART OF THE ARRANGEMENT--THERE'S NO WAY THAT I'LL LET THIS HAPPEN!
WHHUUUMP!
ULTRA MAGNUS, FOR THE BENEFIT AND THE SAFETY OF OUR HOMEWORLD, IT MUST BE DONE. THE AUTOBOTS ARE ENEMIES OF THE STATE, AND WILL REBEL AT THE EARLIEST OPPORTUNITY. THERE IS NO OTHER LOGICAL SOLUTION.
OPTIMUS PRIME AND THE AUTOBOTS ARE TO BE DEACTIVATED UPON ARRIVAL.
NO!
TO BE CONTINUED...

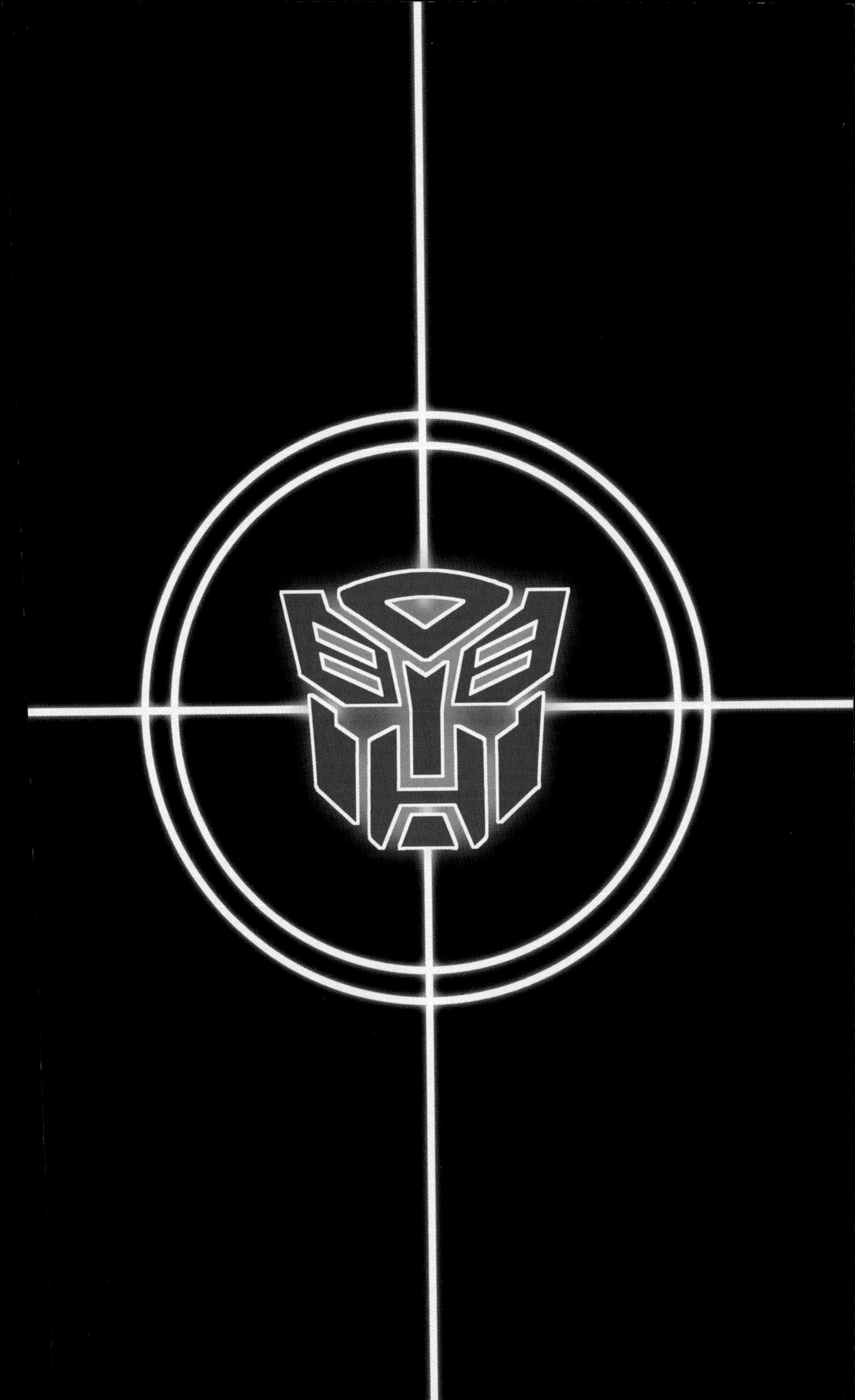

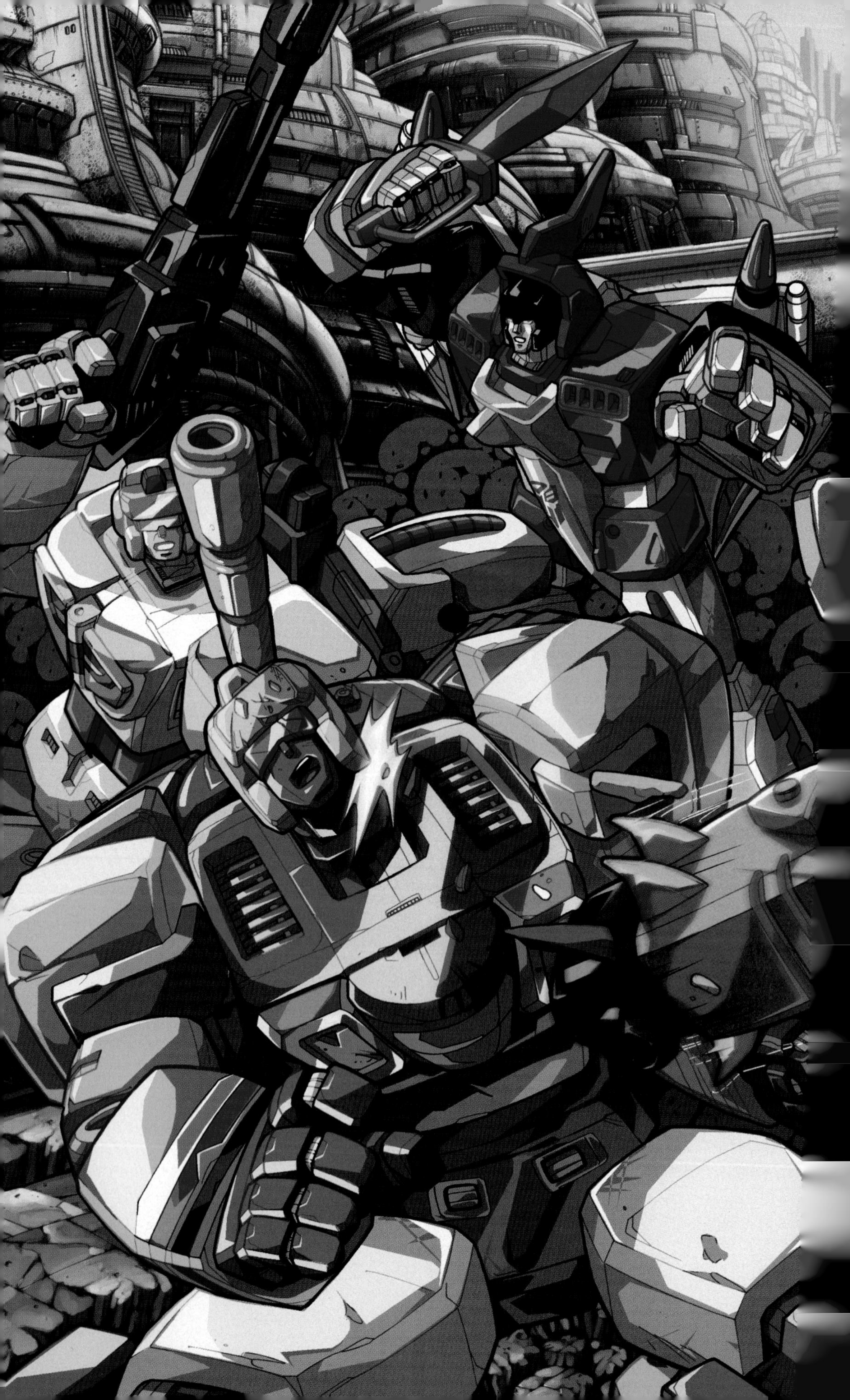

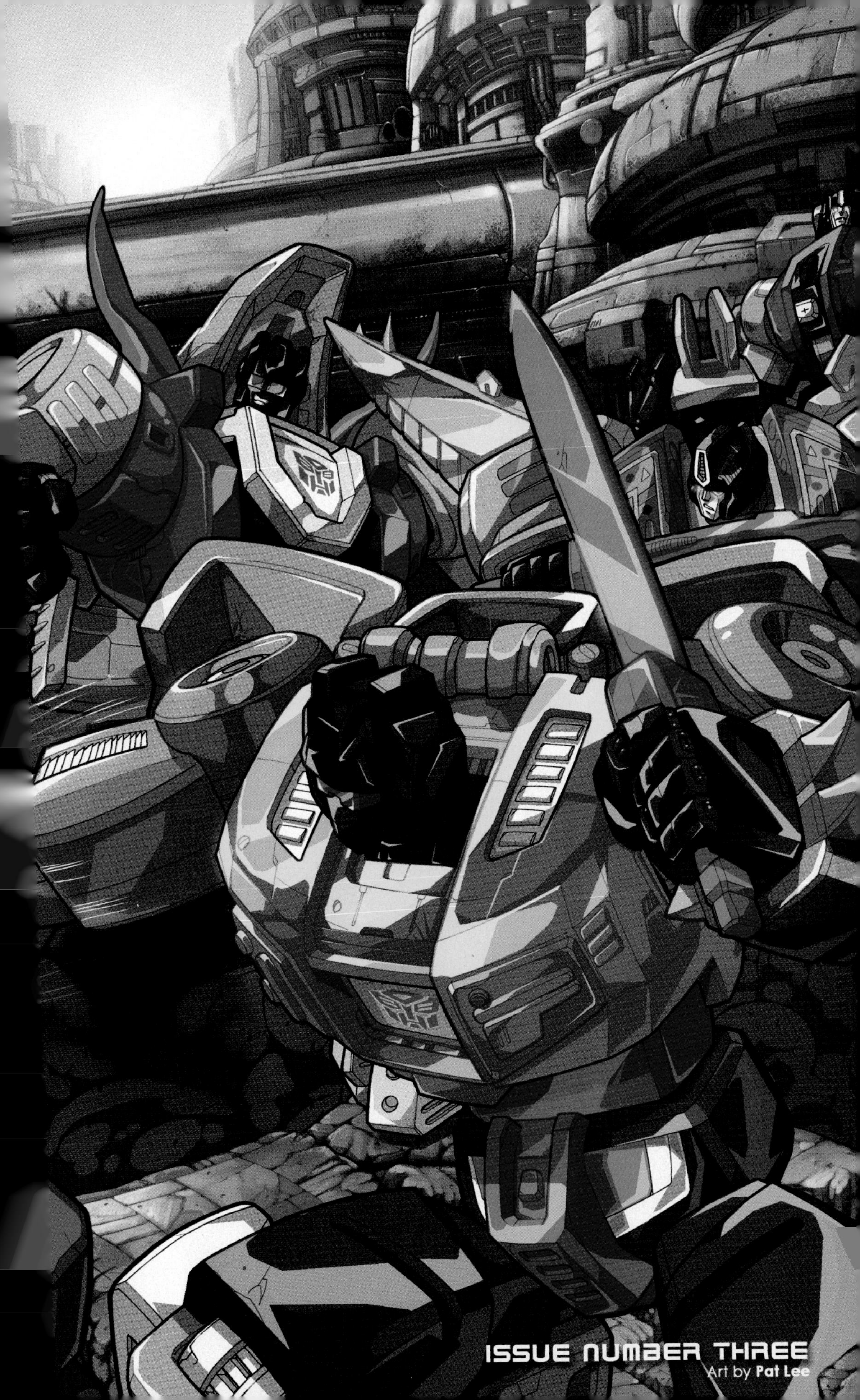

ISSUE NUMBER THREE
Art by **Pat Lee**

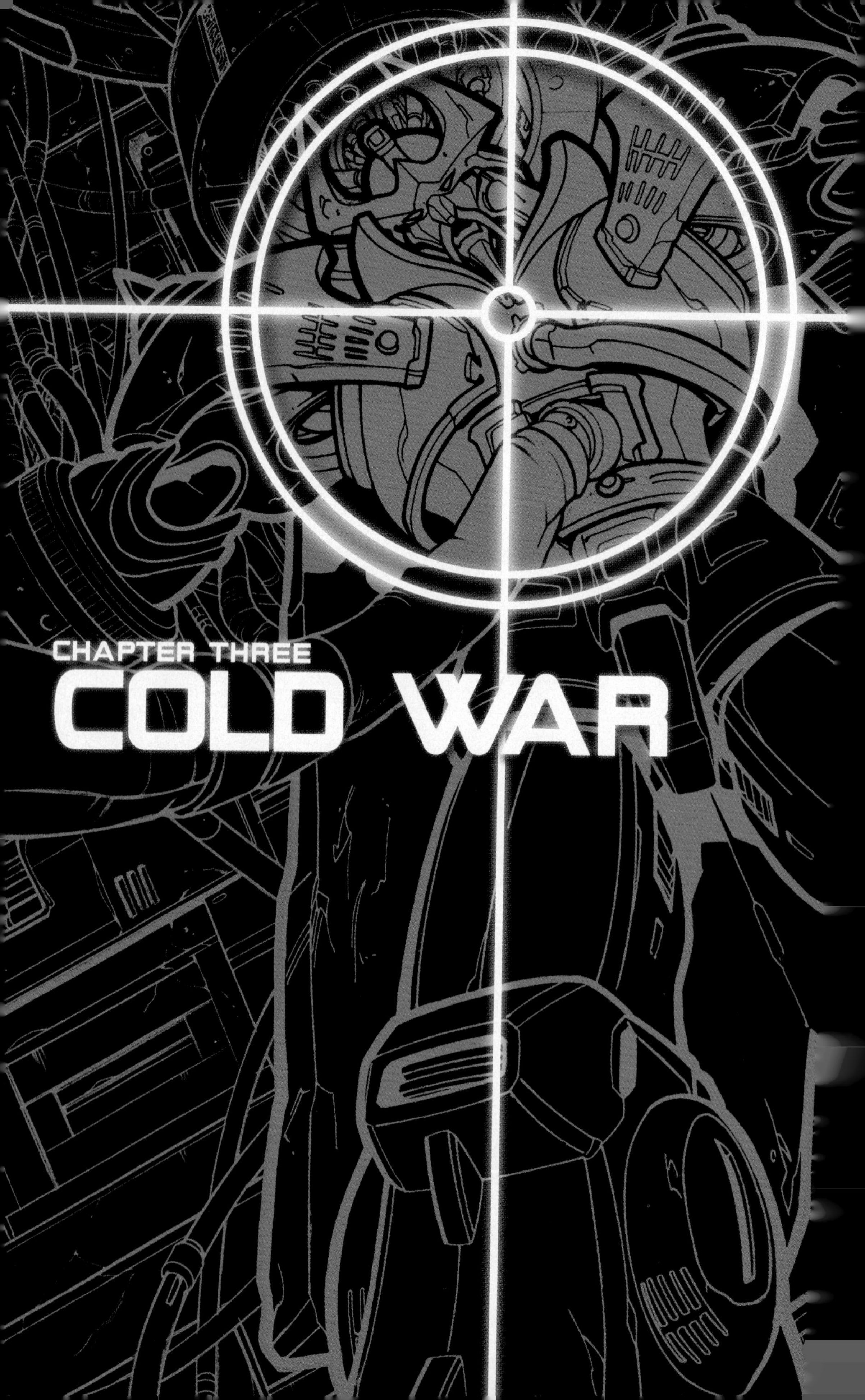
CHAPTER THREE
COLD WAR

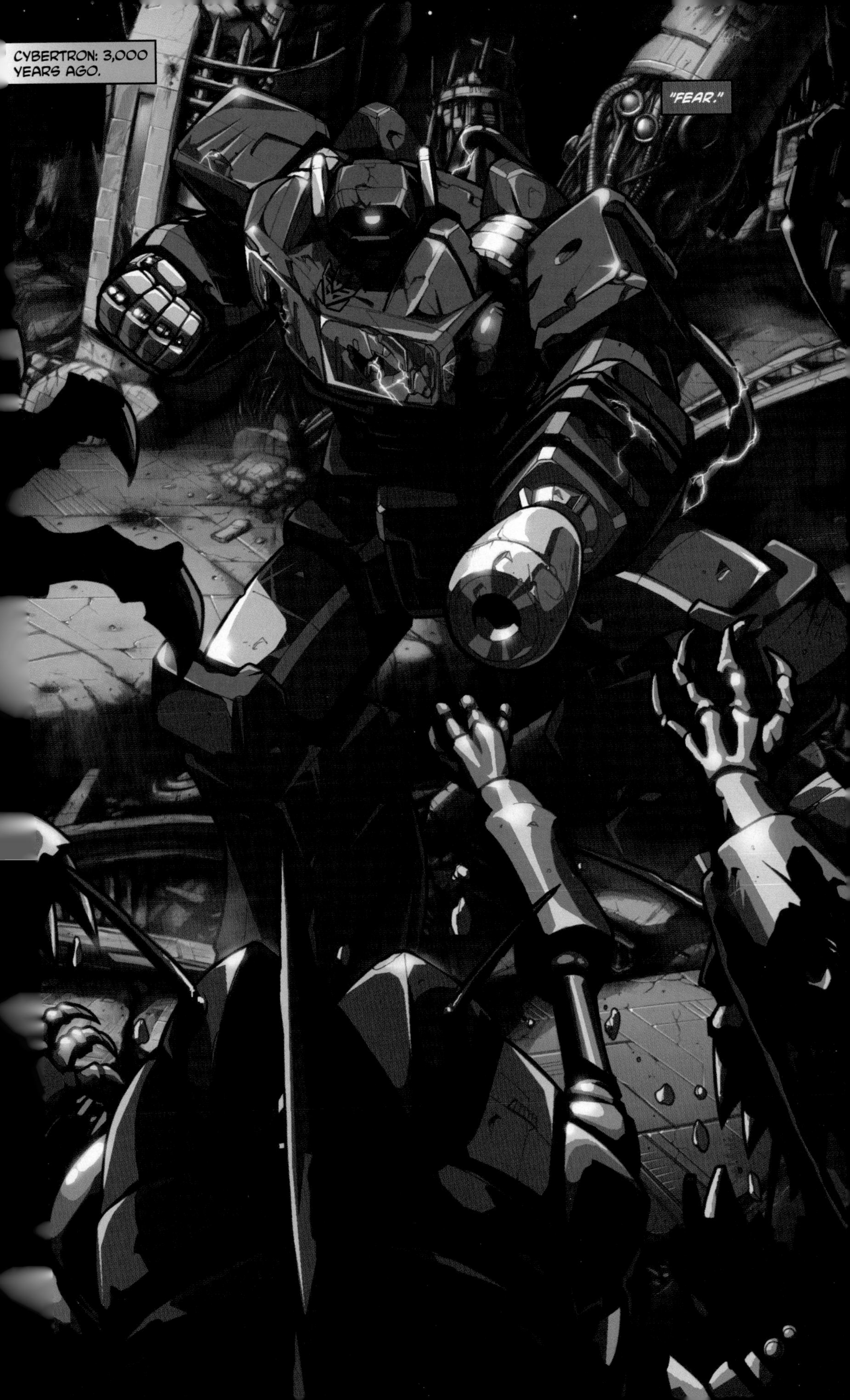
CYBERTRON: 3,000 YEARS AGO.
"FEAR."

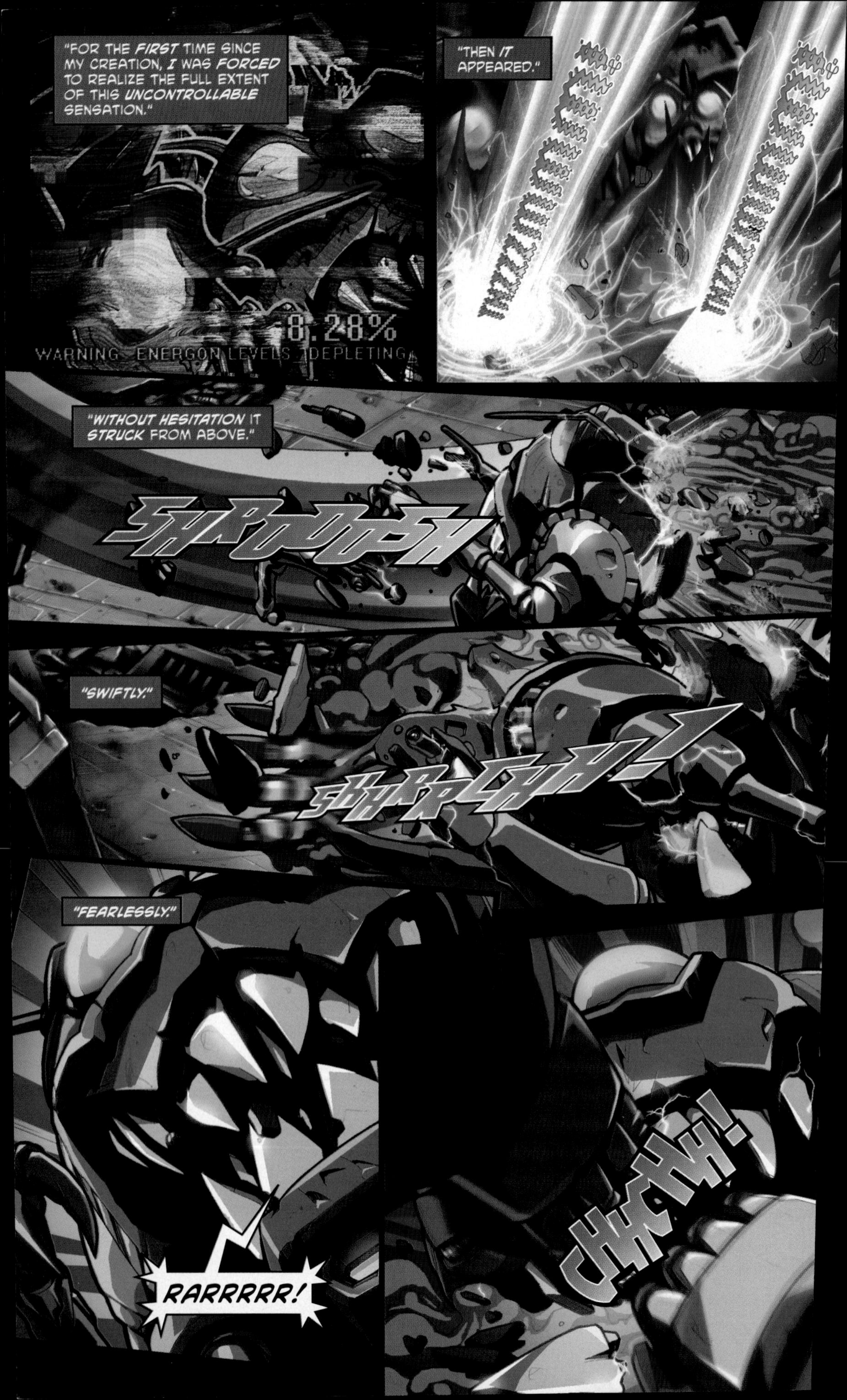
"FOR THE *FIRST* TIME SINCE MY CREATION, *I* WAS *FORCED* TO REALIZE THE FULL EXTENT OF THIS *UNCONTROLLABLE* SENSATION."
8.28%
WARNING ENERGON LEVELS DEPLETING
"THEN *IT* APPEARED."
"*WITHOUT HESITATION* IT *STRUCK* FROM ABOVE."
SHROOOSH
"*SWIFTLY.*"
"*FEARLESSLY.*"
RARRRRR!

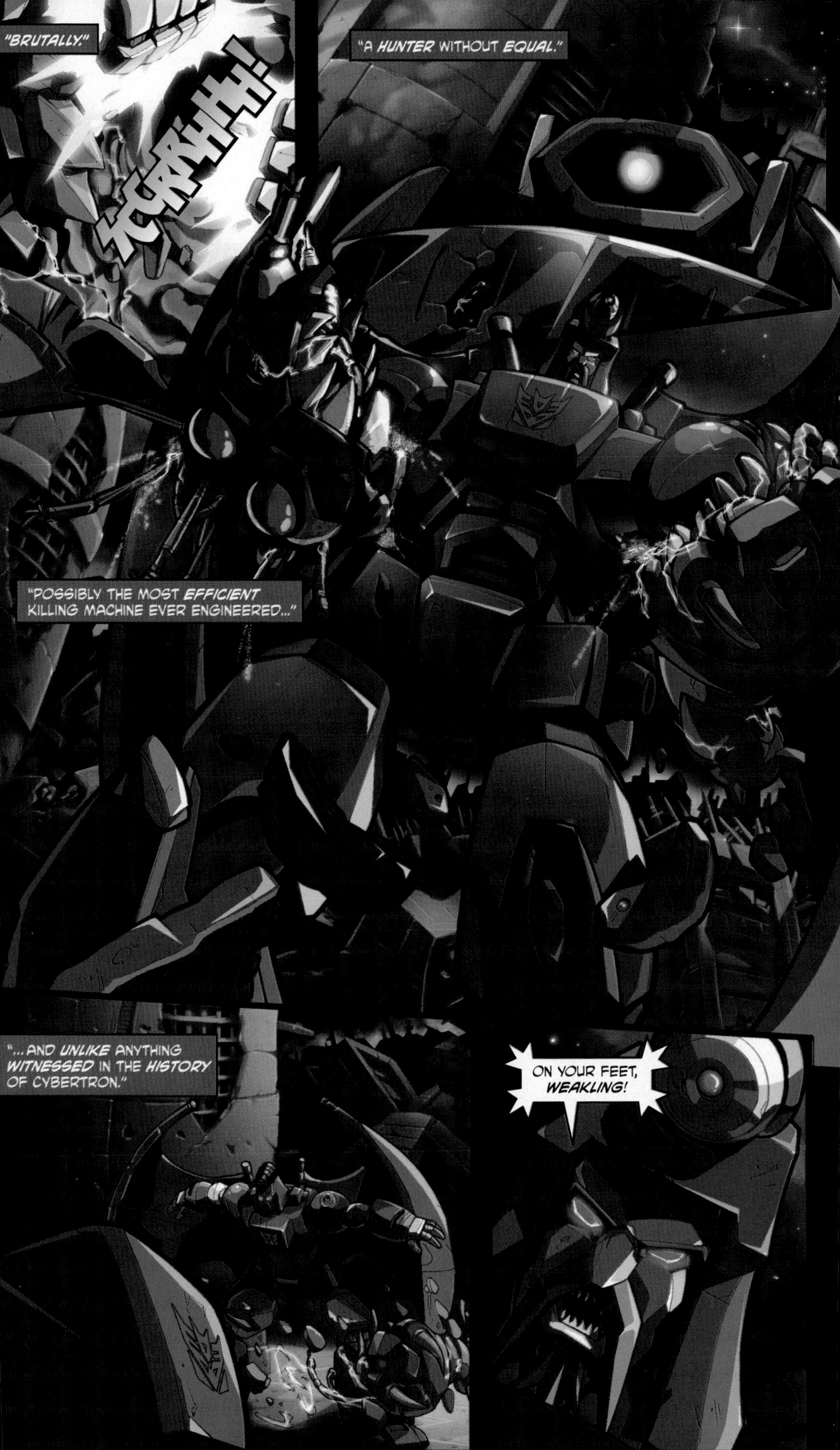
"BRUTALLY."
SCRAAAHHH!
"A HUNTER WITHOUT EQUAL."
"POSSIBLY THE MOST EFFICIENT KILLING MACHINE EVER ENGINEERED..."
"...AND UNLIKE ANYTHING WITNESSED IN THE HISTORY OF CYBERTRON."
ON YOUR FEET, WEAKLING!

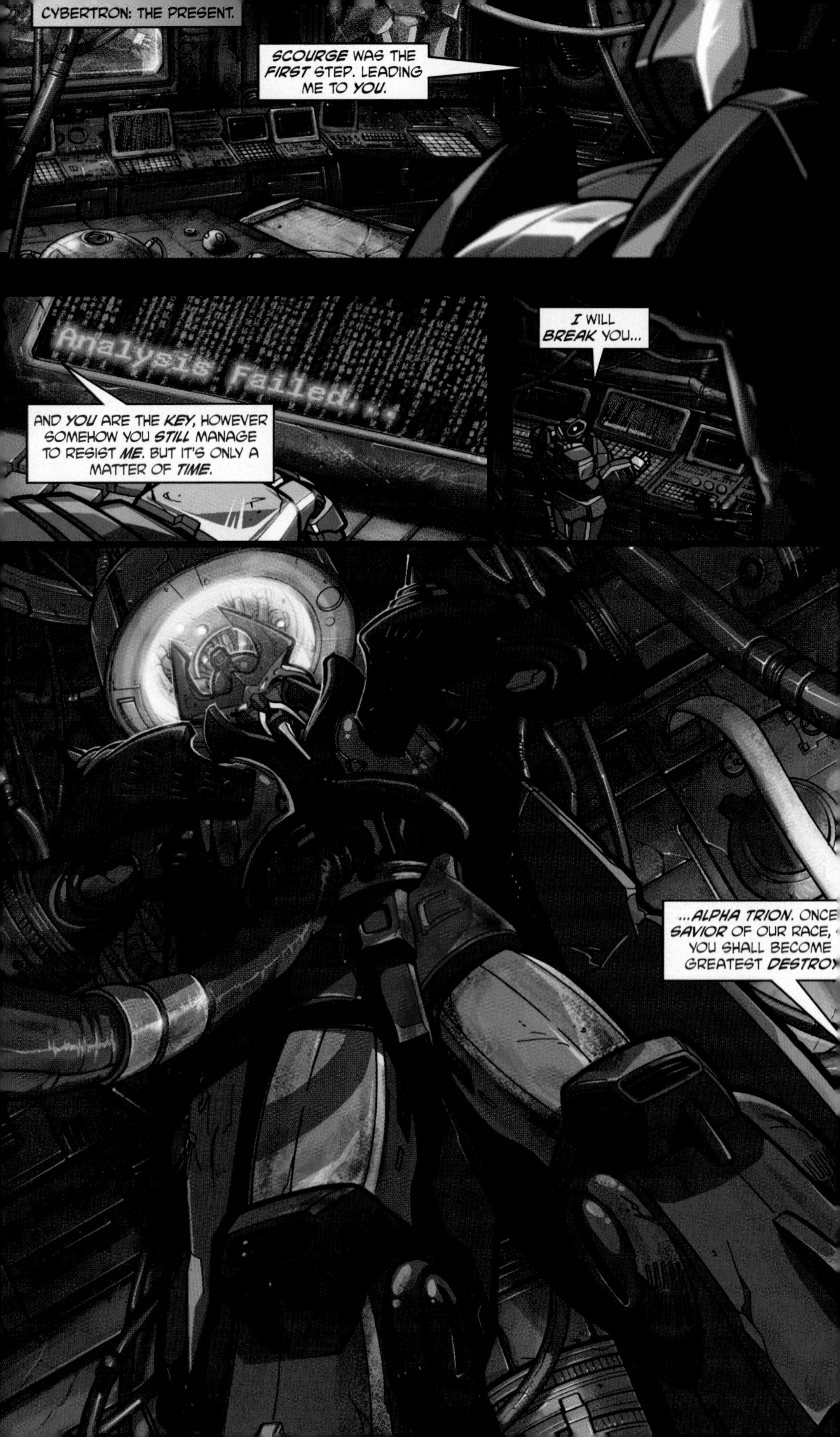
CYBERTRON: THE PRESENT.
SCOURGE WAS THE FIRST STEP. LEADING ME TO YOU.
Analysis Failed...
AND YOU ARE THE KEY, HOWEVER SOMEHOW YOU STILL MANAGE TO RESIST ME. BUT IT'S ONLY A MATTER OF TIME.
I WILL BREAK YOU...
...ALPHA TRION. ONCE SAVIOR OF OUR RACE, YOU SHALL BECOME GREATEST DESTRO

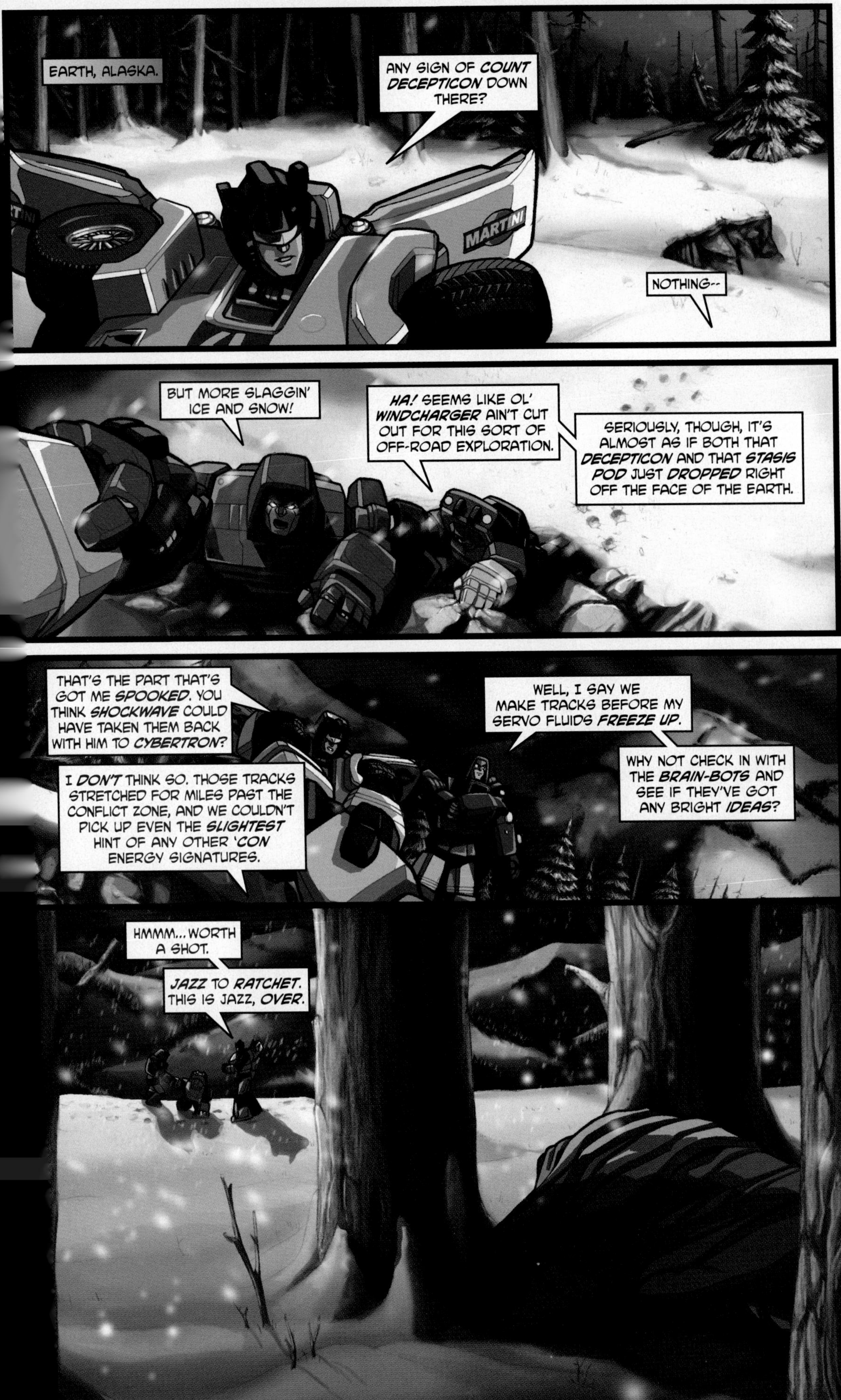

EARTH, ALASKA.
ANY SIGN OF COUNT DECEPTICON DOWN THERE?
NOTHING--
BUT MORE SLAGGIN' ICE AND SNOW!
HA! SEEMS LIKE OL' WINDCHARGER AIN'T CUT OUT FOR THIS SORT OF OFF-ROAD EXPLORATION.
SERIOUSLY, THOUGH, IT'S ALMOST AS IF BOTH THAT DECEPTICON AND THAT STASIS POD JUST DROPPED RIGHT OFF THE FACE OF THE EARTH.
THAT'S THE PART THAT'S GOT ME SPOOKED. YOU THINK SHOCKWAVE COULD HAVE TAKEN THEM BACK WITH HIM TO CYBERTRON?
I DON'T THINK SO. THOSE TRACKS STRETCHED FOR MILES PAST THE CONFLICT ZONE, AND WE COULDN'T PICK UP EVEN THE SLIGHTEST HINT OF ANY OTHER 'CON ENERGY SIGNATURES.
WELL, I SAY WE MAKE TRACKS BEFORE MY SERVO FLUIDS FREEZE UP.
WHY NOT CHECK IN WITH THE BRAIN-BOTS AND SEE IF THEY'VE GOT ANY BRIGHT IDEAS?
HMMM... WORTH A SHOT.
JAZZ TO RATCHET. THIS IS JAZZ, OVER.

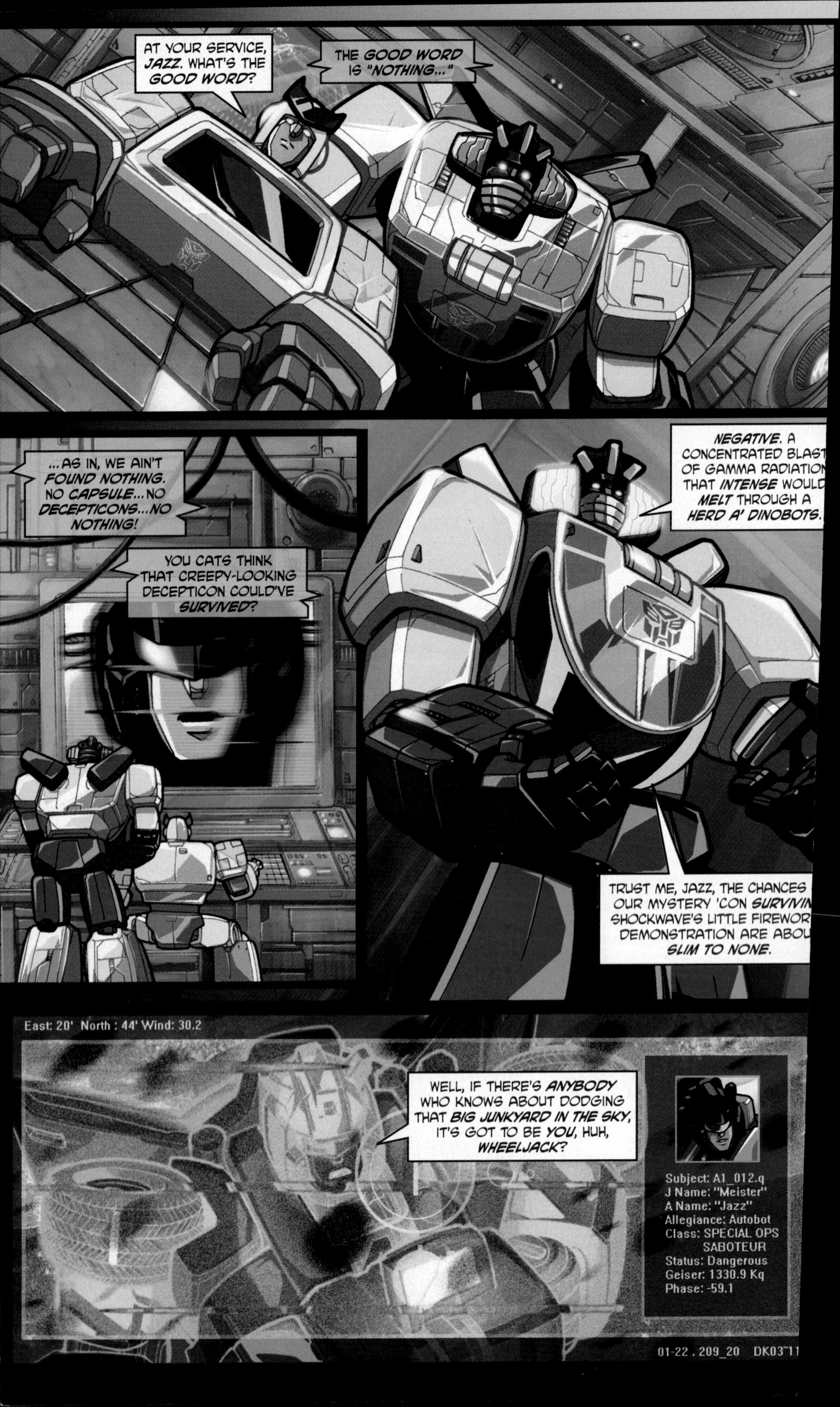

AT YOUR SERVICE, JAZZ. WHAT'S THE GOOD WORD?
THE GOOD WORD IS "NOTHING..."
...AS IN, WE AIN'T FOUND NOTHING. NO CAPSULE...NO DECEPTICONS...NO NOTHING!
YOU CATS THINK THAT CREEPY-LOOKING DECEPTICON COULD'VE SURVIVED?
NEGATIVE. A CONCENTRATED BLAST OF GAMMA RADIATION THAT INTENSE WOULD MELT THROUGH A HERD A' DINOBOTS.
TRUST ME, JAZZ, THE CHANCES OUR MYSTERY 'CON SURVIVIN SHOCKWAVE'S LITTLE FIREWOR DEMONSTRATION ARE ABOU SLIM TO NONE.
East: 20' North : 44' Wind: 30.2
WELL, IF THERE'S ANYBODY WHO KNOWS ABOUT DODGING THAT BIG JUNKYARD IN THE SKY, IT'S GOT TO BE YOU, HUH, WHEELJACK?
Subject: A1_012.q
J Name: "Meister"
A Name: "Jazz"
Allegiance: Autobot
Class: SPECIAL OPS SABOTEUR
Status: Dangerous
Geiser: 1330.9 Kq
Phase: -59.1
01-22 . 209_20 DK03"11

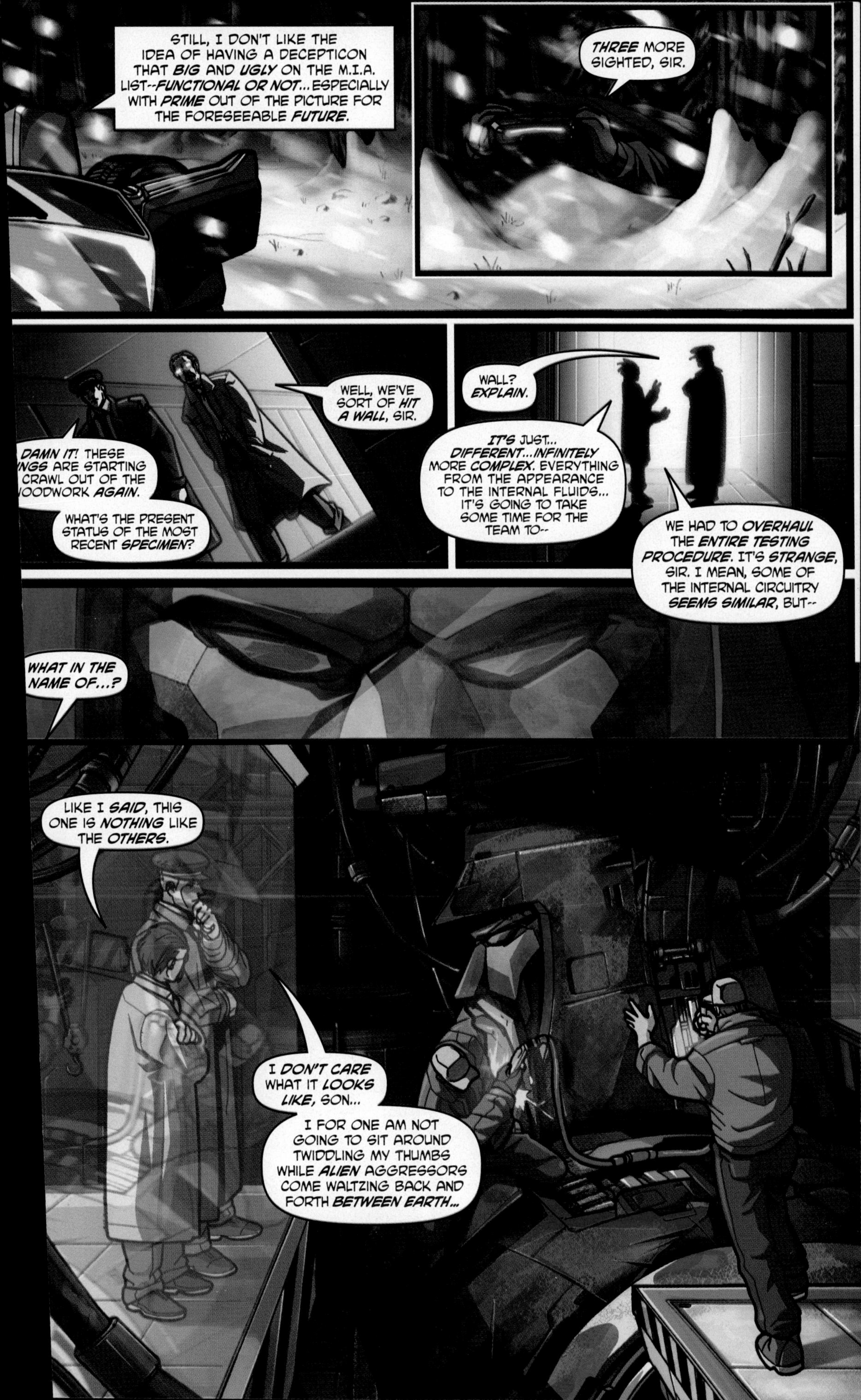
STILL, I DON'T LIKE THE IDEA OF HAVING A DECEPTICON THAT BIG AND UGLY ON THE M.I.A. LIST--FUNCTIONAL OR NOT... ESPECIALLY WITH PRIME OUT OF THE PICTURE FOR THE FORESEEABLE FUTURE.
THREE MORE SIGHTED, SIR.
DAMN IT! THESE ...NGS ARE STARTING ... CRAWL OUT OF THE ...OODWORK AGAIN.
WHAT'S THE PRESENT STATUS OF THE MOST RECENT SPECIMEN?
WELL, WE'VE SORT OF HIT A WALL, SIR.
WALL? EXPLAIN.
IT'S JUST... DIFFERENT...INFINITELY MORE COMPLEX. EVERYTHING FROM THE APPEARANCE TO THE INTERNAL FLUIDS... IT'S GOING TO TAKE SOME TIME FOR THE TEAM TO--
WE HAD TO OVERHAUL THE ENTIRE TESTING PROCEDURE. IT'S STRANGE, SIR. I MEAN, SOME OF THE INTERNAL CIRCUITRY SEEMS SIMILAR, BUT--
WHAT IN THE NAME OF...?
LIKE I SAID, THIS ONE IS NOTHING LIKE THE OTHERS.
I DON'T CARE WHAT IT LOOKS LIKE, SON...
I FOR ONE AM NOT GOING TO SIT AROUND TWIDDLING MY THUMBS WHILE ALIEN AGGRESSORS COME WALTZING BACK AND FORTH BETWEEN EARTH...

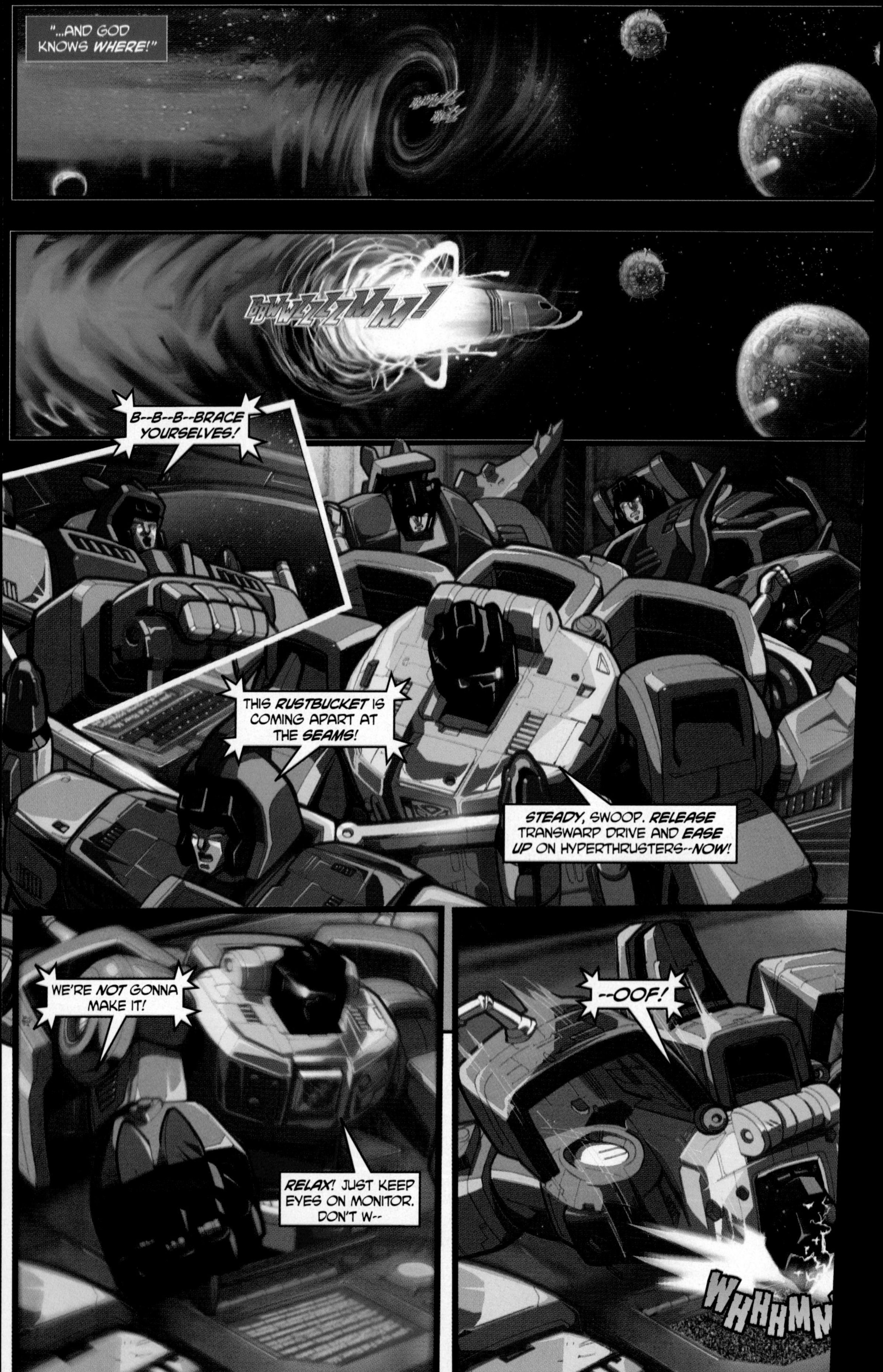
"...AND GOD KNOWS WHERE!"
BBWWZZZMM!
B--B--B--BRACE YOURSELVES!
THIS RUSTBUCKET IS COMING APART AT THE SEAMS!
STEADY, SWOOP. RELEASE TRANSWARP DRIVE AND EASE UP ON HYPERTHRUSTERS--NOW!
WE'RE NOT GONNA MAKE IT!
RELAX! JUST KEEP EYES ON MONITOR. DON'T W--
--OOF!
WHHHMM

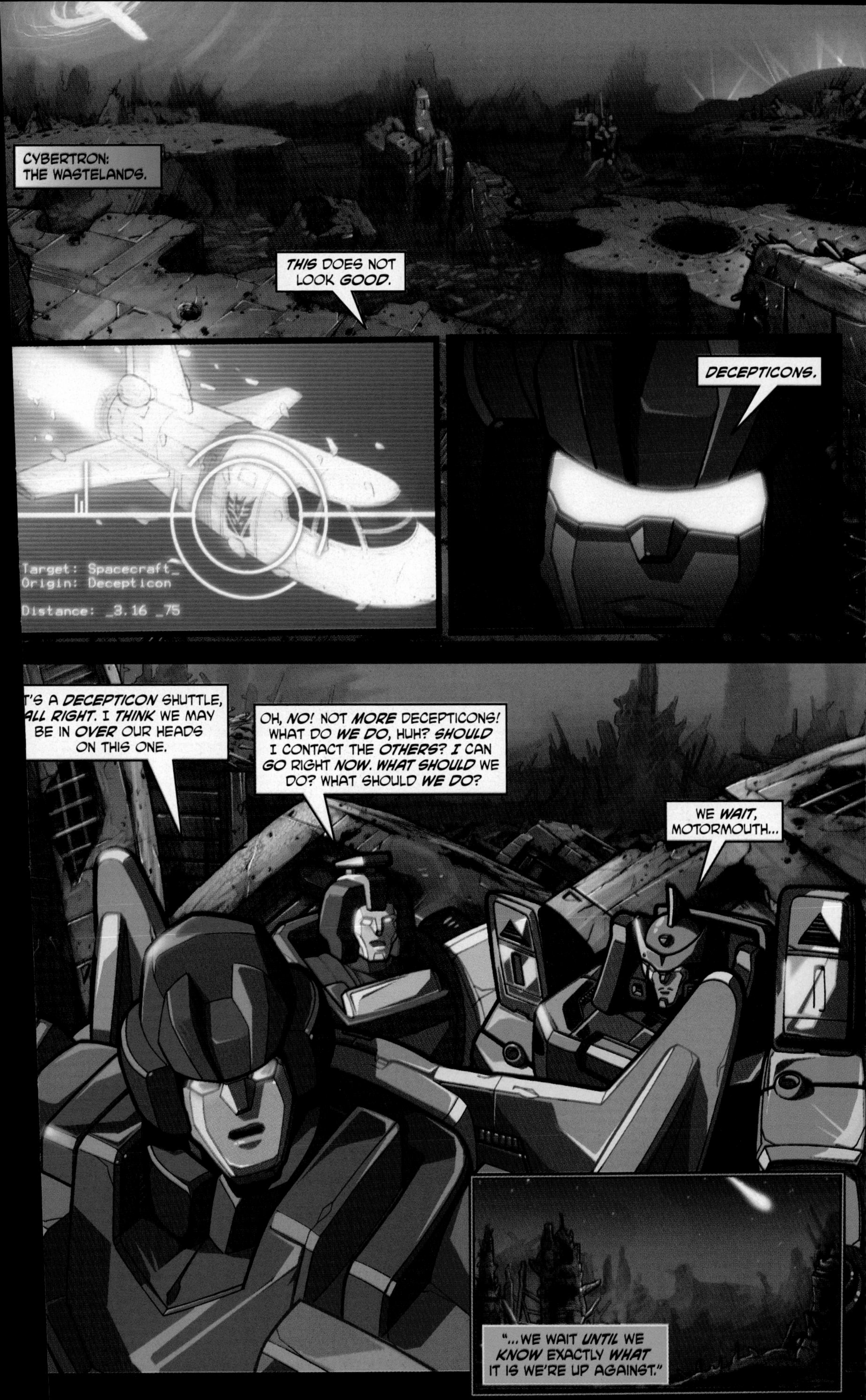
CYBERTRON: THE WASTELANDS.
THIS DOES NOT LOOK GOOD.
Target: Spacecraft_
Origin: Decepticon
Distance: _3.16 _75
DECEPTICONS.
'S A DECEPTICON SHUTTLE, ALL RIGHT. I THINK WE MAY BE IN OVER OUR HEADS ON THIS ONE.
OH, NO! NOT MORE DECEPTICONS! WHAT DO WE DO, HUH? SHOULD I CONTACT THE OTHERS? I CAN GO RIGHT NOW. WHAT SHOULD WE DO? WHAT SHOULD WE DO?
WE WAIT, MOTORMOUTH...
"...WE WAIT UNTIL WE KNOW EXACTLY WHAT IT IS WE'RE UP AGAINST."

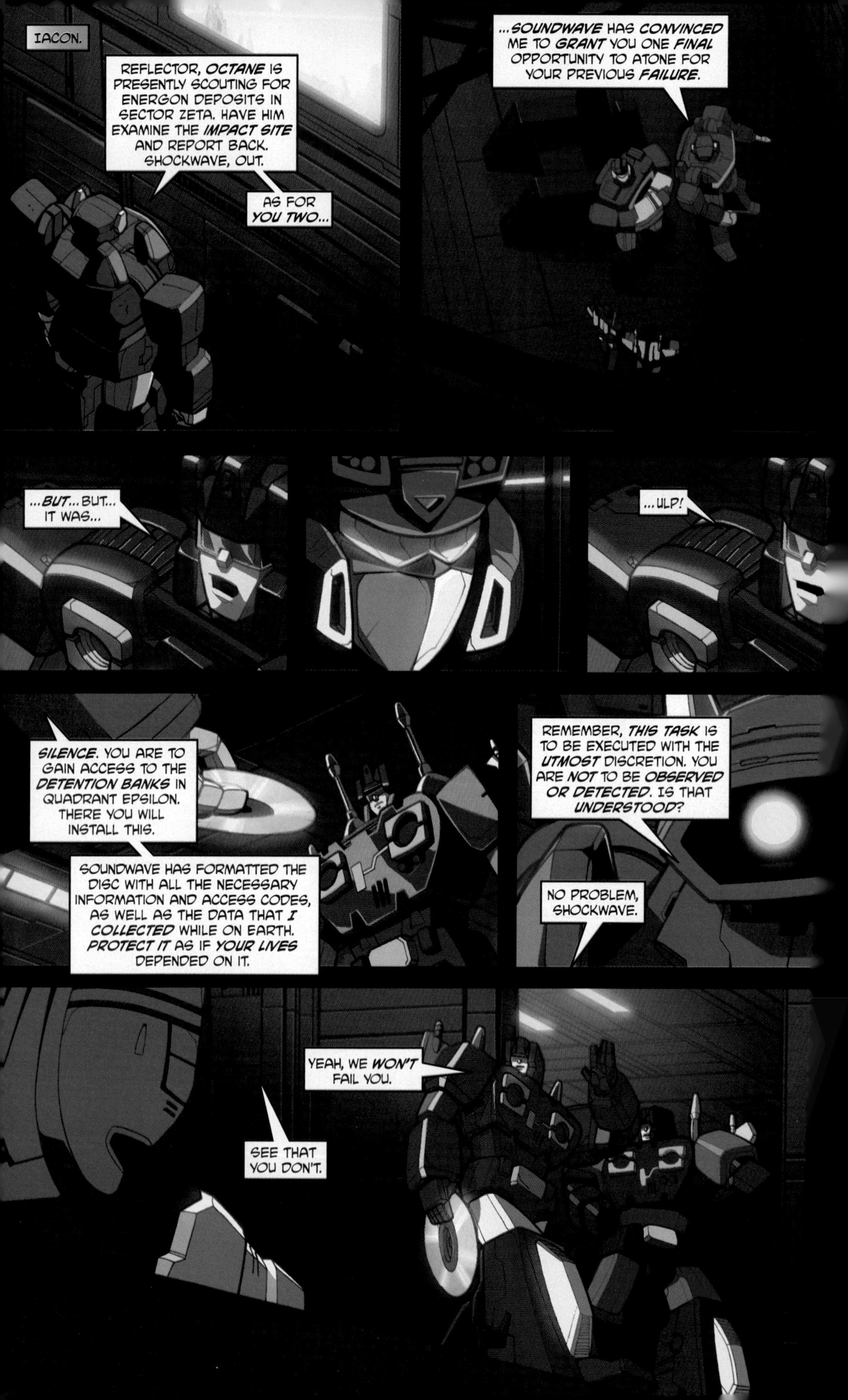
IACON.
REFLECTOR, OCTANE IS PRESENTLY SCOUTING FOR ENERGON DEPOSITS IN SECTOR ZETA. HAVE HIM EXAMINE THE IMPACT SITE AND REPORT BACK. SHOCKWAVE, OUT.
AS FOR YOU TWO...
...SOUNDWAVE HAS CONVINCED ME TO GRANT YOU ONE FINAL OPPORTUNITY TO ATONE FOR YOUR PREVIOUS FAILURE.
...BUT... BUT... IT WAS...
...ULP!
SILENCE. YOU ARE TO GAIN ACCESS TO THE DETENTION BANKS IN QUADRANT EPSILON. THERE YOU WILL INSTALL THIS.
SOUNDWAVE HAS FORMATTED THE DISC WITH ALL THE NECESSARY INFORMATION AND ACCESS CODES, AS WELL AS THE DATA THAT I COLLECTED WHILE ON EARTH. PROTECT IT AS IF YOUR LIVES DEPENDED ON IT.
REMEMBER, THIS TASK IS TO BE EXECUTED WITH THE UTMOST DISCRETION. YOU ARE NOT TO BE OBSERVED OR DETECTED. IS THAT UNDERSTOOD?
NO PROBLEM, SHOCKWAVE.
YEAH, WE WON'T FAIL YOU.
SEE THAT YOU DON'T.

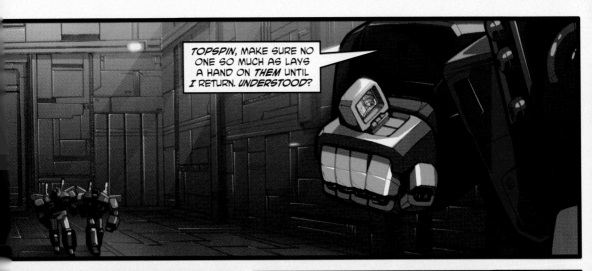

TOPSPIN, MAKE SURE NO ONE SO MUCH AS LAYS A HAND ON *THEM* UNTIL *I* RETURN. *UNDERSTOOD?*

NO *SCREWIN'* AROUND THIS TIME! IF WE *MESS* THIS UP--IT'S *OUR HIDES.*

I KNOW, I KNOW. YOU DON'T HAVE TO--

OOF!

CLANG!

HEY, WATCH WHERE YOU'R--

DON'T *TEST* ME, DECEPTICON.

I'M *NOT* IN THE *MOOD!*

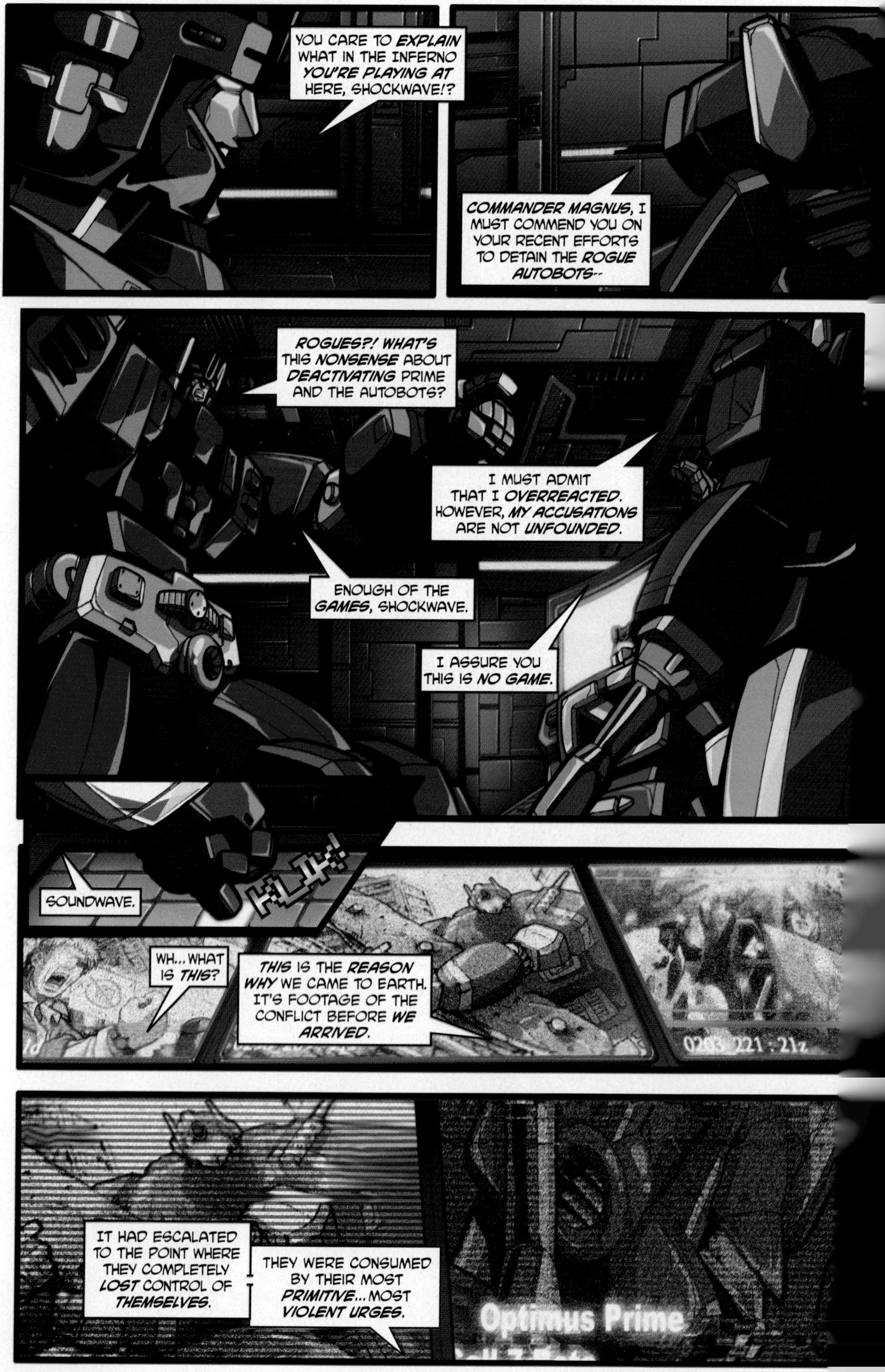
YOU CARE TO EXPLAIN WHAT IN THE INFERNO YOU'RE PLAYING AT HERE, SHOCKWAVE!?
COMMANDER MAGNUS, I MUST COMMEND YOU ON YOUR RECENT EFFORTS TO DETAIN THE ROGUE AUTOBOTS--
ROGUES?! WHAT'S THIS NONSENSE ABOUT DEACTIVATING PRIME AND THE AUTOBOTS?
I MUST ADMIT THAT I OVERREACTED. HOWEVER, MY ACCUSATIONS ARE NOT UNFOUNDED.
ENOUGH OF THE GAMES, SHOCKWAVE.
I ASSURE YOU THIS IS NO GAME.
SOUNDWAVE.
KLIK!
WH... WHAT IS THIS?
THIS IS THE REASON WHY WE CAME TO EARTH. IT'S FOOTAGE OF THE CONFLICT BEFORE WE ARRIVED.
0203 221 : 21z
IT HAD ESCALATED TO THE POINT WHERE THEY COMPLETELY LOST CONTROL OF THEMSELVES.
THEY WERE CONSUMED BY THEIR MOST PRIMITIVE... MOST VIOLENT URGES.
Optimus Prime

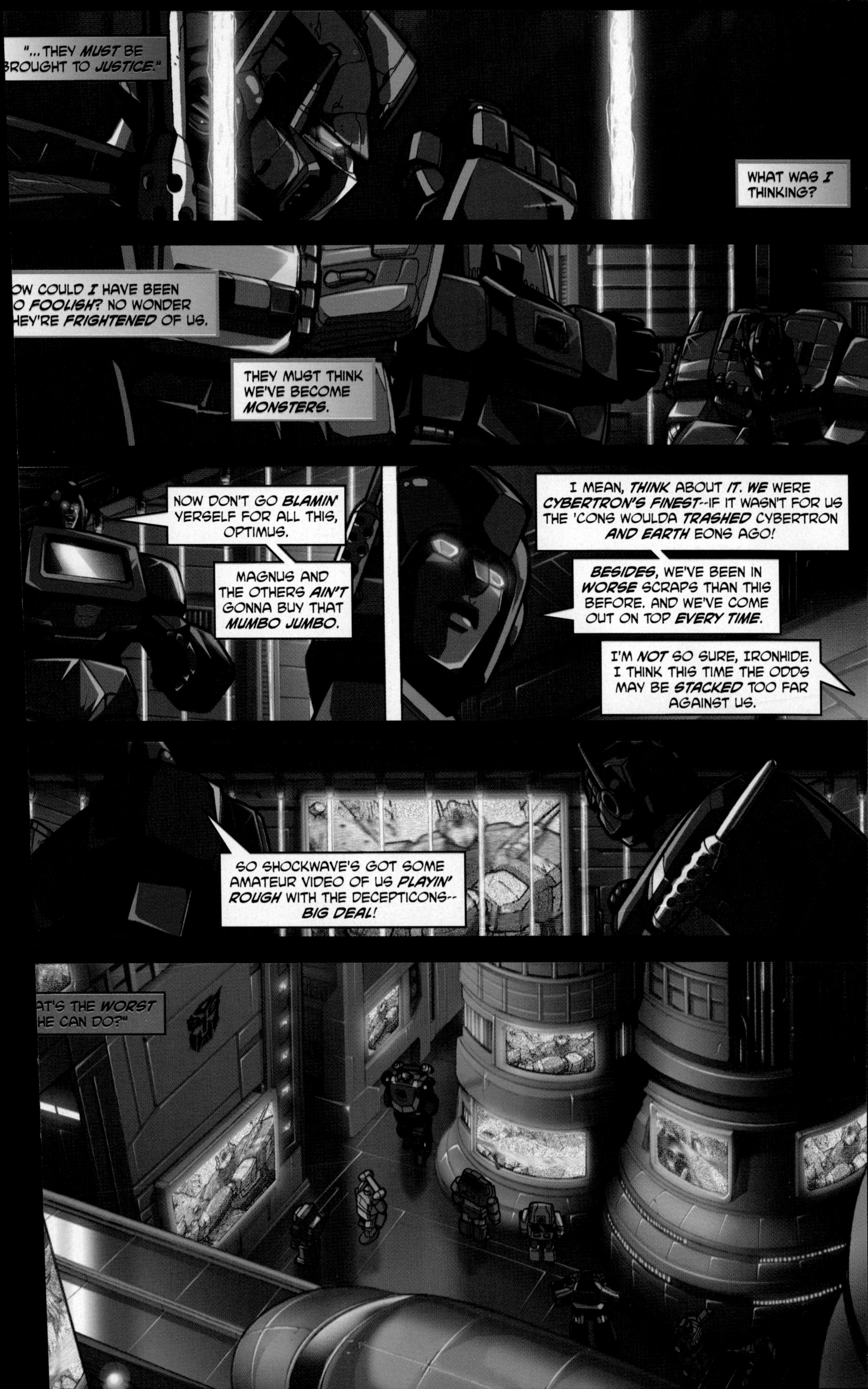
"...THEY MUST BE BROUGHT TO JUSTICE."
WHAT WAS I THINKING?
OW COULD I HAVE BEEN O FOOLISH? NO WONDER HEY'RE FRIGHTENED OF US.
THEY MUST THINK WE'VE BECOME MONSTERS.
NOW DON'T GO BLAMIN' YERSELF FOR ALL THIS, OPTIMUS.
MAGNUS AND THE OTHERS AIN'T GONNA BUY THAT MUMBO JUMBO.
I MEAN, THINK ABOUT IT. WE WERE CYBERTRON'S FINEST--IF IT WASN'T FOR US THE 'CONS WOULDA TRASHED CYBERTRON AND EARTH EONS AGO!
BESIDES, WE'VE BEEN IN WORSE SCRAPS THAN THIS BEFORE. AND WE'VE COME OUT ON TOP EVERY TIME.
I'M NOT SO SURE, IRONHIDE. I THINK THIS TIME THE ODDS MAY BE STACKED TOO FAR AGAINST US.
SO SHOCKWAVE'S GOT SOME AMATEUR VIDEO OF US PLAYIN' ROUGH WITH THE DECEPTICONS--BIG DEAL!
AT'S THE WORST HE CAN DO?"

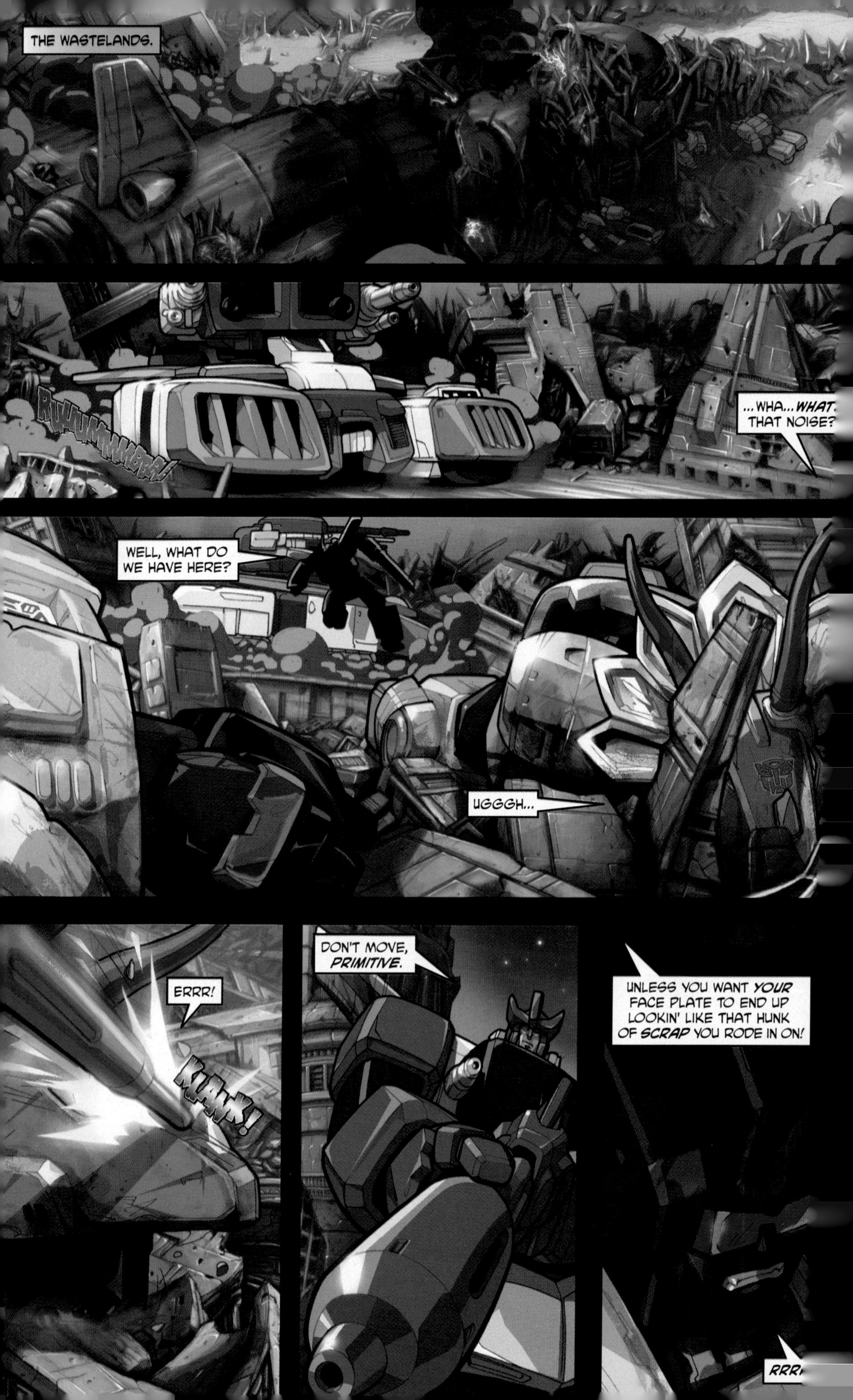
THE WASTELANDS.
RUUUMMMBBB!
...WHA...WHAT... THAT NOISE?
WELL, WHAT DO WE HAVE HERE?
UGGGH...
ERRR!
KLANK!
DON'T MOVE, PRIMITIVE.
UNLESS YOU WANT YOUR FACE PLATE TO END UP LOOKIN' LIKE THAT HUNK OF SCRAP YOU RODE IN ON!
RRR

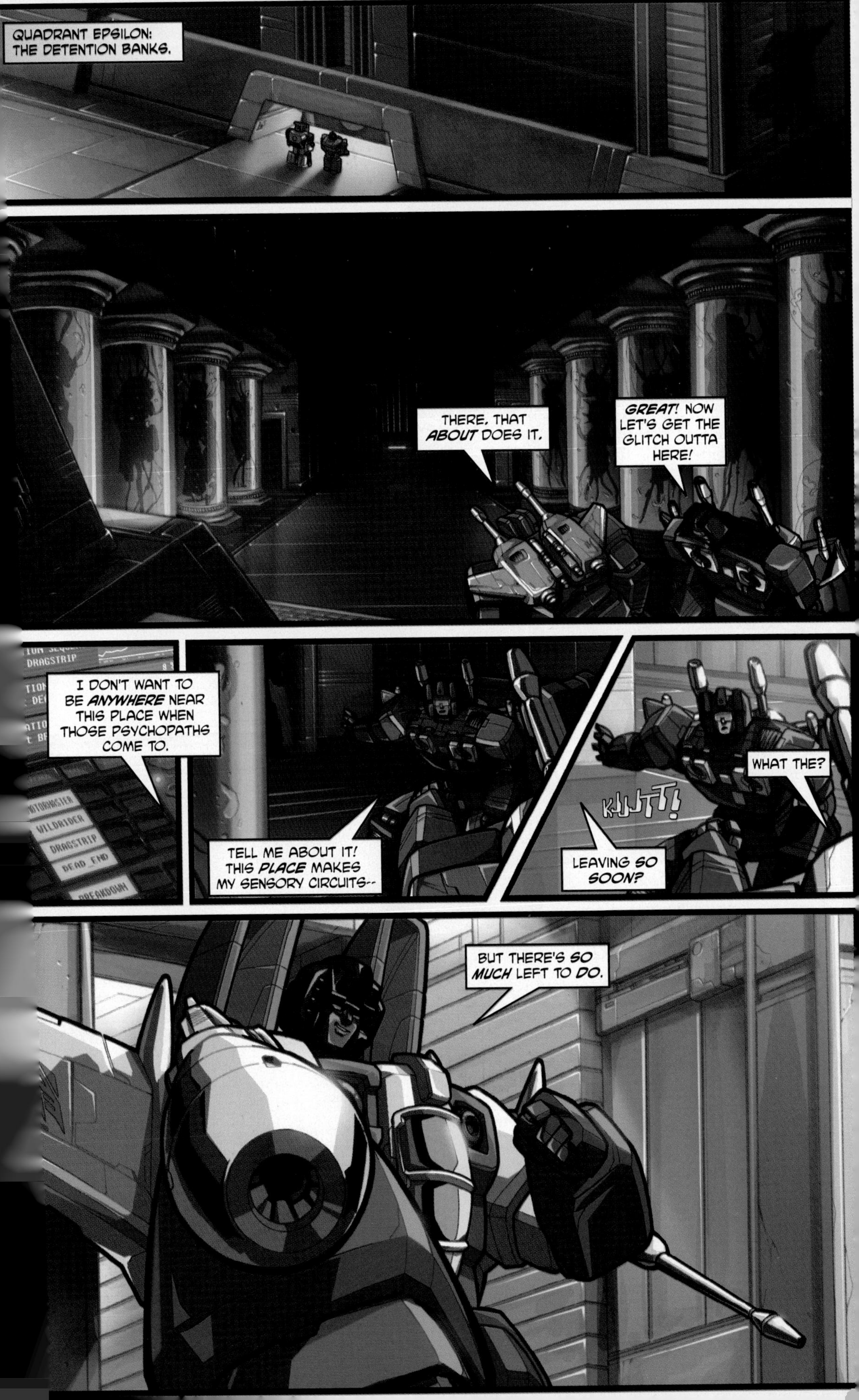
QUADRANT EPSILON: THE DETENTION BANKS.
THERE. THAT ABOUT DOES IT.
GREAT! NOW LET'S GET THE GLITCH OUTTA HERE!
I DON'T WANT TO BE ANYWHERE NEAR THIS PLACE WHEN THOSE PSYCHOPATHS COME TO.
DRAGSTRIP
MOTORMASTER
WILDRIDER
DRAGSTRIP
DEAD END
BREAKDOWN
TELL ME ABOUT IT! THIS PLACE MAKES MY SENSORY CIRCUITS--
KJJJTT!
WHAT THE?
LEAVING SO SOON?
BUT THERE'S SO MUCH LEFT TO DO.

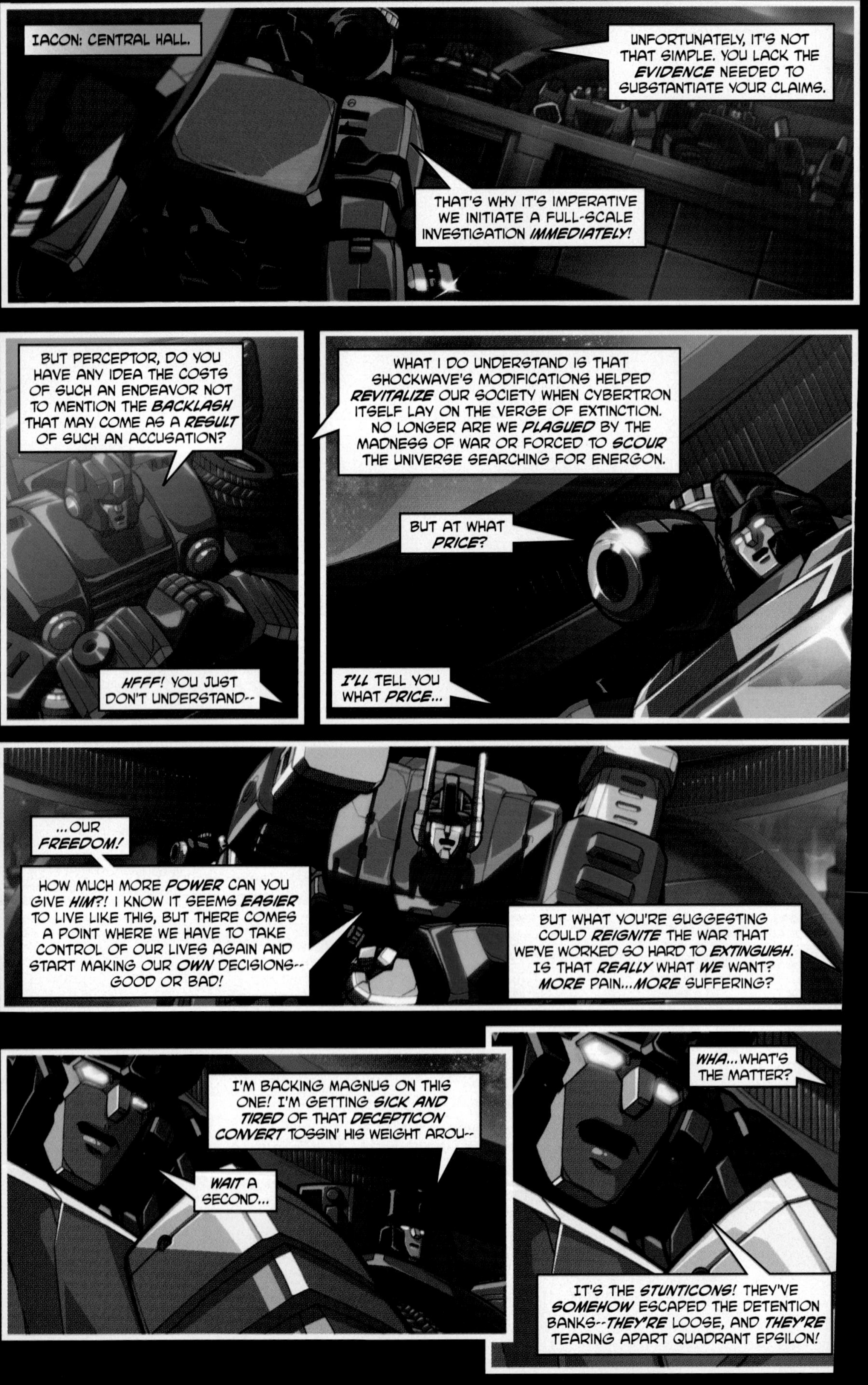
IACON: CENTRAL HALL.
UNFORTUNATELY, IT'S NOT THAT SIMPLE. YOU LACK THE EVIDENCE NEEDED TO SUBSTANTIATE YOUR CLAIMS.
THAT'S WHY IT'S IMPERATIVE WE INITIATE A FULL-SCALE INVESTIGATION IMMEDIATELY!
BUT PERCEPTOR, DO YOU HAVE ANY IDEA THE COSTS OF SUCH AN ENDEAVOR NOT TO MENTION THE BACKLASH THAT MAY COME AS A RESULT OF SUCH AN ACCUSATION?
HFFF! YOU JUST DON'T UNDERSTAND--
WHAT I DO UNDERSTAND IS THAT SHOCKWAVE'S MODIFICATIONS HELPED REVITALIZE OUR SOCIETY WHEN CYBERTRON ITSELF LAY ON THE VERGE OF EXTINCTION. NO LONGER ARE WE PLAGUED BY THE MADNESS OF WAR OR FORCED TO SCOUR THE UNIVERSE SEARCHING FOR ENERGON.
BUT AT WHAT PRICE?
I'LL TELL YOU WHAT PRICE...
...OUR FREEDOM!
HOW MUCH MORE POWER CAN YOU GIVE HIM?! I KNOW IT SEEMS EASIER TO LIVE LIKE THIS, BUT THERE COMES A POINT WHERE WE HAVE TO TAKE CONTROL OF OUR LIVES AGAIN AND START MAKING OUR OWN DECISIONS-- GOOD OR BAD!
BUT WHAT YOU'RE SUGGESTING COULD REIGNITE THE WAR THAT WE'VE WORKED SO HARD TO EXTINGUISH. IS THAT REALLY WHAT WE WANT? MORE PAIN...MORE SUFFERING?
I'M BACKING MAGNUS ON THIS ONE! I'M GETTING SICK AND TIRED OF THAT DECEPTICON CONVERT TOSSIN' HIS WEIGHT AROU--
WAIT A SECOND...
WHA...WHAT'S THE MATTER?
IT'S THE STUNTICONS! THEY'VE SOMEHOW ESCAPED THE DETENTION BANKS--THEY'RE LOOSE, AND THEY'RE TEARING APART QUADRANT EPSILON!

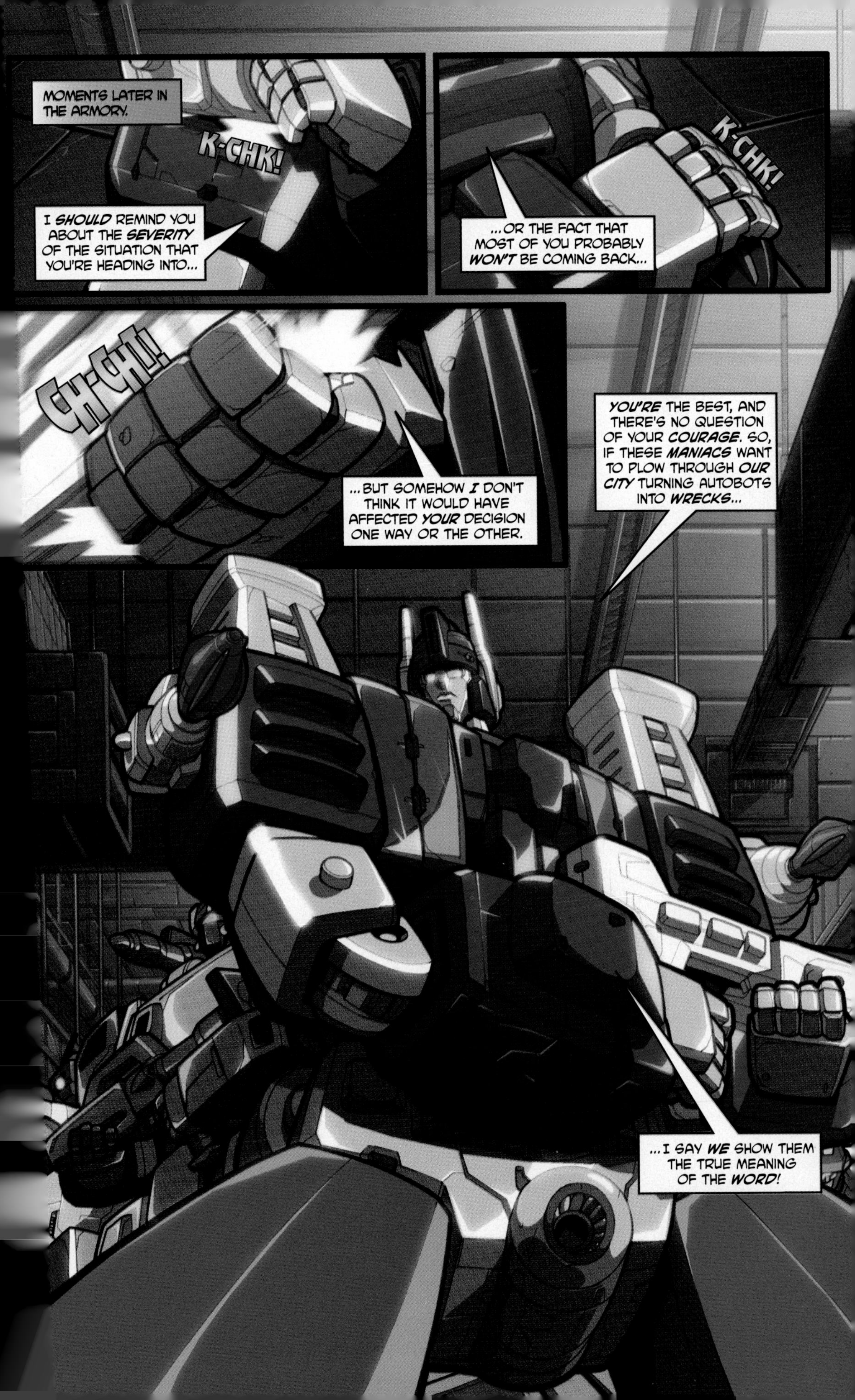
MOMENTS LATER IN THE ARMORY.
K-CHK!
I SHOULD REMIND YOU ABOUT THE SEVERITY OF THE SITUATION THAT YOU'RE HEADING INTO...
K-CHK!
...OR THE FACT THAT MOST OF YOU PROBABLY WON'T BE COMING BACK...
CH-CHT!
...BUT SOMEHOW I DON'T THINK IT WOULD HAVE AFFECTED YOUR DECISION ONE WAY OR THE OTHER.
YOU'RE THE BEST, AND THERE'S NO QUESTION OF YOUR COURAGE. SO, IF THESE MANIACS WANT TO PLOW THROUGH OUR CITY TURNING AUTOBOTS INTO WRECKS...
...I SAY WE SHOW THEM THE TRUE MEANING OF THE WORD!

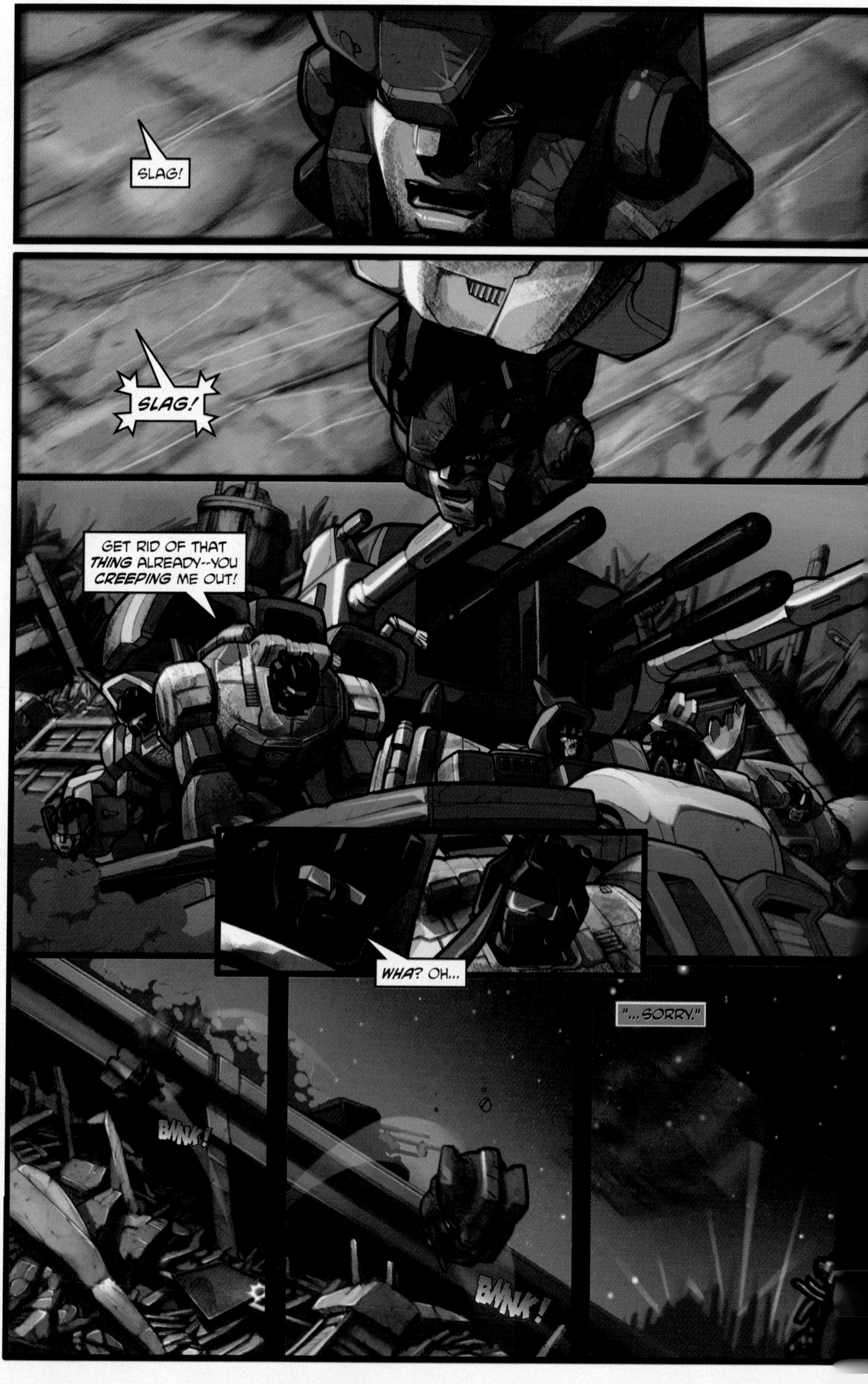
SLAG!
SLAG!
GET RID OF THAT THING ALREADY--YOU CREEPING ME OUT!
WHA? OH...
"...SORRY."
BMNK!
BMNK!

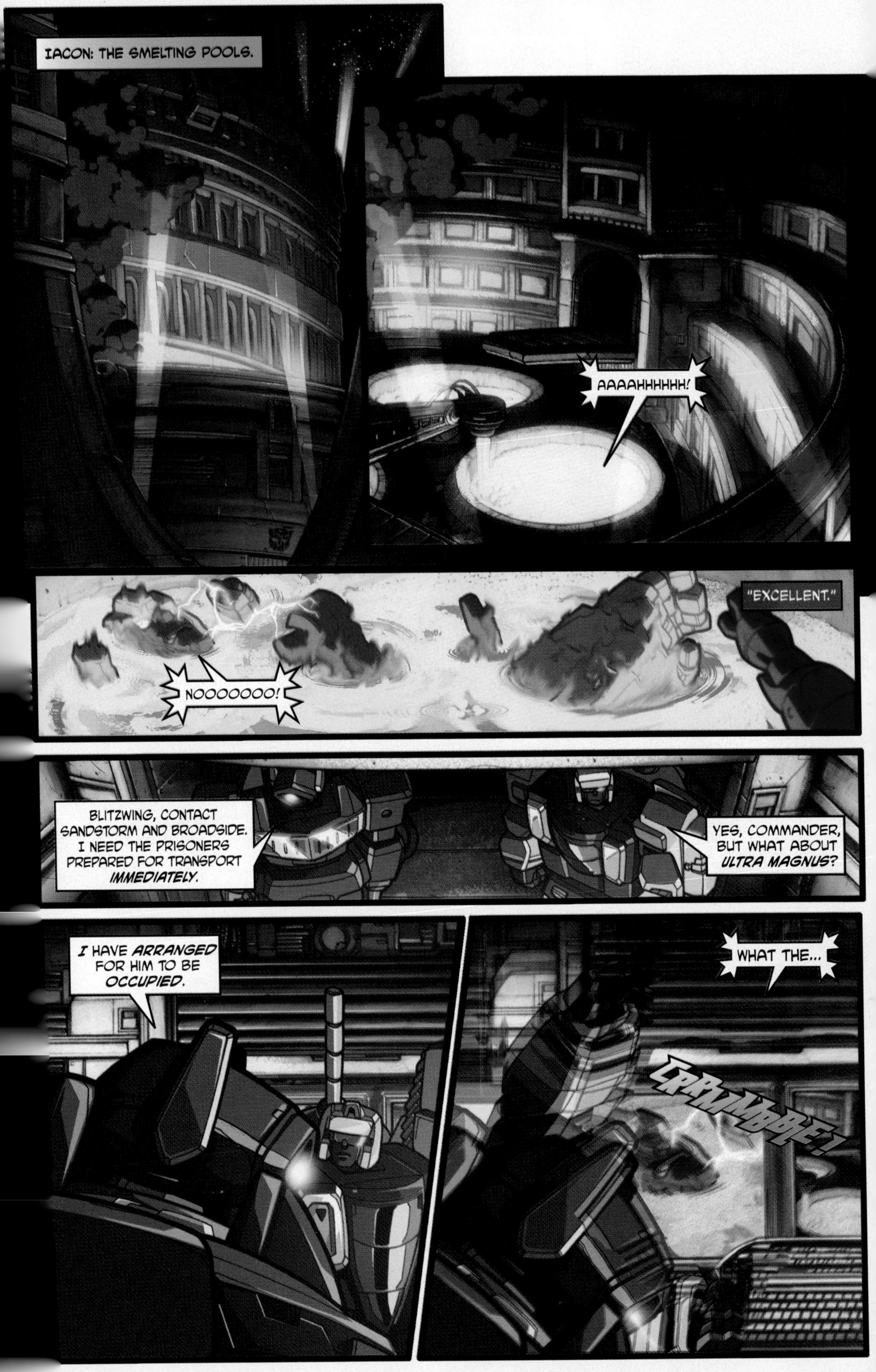
IACON: THE SMELTING POOLS.
AAAAHHHHHH!
"EXCELLENT."
NOOOOOOO!
BLITZWING, CONTACT SANDSTORM AND BROADSIDE. I NEED THE PRISONERS PREPARED FOR TRANSPORT IMMEDIATELY.
YES, COMMANDER, BUT WHAT ABOUT ULTRA MAGNUS?
I HAVE ARRANGED FOR HIM TO BE OCCUPIED.
WHAT THE...
CRRUMBBLE!

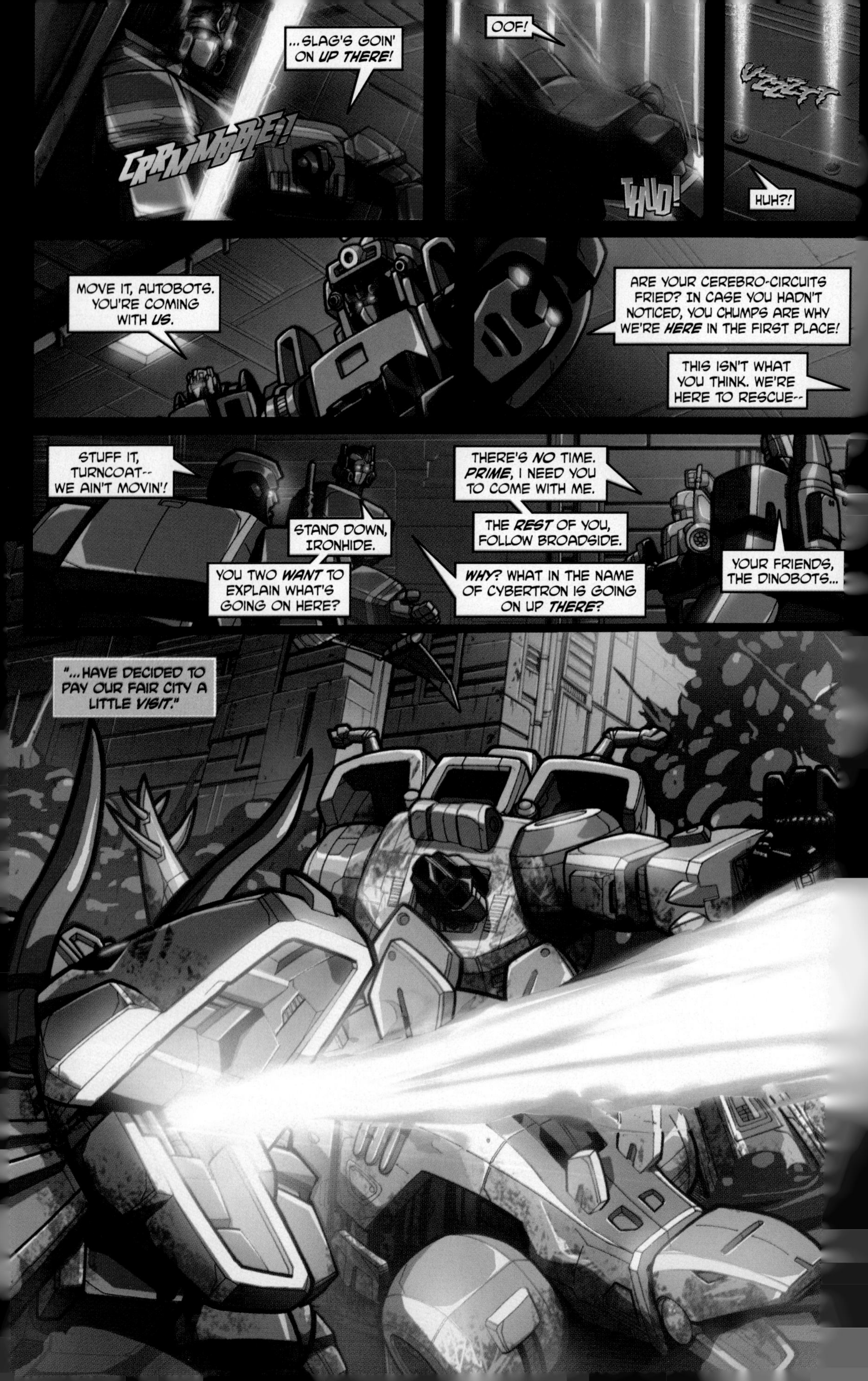
...SLAG'S GOIN' ON UP THERE!
CRRUMBBLE!
OOF!
THUD!
VZZZT
HUH?!
MOVE IT, AUTOBOTS. YOU'RE COMING WITH US.
ARE YOUR CEREBRO-CIRCUITS FRIED? IN CASE YOU HADN'T NOTICED, YOU CHUMPS ARE WHY WE'RE HERE IN THE FIRST PLACE!
THIS ISN'T WHAT YOU THINK. WE'RE HERE TO RESCUE--
STUFF IT, TURNCOAT-- WE AIN'T MOVIN'!
STAND DOWN, IRONHIDE.
YOU TWO WANT TO EXPLAIN WHAT'S GOING ON HERE?
THERE'S NO TIME. PRIME, I NEED YOU TO COME WITH ME.
THE REST OF YOU, FOLLOW BROADSIDE.
WHY? WHAT IN THE NAME OF CYBERTRON IS GOING ON UP THERE?
YOUR FRIENDS, THE DINOBOTS...
"...HAVE DECIDED TO PAY OUR FAIR CITY A LITTLE VISIT."

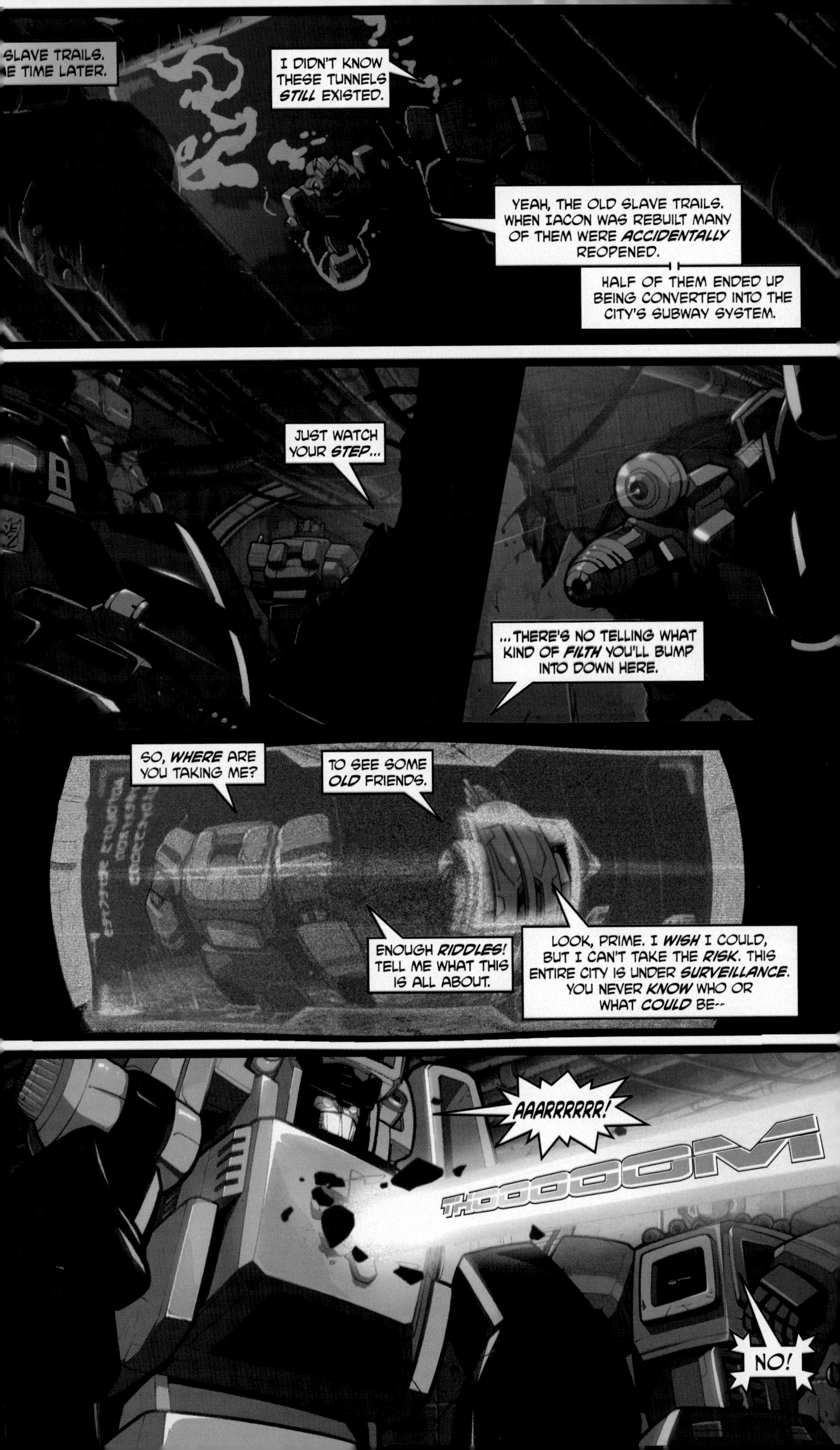
SLAVE TRAILS.
E TIME LATER.
I DIDN'T KNOW THESE TUNNELS STILL EXISTED.
YEAH, THE OLD SLAVE TRAILS. WHEN IACON WAS REBUILT MANY OF THEM WERE ACCIDENTALLY REOPENED.
HALF OF THEM ENDED UP BEING CONVERTED INTO THE CITY'S SUBWAY SYSTEM.
JUST WATCH YOUR STEP...
...THERE'S NO TELLING WHAT KIND OF FILTH YOU'LL BUMP INTO DOWN HERE.
SO, WHERE ARE YOU TAKING ME?
TO SEE SOME OLD FRIENDS.
ENOUGH RIDDLES! TELL ME WHAT THIS IS ALL ABOUT.
LOOK, PRIME. I WISH I COULD, BUT I CAN'T TAKE THE RISK. THIS ENTIRE CITY IS UNDER SURVEILLANCE. YOU NEVER KNOW WHO OR WHAT COULD BE--
AAARRRRRR!
THOOOOOOM
NO!

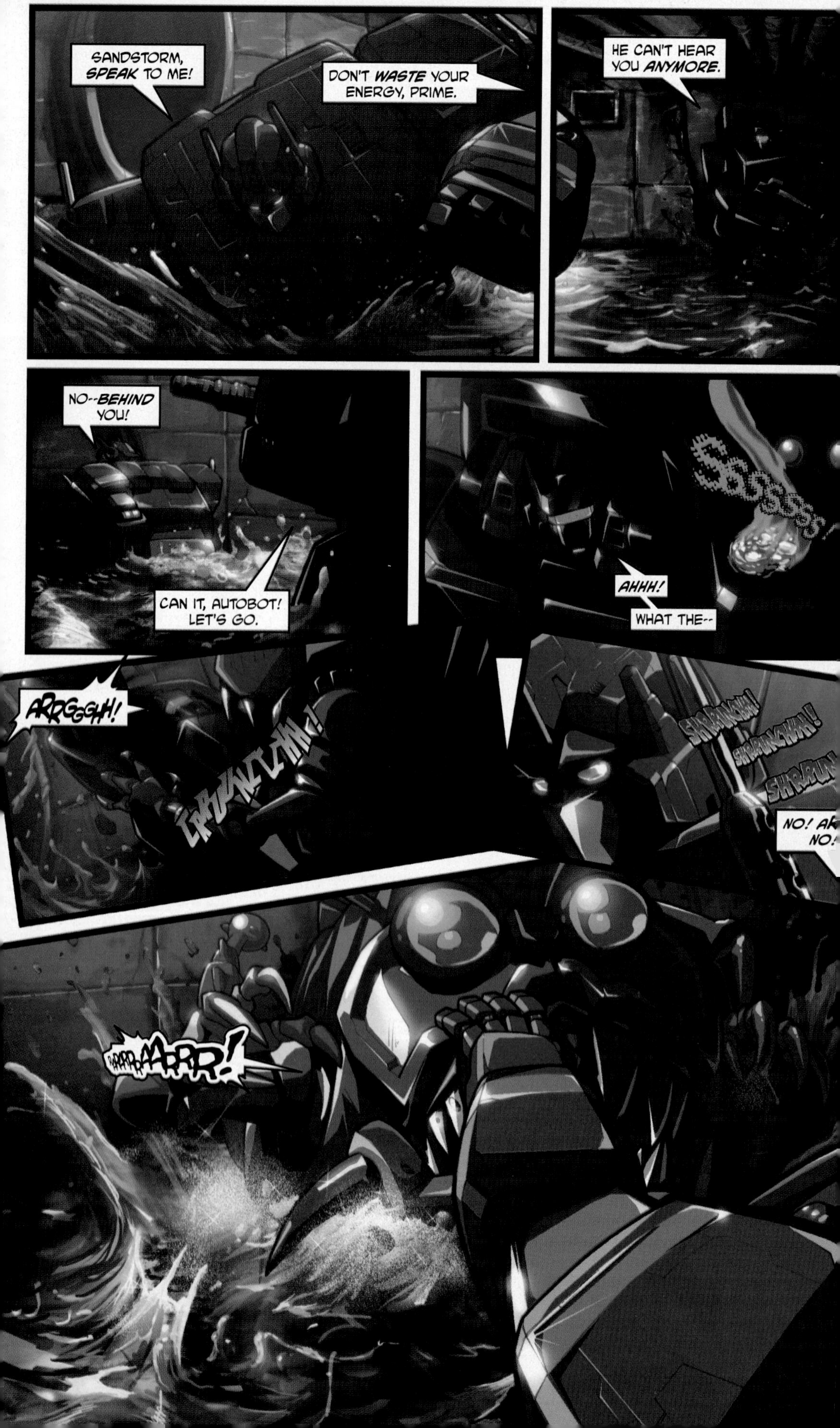
SANDSTORM, *SPEAK* TO ME!
DON'T *WASTE* YOUR ENERGY, PRIME.
HE CAN'T HEAR YOU *ANYMORE*.
NO--*BEHIND* YOU!
CAN IT, AUTOBOT! LET'S GO.
AHHH!
WHAT THE--
ARRGGGH!
SHRRUNCHAK!
SHRRUNCHAK!
NO! AR
NO!
RRRRRRAARRR!

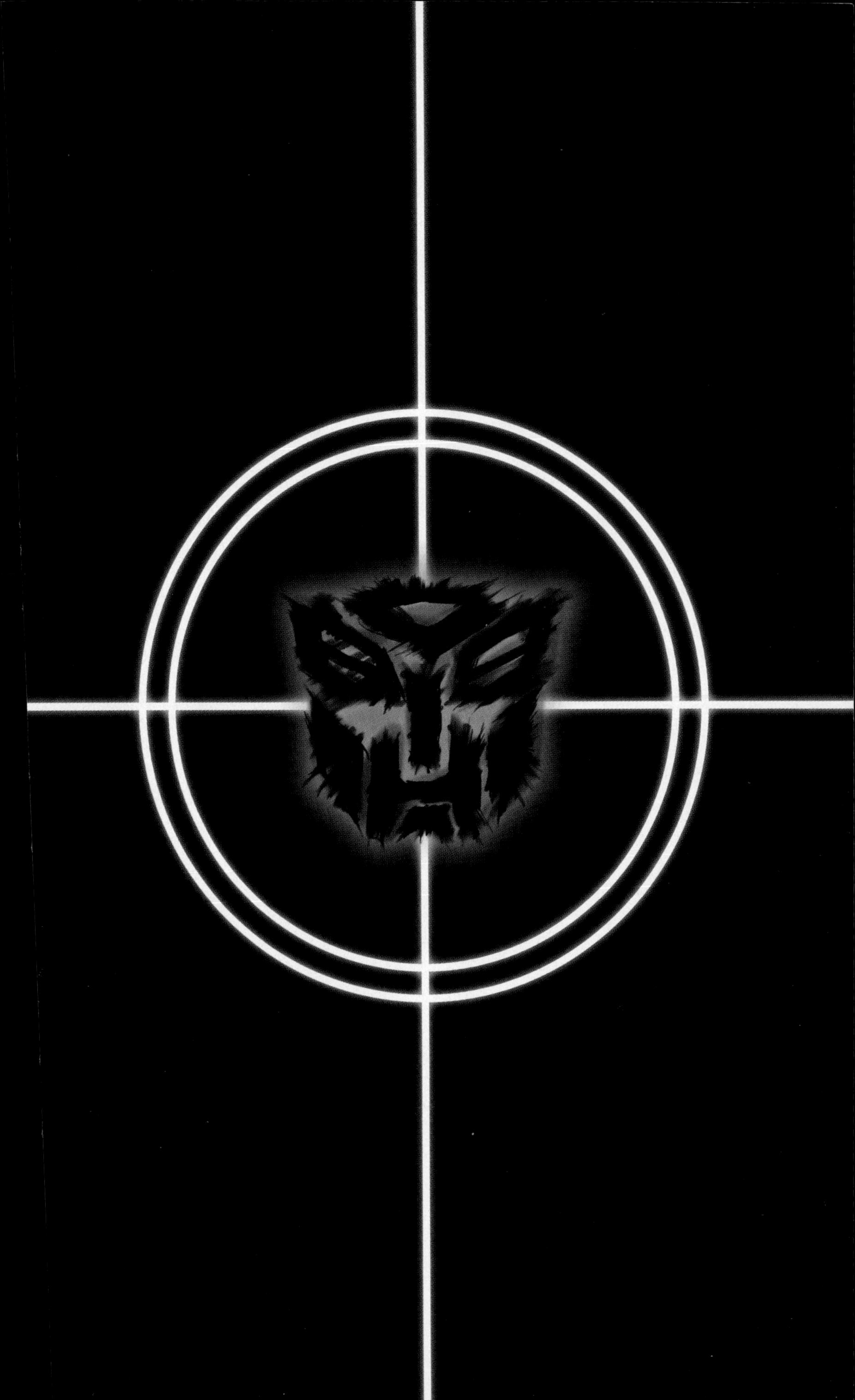

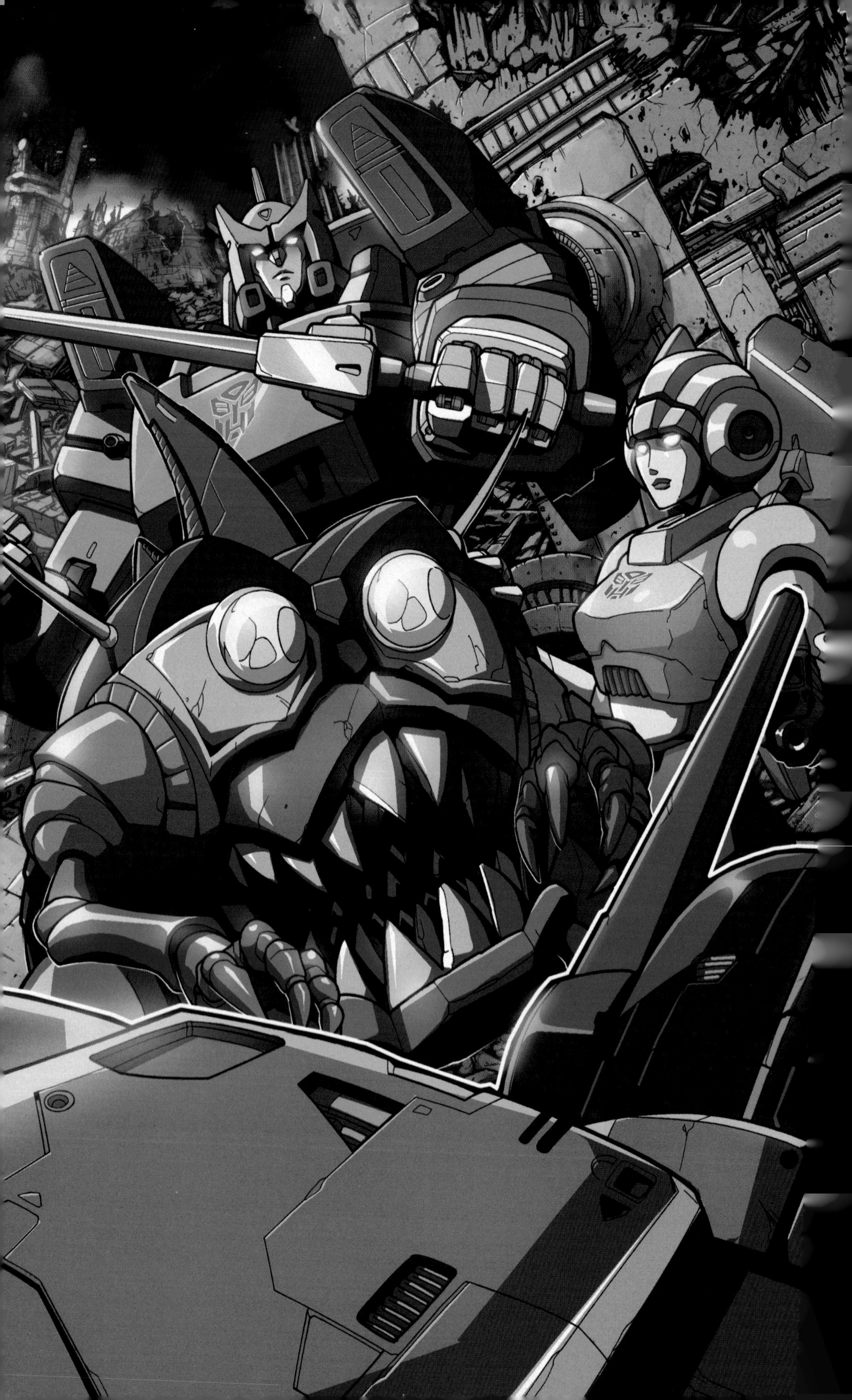

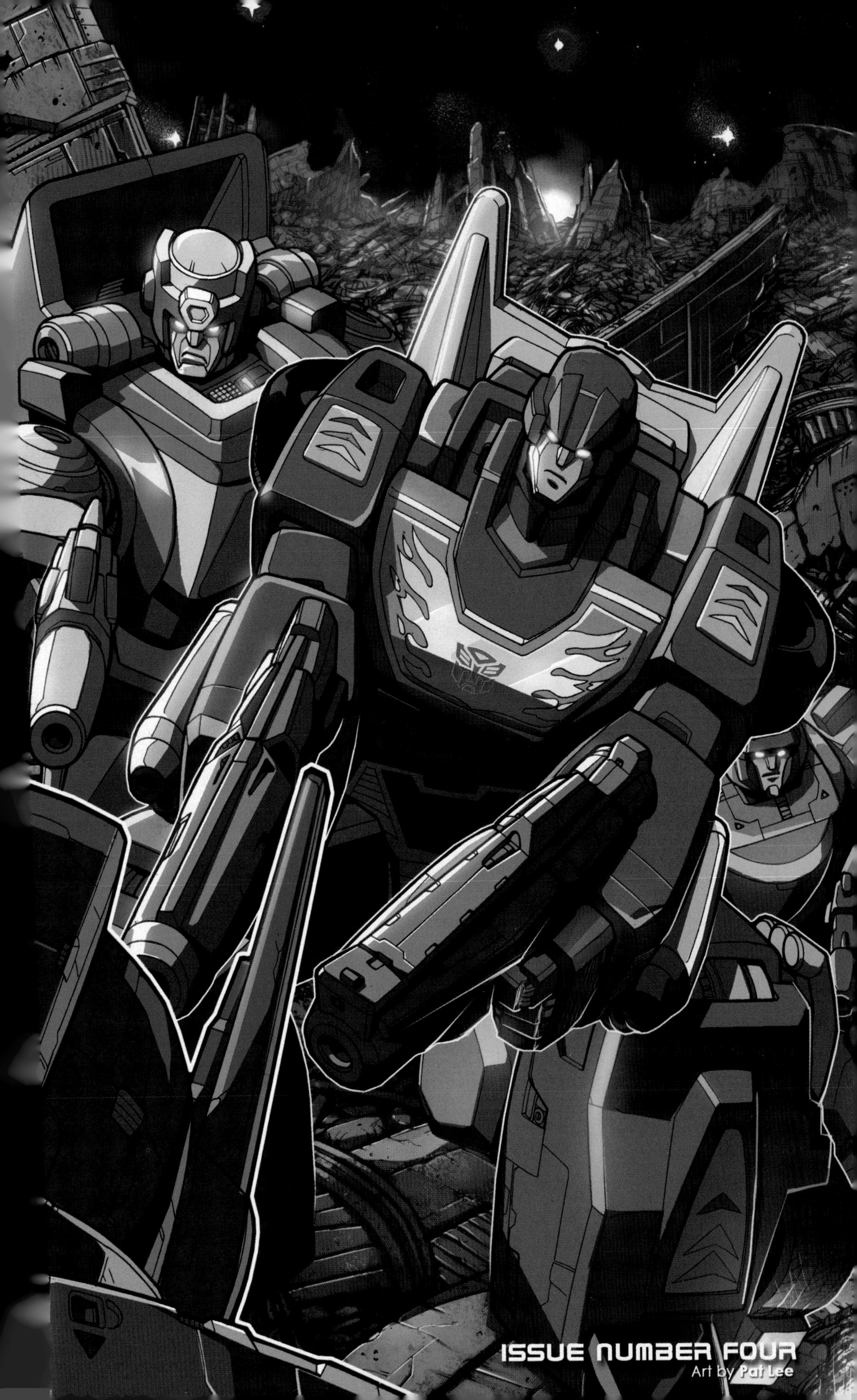
ISSUE NUMBER FOUR
Art by Pat Lee

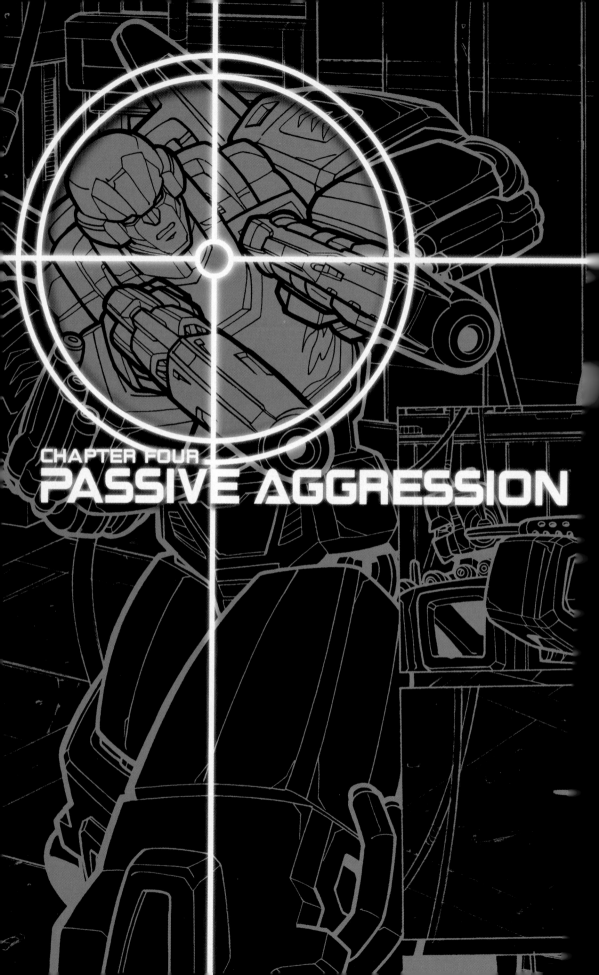

CHAPTER FOUR:
PASSIVE AGGRESSION

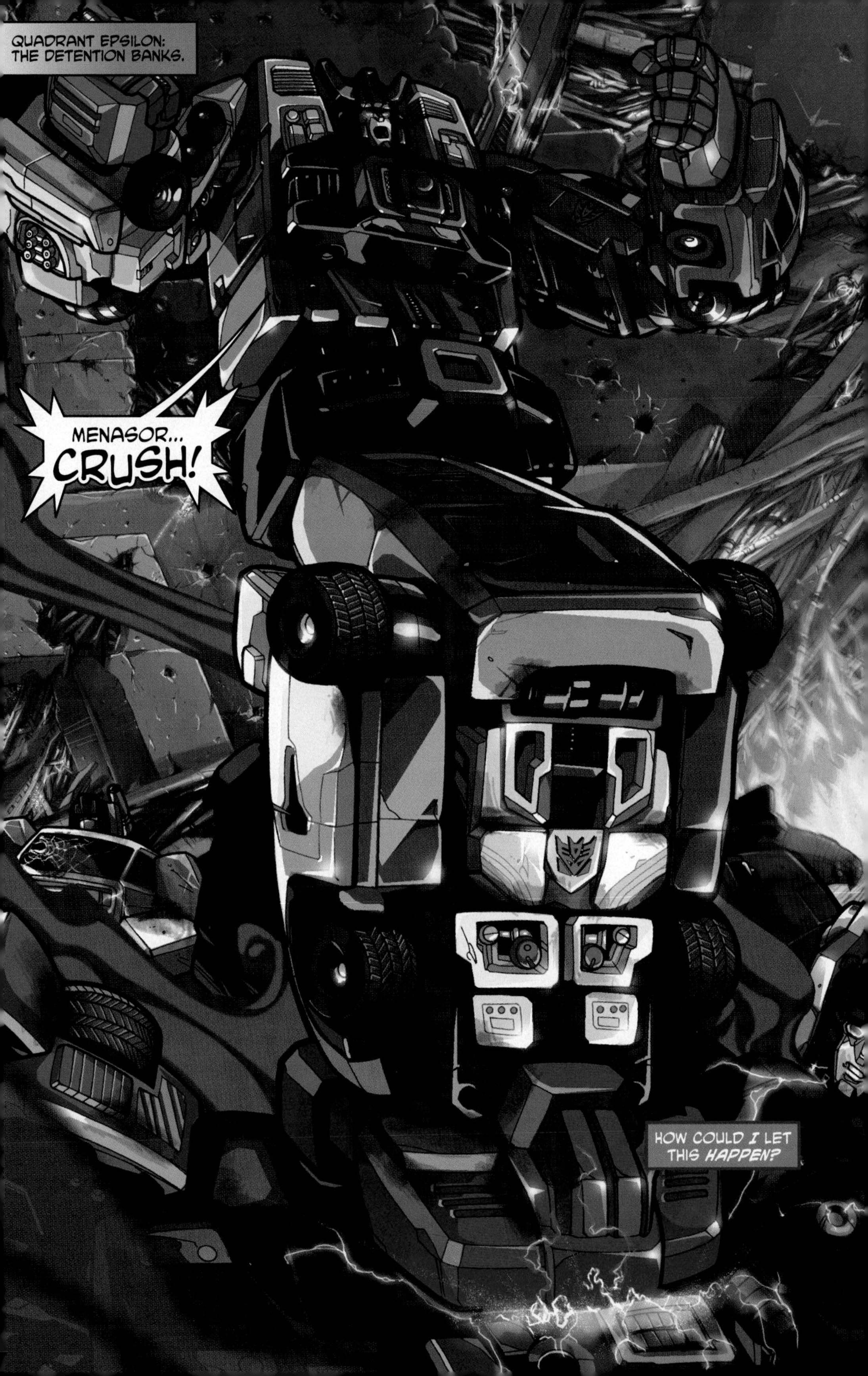
QUADRANT EPSILON: THE DETENTION BANKS.
MENASOR... CRUSH!
HOW COULD *I* LET THIS *HAPPEN?*

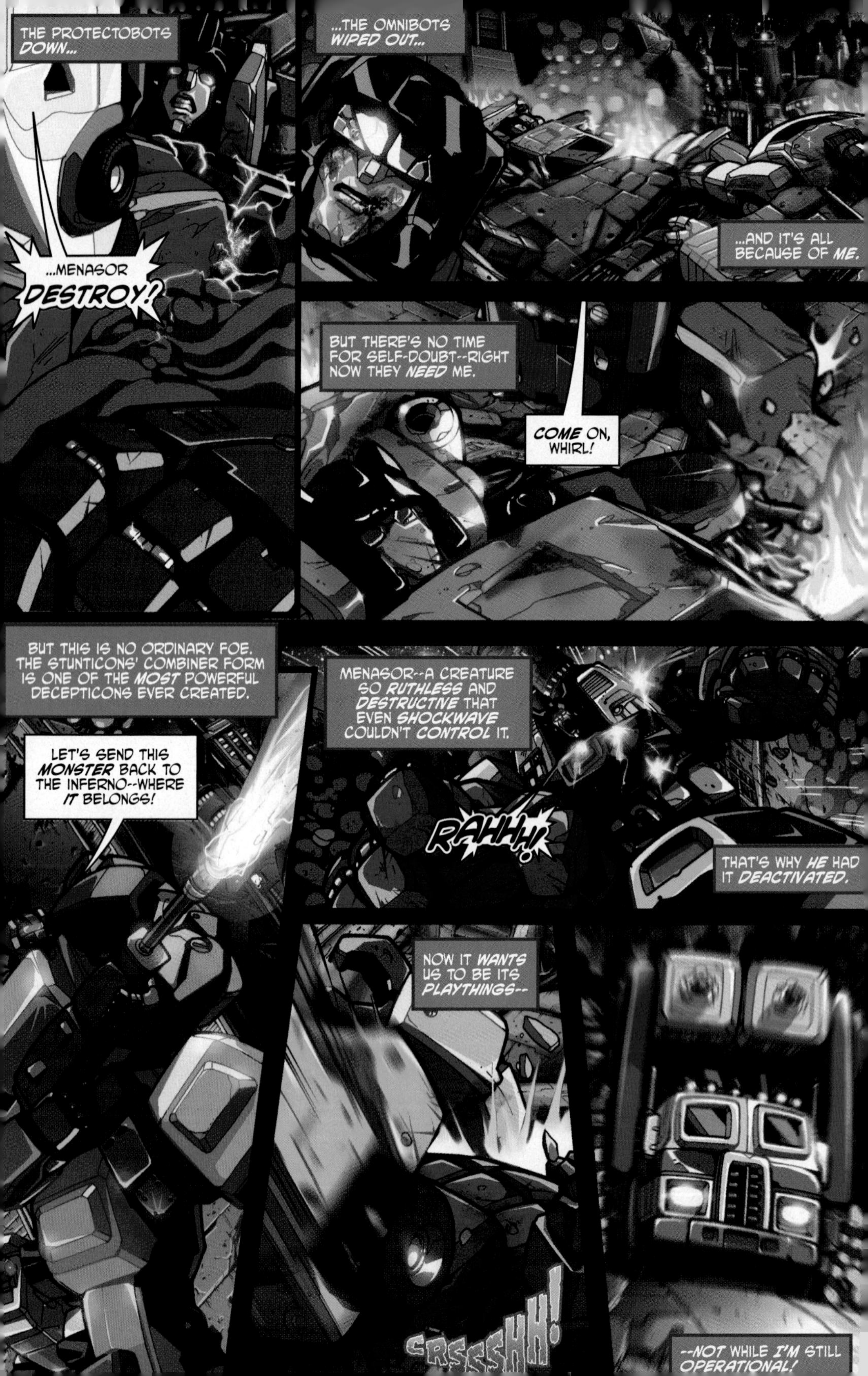
THE PROTECTOBOTS DOWN...
...MENASOR DESTROY!
...THE OMNIBOTS WIPED OUT...
...AND IT'S ALL BECAUSE OF ME.
BUT THERE'S NO TIME FOR SELF-DOUBT--RIGHT NOW THEY NEED ME.
COME ON, WHIRL!
BUT THIS IS NO ORDINARY FOE. THE STUNTICONS' COMBINER FORM IS ONE OF THE MOST POWERFUL DECEPTICONS EVER CREATED.
LET'S SEND THIS MONSTER BACK TO THE INFERNO--WHERE IT BELONGS!
MENASOR--A CREATURE SO RUTHLESS AND DESTRUCTIVE THAT EVEN SHOCKWAVE COULDN'T CONTROL IT.
RAHHH!
THAT'S WHY HE HAD IT DEACTIVATED.
NOW IT WANTS US TO BE ITS PLAYTHINGS--
CRSSSHH!
--NOT WHILE I'M STILL OPERATIONAL!

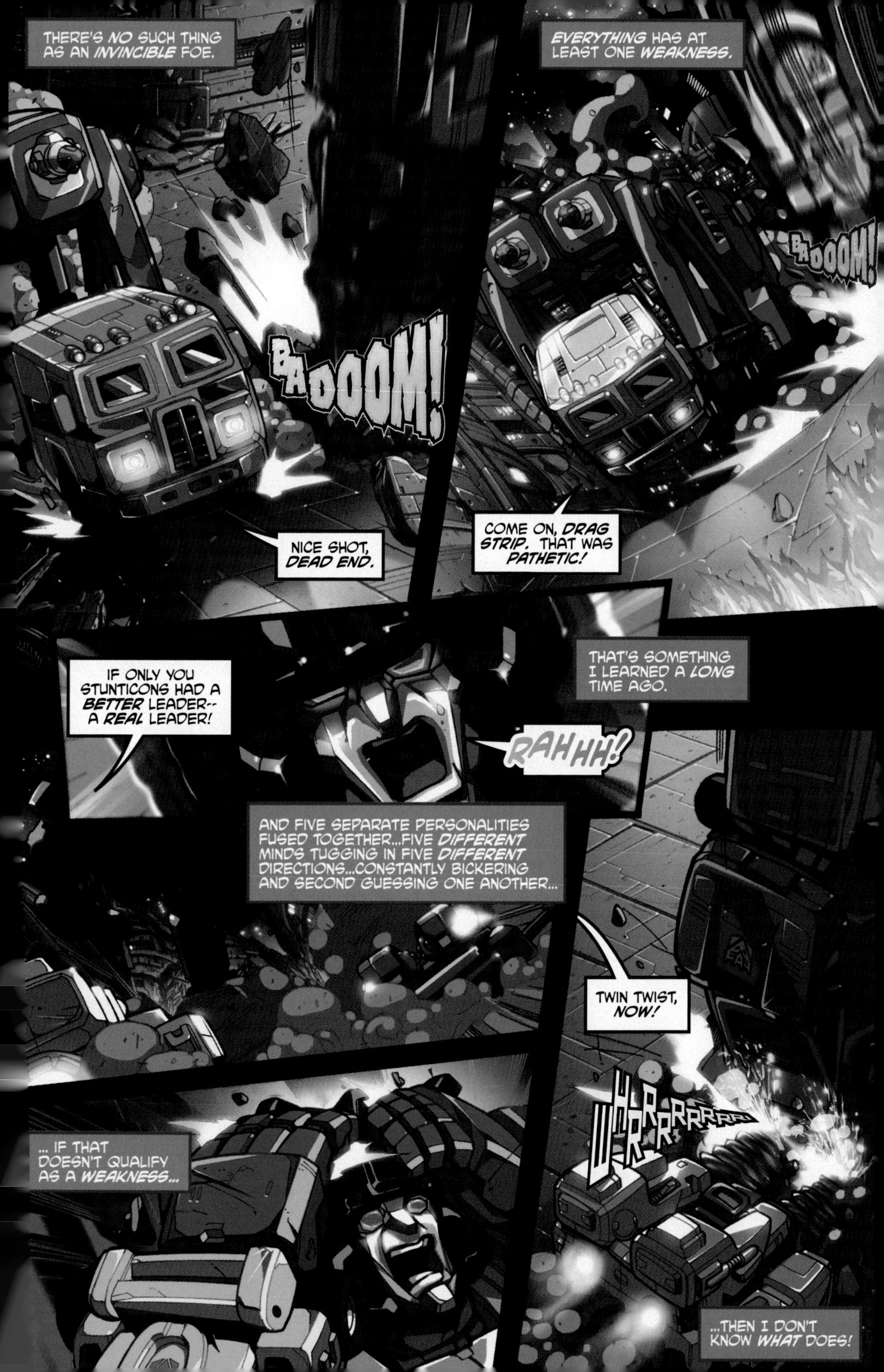
THERE'S NO SUCH THING AS AN INVINCIBLE FOE.
BADOOM!
NICE SHOT, DEAD END.
EVERYTHING HAS AT LEAST ONE WEAKNESS.
BADOOM!
COME ON, DRAG STRIP. THAT WAS PATHETIC!
IF ONLY YOU STUNTICONS HAD A BETTER LEADER-- A REAL LEADER!
RAHHH!
THAT'S SOMETHING I LEARNED A LONG TIME AGO.
AND FIVE SEPARATE PERSONALITIES FUSED TOGETHER...FIVE DIFFERENT MINDS TUGGING IN FIVE DIFFERENT DIRECTIONS...CONSTANTLY BICKERING AND SECOND GUESSING ONE ANOTHER...
TWIN TWIST, NOW!
... IF THAT DOESN'T QUALIFY AS A WEAKNESS...
WHHRRRRRRRRR
...THEN I DON'T KNOW WHAT DOES!

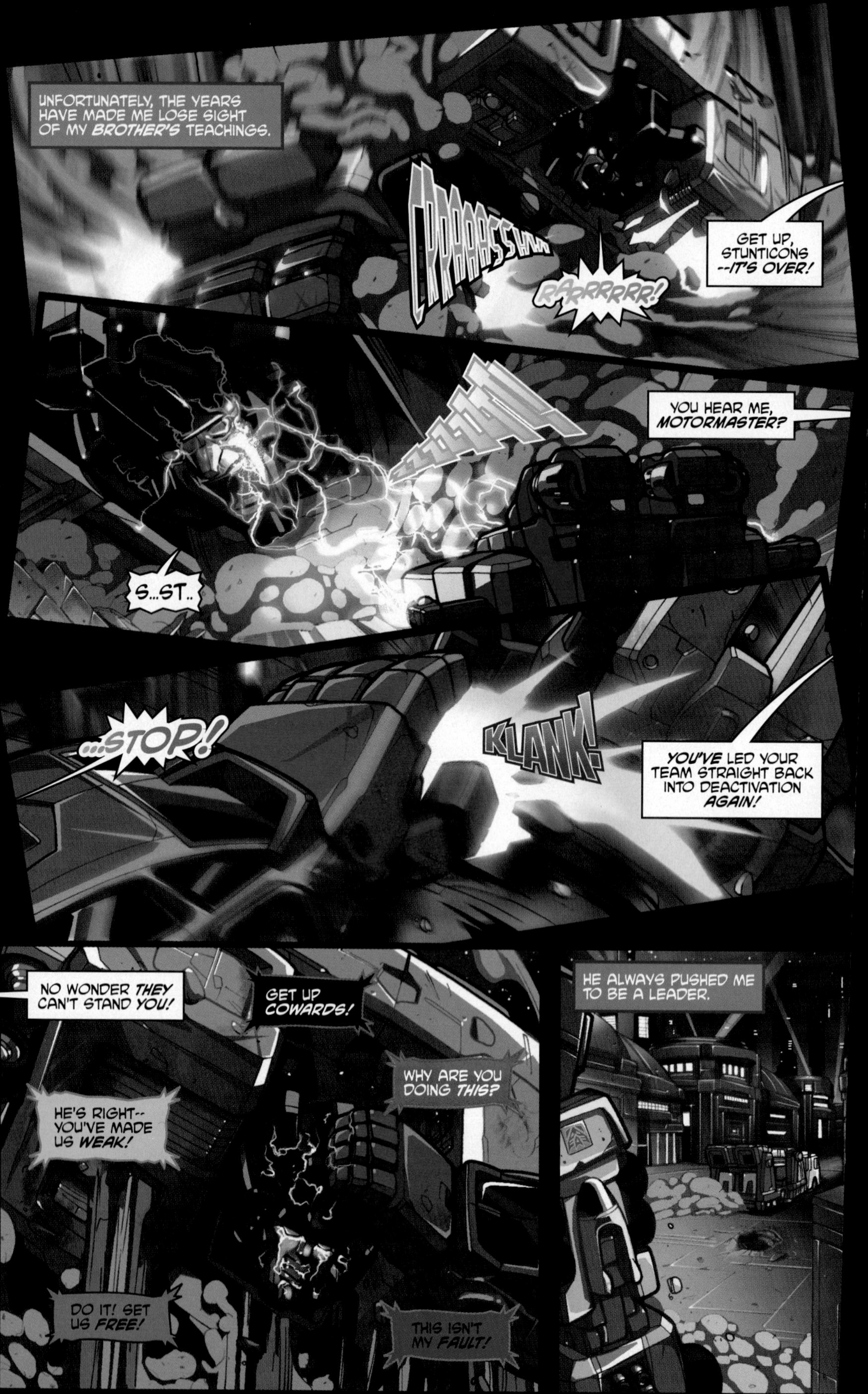

UNFORTUNATELY, THE YEARS HAVE MADE ME LOSE SIGHT OF MY BROTHER'S TEACHINGS.
GET UP, STUNTICONS --IT'S OVER!
RARRRRRR!
YOU HEAR ME, MOTORMASTER?
S...ST...
...STOP!
KLANK!
YOU'VE LED YOUR TEAM STRAIGHT BACK INTO DEACTIVATION AGAIN!
NO WONDER THEY CAN'T STAND YOU!
GET UP COWARDS!
WHY ARE YOU DOING THIS?
HE'S RIGHT-- YOU'VE MADE US WEAK!
DO IT! SET US FREE!
THIS ISN'T MY FAULT!
HE ALWAYS PUSHED ME TO BE A LEADER.

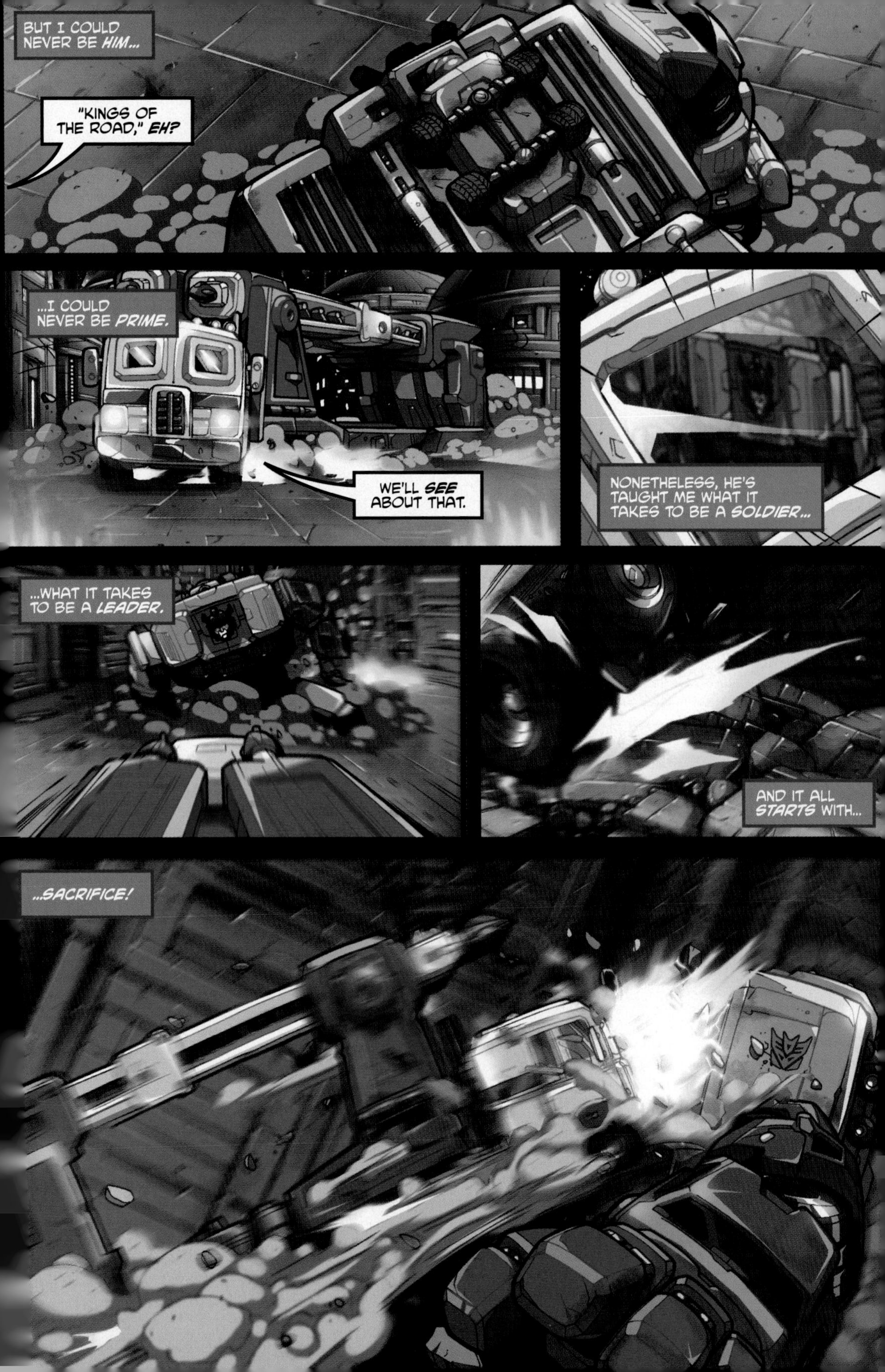
BUT I COULD NEVER BE *HIM*...
"KINGS OF THE ROAD," *EH?*
...I COULD NEVER BE *PRIME.*
WE'LL ***SEE*** ABOUT THAT.
NONETHELESS, HE'S TAUGHT ME WHAT IT TAKES TO BE A *SOLDIER*...
...WHAT IT TAKES TO BE A *LEADER.*
AND IT ALL *STARTS* WITH...
...*SACRIFICE!*

BUT HOW MANY *SACRIFICES* MUST BE MADE? HOW MANY LIVES MUST BE *LOST*?

AT FIRST, I THOUGHT I WAS DOING THE RIGHT THING, BUT AFTER ALL THIS DESTRUCTION... WHAT NOW? IT ALWAYS SEEMS TO END UP THE SAME WAY...*US* AGAINST *THEM*...

...UGHHH...

...AUTOBOT *VERSUS* DECEPTICON... IT'S GONE ON FOR *TOO LONG*... SOMETHING *NEEDS* TO BE DONE...

...BECAUSE SOMEHOW I THINK THIS IS MORE THAN A MERE *COINCIDENCE.*

YOU ALL RIGHT THERE, SOLDIER?

YEAH...I'LL MANAGE. THAT LUNATIC PACKS QUITE THE PUNCH.

MAGNUS!

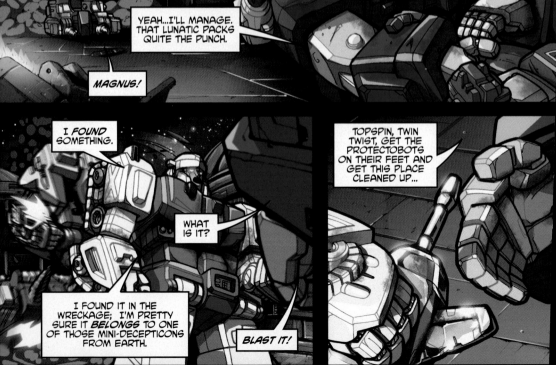

I *FOUND* SOMETHING.

WHAT IS IT?

TOPSPIN, TWIN TWIST, GET THE PROTECTOBOTS ON THEIR FEET AND GET THIS PLACE CLEANED UP...

I FOUND IT IN THE WRECKAGE; I'M PRETTY SURE IT *BELONGS* TO ONE OF THOSE MINI-DECEPTICONS FROM EARTH.

BLAST IT!

"...I'M HEADING BACK TO *IACON* FOR SOME ANSWERS."

SLAG, *KEEP* PUSHING TO CENTRAL TOWER. *ME* HEADED THAT WAY.

WHA...*WHY?!*

NO MORE QUESTIONS-- *JUST GO!*

"*ME* GOT A *HUNCH.*"

DINOBOTS? HOW IS THAT POSSIBLE?

ACTIVATE THE *SENTINELS* IMMEDIATELY--

KA-BOOOOM

AAAAAH!

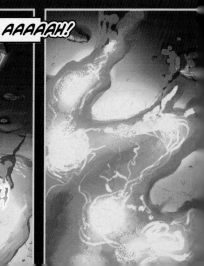

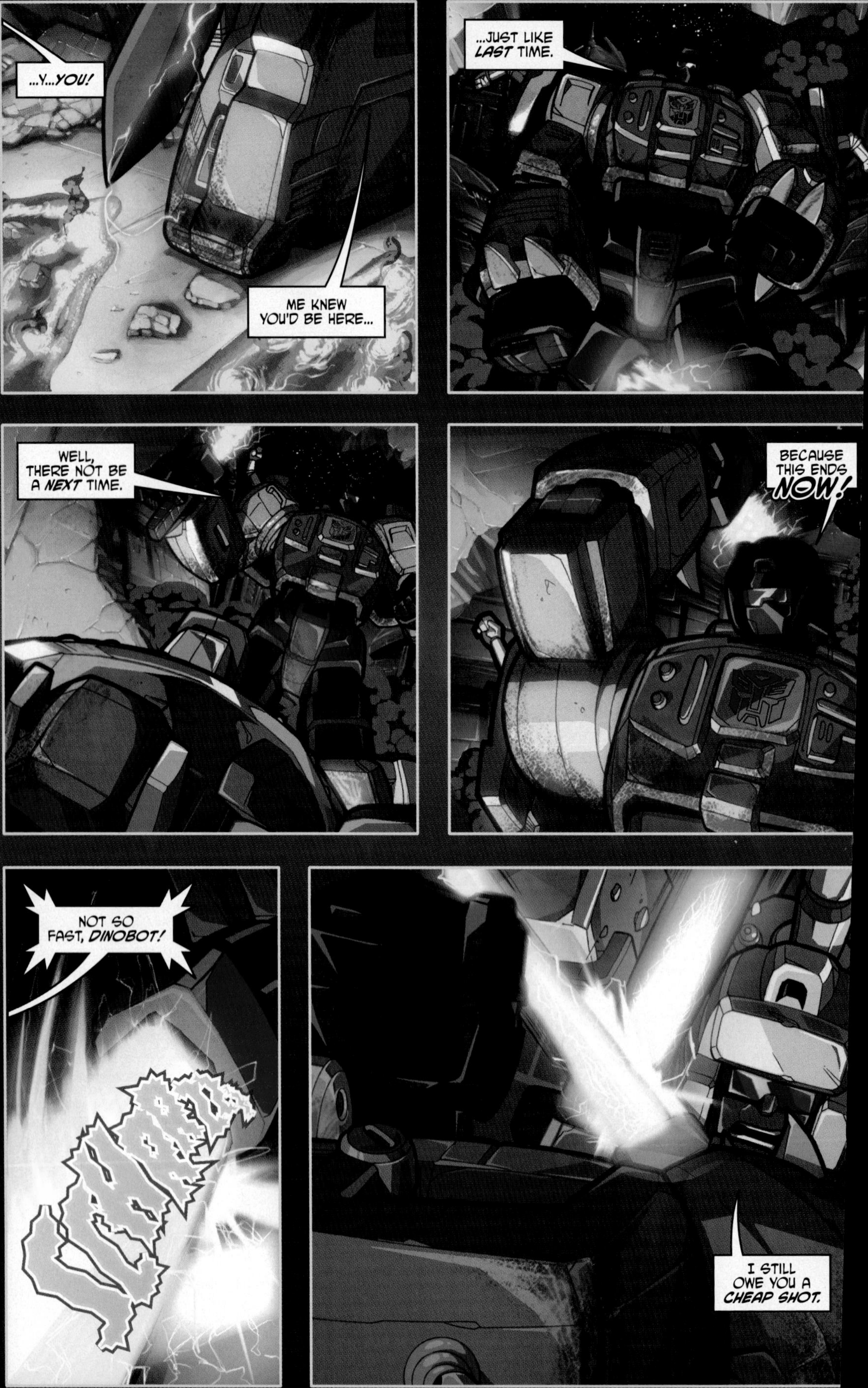
...Y...YOU!
ME KNEW YOU'D BE HERE...
...JUST LIKE LAST TIME.
WELL, THERE NOT BE A NEXT TIME.
BECAUSE THIS ENDS NOW!
NOT SO FAST, DINOBOT!
I STILL OWE YOU A CHEAP SHOT.

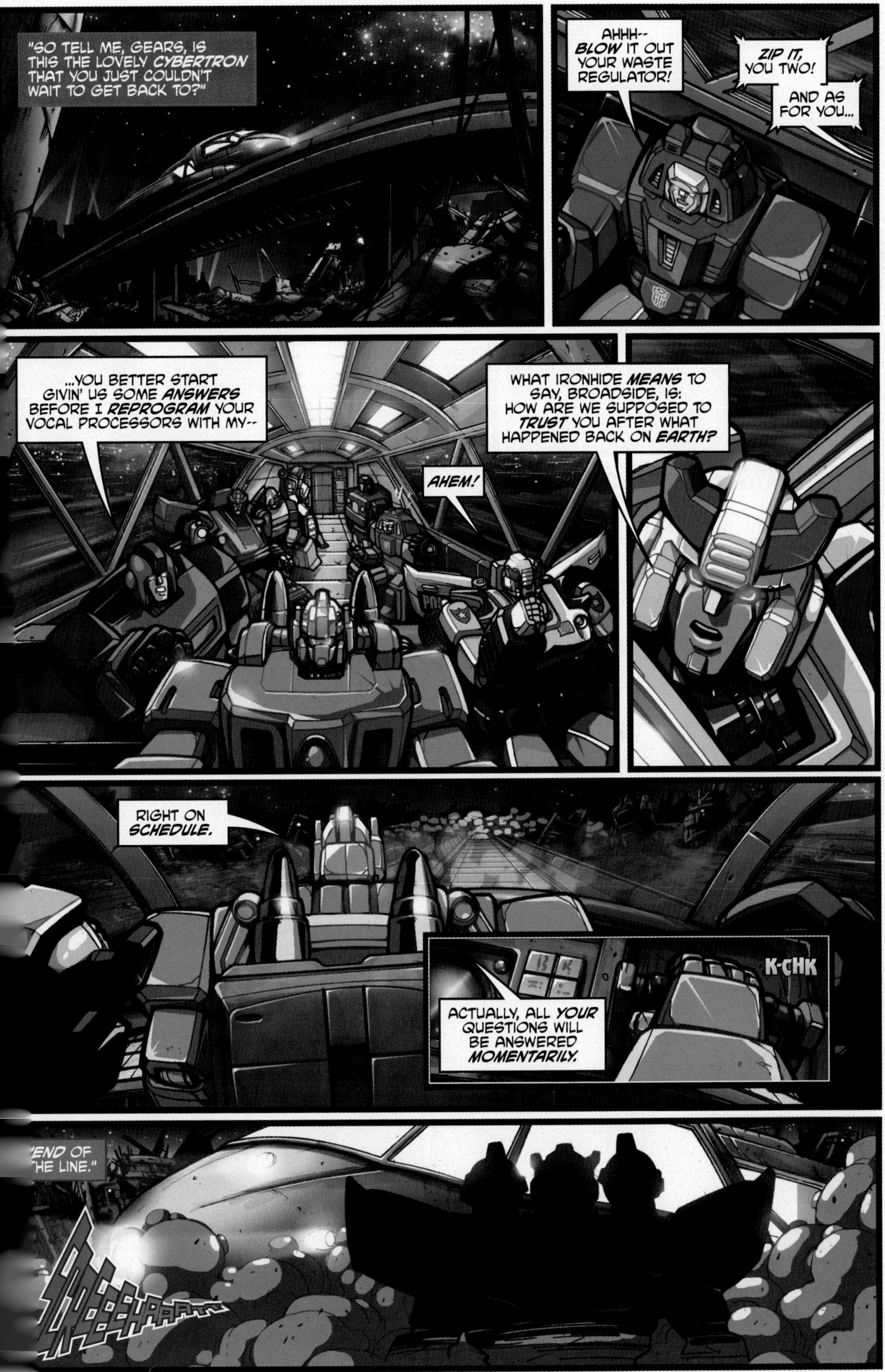
"SO TELL ME, GEARS, IS THIS THE LOVELY CYBERTRON THAT YOU JUST COULDN'T WAIT TO GET BACK TO?"
AHHH-- BLOW IT OUT YOUR WASTE REGULATOR!
ZIP IT, YOU TWO!
AND AS FOR YOU...
...YOU BETTER START GIVIN' US SOME ANSWERS BEFORE I REPROGRAM YOUR VOCAL PROCESSORS WITH MY--
AHEM!
WHAT IRONHIDE MEANS TO SAY, BROADSIDE, IS: HOW ARE WE SUPPOSED TO TRUST YOU AFTER WHAT HAPPENED BACK ON EARTH?
RIGHT ON SCHEDULE.
K-CHK
ACTUALLY, ALL YOUR QUESTIONS WILL BE ANSWERED MOMENTARILY.
END OF THE LINE."

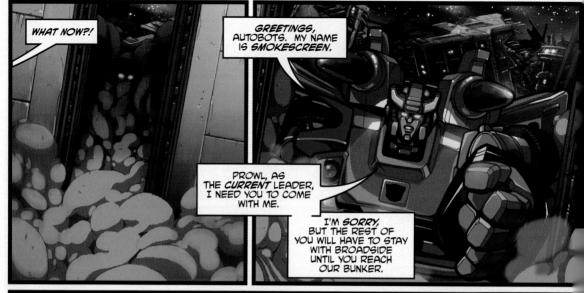

WHAT NOW?!

GREETINGS, AUTOBOTS. MY NAME IS *SMOKESCREEN*.

PROWL, AS THE *CURRENT* LEADER, I NEED YOU TO COME WITH ME.

I'M *SORRY*, BUT THE REST OF YOU WILL HAVE TO STAY WITH BROADSIDE UNTIL YOU REACH OUR BUNKER.

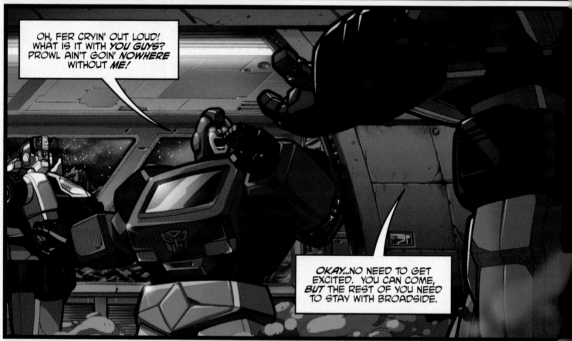

OH, FER CRYIN' OUT LOUD! WHAT IS IT WITH *YOU GUYS*? PROWL AIN'T GOIN' *NOWHERE* WITHOUT *ME*!

OKAY...NO NEED TO GET EXCITED. YOU CAN COME, *BUT* THE REST OF YOU NEED TO STAY WITH BROADSIDE.

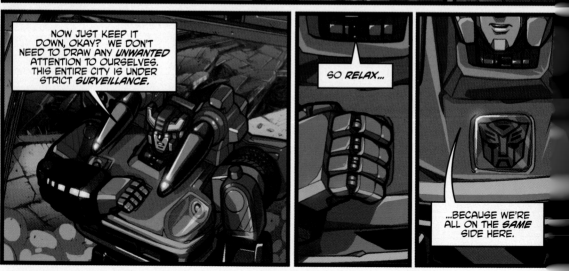

NOW JUST KEEP IT DOWN, OKAY? WE DON'T NEED TO DRAW ANY *UNWANTED* ATTENTION TO OURSELVES. THIS ENTIRE CITY IS UNDER STRICT *SURVEILLANCE*.

SO *RELAX*...

...BECAUSE WE'RE ALL ON THE *SAME* SIDE HERE.

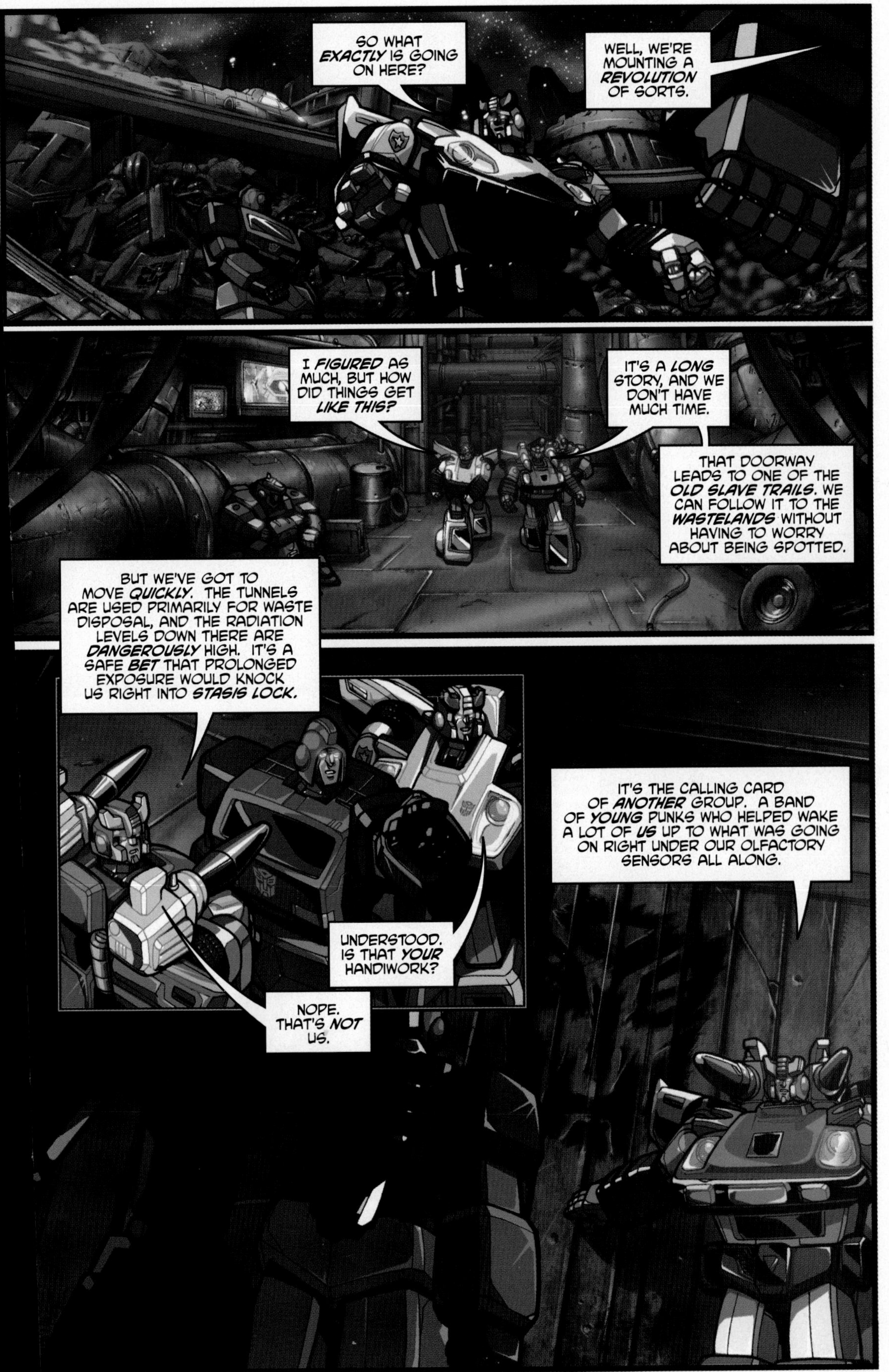
SO WHAT EXACTLY IS GOING ON HERE?
WELL, WE'RE MOUNTING A REVOLUTION OF SORTS.
I FIGURED AS MUCH, BUT HOW DID THINGS GET LIKE THIS?
IT'S A LONG STORY, AND WE DON'T HAVE MUCH TIME.
THAT DOORWAY LEADS TO ONE OF THE OLD SLAVE TRAILS. WE CAN FOLLOW IT TO THE WASTELANDS WITHOUT HAVING TO WORRY ABOUT BEING SPOTTED.
BUT WE'VE GOT TO MOVE QUICKLY. THE TUNNELS ARE USED PRIMARILY FOR WASTE DISPOSAL, AND THE RADIATION LEVELS DOWN THERE ARE DANGEROUSLY HIGH. IT'S A SAFE BET THAT PROLONGED EXPOSURE WOULD KNOCK US RIGHT INTO STASIS LOCK.
UNDERSTOOD. IS THAT YOUR HANDIWORK?
NOPE. THAT'S NOT US.
IT'S THE CALLING CARD OF ANOTHER GROUP. A BAND OF YOUNG PUNKS WHO HELPED WAKE A LOT OF US UP TO WHAT WAS GOING ON RIGHT UNDER OUR OLFACTORY SENSORS ALL ALONG.

"UNFORTUNATELY, *SUBTLETY* ISN'T THEIR FORTE."

...NNN...N...WH......

"NEITHER IS *PATIENCE* OR *RATIONAL* THINKING FOR THAT MATTER."

...WHAT'S...GO... GOING ON...

"THAT'S WHY I'M *HOPING* THAT *WE'RE* ALL STILL ON THE *SAME PAGE.*"

...HERE?

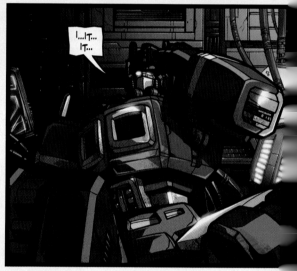

I...IT... IT...

...IT'S THAT...

HSSH!

...MONSTER!

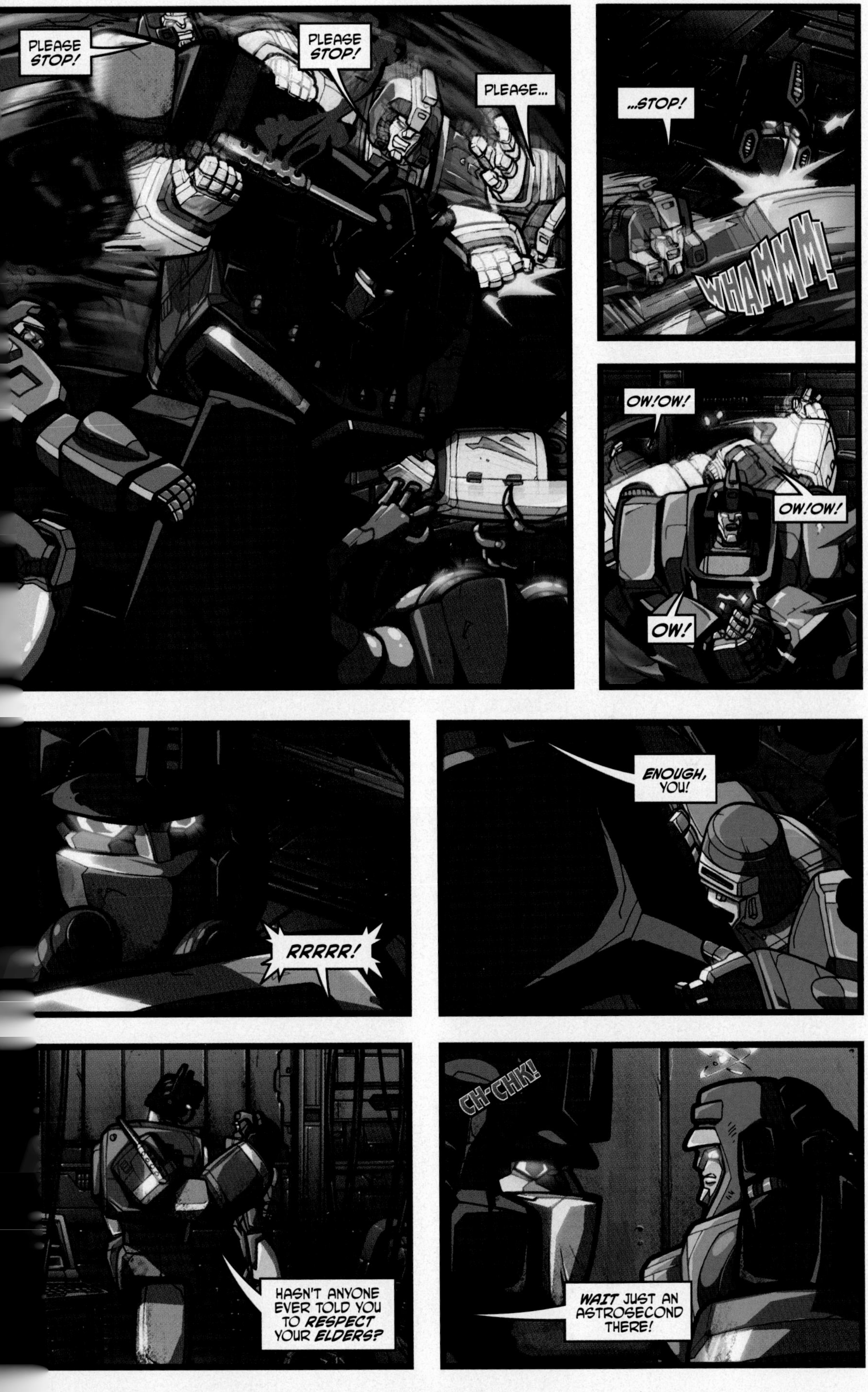
PLEASE STOP!
PLEASE STOP!
PLEASE...
...STOP!
WHAMMM!
OW!OW!
OW!OW!
OW!
RRRRR!
ENOUGH, YOU!
HASN'T ANYONE EVER TOLD YOU TO RESPECT YOUR ELDERS?
CH-CHK!
WAIT JUST AN ASTROSECOND THERE!

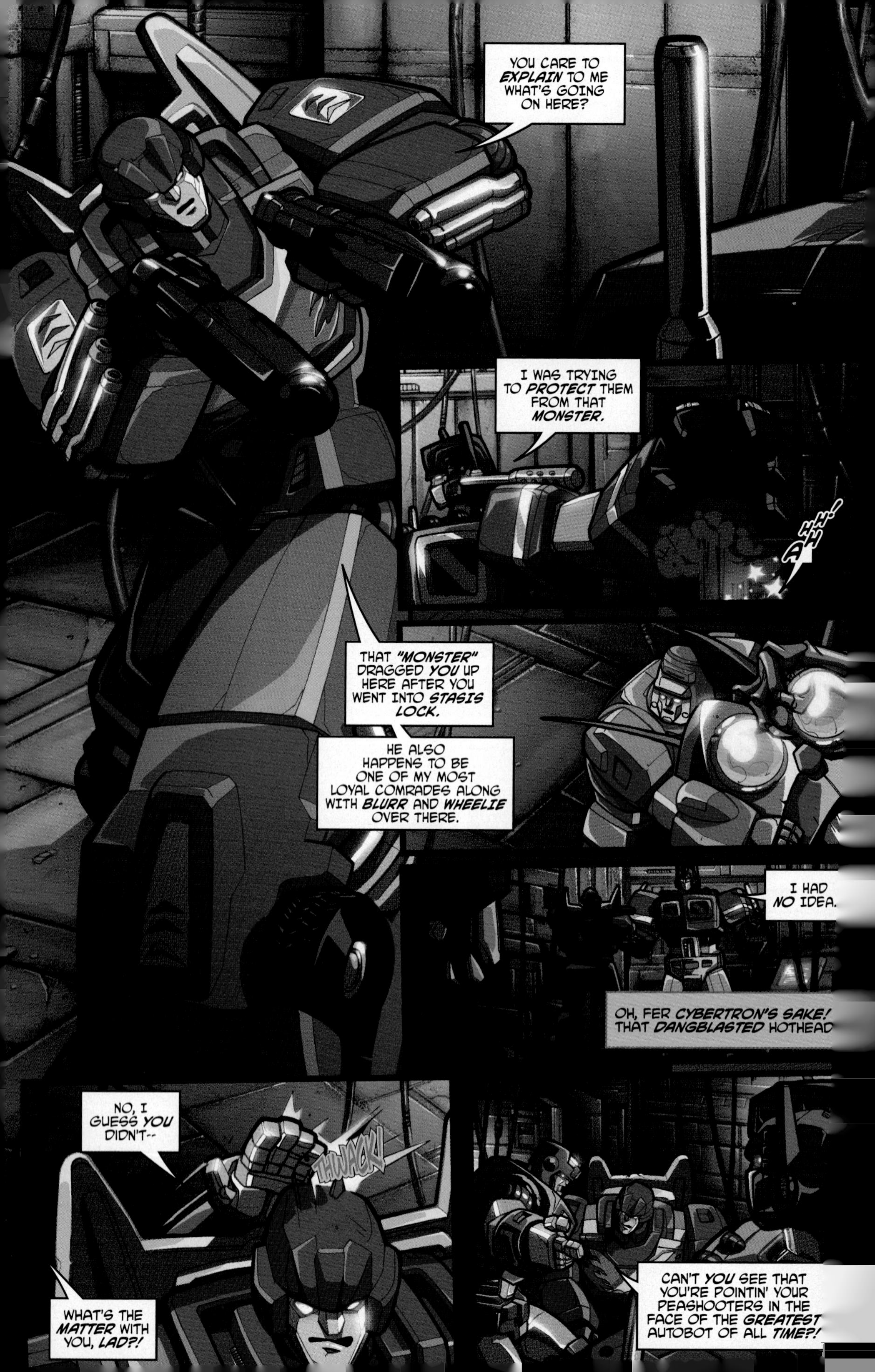
YOU CARE TO EXPLAIN TO ME WHAT'S GOING ON HERE?
I WAS TRYING TO PROTECT THEM FROM THAT MONSTER.
AHHH!
THAT "MONSTER" DRAGGED YOU UP HERE AFTER YOU WENT INTO STASIS LOCK.
HE ALSO HAPPENS TO BE ONE OF MY MOST LOYAL COMRADES ALONG WITH BLURR AND WHEELIE OVER THERE.
I HAD NO IDEA.
OH, FER CYBERTRON'S SAKE! THAT DANGBLASTED HOTHEAD
NO, I GUESS YOU DIDN'T--
THWACK!
WHAT'S THE MATTER WITH YOU, LAD?!
CAN'T YOU SEE THAT YOU'RE POINTIN' YOUR PEASHOOTERS IN THE FACE OF THE GREATEST AUTOBOT OF ALL TIME?!

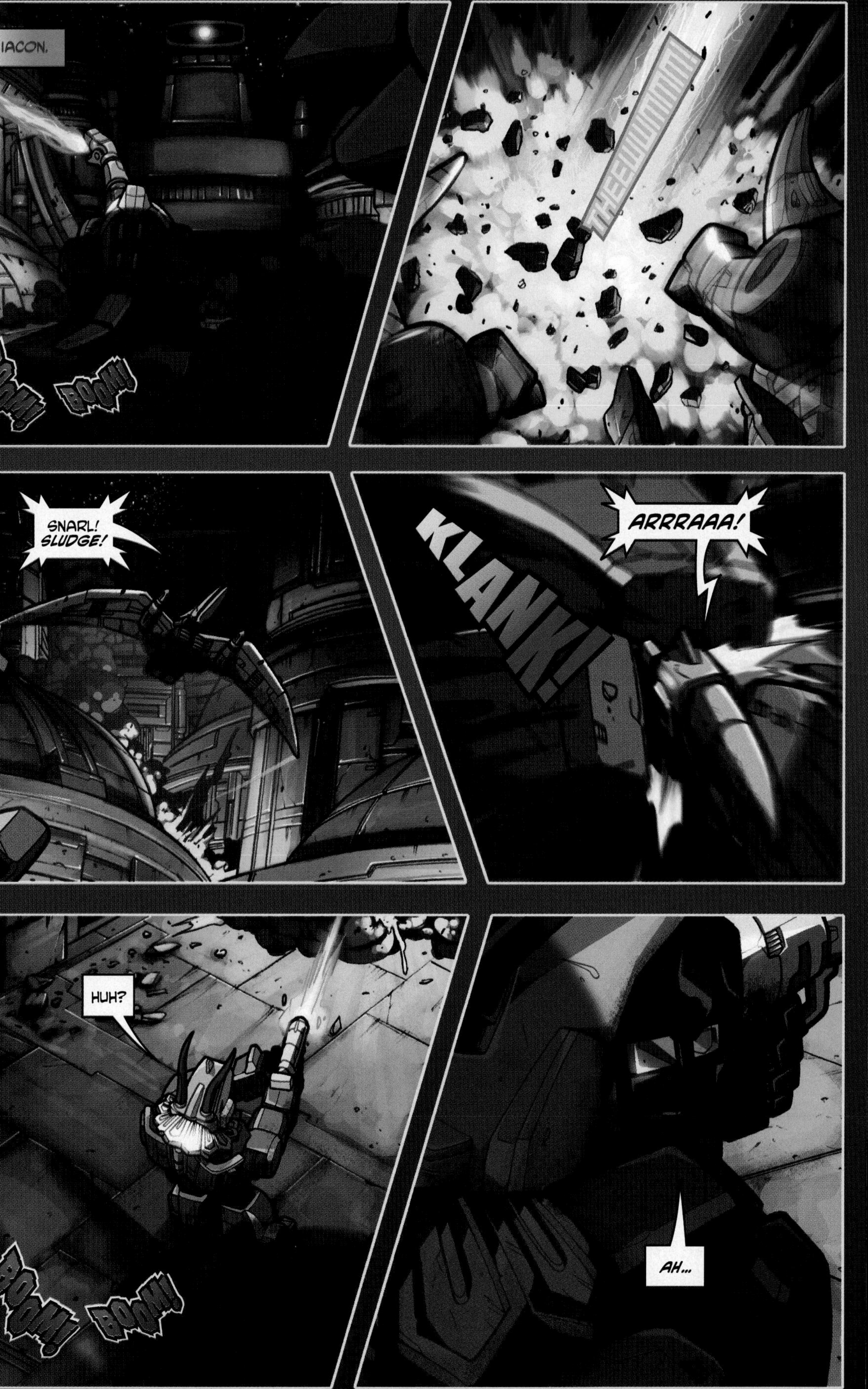
IACON.
BOOM!
SNARL! SLUDGE!
KLANK!
ARRRAAA!
HUH?
BOOM!
AH...

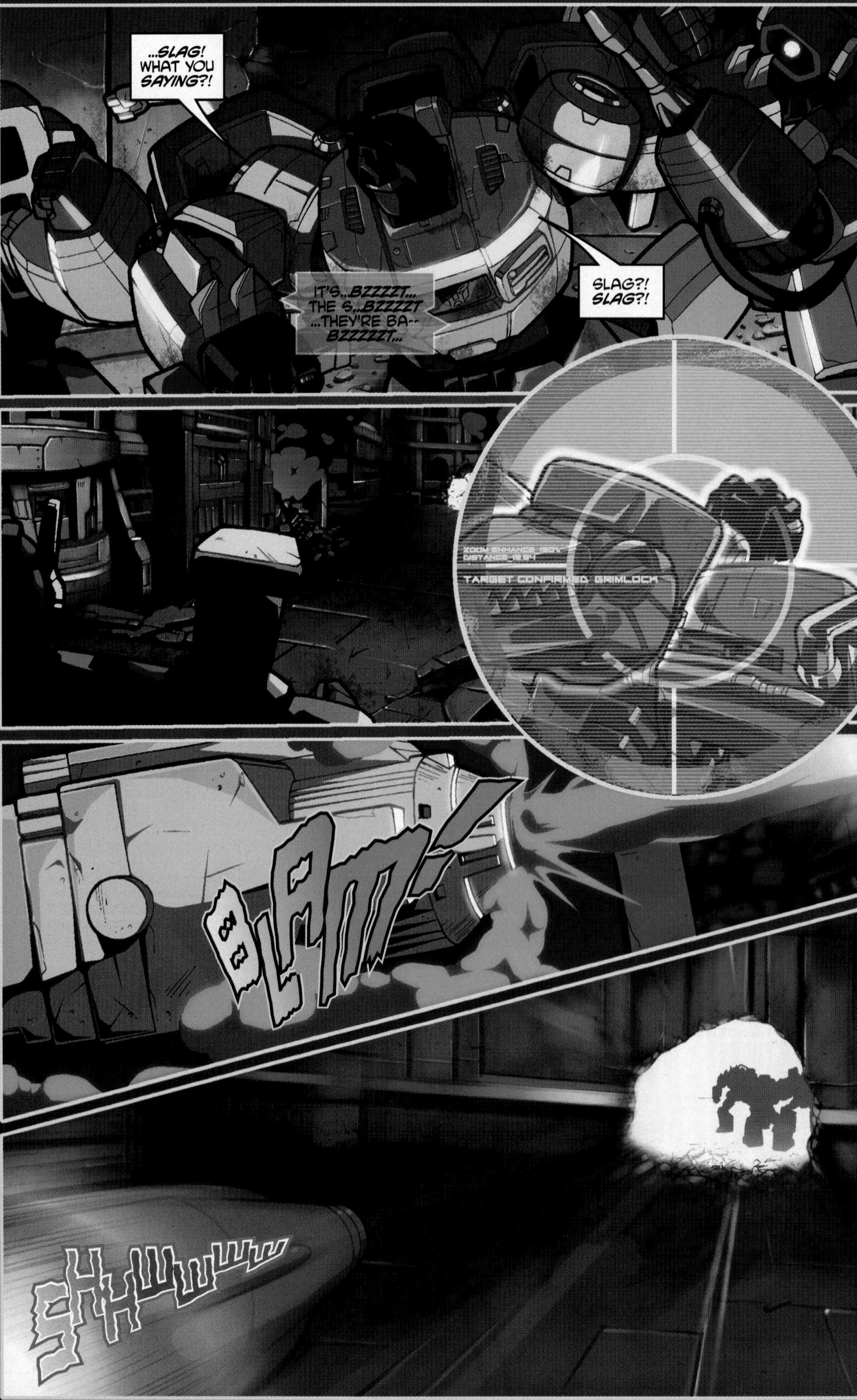
...SLAG! WHAT YOU SAYING?!
IT'S...BZZZZT... THE S...BZZZZT ...THEY'RE BA-- BZZZZZT...
SLAG?! SLAG?!
TARGET CONFIRMED GRIMLOCK
BLAM!
SHWWWWW

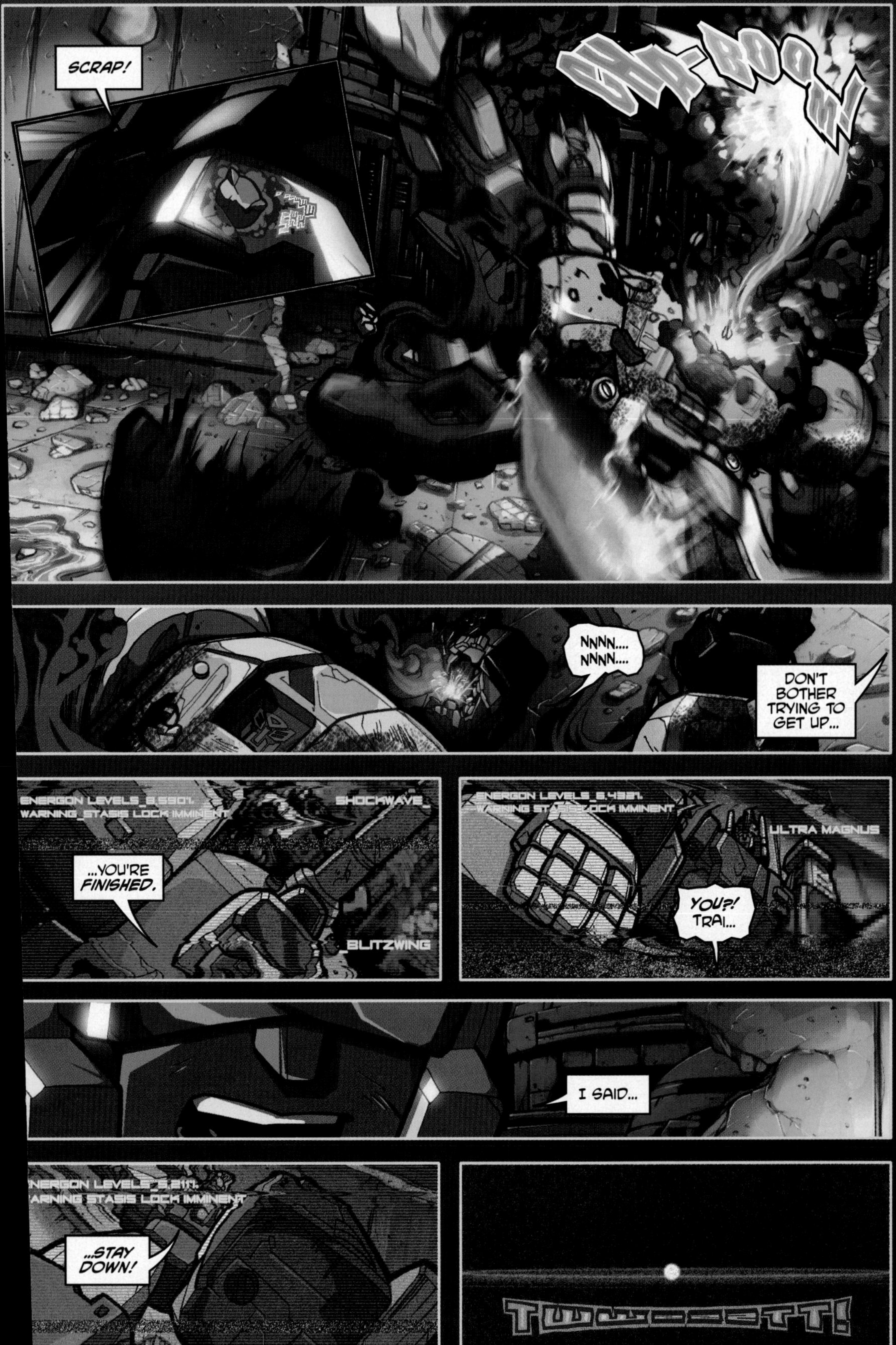
SCRAP!
CHA-BOOM!
NNNN.... NNNN....
DON'T BOTHER TRYING TO GET UP...
WARNING_STASIS LOCK IMMINENT
SHOCKWAVE_
...YOU'RE FINISHED.
_BLITZWING
ULTRA MAGNUS
YOU?! TRAI...
I SAID...
...STAY DOWN!

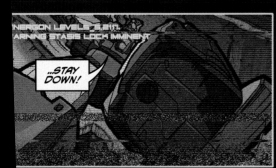

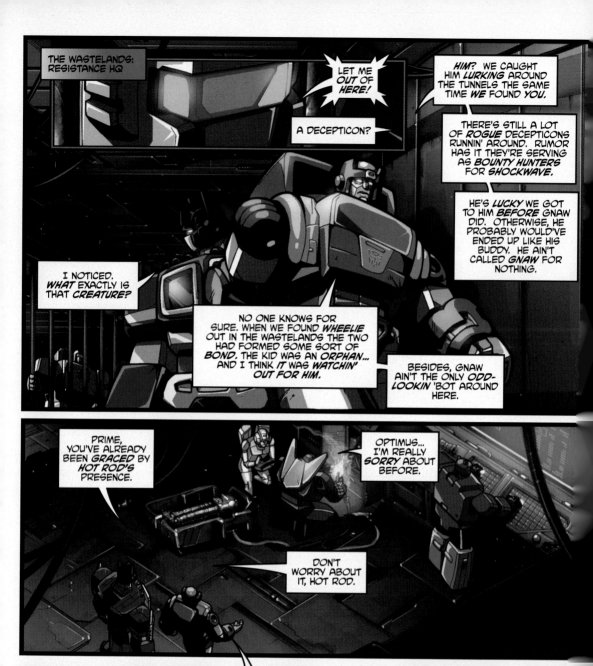

THE WASTELANDS: RESISTANCE HQ

LET ME OUT OF HERE!

A DECEPTICON?

HIM? WE CAUGHT HIM *LURKING* AROUND THE TUNNELS THE SAME TIME *WE* FOUND *YOU.*

THERE'S STILL A LOT OF *ROGUE* DECEPTICONS RUNNIN' AROUND. RUMOR HAS IT THEY'RE SERVING AS *BOUNTY HUNTERS* FOR *SHOCKWAVE.*

HE'S *LUCKY* WE GOT TO HIM *BEFORE* GNAW DID. OTHERWISE, HE PROBABLY WOULD'VE ENDED UP LIKE HIS BUDDY. HE AIN'T CALLED *GNAW* FOR NOTHING.

I NOTICED. *WHAT* EXACTLY IS THAT *CREATURE?*

NO ONE KNOWS FOR SURE. WHEN WE FOUND *WHEELIE* OUT IN THE WASTELANDS THE TWO HAD FORMED SOME SORT OF *BOND.* THE KID WAS AN ORPHAN... AND I THINK *IT WAS WATCHIN'* OUT FOR HIM.

BESIDES, GNAW AIN'T THE ONLY *ODD-LOOKIN* 'BOT AROUND HERE.

PRIME, YOU'VE ALREADY BEEN *GRACED* BY *HOT ROD'S* PRESENCE.

OPTIMUS... I'M REALLY *SORRY* ABOUT BEFORE.

DON'T WORRY ABOUT IT, HOT ROD.

AND THIS IS ARCEE.

PLEASURE TO MEET *YOU.*

AHEM!

UM...EXCUSE US, BUT THERE'S STILL *WORK* THAT *NEEDS* TO BE DONE HERE.

DON'T MIND HOT ROD. HIS POWER CONVERTERS ALWAYS GET A LITTLE *TORQUED* WHENEVER ANYBODY EVEN LOOKS AT *HIS* FAVORITE GAL.

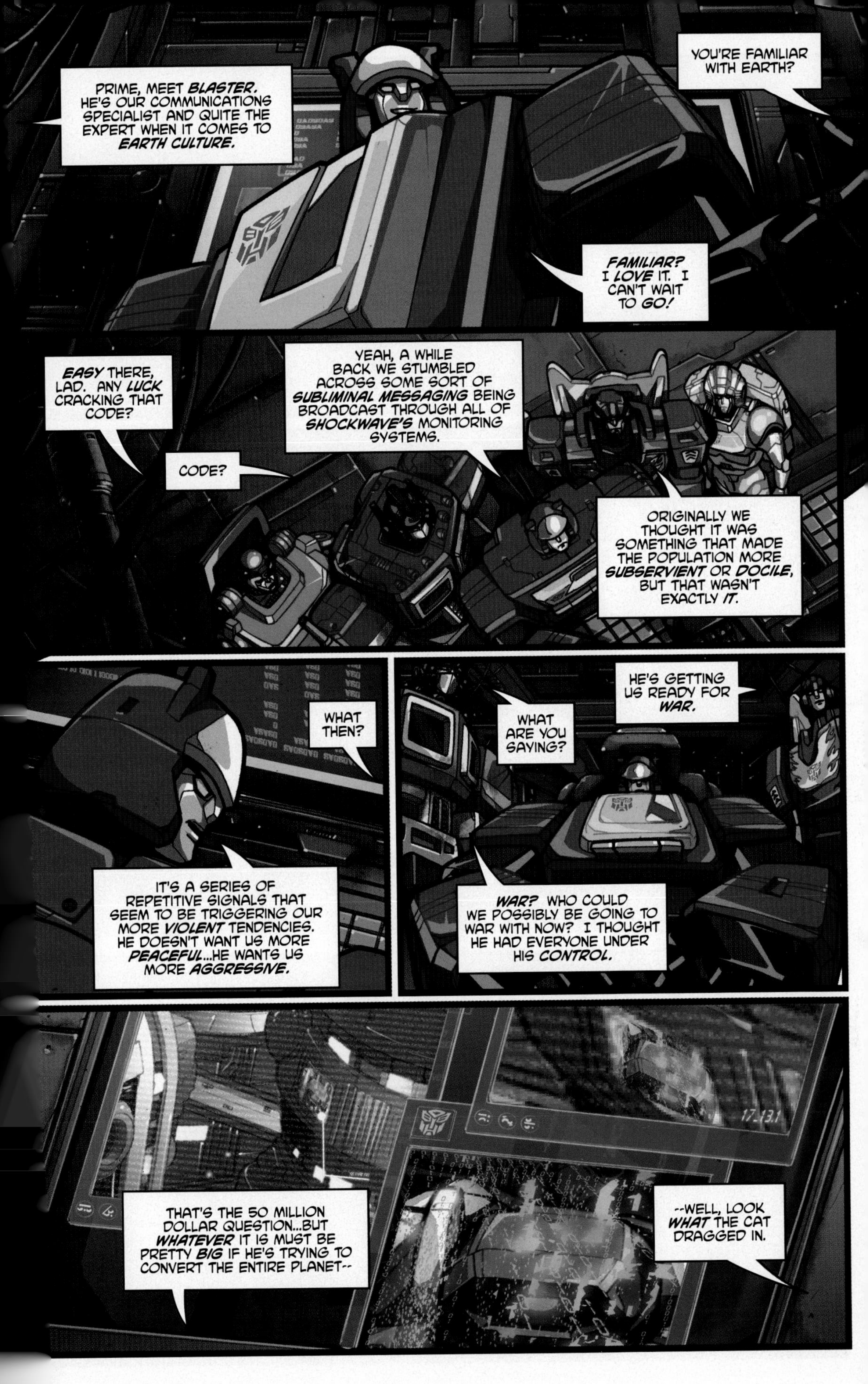
PRIME, MEET BLASTER. HE'S OUR COMMUNICATIONS SPECIALIST AND QUITE THE EXPERT WHEN IT COMES TO EARTH CULTURE.
YOU'RE FAMILIAR WITH EARTH?
FAMILIAR? I LOVE IT. I CAN'T WAIT TO GO!
EASY THERE, LAD. ANY LUCK CRACKING THAT CODE?
CODE?
YEAH, A WHILE BACK WE STUMBLED ACROSS SOME SORT OF SUBLIMINAL MESSAGING BEING BROADCAST THROUGH ALL OF SHOCKWAVE'S MONITORING SYSTEMS.
ORIGINALLY WE THOUGHT IT WAS SOMETHING THAT MADE THE POPULATION MORE SUBSERVIENT OR DOCILE, BUT THAT WASN'T EXACTLY IT.
WHAT THEN?
IT'S A SERIES OF REPETITIVE SIGNALS THAT SEEM TO BE TRIGGERING OUR MORE VIOLENT TENDENCIES. HE DOESN'T WANT US MORE PEACEFUL...HE WANTS US MORE AGGRESSIVE.
WHAT ARE YOU SAYING?
HE'S GETTING US READY FOR WAR.
WAR? WHO COULD WE POSSIBLY BE GOING TO WAR WITH NOW? I THOUGHT HE HAD EVERYONE UNDER HIS CONTROL.
THAT'S THE 50 MILLION DOLLAR QUESTION...BUT WHATEVER IT IS MUST BE PRETTY BIG IF HE'S TRYING TO CONVERT THE ENTIRE PLANET--
--WELL, LOOK WHAT THE CAT DRAGGED IN.
17.13.1

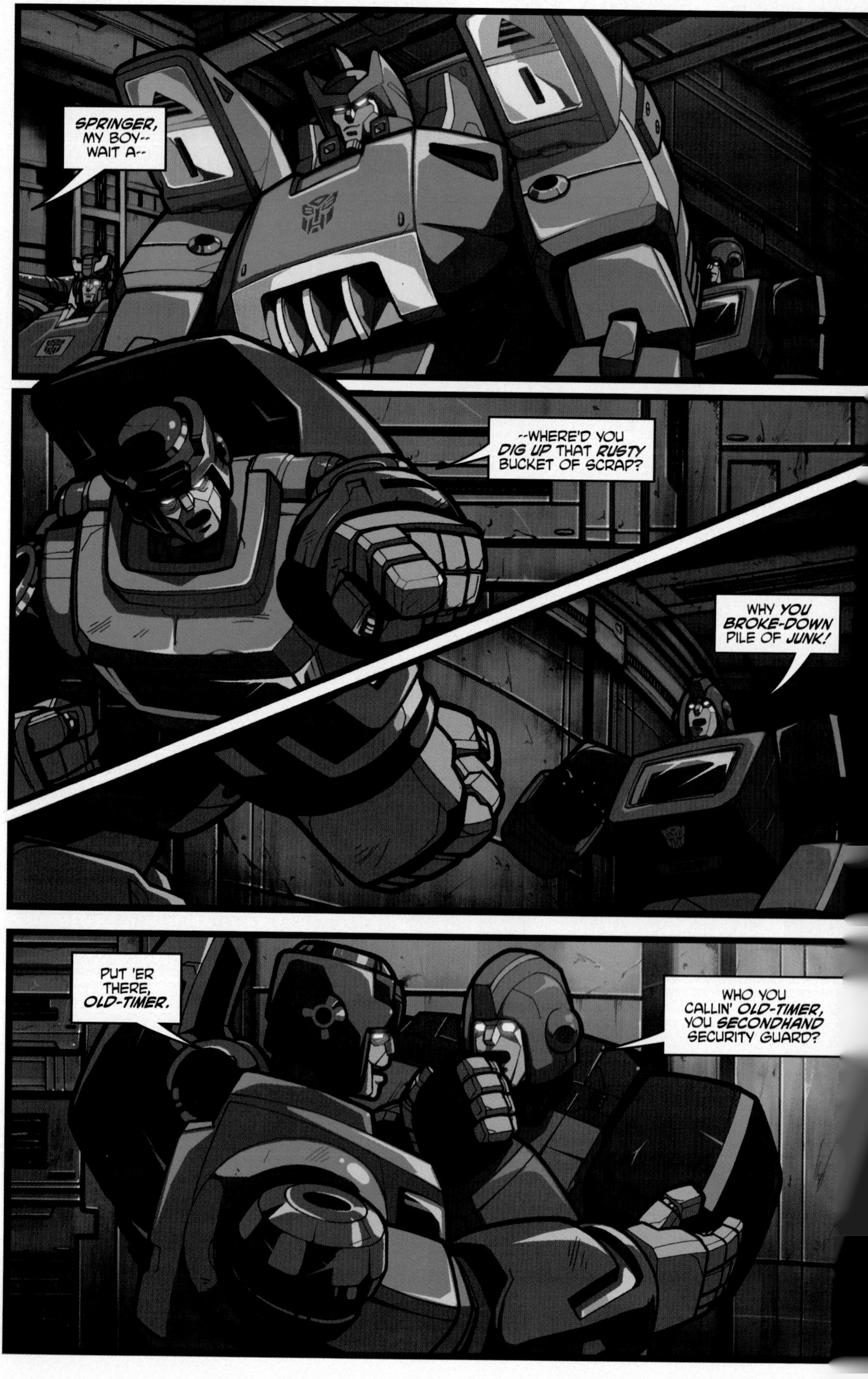
SPRINGER, MY BOY-- WAIT A--
--WHERE'D YOU DIG UP THAT RUSTY BUCKET OF SCRAP?
WHY YOU BROKE-DOWN PILE OF JUNK!
PUT 'ER THERE, OLD-TIMER.
WHO YOU CALLIN' OLD-TIMER, YOU SECONDHAND SECURITY GUARD?

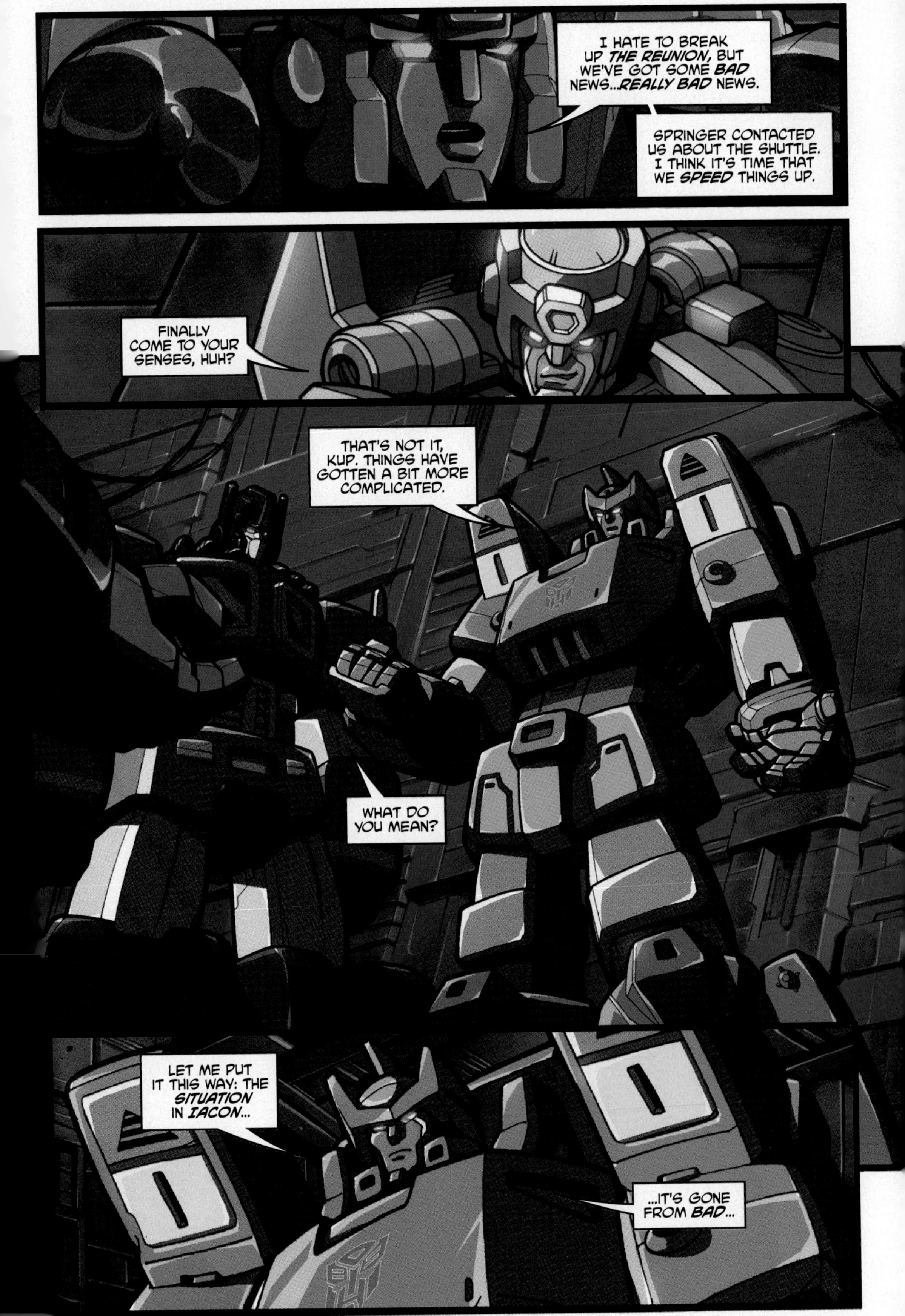
I HATE TO BREAK UP *THE REUNION*, BUT WE'VE GOT SOME *BAD* NEWS...*REALLY BAD* NEWS.
SPRINGER CONTACTED US ABOUT THE SHUTTLE. I THINK IT'S TIME THAT WE *SPEED* THINGS UP.
FINALLY COME TO YOUR SENSES, HUH?
THAT'S NOT IT, KUP. THINGS HAVE GOTTEN A BIT MORE COMPLICATED.
WHAT DO YOU MEAN?
LET ME PUT IT THIS WAY: THE *SITUATION* IN *IACON*...
...IT'S GONE FROM *BAD*...

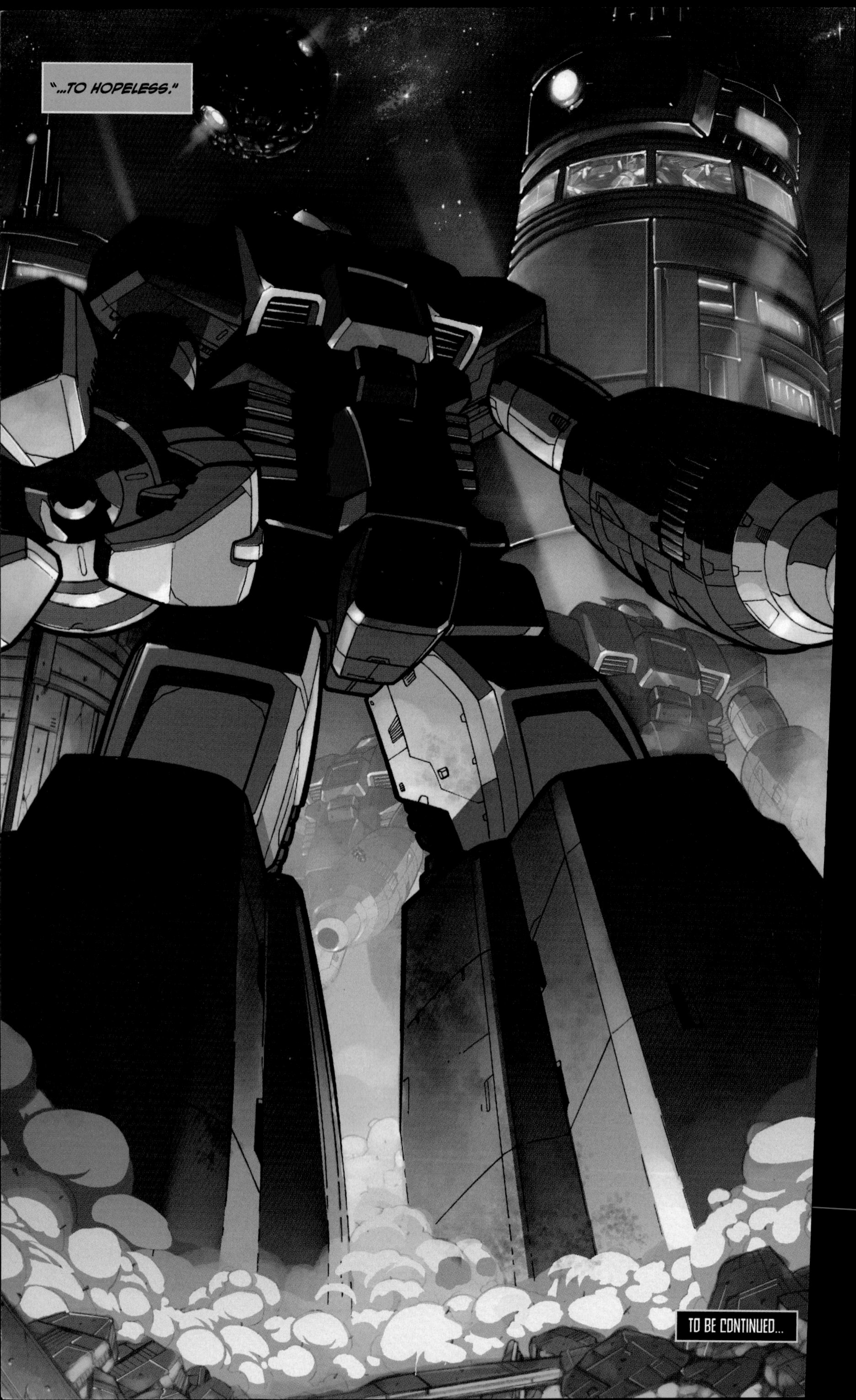
"...TO HOPELESS."
TO BE CONTINUED...

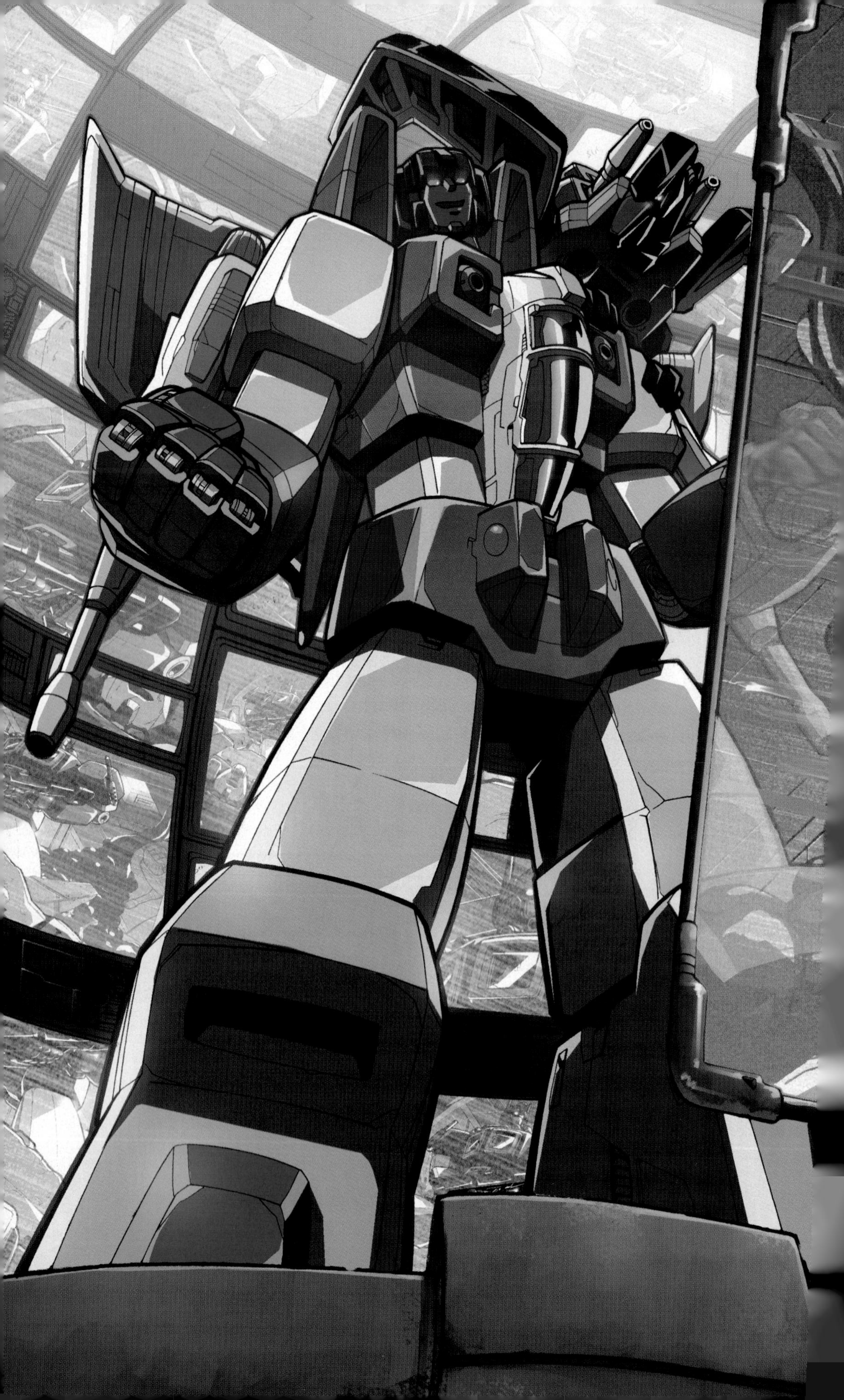

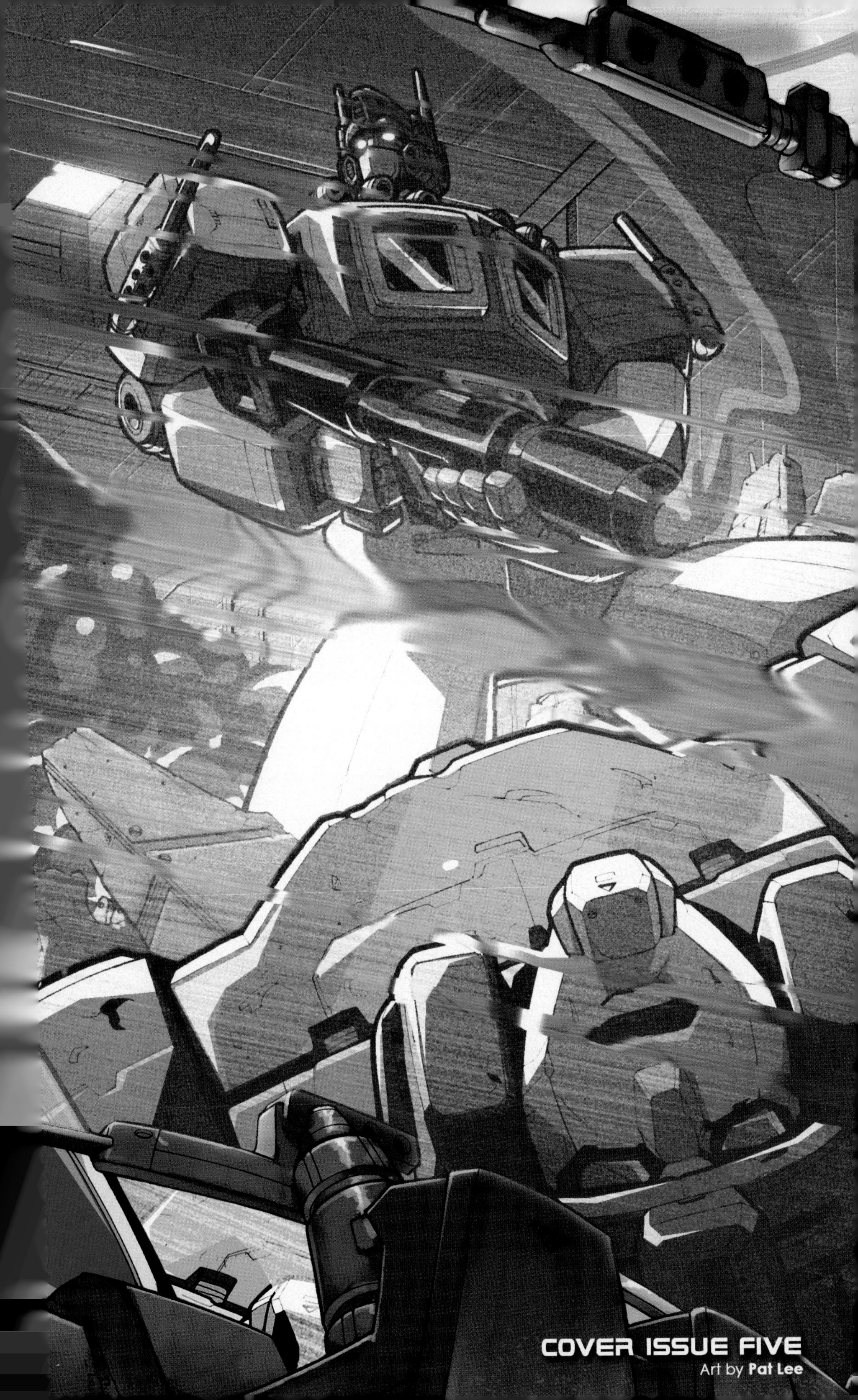

COVER ISSUE FIVE

Art by **Pat Lee**

CHAPTER FIVE
COUNTDOWN TO EXTINCTION

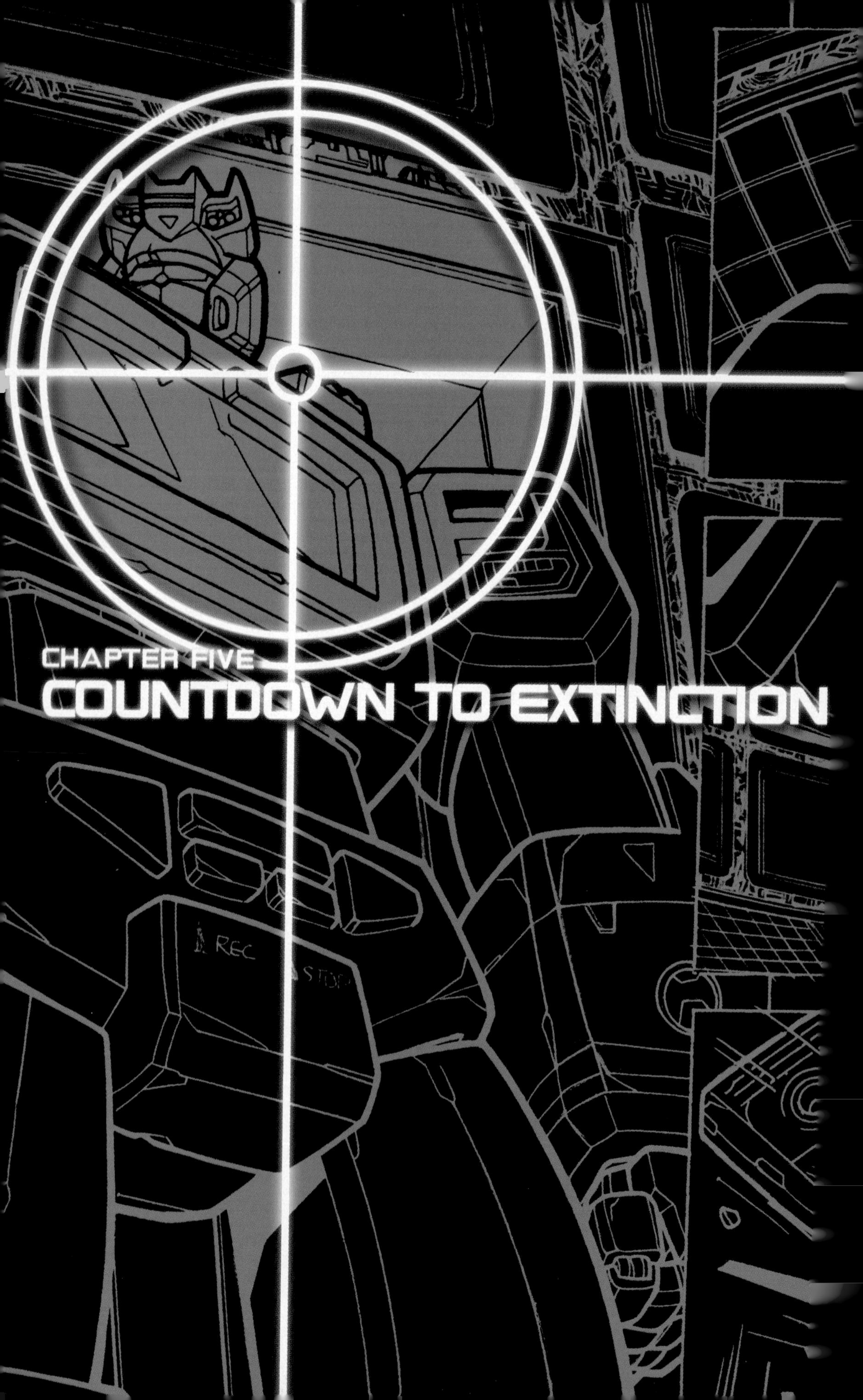
REC

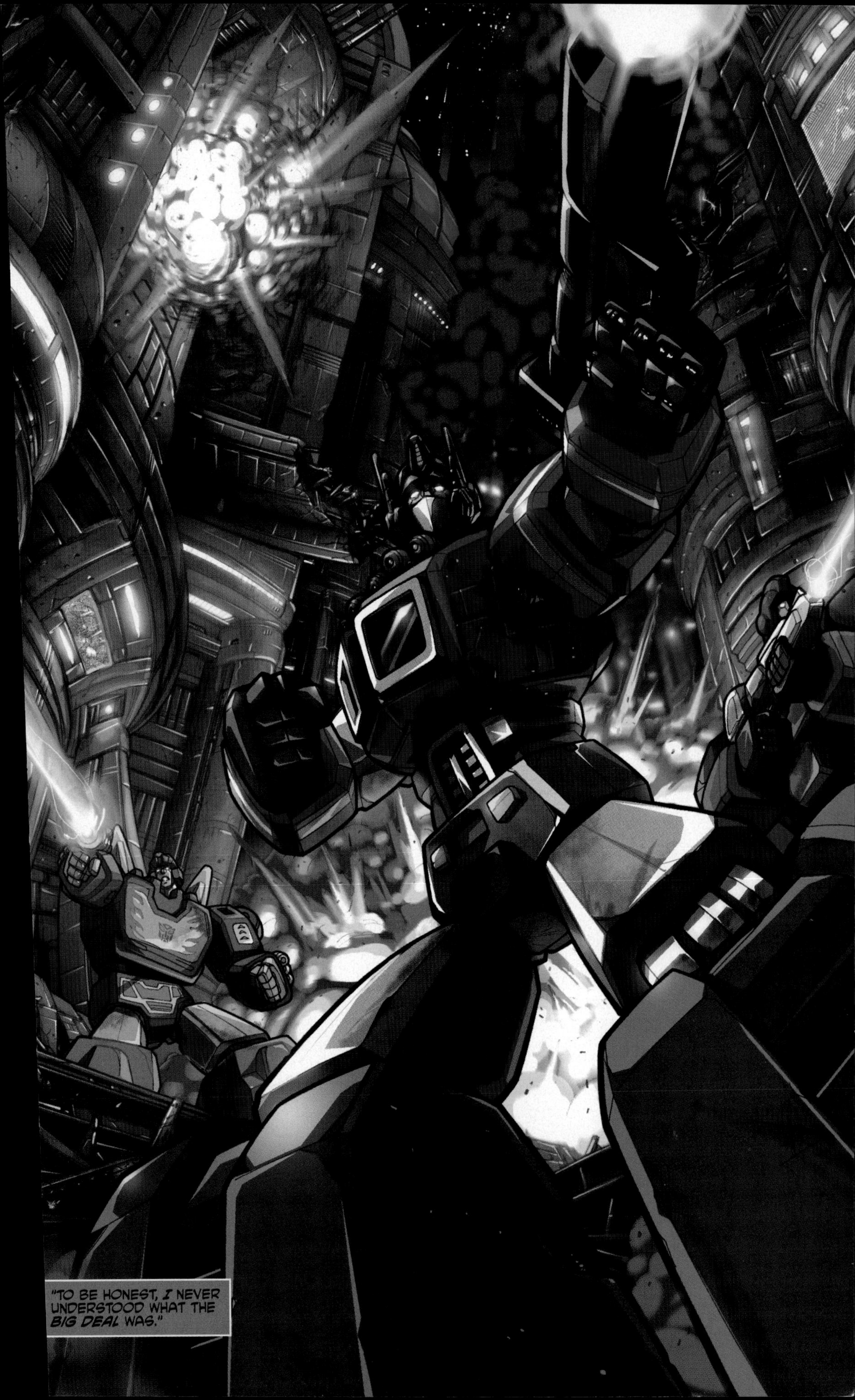
"TO BE HONEST, I NEVER UNDERSTOOD WHAT THE BIG DEAL WAS."

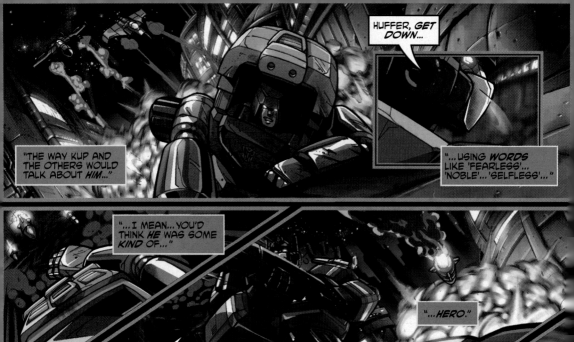

HUFFER, GET DOWN...

"THE WAY KUP AND THE OTHERS WOULD TALK ABOUT *HIM*..."

"...USING *WORDS* LIKE 'FEARLESS'... 'NOBLE'... 'SELFLESS'..."

"...I MEAN...YOU'D THINK *HE* WAS SOME KIND OF..."

"...HERO."

...NOW!

ARRR!

PCHOOM!

OPTIMUS!

HOT ROD... I'LL...BE... FINE.

HOW 'BOUT YOU, HUFFER?

YEAH. I'M OKAY.

BUT *YOUR SIDE*—

THERE'S NO TIME.

AUTOBOTS, MOVE OUT!

"NOW I KNOW."

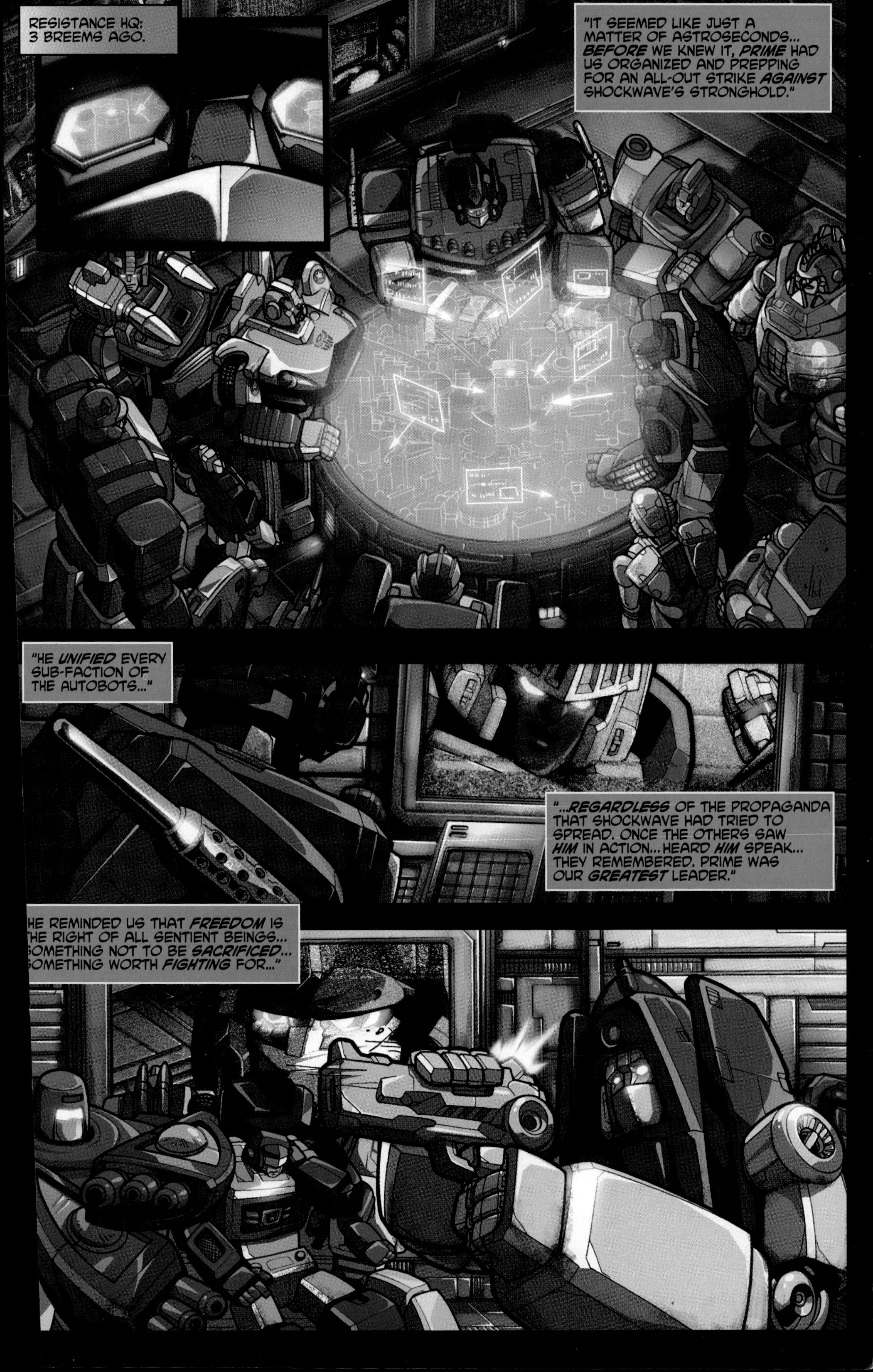
RESISTANCE HQ: 3 BREEMS AGO.
"IT SEEMED LIKE JUST A MATTER OF ASTROSECONDS... BEFORE WE KNEW IT, PRIME HAD US ORGANIZED AND PREPPING FOR AN ALL-OUT STRIKE AGAINST SHOCKWAVE'S STRONGHOLD."
"HE UNIFIED EVERY SUB-FACTION OF THE AUTOBOTS..."
"...REGARDLESS OF THE PROPAGANDA THAT SHOCKWAVE HAD TRIED TO SPREAD. ONCE THE OTHERS SAW HIM IN ACTION... HEARD HIM SPEAK... THEY REMEMBERED. PRIME WAS OUR GREATEST LEADER."
HE REMINDED US THAT FREEDOM IS THE RIGHT OF ALL SENTIENT BEINGS... SOMETHING NOT TO BE SACRIFICED... SOMETHING WORTH FIGHTING FOR..."

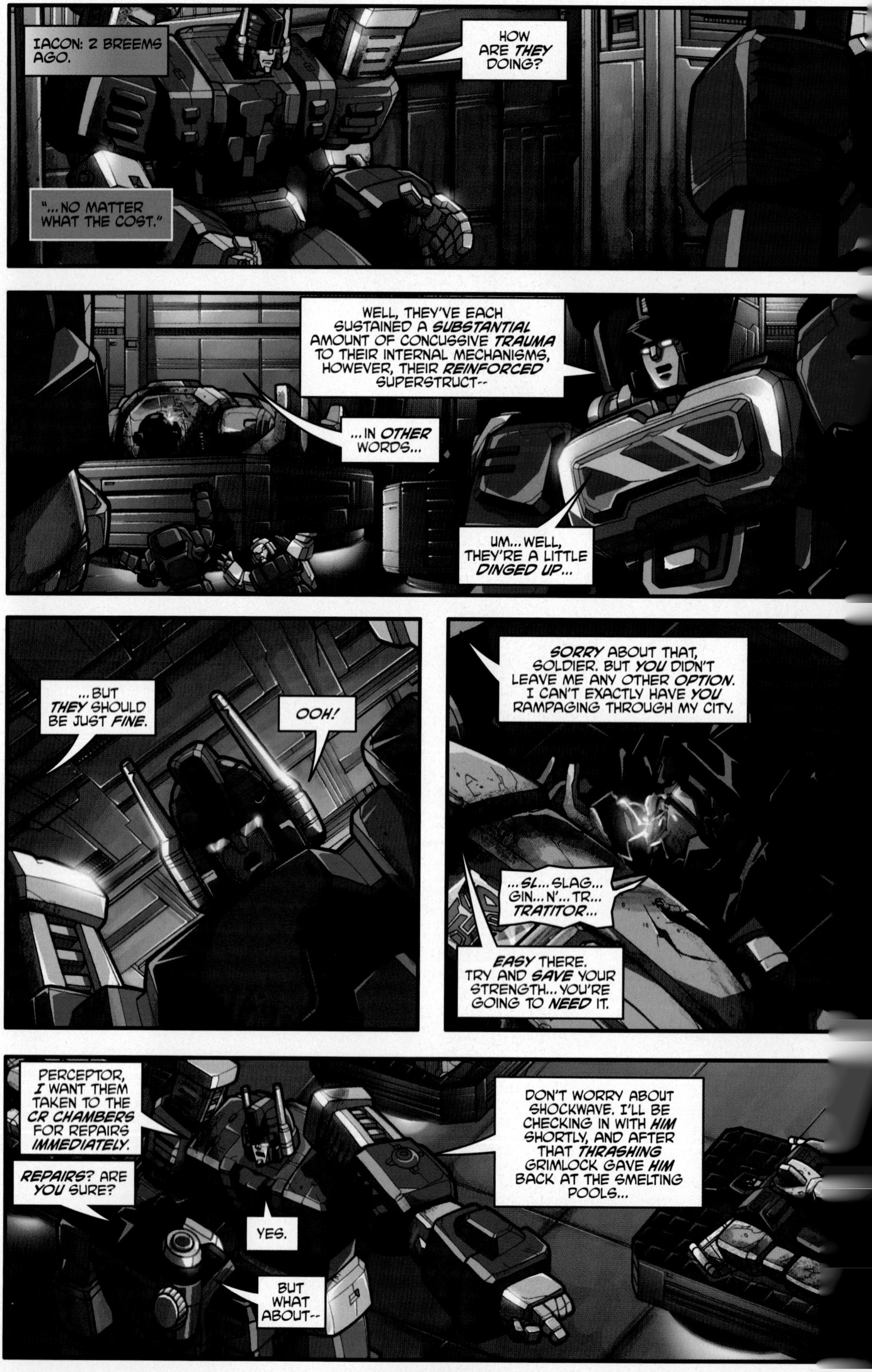
IACON: 2 BREEMS AGO.
HOW ARE THEY DOING?
"...NO MATTER WHAT THE COST."
WELL, THEY'VE EACH SUSTAINED A SUBSTANTIAL AMOUNT OF CONCUSSIVE TRAUMA TO THEIR INTERNAL MECHANISMS, HOWEVER, THEIR REINFORCED SUPERSTRUCT--
...IN OTHER WORDS...
UM...WELL, THEY'RE A LITTLE DINGED UP...
...BUT THEY SHOULD BE JUST FINE.
OOH!
SORRY ABOUT THAT, SOLDIER. BUT YOU DIDN'T LEAVE ME ANY OTHER OPTION. I CAN'T EXACTLY HAVE YOU RAMPAGING THROUGH MY CITY.
...SL...SLAG... GIN...N'...TR... TRATITOR...
EASY THERE. TRY AND SAVE YOUR STRENGTH...YOU'RE GOING TO NEED IT.
PERCEPTOR, I WANT THEM TAKEN TO THE CR CHAMBERS FOR REPAIRS IMMEDIATELY.
REPAIRS? ARE YOU SURE?
YES.
BUT WHAT ABOUT--
DON'T WORRY ABOUT SHOCKWAVE. I'LL BE CHECKING IN WITH HIM SHORTLY, AND AFTER THAT THRASHING GRIMLOCK GAVE HIM BACK AT THE SMELTING POOLS...

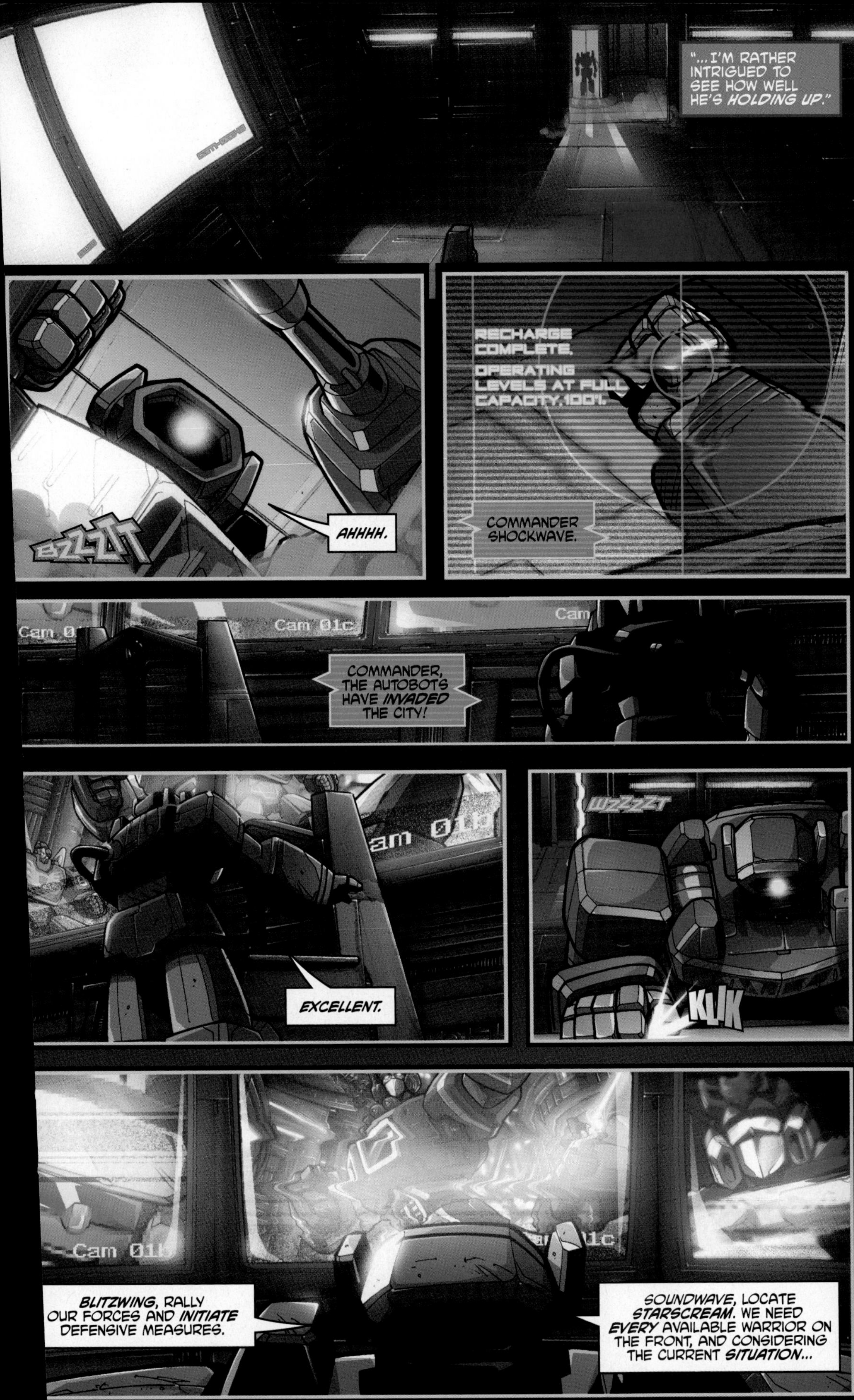

"...I'M RATHER INTRIGUED TO SEE HOW WELL HE'S *HOLDING UP.*"
BZZZT
AHHHH.
RECHARGE COMPLETE.
OPERATING LEVELS AT FULL CAPACITY.100%.
COMMANDER SHOCKWAVE.
Cam 01c
COMMANDER, THE AUTOBOTS HAVE *INVADED* THE CITY!
EXCELLENT.
WZZZT
KLIK
Cam 01b
BLITZWING, RALLY OUR FORCES AND *INITIATE* DEFENSIVE MEASURES.
SOUNDWAVE, LOCATE *STARSCREAM*. WE NEED *EVERY* AVAILABLE WARRIOR ON THE FRONT, AND CONSIDERING THE CURRENT *SITUATION*...

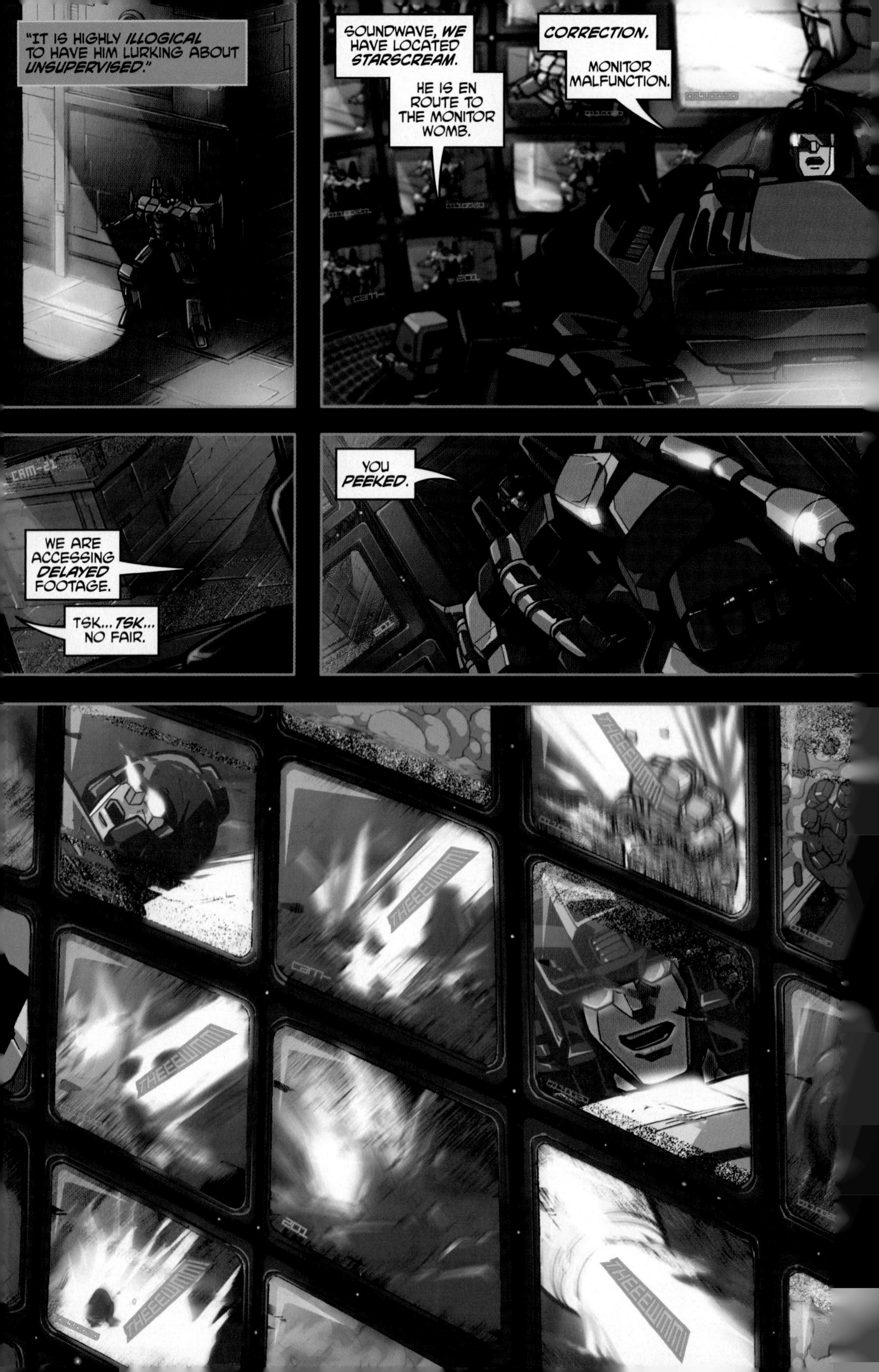
"IT IS HIGHLY *ILLOGICAL* TO HAVE HIM LURKING ABOUT *UNSUPERVISED*."
SOUNDWAVE, *WE* HAVE LOCATED *STARSCREAM*.
HE IS EN ROUTE TO THE MONITOR WOMB.
CORRECTION.
MONITOR MALFUNCTION.
CAM-21
WE ARE ACCESSING *DELAYED* FOOTAGE.
TSK... *TSK*... NO FAIR.
YOU *PEEKED*.
THEEEWMM

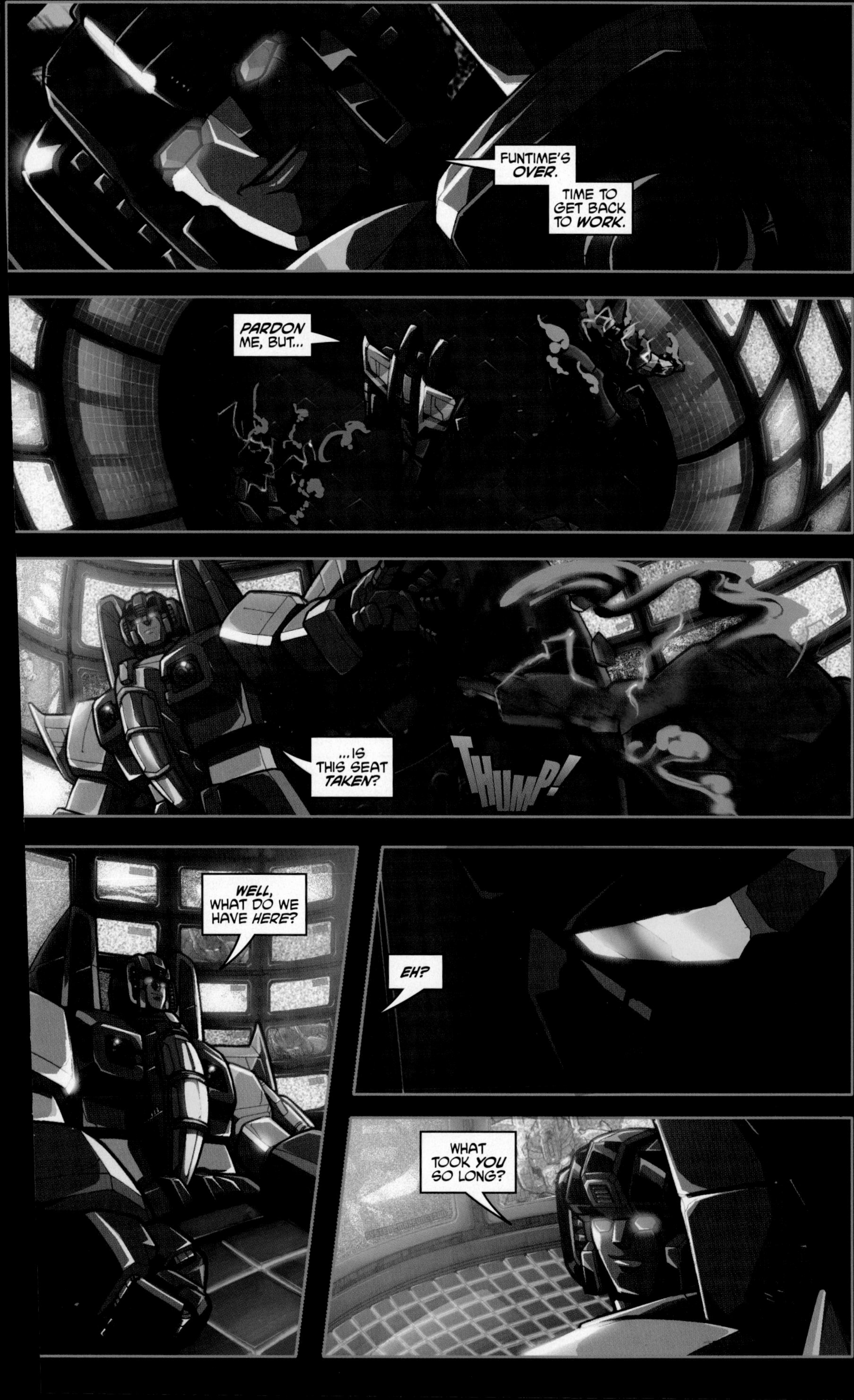
FUNTIME'S OVER.
TIME TO GET BACK TO WORK.
PARDON ME, BUT...
...IS THIS SEAT TAKEN?
THUMP!
WELL, WHAT DO WE HAVE HERE?
EH?
WHAT TOOK YOU SO LONG?

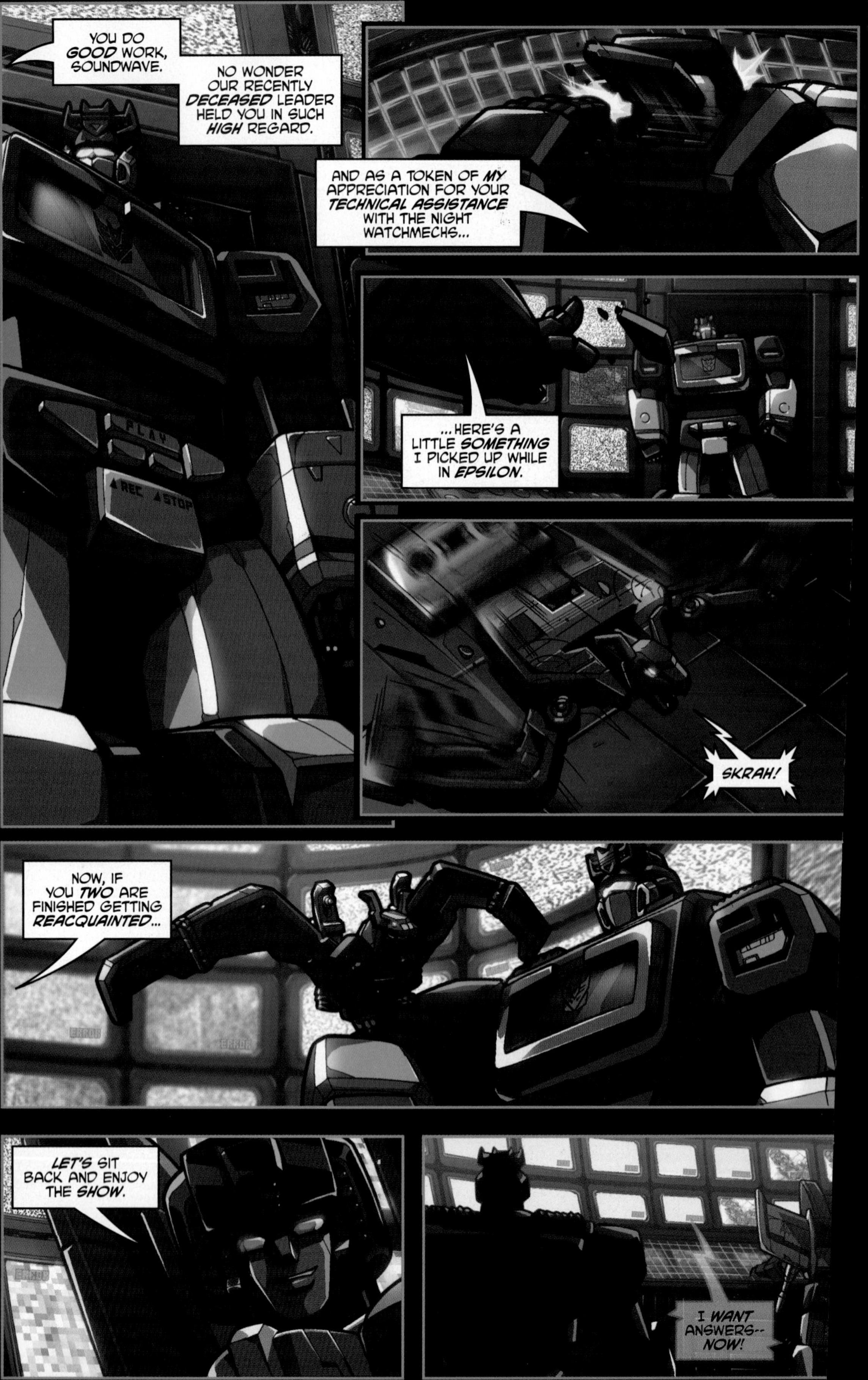
YOU DO GOOD WORK, SOUNDWAVE.
NO WONDER OUR RECENTLY DECEASED LEADER HELD YOU IN SUCH HIGH REGARD.
AND AS A TOKEN OF MY APPRECIATION FOR YOUR TECHNICAL ASSISTANCE WITH THE NIGHT WATCHMECHS...
...HERE'S A LITTLE SOMETHING I PICKED UP WHILE IN EPSILON.
SKRAH!
NOW, IF YOU TWO ARE FINISHED GETTING REACQUAINTED...
LET'S SIT BACK AND ENJOY THE SHOW.
I WANT ANSWERS-- NOW!

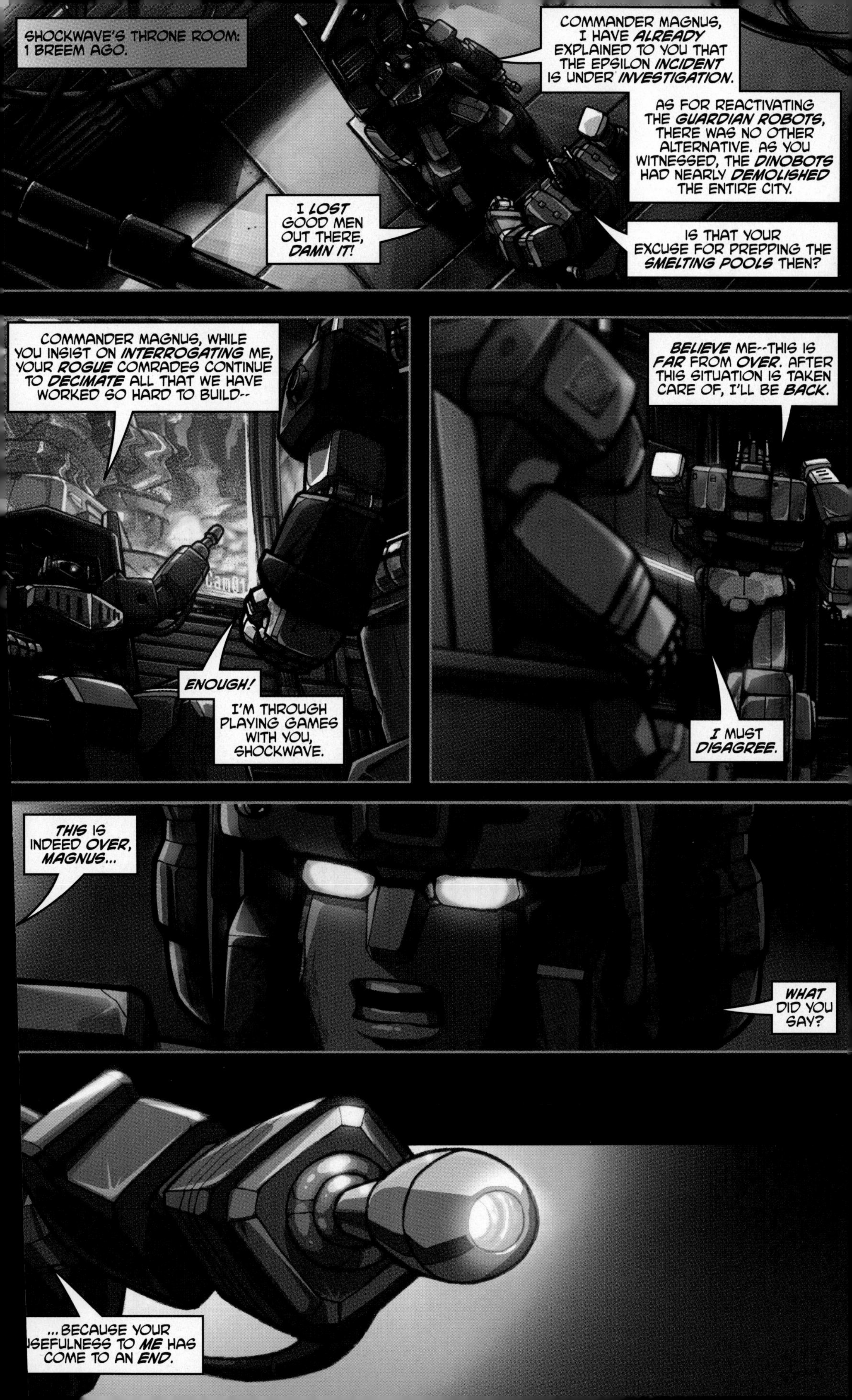
SHOCKWAVE'S THRONE ROOM: 1 BREEM AGO.
COMMANDER MAGNUS, I HAVE ALREADY EXPLAINED TO YOU THAT THE EPSILON INCIDENT IS UNDER INVESTIGATION.
AS FOR REACTIVATING THE GUARDIAN ROBOTS, THERE WAS NO OTHER ALTERNATIVE. AS YOU WITNESSED, THE DINOBOTS HAD NEARLY DEMOLISHED THE ENTIRE CITY.
I LOST GOOD MEN OUT THERE, DAMN IT!
IS THAT YOUR EXCUSE FOR PREPPING THE SMELTING POOLS THEN?
COMMANDER MAGNUS, WHILE YOU INSIST ON INTERROGATING ME, YOUR ROGUE COMRADES CONTINUE TO DECIMATE ALL THAT WE HAVE WORKED SO HARD TO BUILD--
ENOUGH!
I'M THROUGH PLAYING GAMES WITH YOU, SHOCKWAVE.
BELIEVE ME--THIS IS FAR FROM OVER. AFTER THIS SITUATION IS TAKEN CARE OF, I'LL BE BACK.
I MUST DISAGREE.
THIS IS INDEED OVER, MAGNUS...
WHAT DID YOU SAY?
...BECAUSE YOUR USEFULNESS TO ME HAS COME TO AN END.

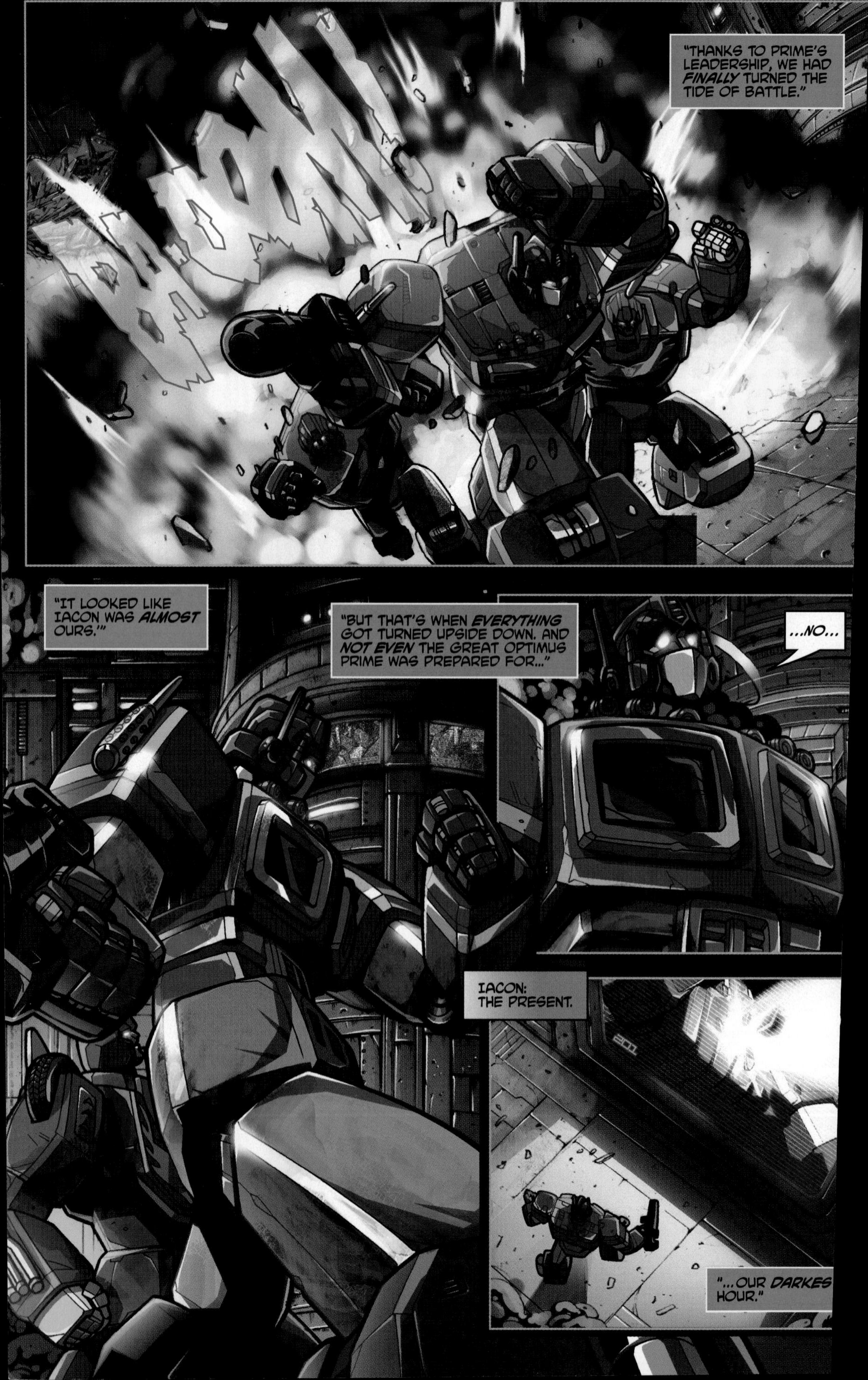
"THANKS TO PRIME'S LEADERSHIP, WE HAD *FINALLY* TURNED THE TIDE OF BATTLE."
"IT LOOKED LIKE IACON WAS *ALMOST* OURS."
"BUT THAT'S WHEN *EVERYTHING* GOT TURNED UPSIDE DOWN. AND *NOT EVEN* THE GREAT OPTIMUS PRIME WAS PREPARED FOR..."
...NO...
IACON: THE PRESENT.
"...OUR *DARKES* HOUR."

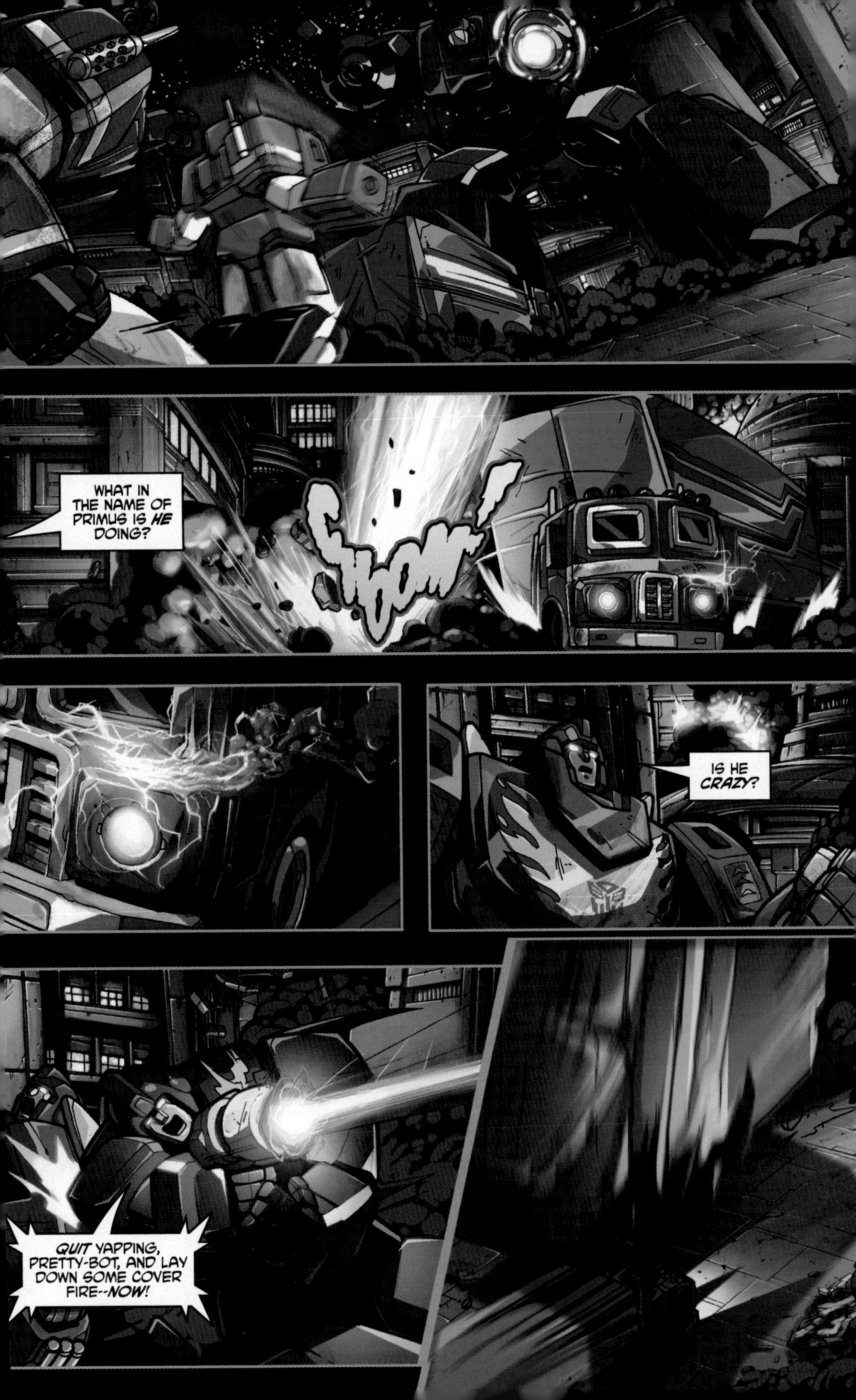
WHAT IN THE NAME OF PRIMUS IS *HE* DOING?
CHOOM!
IS HE *CRAZY?*
QUIT YAPPING, PRETTY-BOT, AND LAY DOWN SOME COVER FIRE--*NOW!*

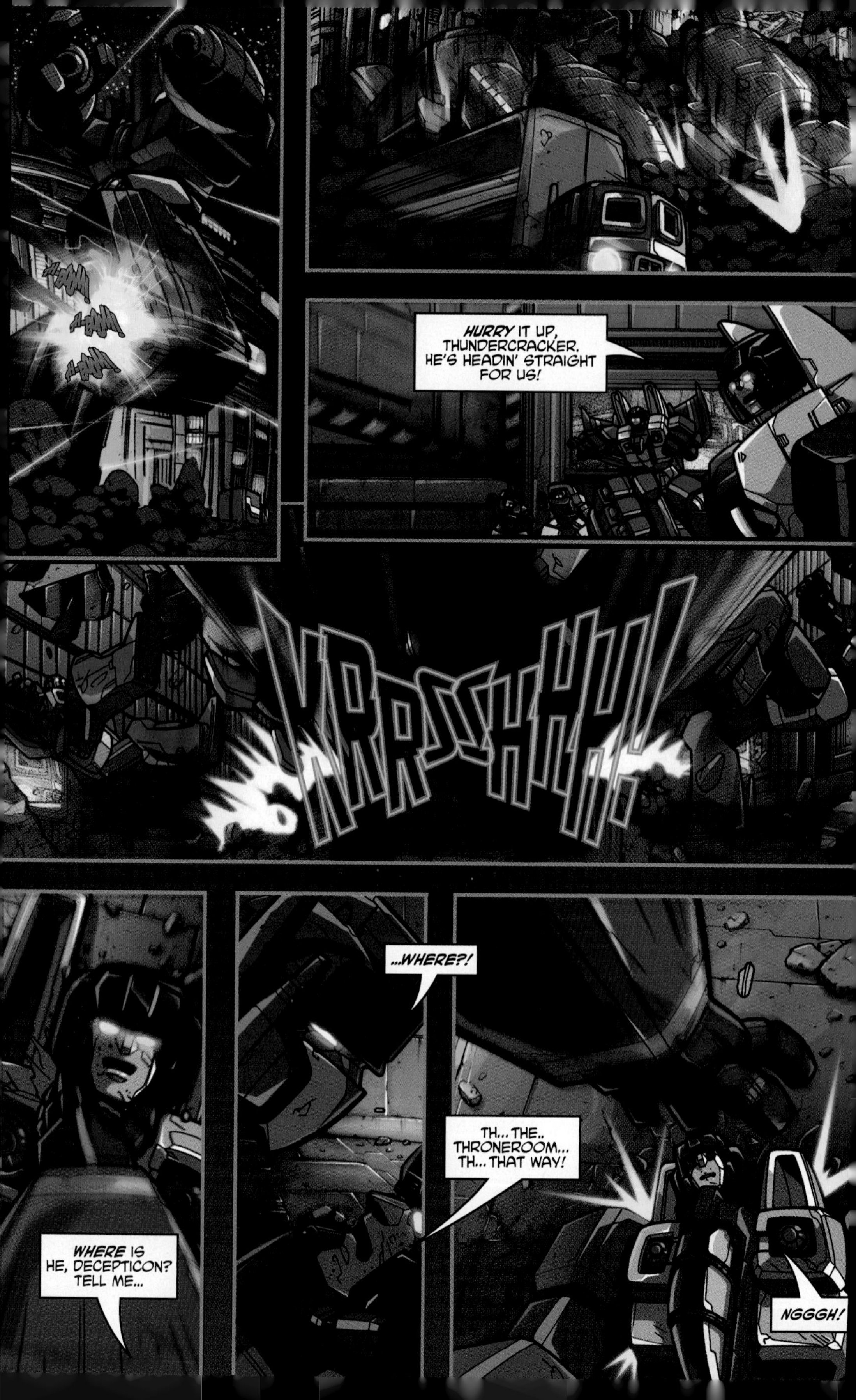

KA-BOOM!
KA-BAM!
KA-BAM!
HURRY IT UP, THUNDERCRACKER. HE'S HEADIN' STRAIGHT FOR US!
KRRSSHHH!!
WHERE IS HE, DECEPTICON? TELL ME...
...WHERE?!
TH... THE.. THRONEROOM... TH... THAT WAY!
NGGGH!

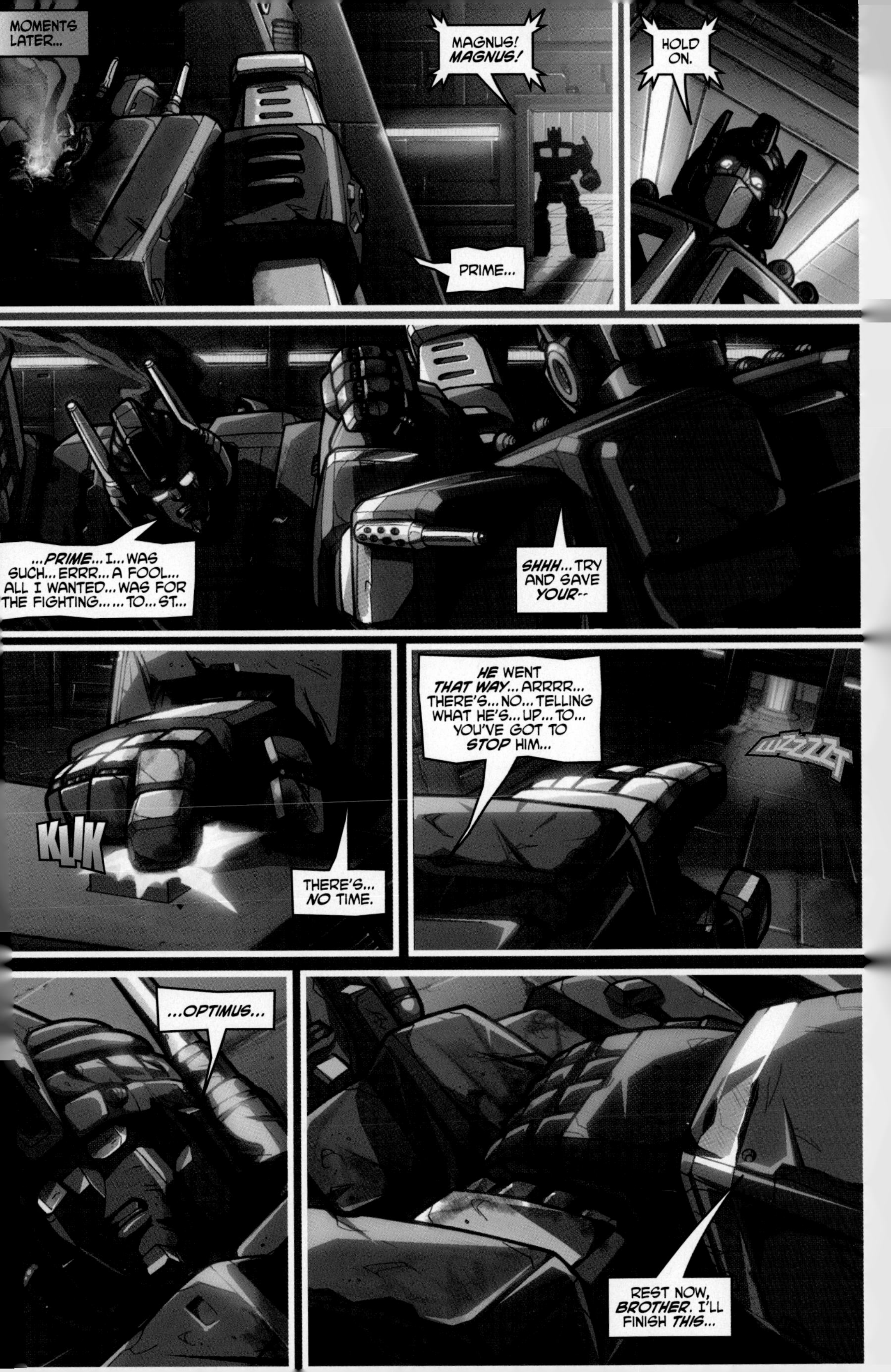
MOMENTS LATER...
MAGNUS! MAGNUS!
PRIME...
HOLD ON.
...PRIME... I... WAS SUCH... ERRR... A FOOL... ALL I WANTED... WAS FOR THE FIGHTING... ... TO... ST...
SHHH... TRY AND SAVE YOUR--
KLIK
THERE'S... NO TIME.
HE WENT THAT WAY... ARRRR... THERE'S... NO... TELLING WHAT HE'S... UP... TO... YOU'VE GOT TO STOP HIM...
WZZZT
...OPTIMUS...
REST NOW, BROTHER. I'LL FINISH THIS...

...I PROMISE.

A HIDDEN CHAMBER?

WHAT ON CYBERTRON...?

CH-CHK!

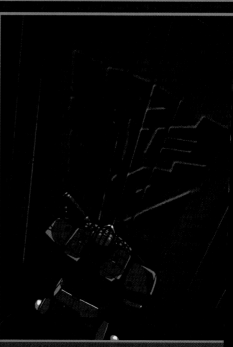

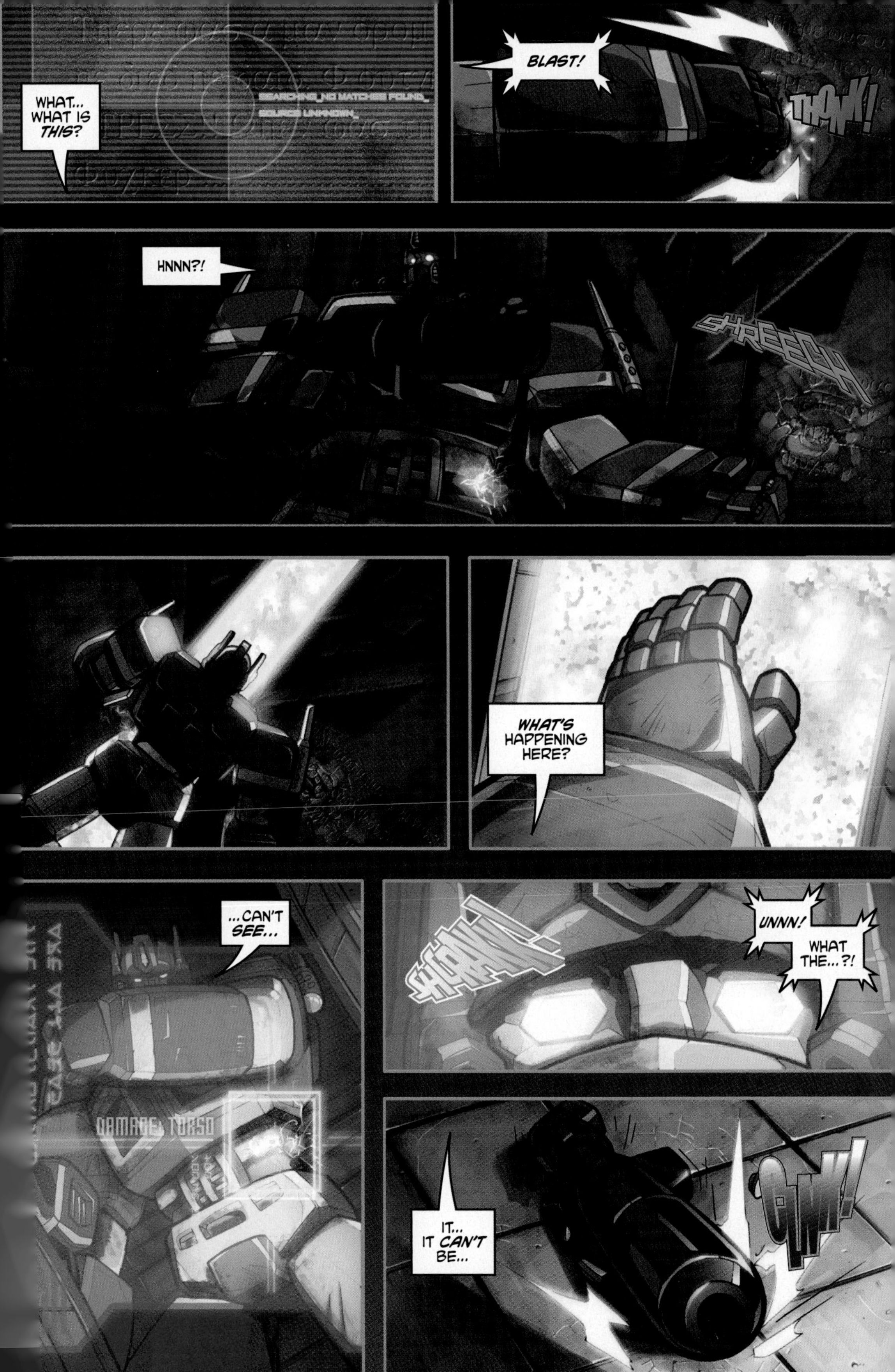
WHAT... WHAT IS THIS?
SEARCHING_NO MATCHES FOUND_
SOURCE UNKNOWN_
BLAST!
THONK!
HNNN?!
SHREECH
WHAT'S HAPPENING HERE?
...CAN'T SEE...
DAMAGE: TORSO
SHCRAKK!
UNNN!
WHAT THE...?!
IT... IT CAN'T BE...
CLUNK!

NO!

X-RAY ISO'L, TARGET IRONHIDE

CHHRT!

X-KOSH!

A BLAST OF *LIQUID NITROGEN*...NICE TRICK, OLD-TIMER! YOU'RE JUST FULL OF SURPRISES.

THANKS. YOU WEREN'T *HALF-BAD* YOURSELF--

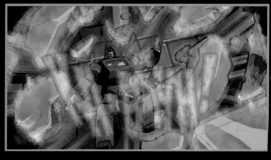

SKIP THE PLEASANTRIES, YOU TWO...

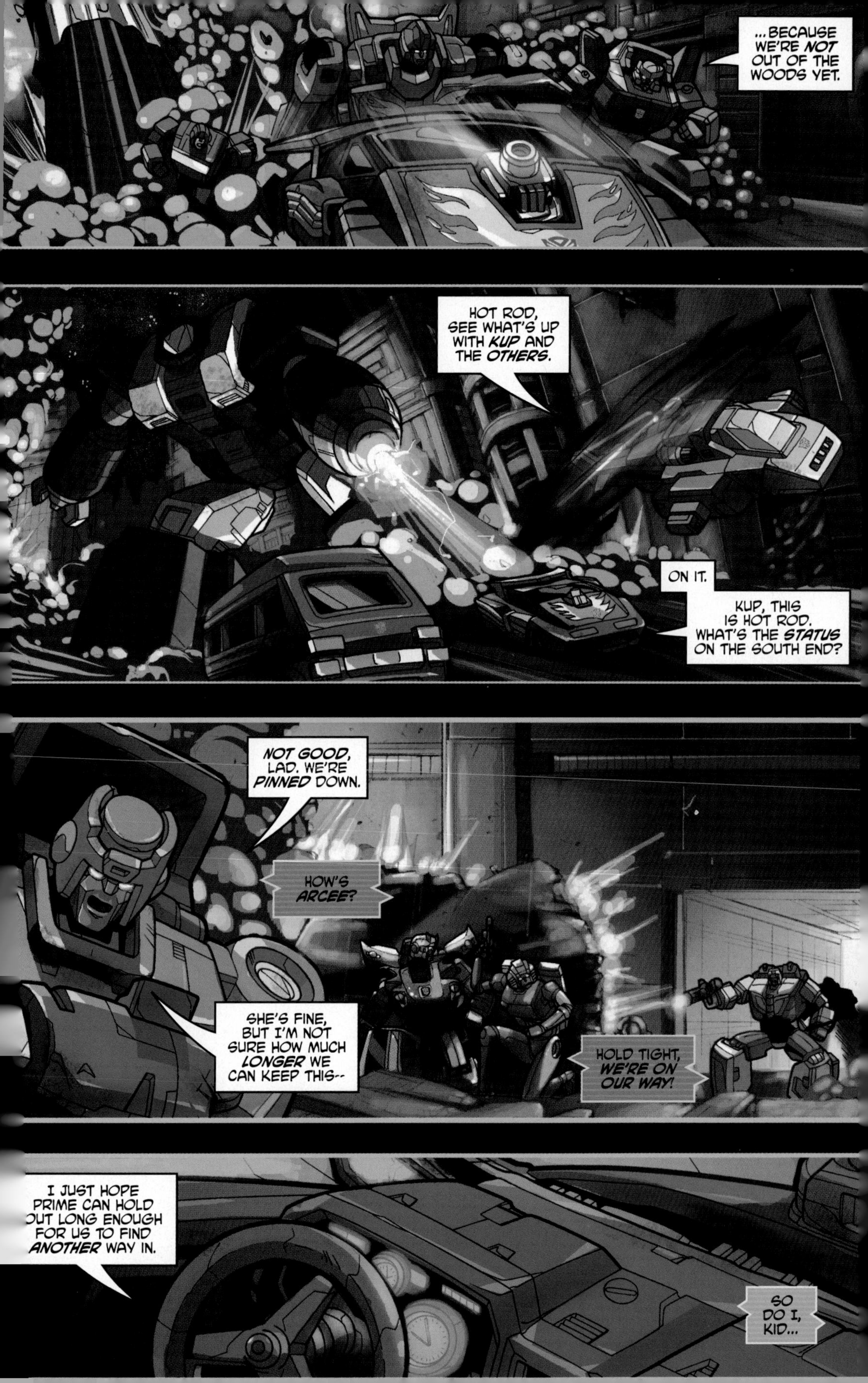
...BECAUSE WE'RE NOT OUT OF THE WOODS YET.
HOT ROD, SEE WHAT'S UP WITH KUP AND THE OTHERS.
ON IT.
KUP, THIS IS HOT ROD. WHAT'S THE STATUS ON THE SOUTH END?
NOT GOOD, LAD. WE'RE PINNED DOWN.
HOW'S ARCEE?
SHE'S FINE, BUT I'M NOT SURE HOW MUCH LONGER WE CAN KEEP THIS--
HOLD TIGHT, WE'RE ON OUR WAY!
I JUST HOPE PRIME CAN HOLD OUT LONG ENOUGH FOR US TO FIND ANOTHER WAY IN.
SO DO I, KID...

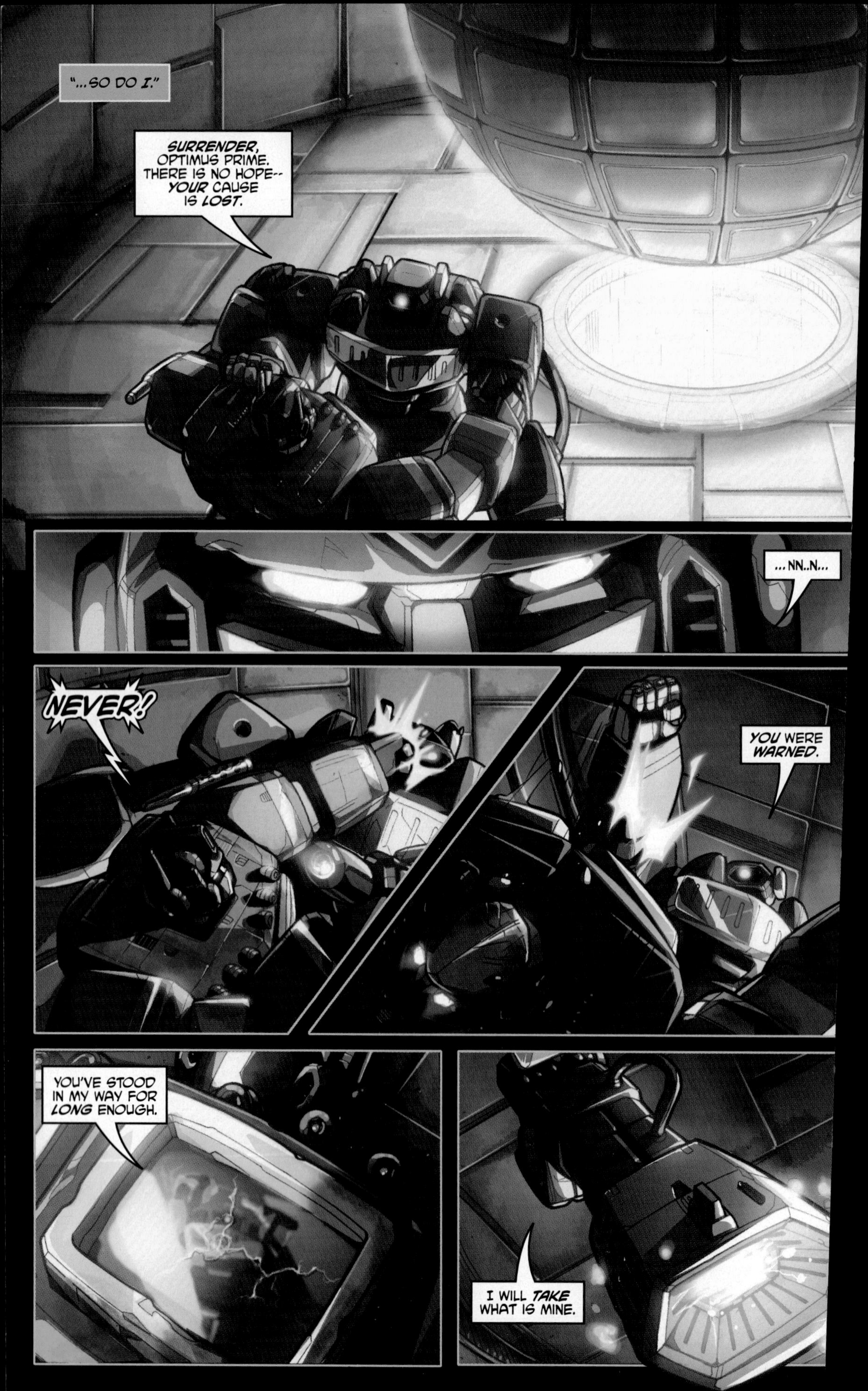
"...SO DO I."
SURRENDER, OPTIMUS PRIME. THERE IS NO HOPE-- YOUR CAUSE IS LOST.
...NN..N...
NEVER!
YOU WERE WARNED.
YOU'VE STOOD IN MY WAY FOR LONG ENOUGH.
I WILL TAKE WHAT IS MINE.

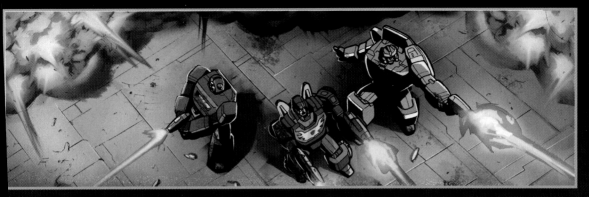

HUH?!

WHAT--

--IN THE NAME OF--

--THE MATRIX--

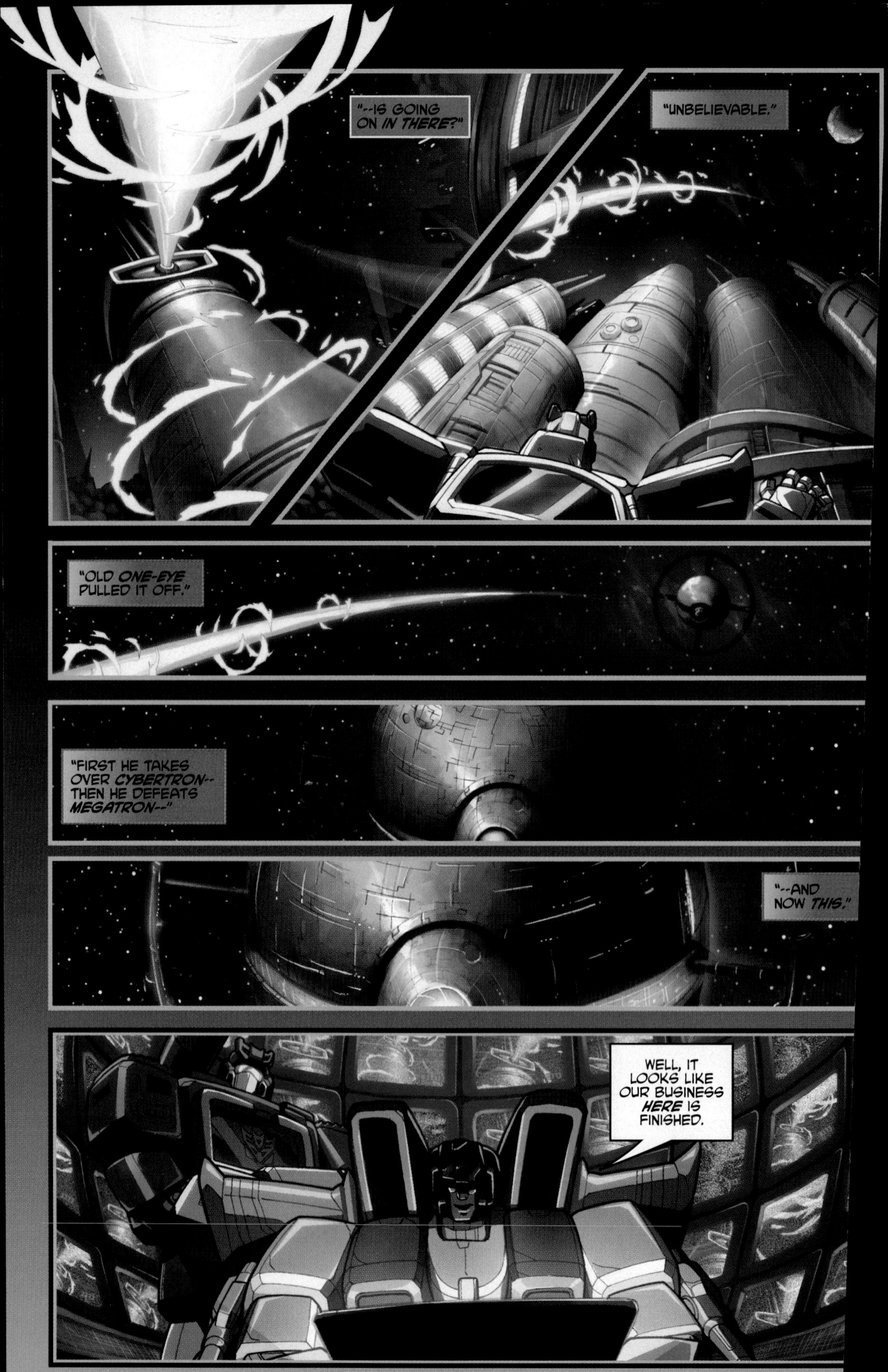
"--IS GOING ON IN THERE?"
"UNBELIEVABLE."
"OLD ONE-EYE PULLED IT OFF."
"FIRST HE TAKES OVER CYBERTRON-- THEN HE DEFEATS MEGATRON--"
"--AND NOW THIS."
WELL, IT LOOKS LIKE OUR BUSINESS HERE IS FINISHED.

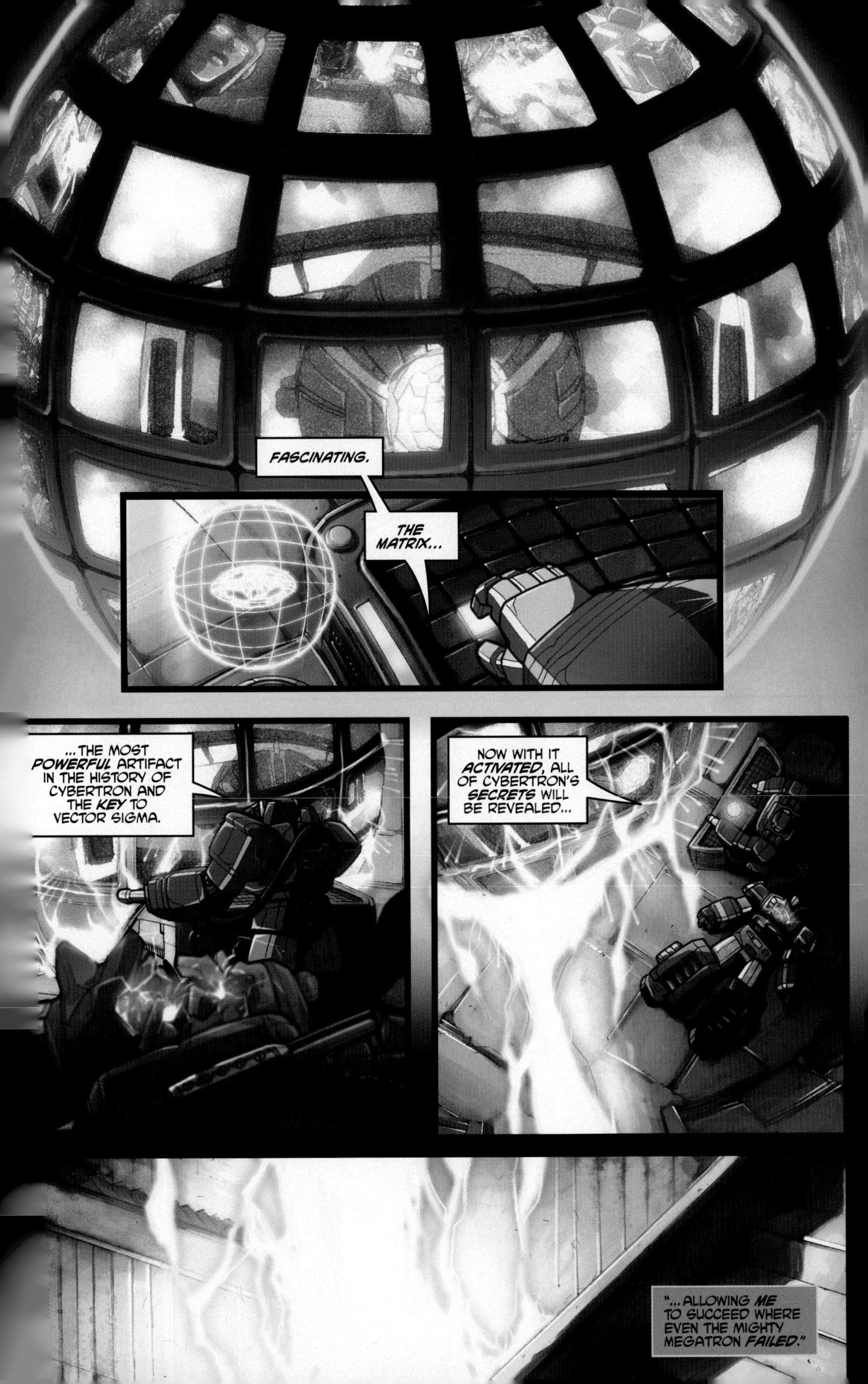
FASCINATING.
THE MATRIX...
...THE MOST POWERFUL ARTIFACT IN THE HISTORY OF CYBERTRON AND THE KEY TO VECTOR SIGMA.
NOW WITH IT ACTIVATED, ALL OF CYBERTRON'S SECRETS WILL BE REVEALED...
"...ALLOWING ME TO SUCCEED WHERE EVEN THE MIGHTY MEGATRON FAILED."

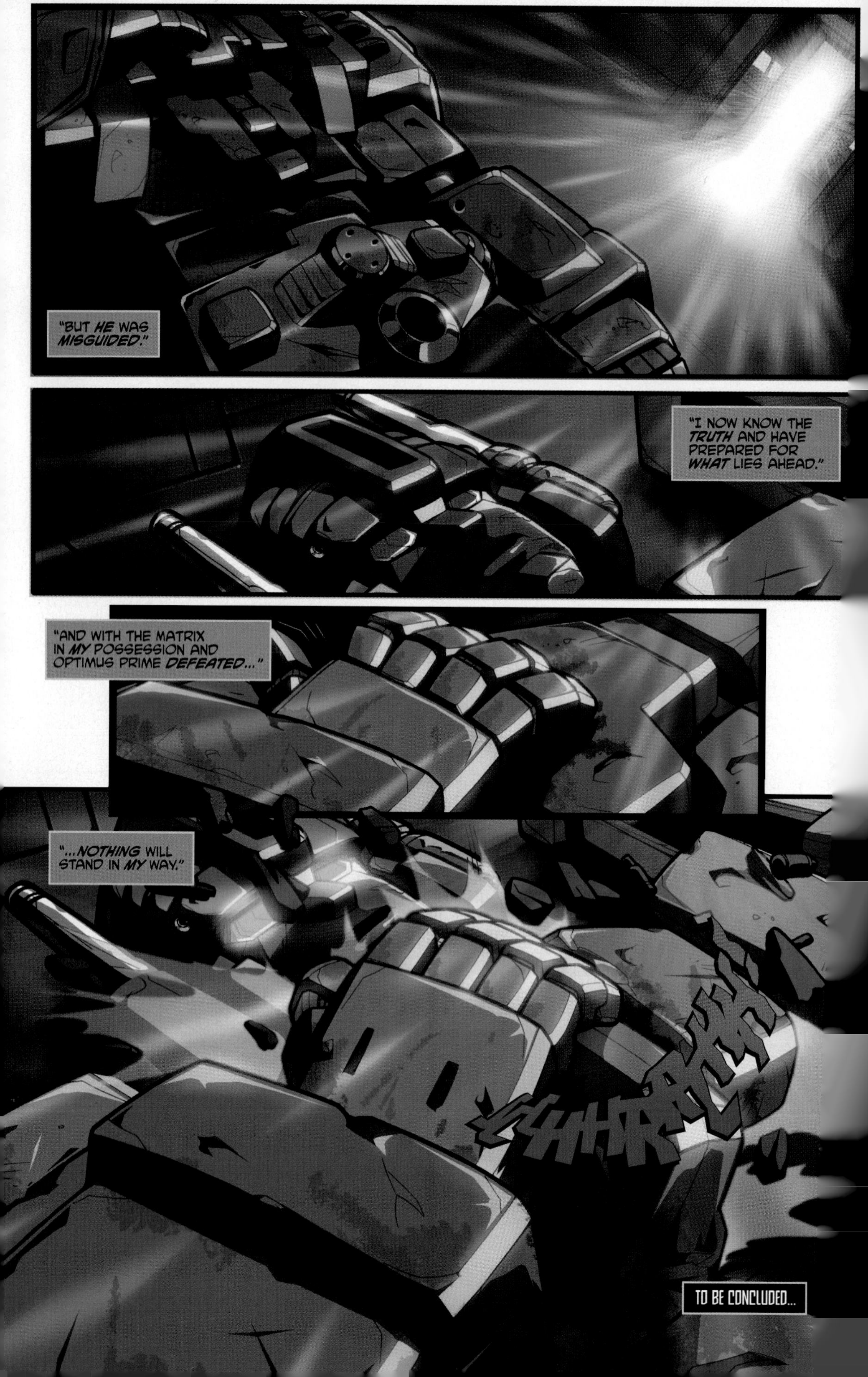
"BUT *HE* WAS *MISGUIDED*."
"I NOW KNOW THE *TRUTH* AND HAVE PREPARED FOR *WHAT* LIES AHEAD."
"AND WITH THE MATRIX IN *MY* POSSESSION AND OPTIMUS PRIME *DEFEATED*..."
"...*NOTHING* WILL STAND IN *MY* WAY."
TO BE CONCLUDED...

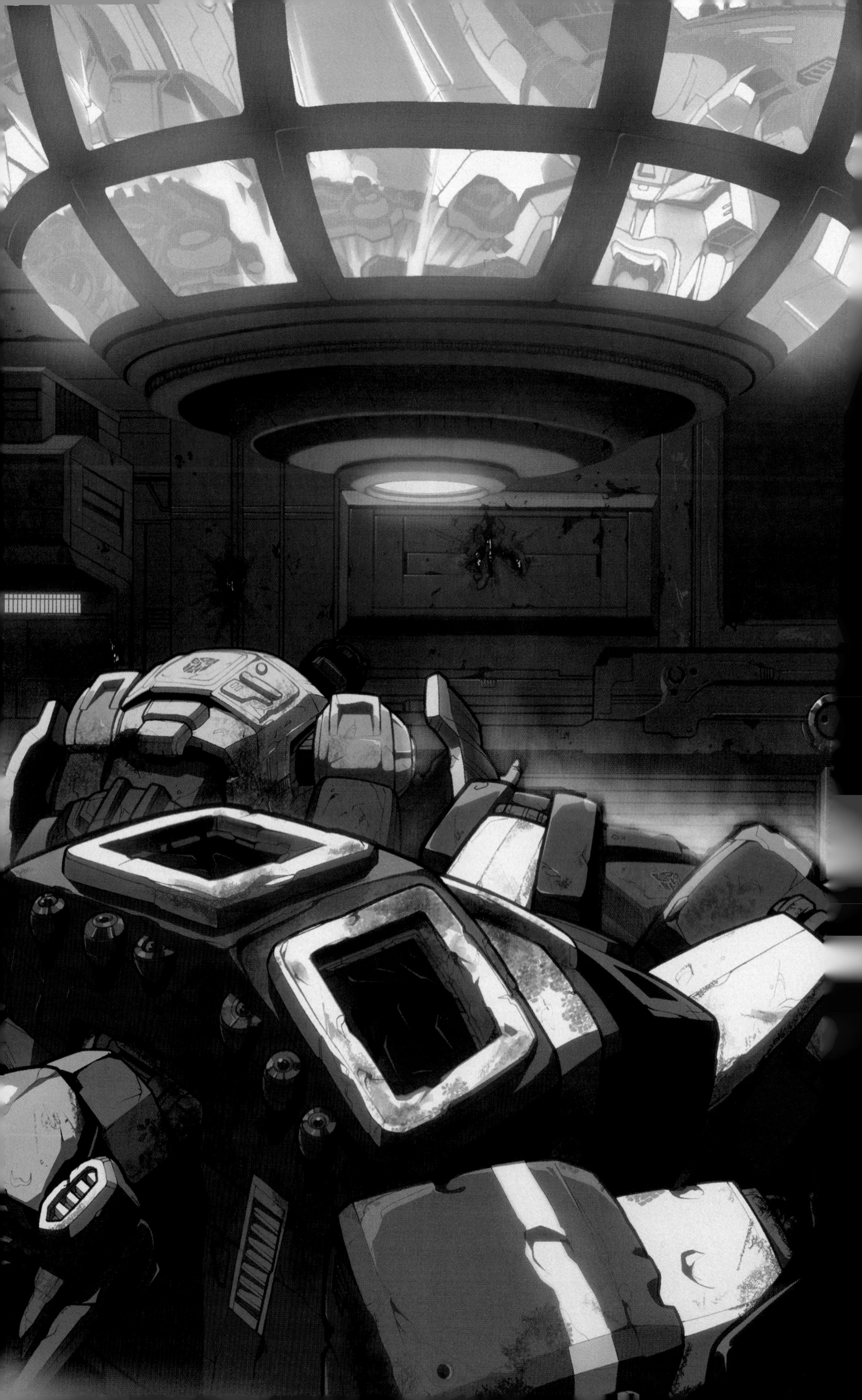

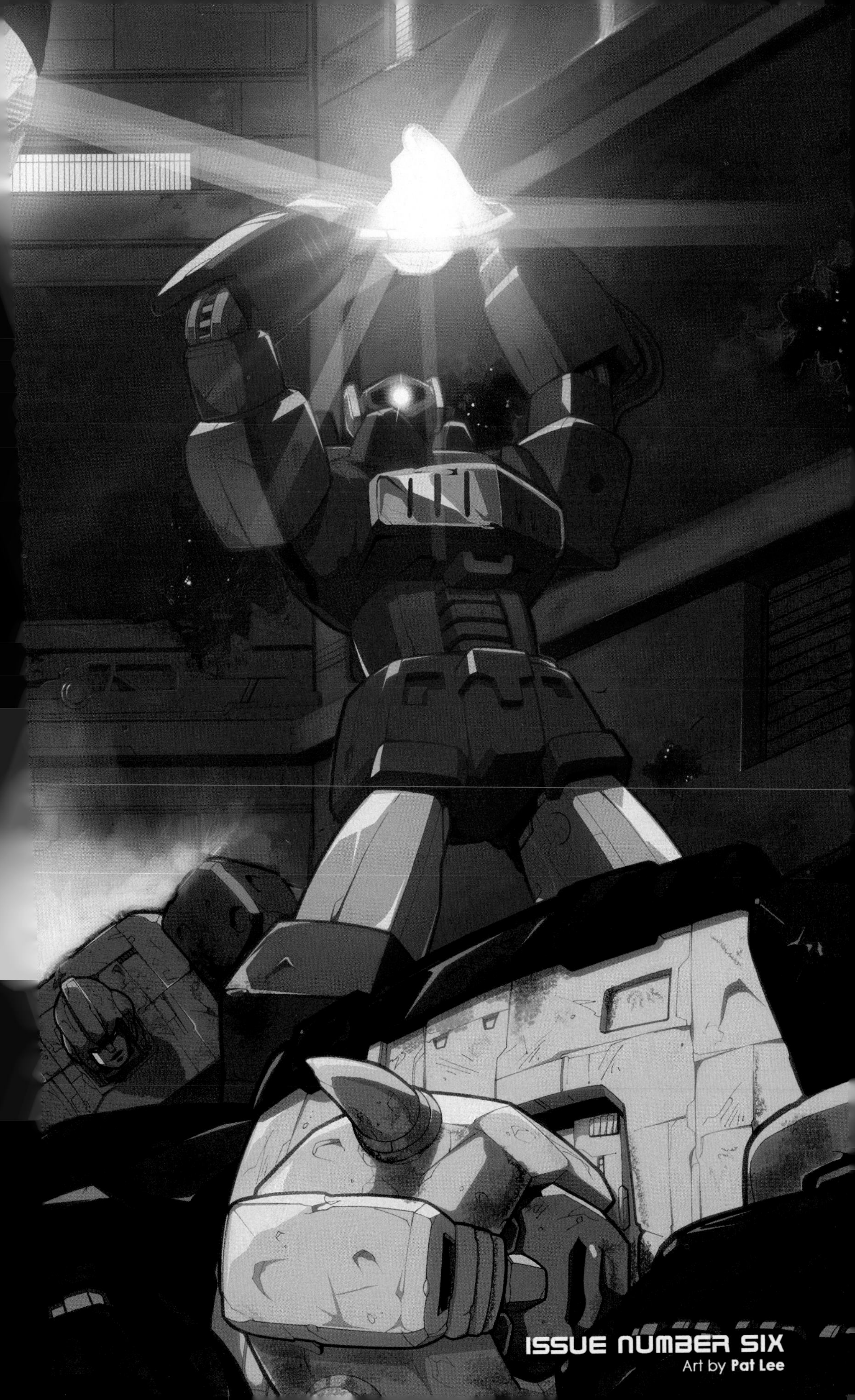

ISSUE NUMBER SIX

Art by **Pat Lee**

CHAPTER SIX
REVELATION

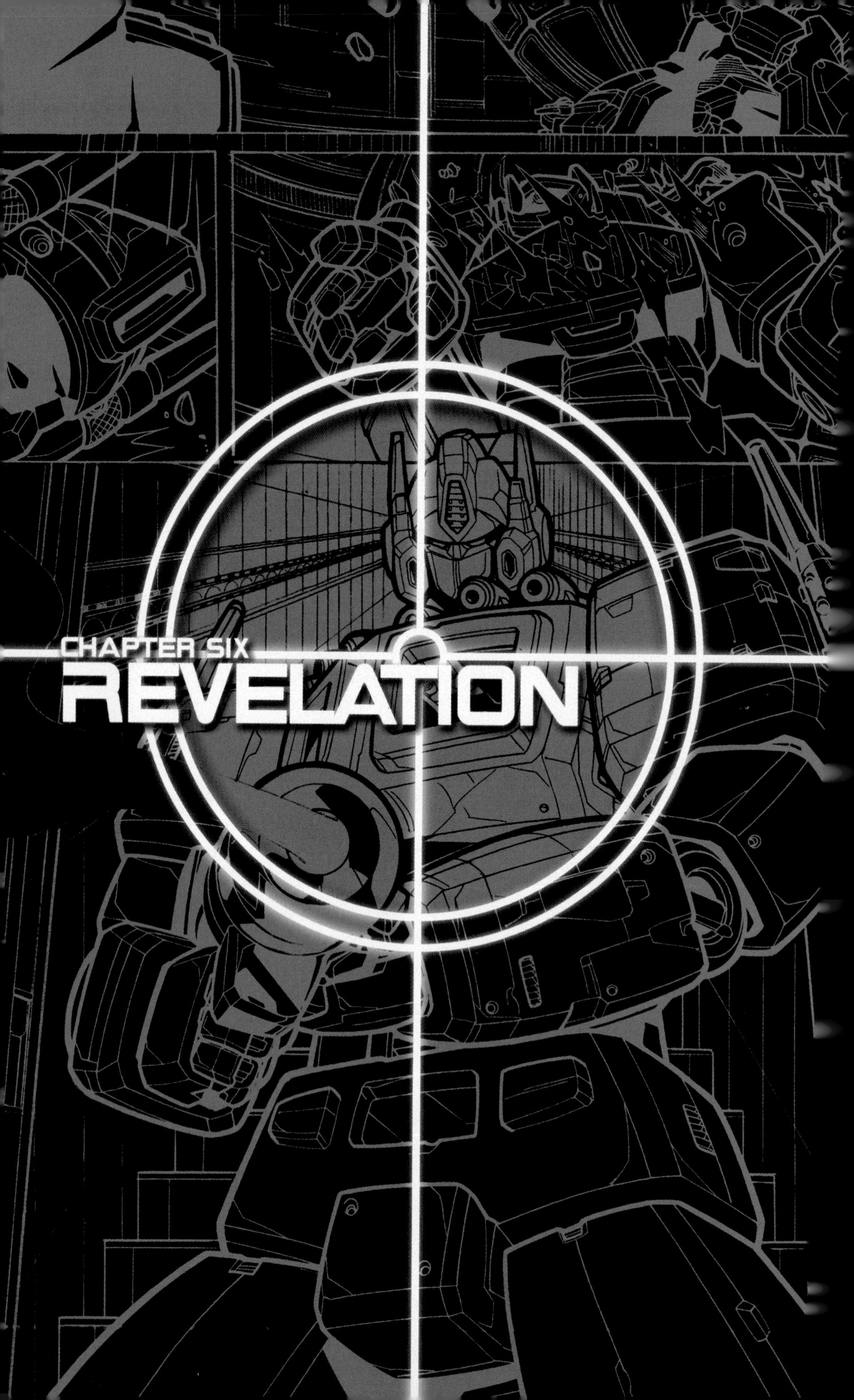

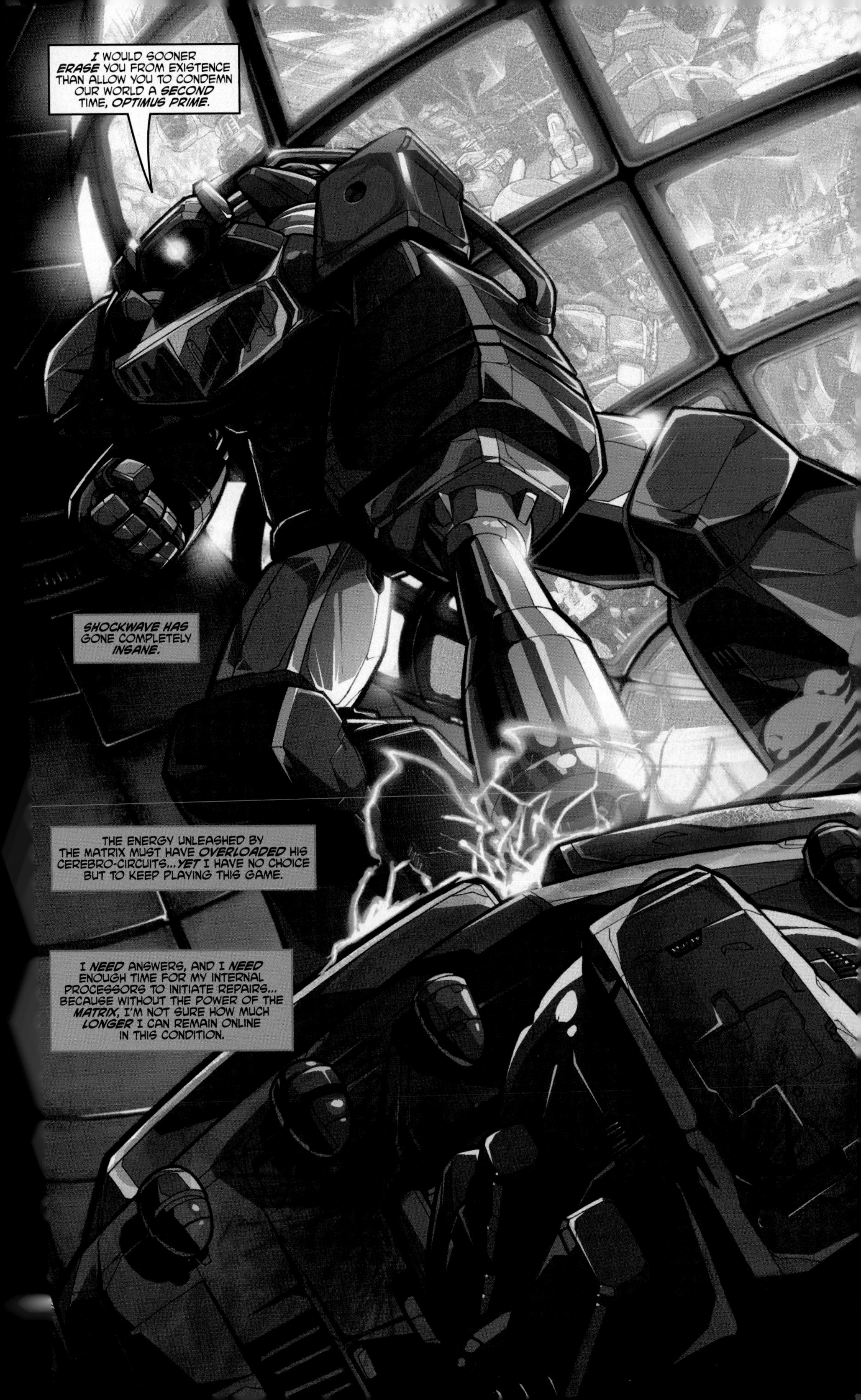
I WOULD SOONER *ERASE* YOU FROM EXISTENCE THAN ALLOW YOU TO CONDEMN OUR WORLD A *SECOND* TIME, *OPTIMUS PRIME*.
SHOCKWAVE HAS GONE COMPLETELY *INSANE.*
THE ENERGY UNLEASHED BY THE MATRIX MUST HAVE *OVERLOADED* HIS CEREBRO-CIRCUITS...*YET* I HAVE NO CHOICE BUT TO KEEP PLAYING THIS GAME.
I *NEED* ANSWERS, AND I *NEED* ENOUGH TIME FOR MY INTERNAL PROCESSORS TO INITIATE REPAIRS... BECAUSE WITHOUT THE POWER OF THE *MATRIX*, I'M NOT SURE HOW MUCH *LONGER* I CAN REMAIN ONLINE IN THIS CONDITION.

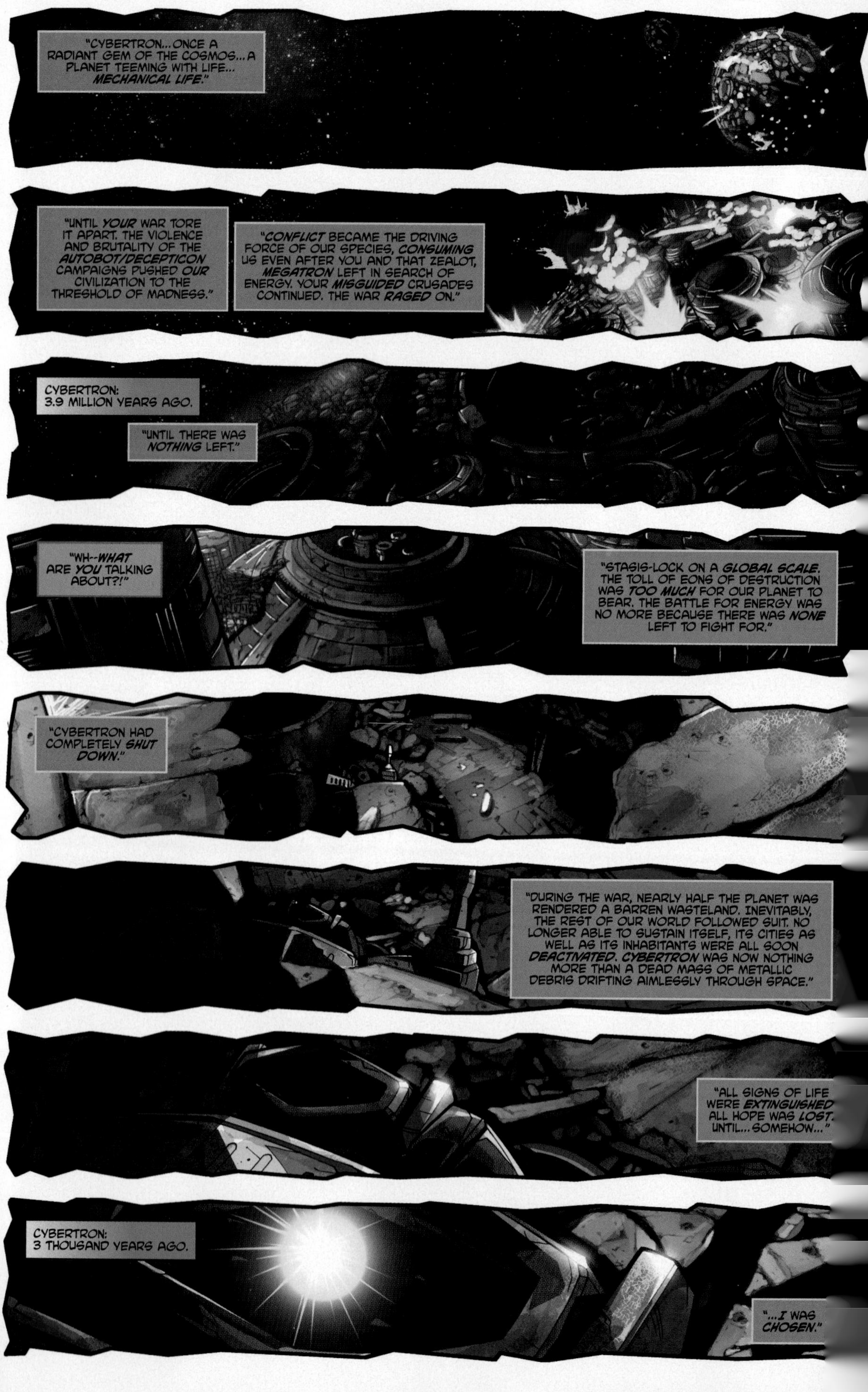
"CYBERTRON...ONCE A RADIANT GEM OF THE COSMOS...A PLANET TEEMING WITH LIFE... MECHANICAL LIFE."
"UNTIL YOUR WAR TORE IT APART. THE VIOLENCE AND BRUTALITY OF THE AUTOBOT/DECEPTICON CAMPAIGNS PUSHED OUR CIVILIZATION TO THE THRESHOLD OF MADNESS."
"CONFLICT BECAME THE DRIVING FORCE OF OUR SPECIES, CONSUMING US EVEN AFTER YOU AND THAT ZEALOT, MEGATRON LEFT IN SEARCH OF ENERGY. YOUR MISGUIDED CRUSADES CONTINUED. THE WAR RAGED ON."
CYBERTRON: 3.9 MILLION YEARS AGO.
"UNTIL THERE WAS NOTHING LEFT."
"WH--WHAT ARE YOU TALKING ABOUT?!"
"STASIS-LOCK ON A GLOBAL SCALE. THE TOLL OF EONS OF DESTRUCTION WAS TOO MUCH FOR OUR PLANET TO BEAR. THE BATTLE FOR ENERGY WAS NO MORE BECAUSE THERE WAS NONE LEFT TO FIGHT FOR."
"CYBERTRON HAD COMPLETELY SHUT DOWN."
"DURING THE WAR, NEARLY HALF THE PLANET WAS RENDERED A BARREN WASTELAND. INEVITABLY, THE REST OF OUR WORLD FOLLOWED SUIT. NO LONGER ABLE TO SUSTAIN ITSELF, ITS CITIES AS WELL AS ITS INHABITANTS WERE ALL SOON DEACTIVATED. CYBERTRON WAS NOW NOTHING MORE THAN A DEAD MASS OF METALLIC DEBRIS DRIFTING AIMLESSLY THROUGH SPACE."
"ALL SIGNS OF LIFE WERE EXTINGUISHED. ALL HOPE WAS LOST. UNTIL...SOMEHOW..."
CYBERTRON: 3 THOUSAND YEARS AGO.
"...I WAS CHOSEN."

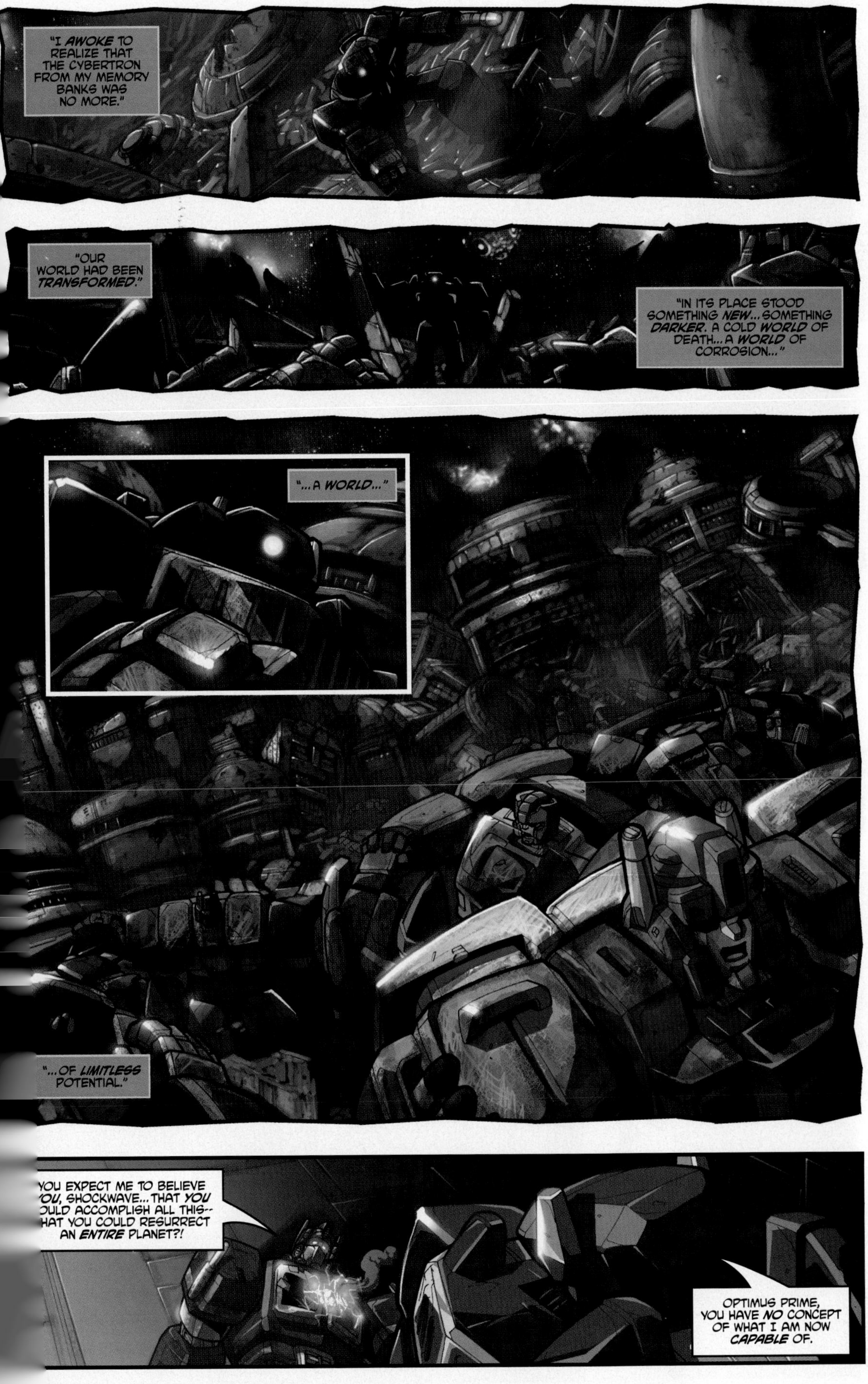
"I AWOKE TO REALIZE THAT THE CYBERTRON FROM MY MEMORY BANKS WAS NO MORE."
"OUR WORLD HAD BEEN TRANSFORMED."
"IN ITS PLACE STOOD SOMETHING NEW...SOMETHING DARKER. A COLD WORLD OF DEATH...A WORLD OF CORROSION..."
"...A WORLD..."
"...OF LIMITLESS POTENTIAL."
YOU EXPECT ME TO BELIEVE YOU, SHOCKWAVE...THAT YOU OULD ACCOMPLISH ALL THIS-- HAT YOU COULD RESURRECT AN ENTIRE PLANET?!
OPTIMUS PRIME, YOU HAVE NO CONCEPT OF WHAT I AM NOW CAPABLE OF.

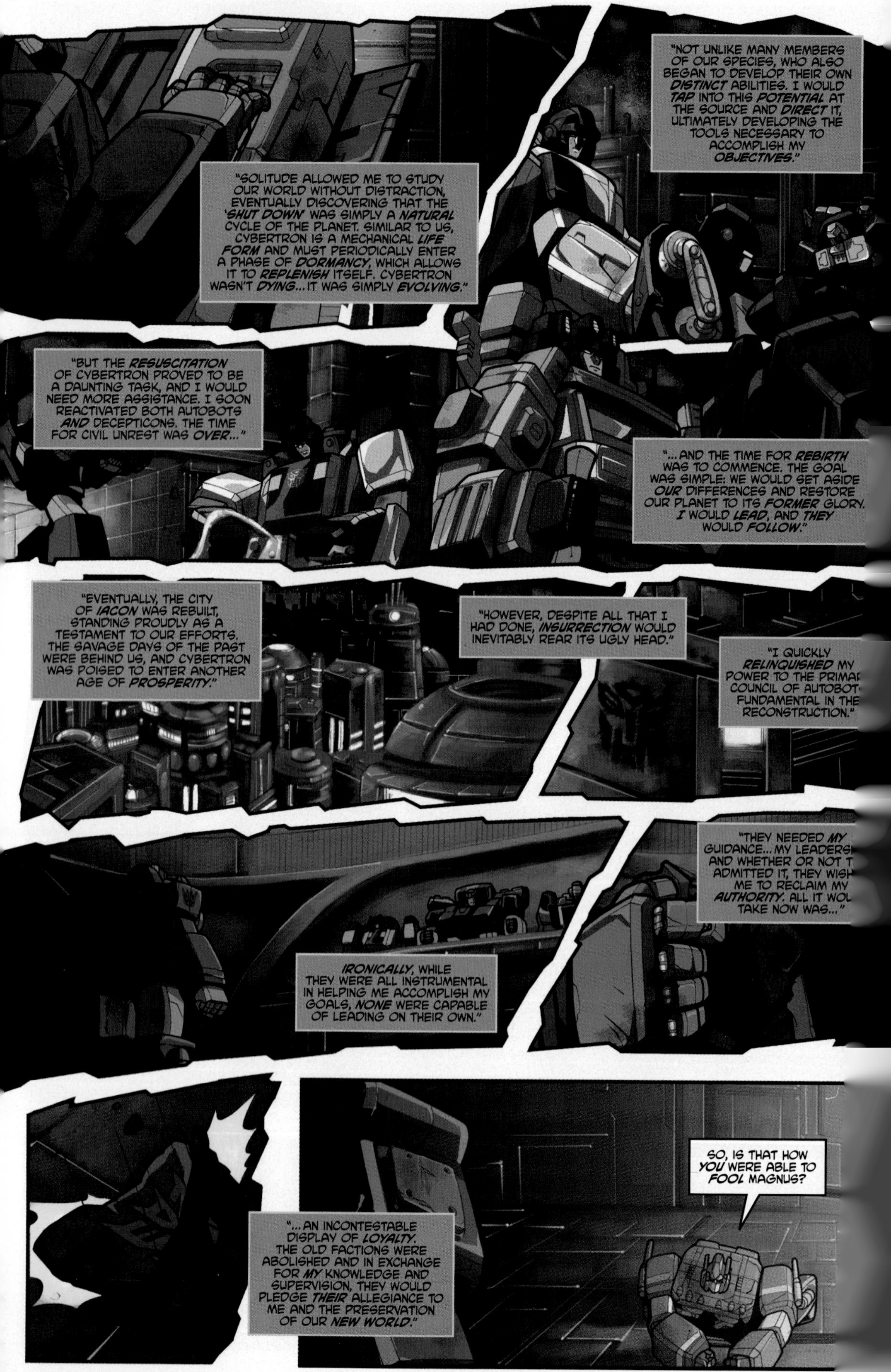
"SOLITUDE ALLOWED ME TO STUDY OUR WORLD WITHOUT DISTRACTION, EVENTUALLY DISCOVERING THAT THE 'SHUT DOWN' WAS SIMPLY A NATURAL CYCLE OF THE PLANET. SIMILAR TO US, CYBERTRON IS A MECHANICAL LIFE FORM AND MUST PERIODICALLY ENTER A PHASE OF DORMANCY, WHICH ALLOWS IT TO REPLENISH ITSELF. CYBERTRON WASN'T DYING... IT WAS SIMPLY EVOLVING."
"NOT UNLIKE MANY MEMBERS OF OUR SPECIES, WHO ALSO BEGAN TO DEVELOP THEIR OWN DISTINCT ABILITIES. I WOULD TAP INTO THIS POTENTIAL AT THE SOURCE AND DIRECT IT, ULTIMATELY DEVELOPING THE TOOLS NECESSARY TO ACCOMPLISH MY OBJECTIVES."
"BUT THE RESUSCITATION OF CYBERTRON PROVED TO BE A DAUNTING TASK, AND I WOULD NEED MORE ASSISTANCE. I SOON REACTIVATED BOTH AUTOBOTS AND DECEPTICONS. THE TIME FOR CIVIL UNREST WAS OVER..."
"...AND THE TIME FOR REBIRTH WAS TO COMMENCE. THE GOAL WAS SIMPLE: WE WOULD SET ASIDE OUR DIFFERENCES AND RESTORE OUR PLANET TO ITS FORMER GLORY. I WOULD LEAD, AND THEY WOULD FOLLOW."
"EVENTUALLY, THE CITY OF IACON WAS REBUILT, STANDING PROUDLY AS A TESTAMENT TO OUR EFFORTS. THE SAVAGE DAYS OF THE PAST WERE BEHIND US, AND CYBERTRON WAS POISED TO ENTER ANOTHER AGE OF PROSPERITY."
"HOWEVER, DESPITE ALL THAT I HAD DONE, INSURRECTION WOULD INEVITABLY REAR ITS UGLY HEAD."
"I QUICKLY RELINQUISHED MY POWER TO THE PRIMAR COUNCIL OF AUTOBOT FUNDAMENTAL IN THE RECONSTRUCTION."
IRONICALLY, WHILE THEY WERE ALL INSTRUMENTAL IN HELPING ME ACCOMPLISH MY GOALS, NONE WERE CAPABLE OF LEADING ON THEIR OWN."
"THEY NEEDED MY GUIDANCE... MY LEADERS AND WHETHER OR NOT T ADMITTED IT, THEY WISH ME TO RECLAIM MY AUTHORITY. ALL IT WOU TAKE NOW WAS..."
"...AN INCONTESTABLE DISPLAY OF LOYALTY. THE OLD FACTIONS WERE ABOLISHED AND IN EXCHANGE FOR MY KNOWLEDGE AND SUPERVISION, THEY WOULD PLEDGE THEIR ALLEGIANCE TO ME AND THE PRESERVATION OF OUR NEW WORLD."
SO, IS THAT HOW YOU WERE ABLE TO FOOL MAGNUS?

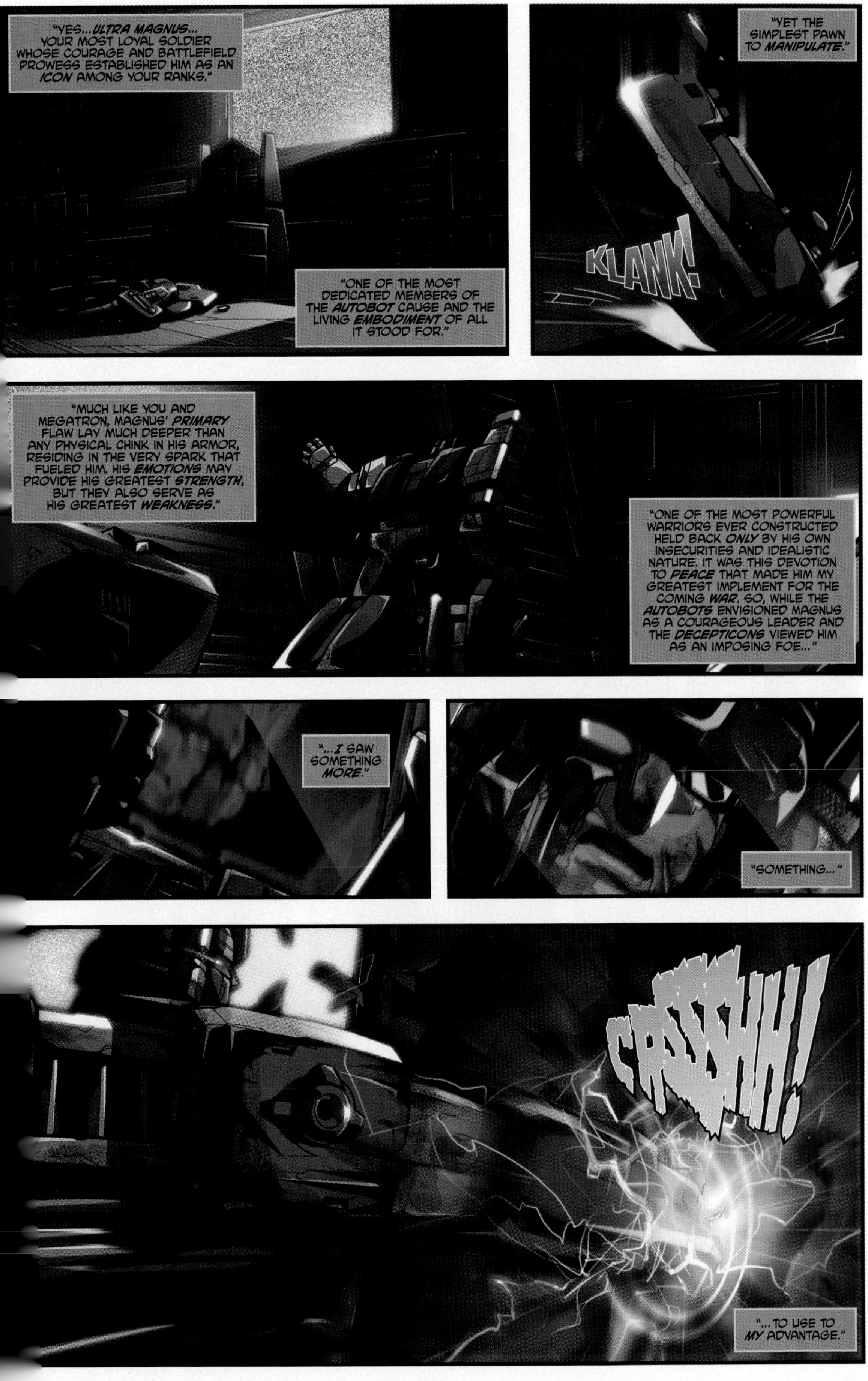
"YES...ULTRA MAGNUS... YOUR MOST LOYAL SOLDIER WHOSE COURAGE AND BATTLEFIELD PROWESS ESTABLISHED HIM AS AN ICON AMONG YOUR RANKS."
"ONE OF THE MOST DEDICATED MEMBERS OF THE AUTOBOT CAUSE AND THE LIVING EMBODIMENT OF ALL IT STOOD FOR."
"YET THE SIMPLEST PAWN TO MANIPULATE."
KLANK!
"MUCH LIKE YOU AND MEGATRON, MAGNUS' PRIMARY FLAW LAY MUCH DEEPER THAN ANY PHYSICAL CHINK IN HIS ARMOR, RESIDING IN THE VERY SPARK THAT FUELED HIM. HIS EMOTIONS MAY PROVIDE HIS GREATEST STRENGTH, BUT THEY ALSO SERVE AS HIS GREATEST WEAKNESS."
"ONE OF THE MOST POWERFUL WARRIORS EVER CONSTRUCTED HELD BACK ONLY BY HIS OWN INSECURITIES AND IDEALISTIC NATURE. IT WAS THIS DEVOTION TO PEACE THAT MADE HIM MY GREATEST IMPLEMENT FOR THE COMING WAR. SO, WHILE THE AUTOBOTS ENVISIONED MAGNUS AS A COURAGEOUS LEADER AND THE DECEPTICONS VIEWED HIM AS AN IMPOSING FOE..."
"...I SAW SOMETHING MORE."
"SOMETHING..."
CRSSHH!
"...TO USE TO MY ADVANTAGE."

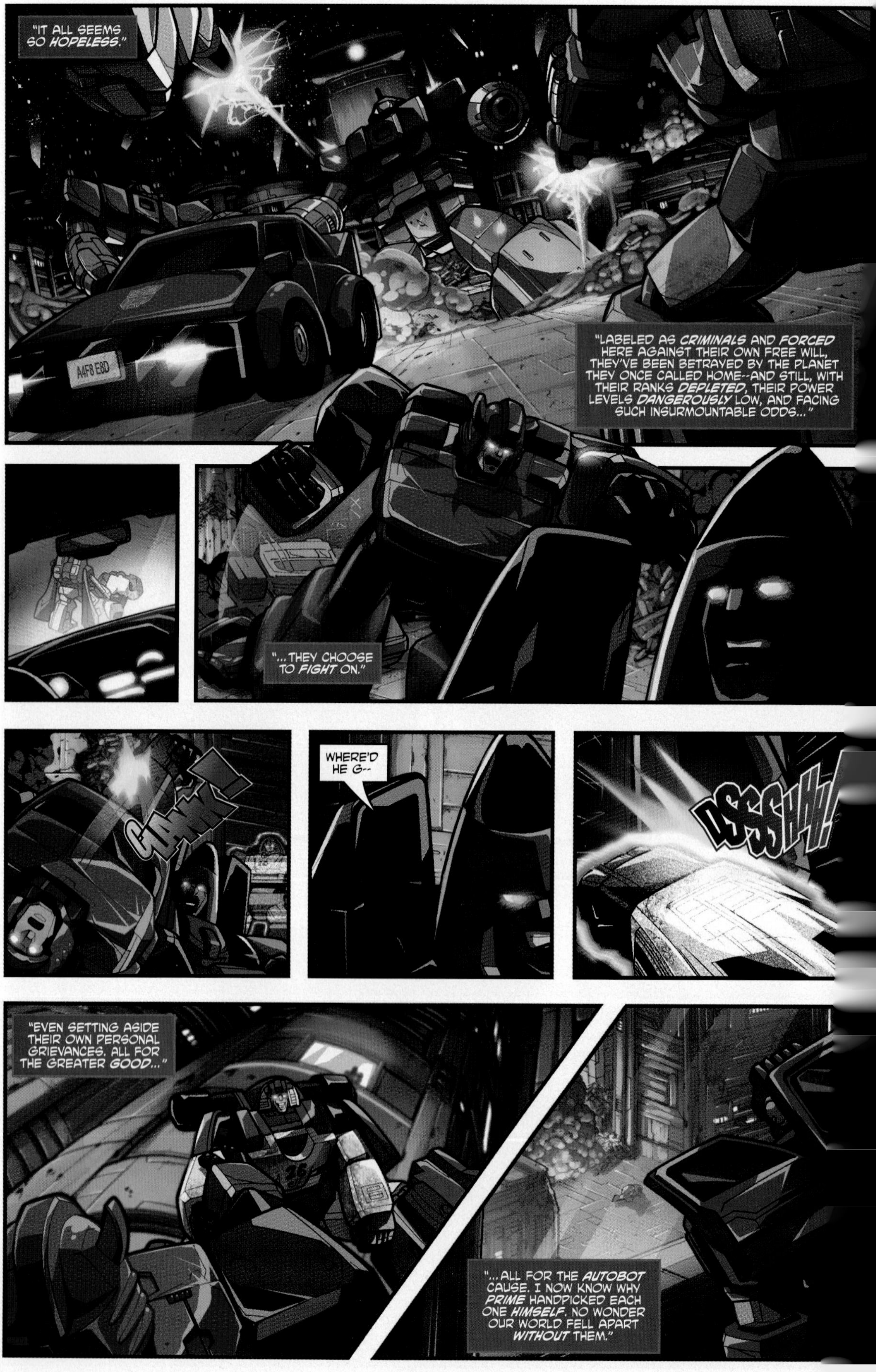

"IT ALL SEEMS SO *HOPELESS*."
A4F8 E8D
"LABELED AS *CRIMINALS* AND *FORCED* HERE AGAINST THEIR OWN FREE WILL, THEY'VE BEEN BETRAYED BY THE PLANET THEY ONCE CALLED HOME--AND STILL, WITH THEIR RANKS *DEPLETED*, THEIR POWER LEVELS *DANGEROUSLY* LOW, AND FACING SUCH INSURMOUNTABLE ODDS..."
"...THEY CHOOSE TO *FIGHT* ON."
WHERE'D HE G--
"EVEN SETTING ASIDE THEIR OWN PERSONAL GRIEVANCES. ALL FOR THE GREATER *GOOD*..."
"...ALL FOR THE *AUTOBOT* CAUSE. I NOW KNOW WHY *PRIME* HANDPICKED EACH ONE *HIMSELF*. NO WONDER OUR WORLD FELL APART *WITHOUT* THEM."

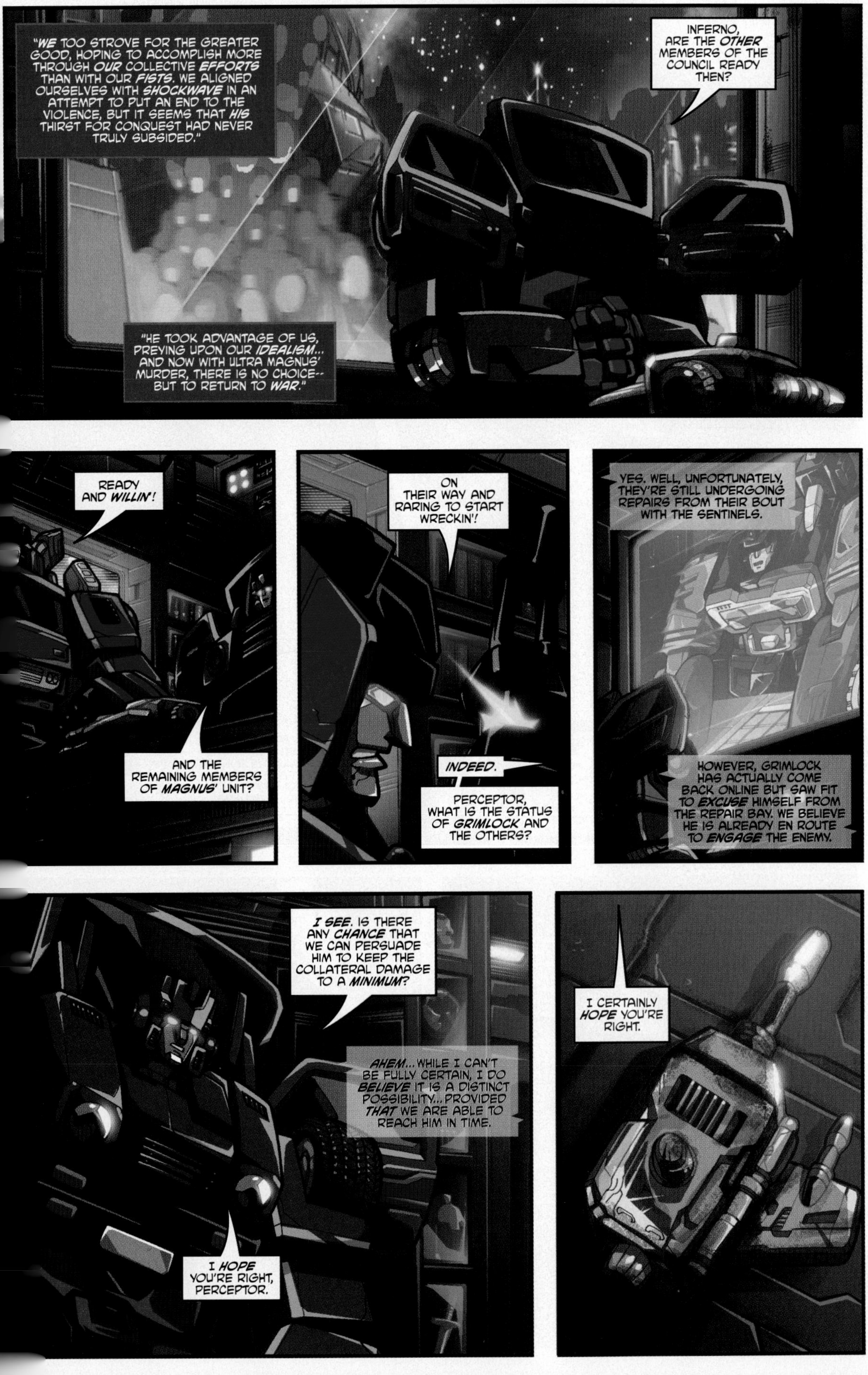
"WE TOO STROVE FOR THE GREATER GOOD, HOPING TO ACCOMPLISH MORE THROUGH OUR COLLECTIVE EFFORTS THAN WITH OUR FISTS. WE ALIGNED OURSELVES WITH SHOCKWAVE IN AN ATTEMPT TO PUT AN END TO THE VIOLENCE, BUT IT SEEMS THAT HIS THIRST FOR CONQUEST HAD NEVER TRULY SUBSIDED."
"HE TOOK ADVANTAGE OF US, PREYING UPON OUR IDEALISM... AND NOW WITH ULTRA MAGNUS' MURDER, THERE IS NO CHOICE-- BUT TO RETURN TO WAR."
INFERNO, ARE THE OTHER MEMBERS OF THE COUNCIL READY THEN?
READY AND WILLIN'!
AND THE REMAINING MEMBERS OF MAGNUS' UNIT?
ON THEIR WAY AND RARING TO START WRECKIN'!
INDEED.
PERCEPTOR, WHAT IS THE STATUS OF GRIMLOCK AND THE OTHERS?
YES. WELL, UNFORTUNATELY, THEY'RE STILL UNDERGOING REPAIRS FROM THEIR BOUT WITH THE SENTINELS.
HOWEVER, GRIMLOCK HAS ACTUALLY COME BACK ONLINE BUT SAW FIT TO EXCUSE HIMSELF FROM THE REPAIR BAY. WE BELIEVE HE IS ALREADY EN ROUTE TO ENGAGE THE ENEMY.
I SEE. IS THERE ANY CHANCE THAT WE CAN PERSUADE HIM TO KEEP THE COLLATERAL DAMAGE TO A MINIMUM?
AHEM... WHILE I CAN'T BE FULLY CERTAIN, I DO BELIEVE IT IS A DISTINCT POSSIBILITY... PROVIDED THAT WE ARE ABLE TO REACH HIM IN TIME.
I HOPE YOU'RE RIGHT, PERCEPTOR.
I CERTAINLY HOPE YOU'RE RIGHT.

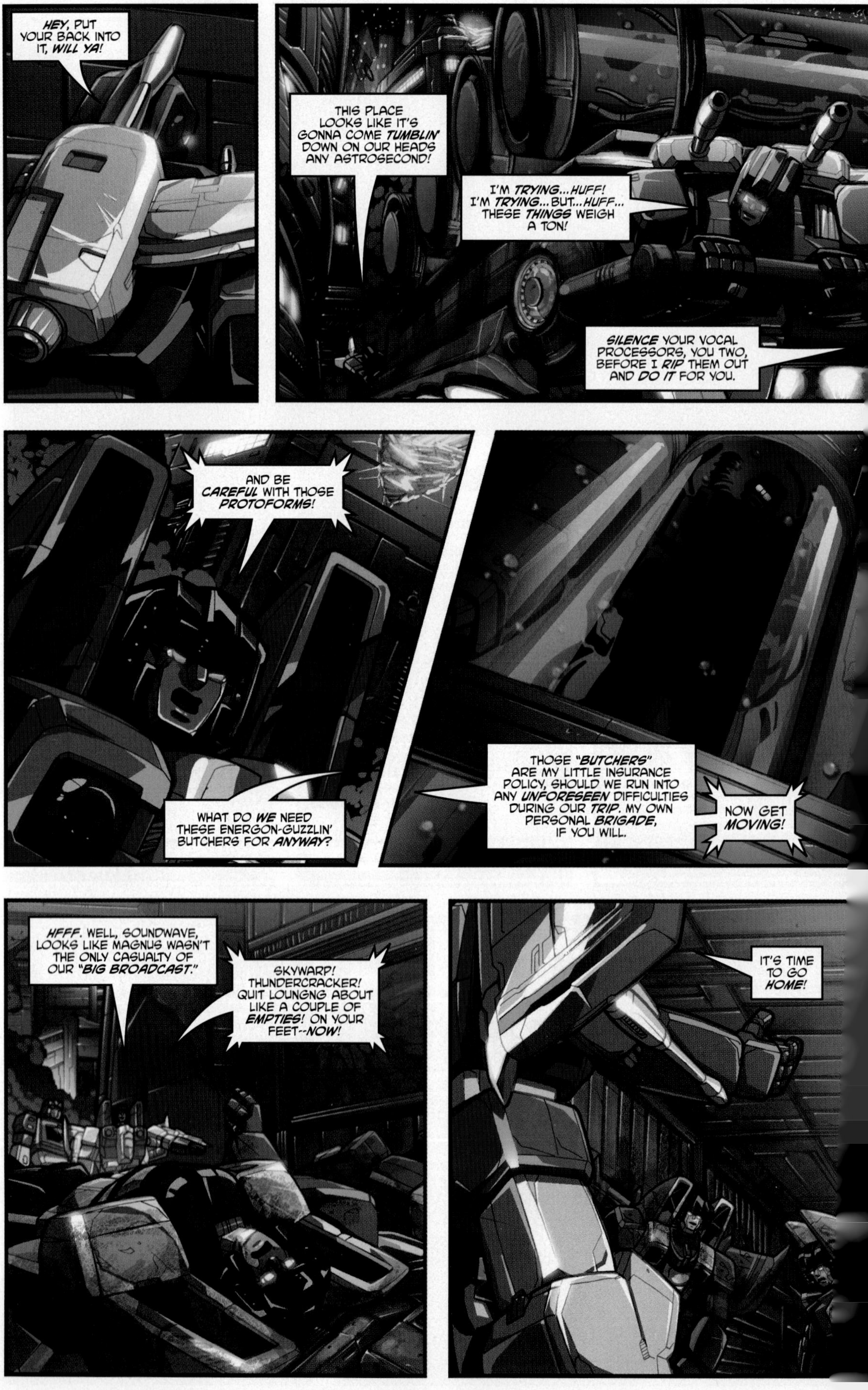
HEY, PUT YOUR BACK INTO IT, WILL YA!
THIS PLACE LOOKS LIKE IT'S GONNA COME TUMBLIN' DOWN ON OUR HEADS ANY ASTROSECOND!
I'M TRYING... HUFF! I'M TRYING... BUT... HUFF... THESE THINGS WEIGH A TON!
SILENCE YOUR VOCAL PROCESSORS, YOU TWO, BEFORE I RIP THEM OUT AND DO IT FOR YOU.
AND BE CAREFUL WITH THOSE PROTOFORMS!
WHAT DO WE NEED THESE ENERGON-GUZZLIN' BUTCHERS FOR ANYWAY?
THOSE "BUTCHERS" ARE MY LITTLE INSURANCE POLICY, SHOULD WE RUN INTO ANY UNFORESEEN DIFFICULTIES DURING OUR TRIP. MY OWN PERSONAL BRIGADE, IF YOU WILL.
NOW GET MOVING!
HFFF. WELL, SOUNDWAVE, LOOKS LIKE MAGNUS WASN'T THE ONLY CASUALTY OF OUR "BIG BROADCAST."
SKYWARP! THUNDERCRACKER! QUIT LOUNGNG ABOUT LIKE A COUPLE OF EMPTIES! ON YOUR FEET--NOW!
IT'S TIME TO GO HOME!

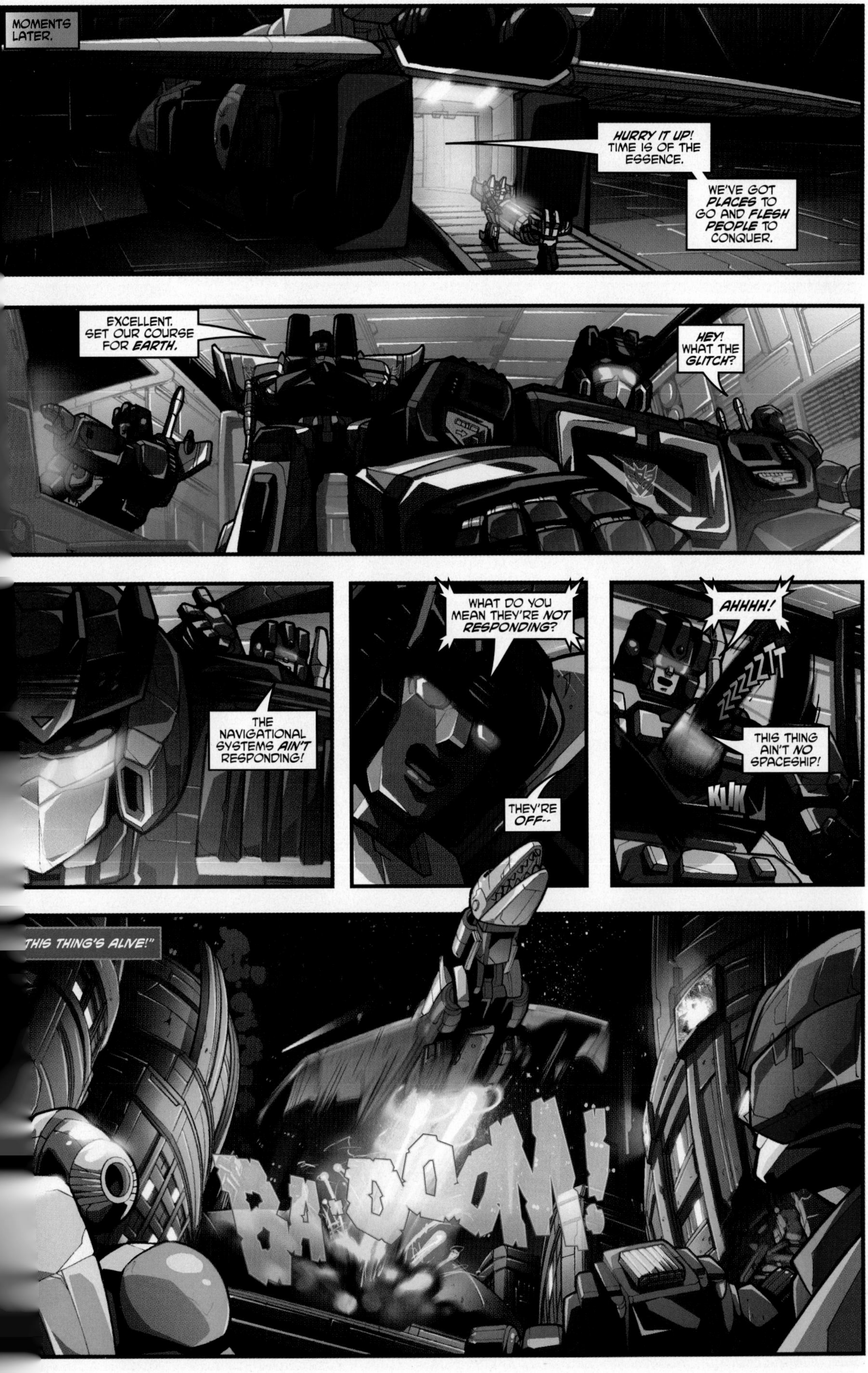
MOMENTS LATER.
HURRY IT UP! TIME IS OF THE ESSENCE.
WE'VE GOT PLACES TO GO AND FLESH PEOPLE TO CONQUER.
EXCELLENT. SET OUR COURSE FOR EARTH.
HEY! WHAT THE GLITCH?
THE NAVIGATIONAL SYSTEMS AIN'T RESPONDING!
WHAT DO YOU MEAN THEY'RE NOT RESPONDING?
THEY'RE OFF--
AHHHH!
ZZZZZZZT
THIS THING AIN'T NO SPACESHIP!
KLIK
"THIS THING'S ALIVE!"
BA-DOOM!

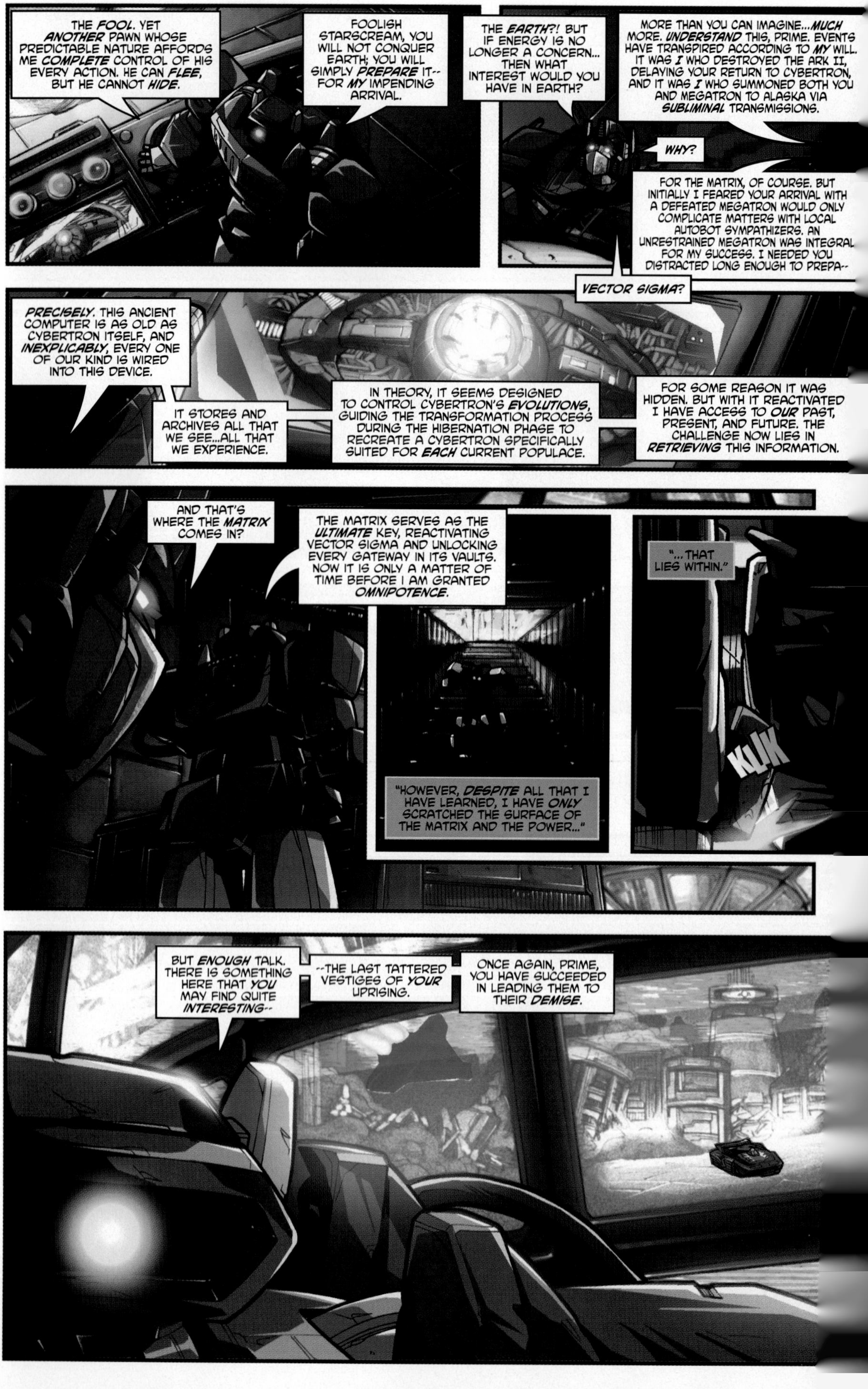
THE FOOL. YET ANOTHER PAWN WHOSE PREDICTABLE NATURE AFFORDS ME COMPLETE CONTROL OF HIS EVERY ACTION. HE CAN FLEE, BUT HE CANNOT HIDE.
FOOLISH STARSCREAM, YOU WILL NOT CONQUER EARTH; YOU WILL SIMPLY PREPARE IT-- FOR MY IMPENDING ARRIVAL.
THE EARTH?! BUT IF ENERGY IS NO LONGER A CONCERN... THEN WHAT INTEREST WOULD YOU HAVE IN EARTH?
MORE THAN YOU CAN IMAGINE...MUCH MORE. UNDERSTAND THIS, PRIME. EVENTS HAVE TRANSPIRED ACCORDING TO MY WILL. IT WAS I WHO DESTROYED THE ARK II, DELAYING YOUR RETURN TO CYBERTRON, AND IT WAS I WHO SUMMONED BOTH YOU AND MEGATRON TO ALASKA VIA SUBLIMINAL TRANSMISSIONS.
WHY?
FOR THE MATRIX, OF COURSE. BUT INITIALLY I FEARED YOUR ARRIVAL WITH A DEFEATED MEGATRON WOULD ONLY COMPLICATE MATTERS WITH LOCAL AUTOBOT SYMPATHIZERS. AN UNRESTRAINED MEGATRON WAS INTEGRAL FOR MY SUCCESS. I NEEDED YOU DISTRACTED LONG ENOUGH TO PREPA--
VECTOR SIGMA?
PRECISELY. THIS ANCIENT COMPUTER IS AS OLD AS CYBERTRON ITSELF, AND INEXPLICABLY, EVERY ONE OF OUR KIND IS WIRED INTO THIS DEVICE.
IT STORES AND ARCHIVES ALL THAT WE SEE...ALL THAT WE EXPERIENCE.
IN THEORY, IT SEEMS DESIGNED TO CONTROL CYBERTRON'S EVOLUTIONS, GUIDING THE TRANSFORMATION PROCESS DURING THE HIBERNATION PHASE TO RECREATE A CYBERTRON SPECIFICALLY SUITED FOR EACH CURRENT POPULACE.
FOR SOME REASON IT WAS HIDDEN. BUT WITH IT REACTIVATED I HAVE ACCESS TO OUR PAST, PRESENT, AND FUTURE. THE CHALLENGE NOW LIES IN RETRIEVING THIS INFORMATION.
AND THAT'S WHERE THE MATRIX COMES IN?
THE MATRIX SERVES AS THE ULTIMATE KEY, REACTIVATING VECTOR SIGMA AND UNLOCKING EVERY GATEWAY IN ITS VAULTS. NOW IT IS ONLY A MATTER OF TIME BEFORE I AM GRANTED OMNIPOTENCE.
"HOWEVER, DESPITE ALL THAT I HAVE LEARNED, I HAVE ONLY SCRATCHED THE SURFACE OF THE MATRIX AND THE POWER..."
"...THAT LIES WITHIN."
KLIK
BUT ENOUGH TALK. THERE IS SOMETHING HERE THAT YOU MAY FIND QUITE INTERESTING--
--THE LAST TATTERED VESTIGES OF YOUR UPRISING.
ONCE AGAIN, PRIME, YOU HAVE SUCCEEDED IN LEADING THEM TO THEIR DEMISE.

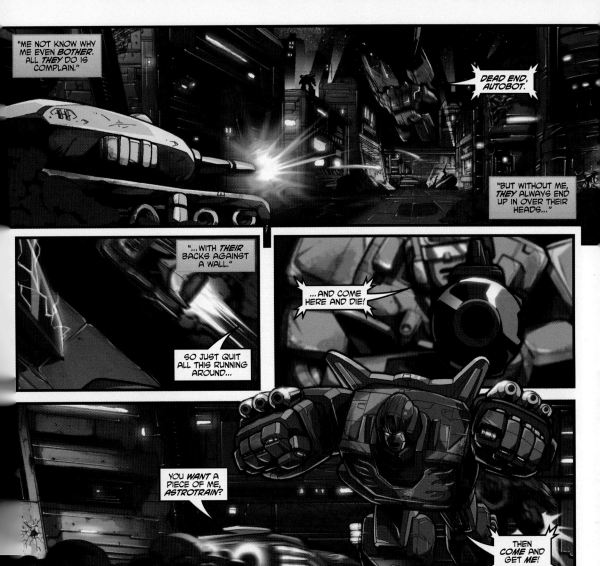

"ME NOT KNOW WHY ME EVEN *BOTHER.* ALL *THEY* DO IS COMPLAIN."

DEAD END, AUTOBOT.

"BUT WITHOUT ME, *THEY* ALWAYS END UP IN OVER THEIR HEADS..."

"...WITH *THEIR* BACKS AGAINST A WALL."

...AND COME HERE AND DIE!

SO JUST QUIT ALL THIS RUNNING AROUND...

YOU *WANT* A PIECE OF ME, *ASTROTRAIN?*

THEN *COME* AND GET *ME!*

"ALWAYS..."

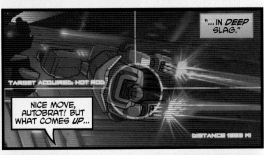

"...IN *DEEP* SLAG."

TARGET ACQUIRED: HOT ROD

NICE MOVE, AUTOBRAT! BUT WHAT COMES *UP*...

DISTANCE 1989 MI

TARGET: SEARCHING.   TARGET ACQUIRED: GRIMLOCK.

...MUST COME DOW--

DISTANCE 41 MI

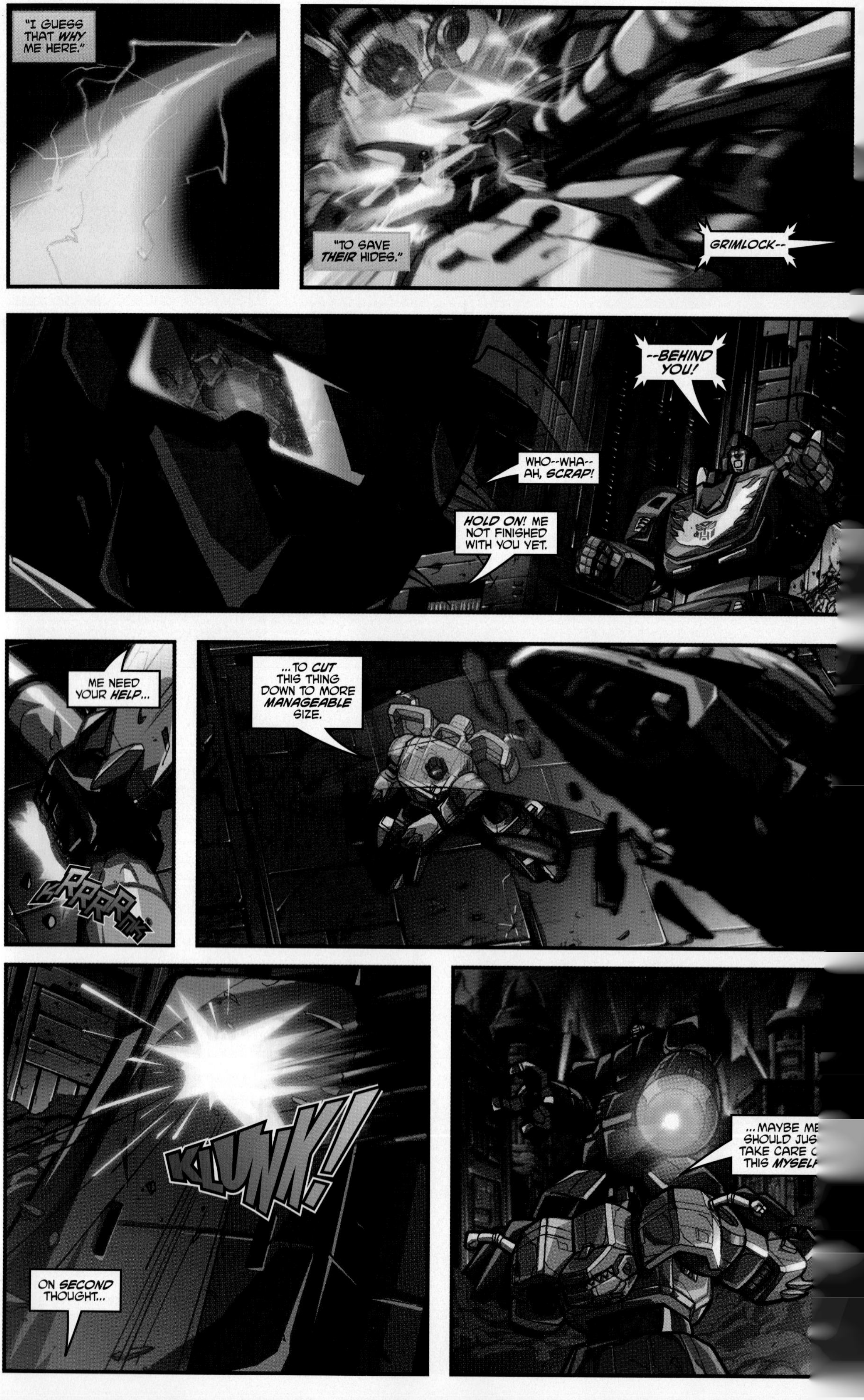
"I GUESS THAT WHY ME HERE."
"TO SAVE THEIR HIDES."
GRIMLOCK--
--BEHIND YOU!
WHO--WHA-- AH, SCRAP!
HOLD ON! ME NOT FINISHED WITH YOU YET.
ME NEED YOUR HELP...
KRRRRNK
...TO CUT THIS THING DOWN TO MORE MANAGEABLE SIZE.
KLUNK!!
ON SECOND THOUGHT...
...MAYBE ME SHOULD JUS TAKE CARE O THIS MYSEL

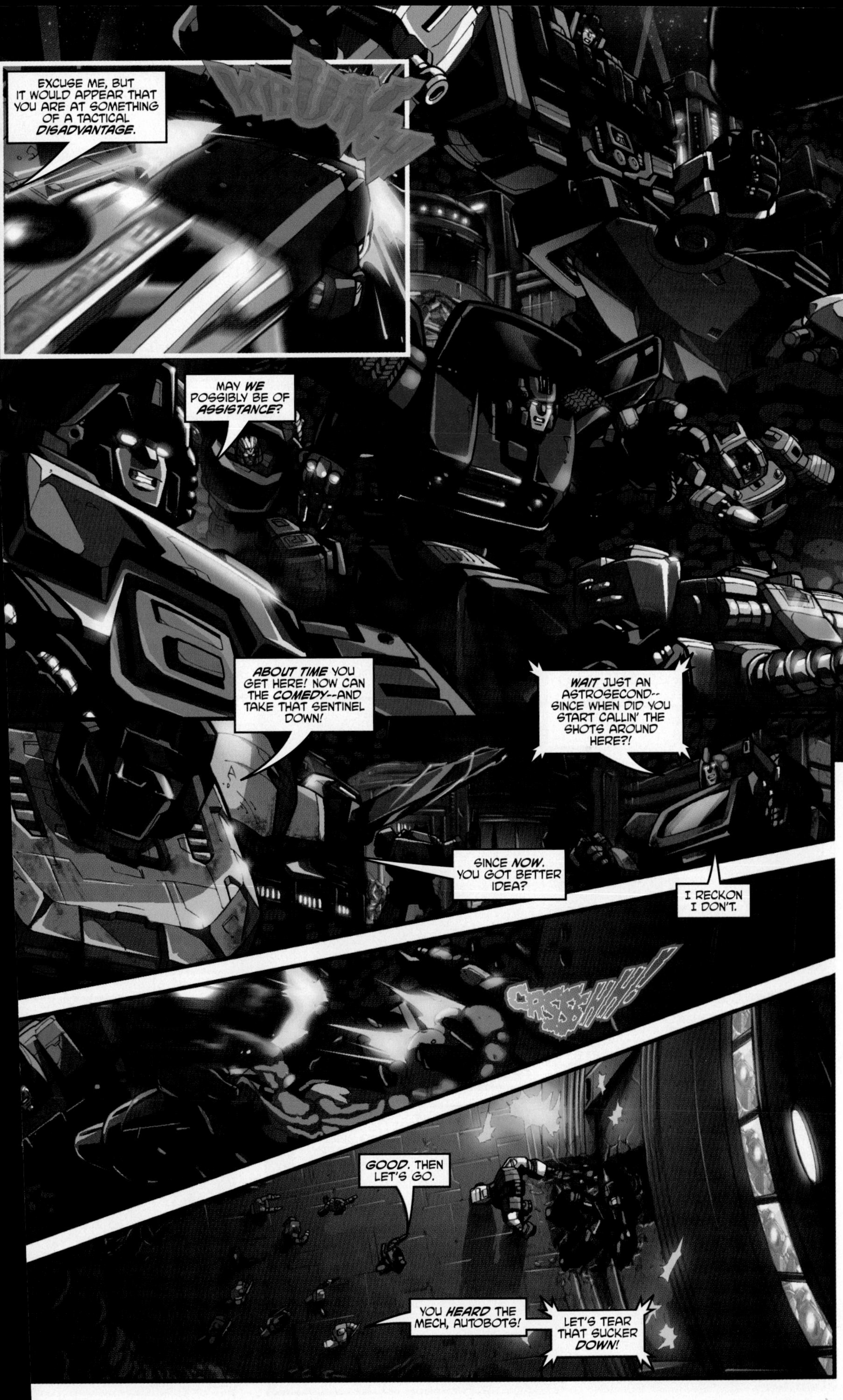
EXCUSE ME, BUT IT WOULD APPEAR THAT YOU ARE AT SOMETHING OF A TACTICAL *DISADVANTAGE*.
MAY *WE* POSSIBLY BE OF *ASSISTANCE*?
ABOUT TIME YOU GET HERE! NOW CAN THE *COMEDY*--AND TAKE THAT SENTINEL DOWN!
WAIT JUST AN ASTROSECOND-- SINCE WHEN DID YOU START CALLIN' THE SHOTS AROUND HERE?!
SINCE *NOW*. YOU GOT BETTER IDEA?
I RECKON I DON'T.
GOOD. THEN LET'S GO.
YOU *HEARD* THE MECH, AUTOBOTS!
LET'S TEAR THAT SUCKER *DOWN*!

BLAST! THEY *DARE* BETRAY ME!

EVEN THE BEST-LAID PLANS AREN'T *FOOLPROOF*, SHOCKWAVE. THE AUTOBOTS, WILL *STORM* THIS TOWER ANY SECOND.

YOU'RE *FINISHED*.

THAT IS THE *LEAST* OF MY CONCERNS. MUCH LIKE YOU, THIS *TOWER* IS *EXPENDABLE*.

I HAVE *UPLOADED* THE CORE CONSCIOUSNESS OF VECTOR SIGMA TO MY *LABORATORY*. MY OBJECTIVE HERE IS ACCOMPLISHED.

IF I WERE YOU I WOULD SPEND YOUR REMAINING MOMENTS REMINISCING ABOUT YOUR BELOVED EARTH--BECAUSE IT TOO WILL BE *MINE*.

AND HOW DO YOU *INTEND* TO DO THAT?

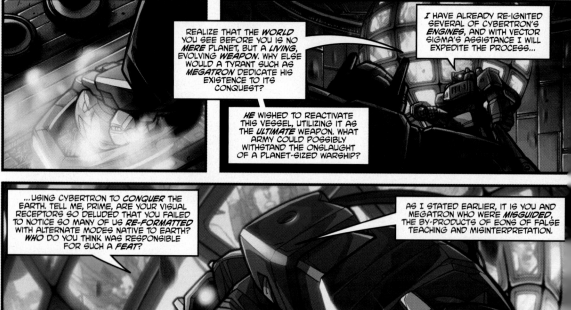

REALIZE THAT THE *WORLD* YOU SEE BEFORE YOU IS NO *MERE* PLANET, BUT A *LIVING*, EVOLVING *WEAPON*. WHY ELSE WOULD A TYRANT SUCH AS *MEGATRON* DEDICATE HIS EXISTENCE TO ITS CONQUEST?

HE WISHED TO REACTIVATE THIS VESSEL, UTILIZING IT AS THE *ULTIMATE* WEAPON. WHAT ARMY COULD POSSIBLY WITHSTAND THE ONSLAUGHT OF A PLANET-SIZED WARSHIP?

I HAVE ALREADY RE-IGNITED SEVERAL OF CYBERTRON'S *ENGINES*, AND WITH VECTOR SIGMA'S ASSISTANCE I WILL EXPEDITE THE PROCESS...

...USING CYBERTRON TO *CONQUER* THE EARTH. TELL ME, PRIME, ARE YOUR VISUAL RECEPTORS SO DELUDED THAT YOU FAILED TO NOTICE SO MANY OF US *RE-FORMATTED* WITH ALTERNATE MODES NATIVE TO EARTH? *WHO* DO YOU THINK WAS RESPONSIBLE FOR SUCH A *FEAT*?

AS I STATED EARLIER, IT IS YOU AND MEGATRON WHO WERE *MISGUIDED*, THE BY-PRODUCTS OF EONS OF FALSE TEACHING AND MISINTERPRETATION.

YOU'RE *MAD*!

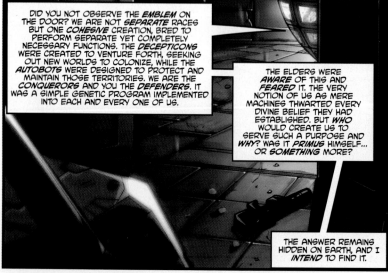

DID YOU NOT OBSERVE THE *EMBLEM* ON THE DOOR? WE ARE NOT *SEPARATE* RACES BUT ONE *COHESIVE* CREATION, BRED TO PERFORM SEPARATE YET COMPLETELY NECESSARY FUNCTIONS. THE *DECEPTICONS* WERE CREATED TO VENTURE FORTH, SEEKING OUT NEW WORLDS TO COLONIZE, WHILE THE *AUTOBOTS* WERE DESIGNED TO PROTECT AND MAINTAIN THOSE TERRITORIES. WE ARE THE *CONQUERORS* AND YOU THE *DEFENDERS*. IT WAS A SIMPLE GENETIC PROGRAM IMPLEMENTED INTO EACH AND EVERY ONE OF US.

THE ELDERS WERE *AWARE* OF THIS AND *FEARED* IT. THE VERY NOTION OF US AS MERE MACHINES THWARTED EVERY DIVINE BELIEF THEY HAD ESTABLISHED. BUT *WHO* WOULD CREATE US TO SERVE SUCH A PURPOSE AND *WHY*? WAS IT *PRIMUS* HIMSELF... OR *SOMETHING* MORE?

THE ANSWER REMAINS HIDDEN ON EARTH, AND I *INTEND* TO FIND IT.

FAREWELL, OPTIMUS PRIME.

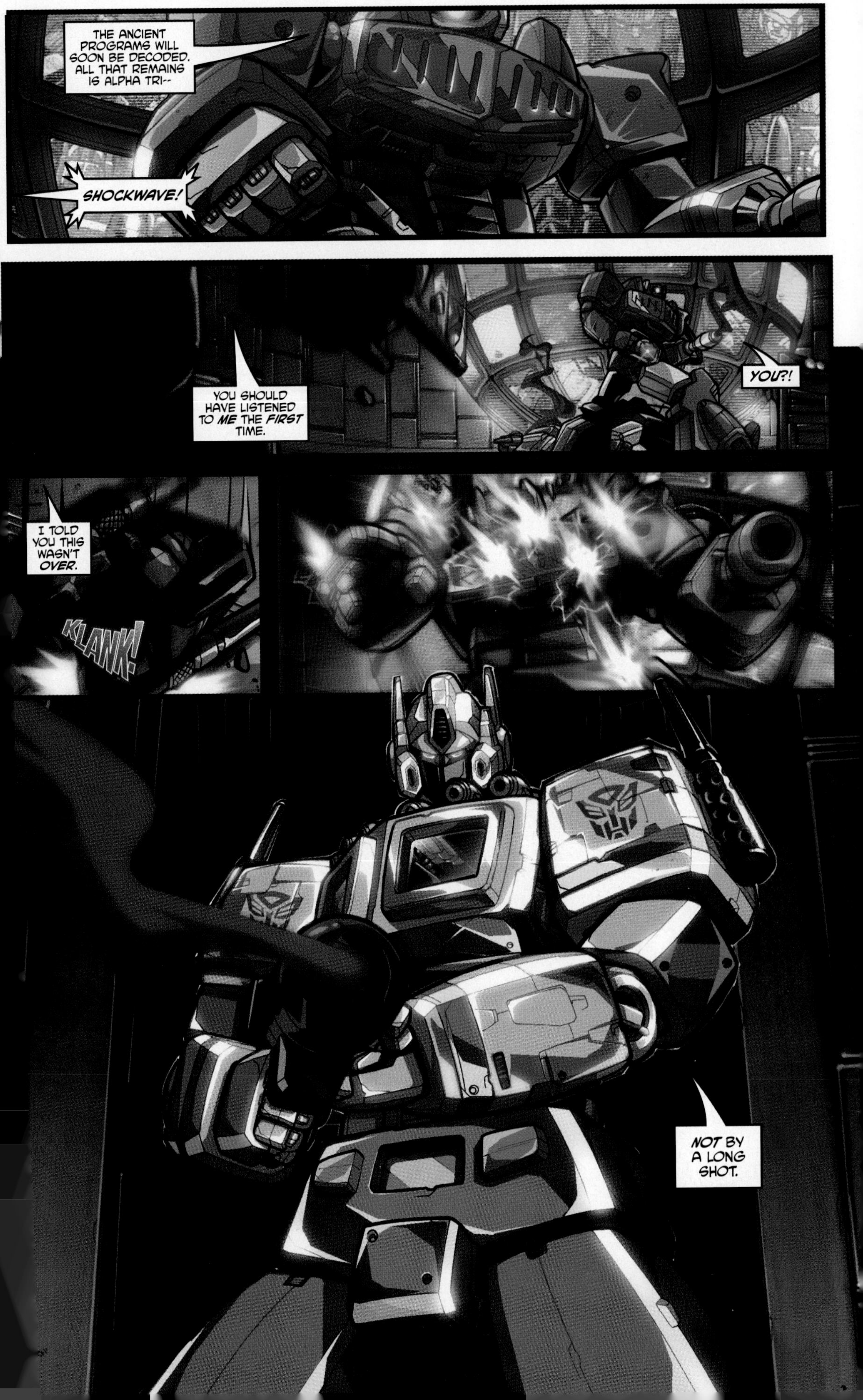
THE ANCIENT PROGRAMS WILL SOON BE DECODED. ALL THAT REMAINS IS ALPHA TRI--
SHOCKWAVE!
YOU SHOULD HAVE LISTENED TO ME THE FIRST TIME.
YOU?!
I TOLD YOU THIS WASN'T OVER.
KLANK!
NOT BY A LONG SHOT.

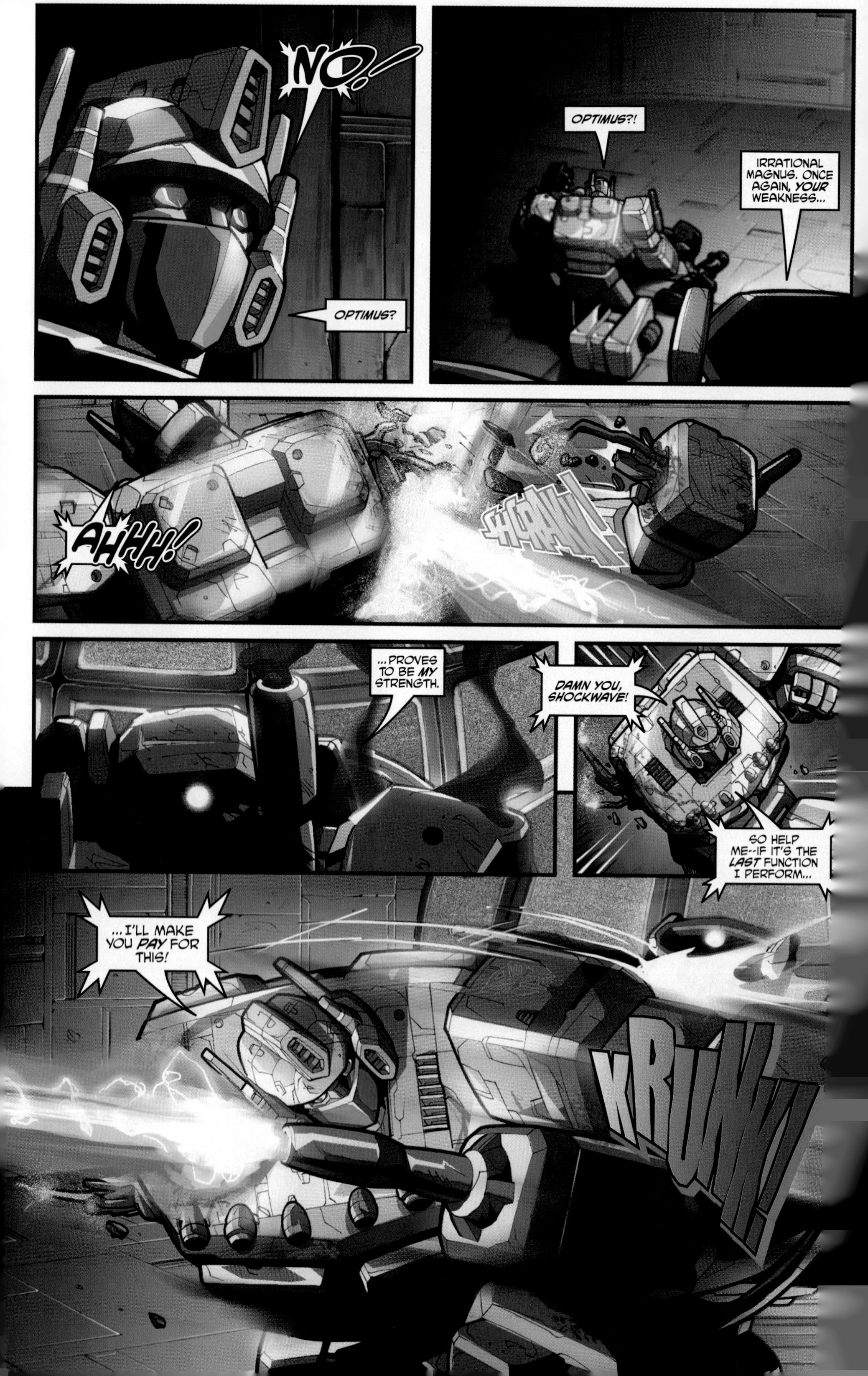
NO!
OPTIMUS?
OPTIMUS?!
IRRATIONAL MAGNUS. ONCE AGAIN, YOUR WEAKNESS...
AHHH!
...PROVES TO BE MY STRENGTH.
DAMN YOU, SHOCKWAVE!
SO HELP ME--IF IT'S THE LAST FUNCTION I PERFORM...
...I'LL MAKE YOU PAY FOR THIS!
KRUNK!

FOR *ALL* OF THIS!

KLANK!

SILENCE!

I HAVE SUFFERED YOUR *INSOLENCE* FOR FAR TOO LONG. THIS PATHETIC LITTLE TIRADE IS *OVER.*

PHYSICALLY, YOU ARE NO MATCH FOR ME!

WHAM

THE *ENERGY TRANSFER MODULES* ENABLE ME TO SIPHON POWER DIRECTLY FROM CYBERTRON AND ITS INHABITANTS, *MAXIMIZING* MY OPERATING SYSTEMS AS WELL AS MAINTAINING ALL *THOSE* WHO HAVE BEEN FORMATTED WITH AN ETM, SPECIFICALLY YOU AND YOUR AUTOBOT BRETHREN--AT A LEVEL THAT I CAN SAFELY *CONTROL.*

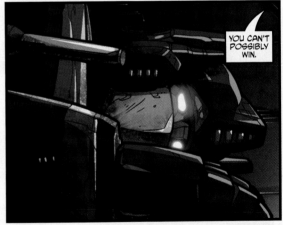

YOU CAN'T POSSIBLY WIN.

...NNN....

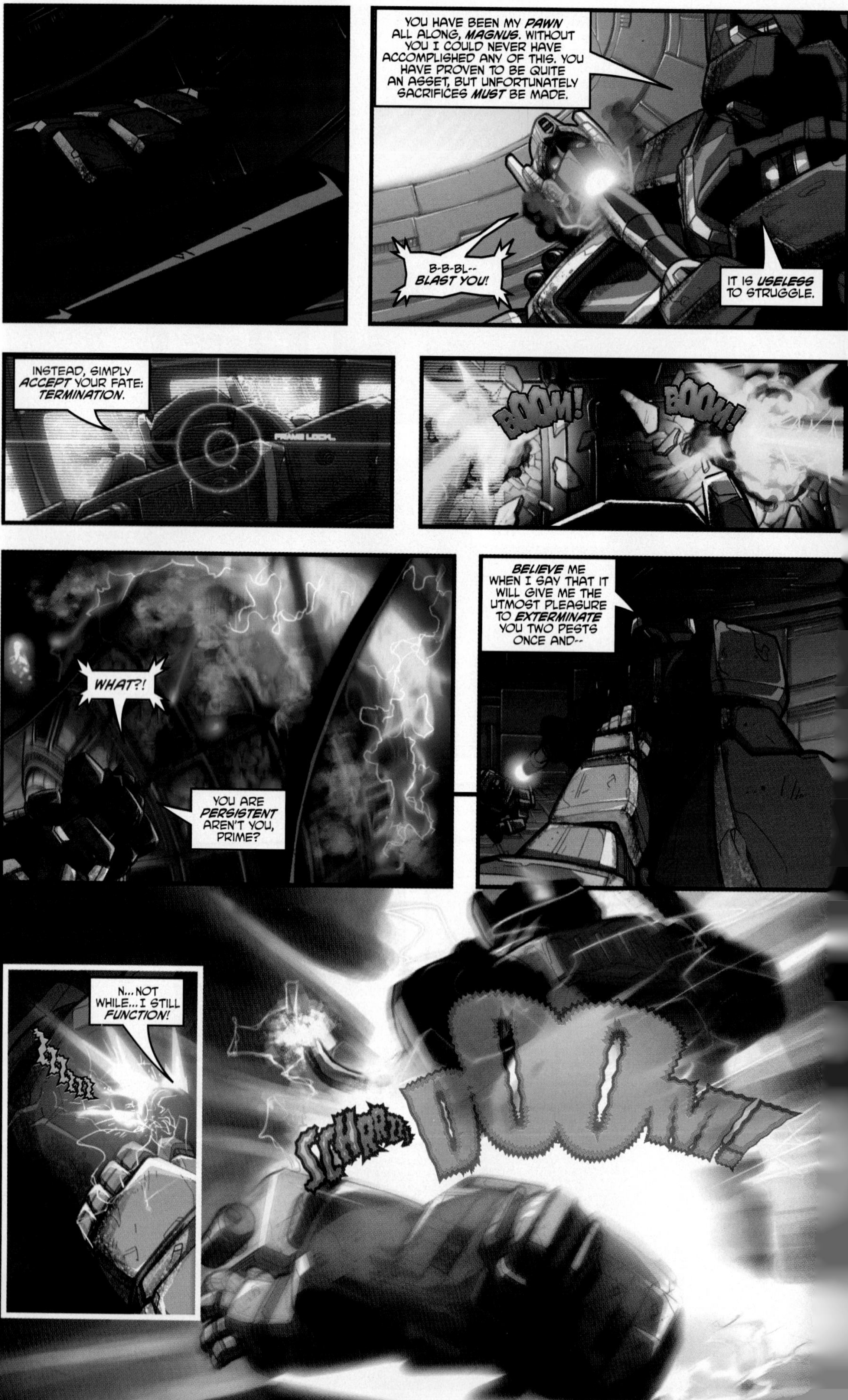
YOU HAVE BEEN MY PAWN ALL ALONG, MAGNUS. WITHOUT YOU I COULD NEVER HAVE ACCOMPLISHED ANY OF THIS. YOU HAVE PROVEN TO BE QUITE AN ASSET, BUT UNFORTUNATELY SACRIFICES MUST BE MADE.
B-B-BL-- BLAST YOU!
IT IS USELESS TO STRUGGLE.
INSTEAD, SIMPLY ACCEPT YOUR FATE: TERMINATION.
FRAME LOCK.
BOOM!
BOOM!
WHAT?!
YOU ARE PERSISTENT AREN'T YOU, PRIME?
BELIEVE ME WHEN I SAY THAT IT WILL GIVE ME THE UTMOST PLEASURE TO EXTERMINATE YOU TWO PESTS ONCE AND--
N...NOT WHILE...I STILL FUNCTION!
SCHRRTT
DOOM!

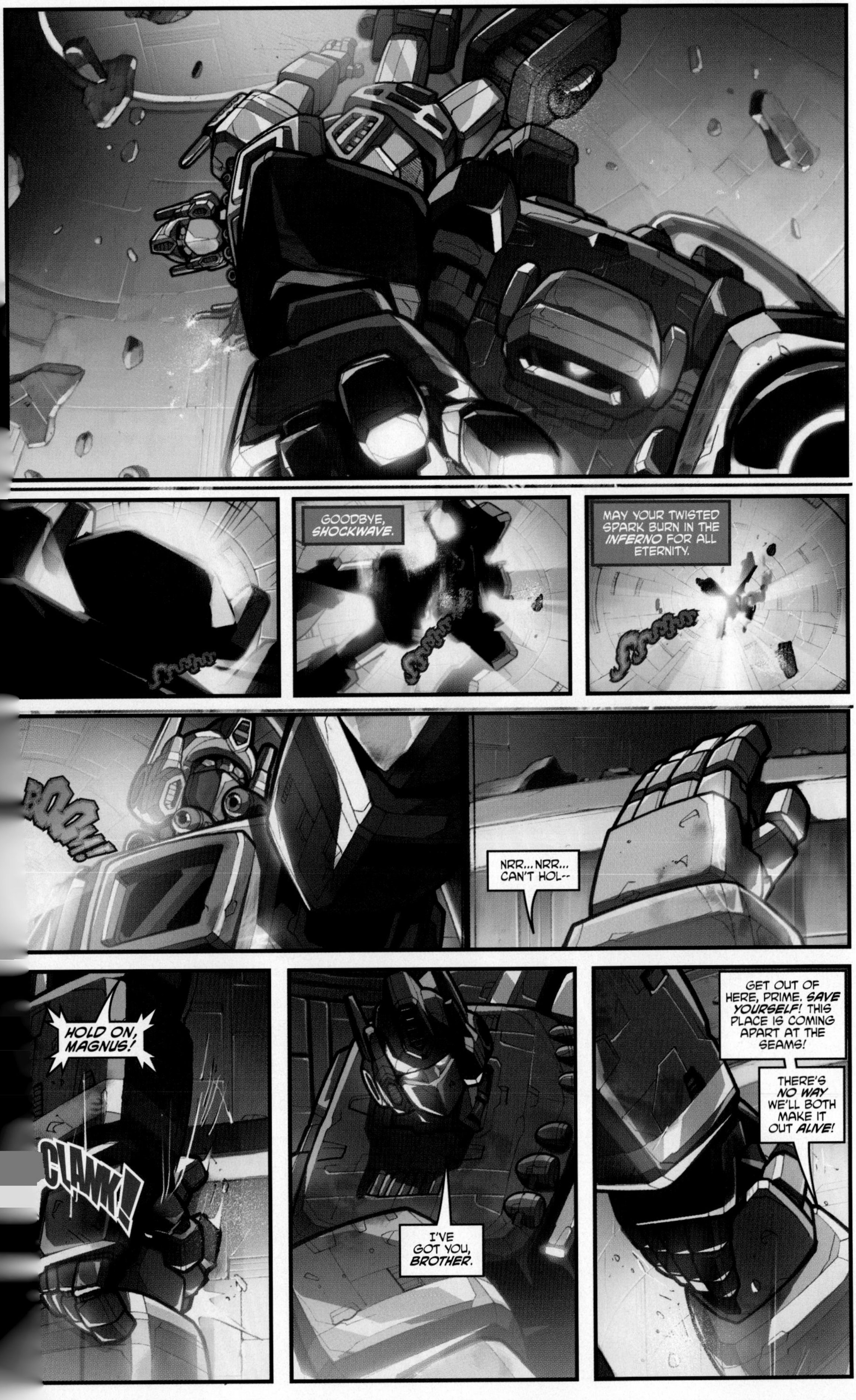

GOODBYE, *SHOCKWAVE*.
MAY YOUR TWISTED SPARK BURN IN THE *INFERNO* FOR ALL ETERNITY.
BOOM!
NRR... NRR... CAN'T HOL--
HOLD ON, MAGNUS!
CLANK!!
I'VE GOT YOU, *BROTHER*.
GET OUT OF HERE, PRIME. *SAVE YOURSELF!* THIS PLACE IS COMING APART AT THE SEAMS!
THERE'S *NO WAY* WE'LL BOTH MAKE IT OUT *ALIVE!*

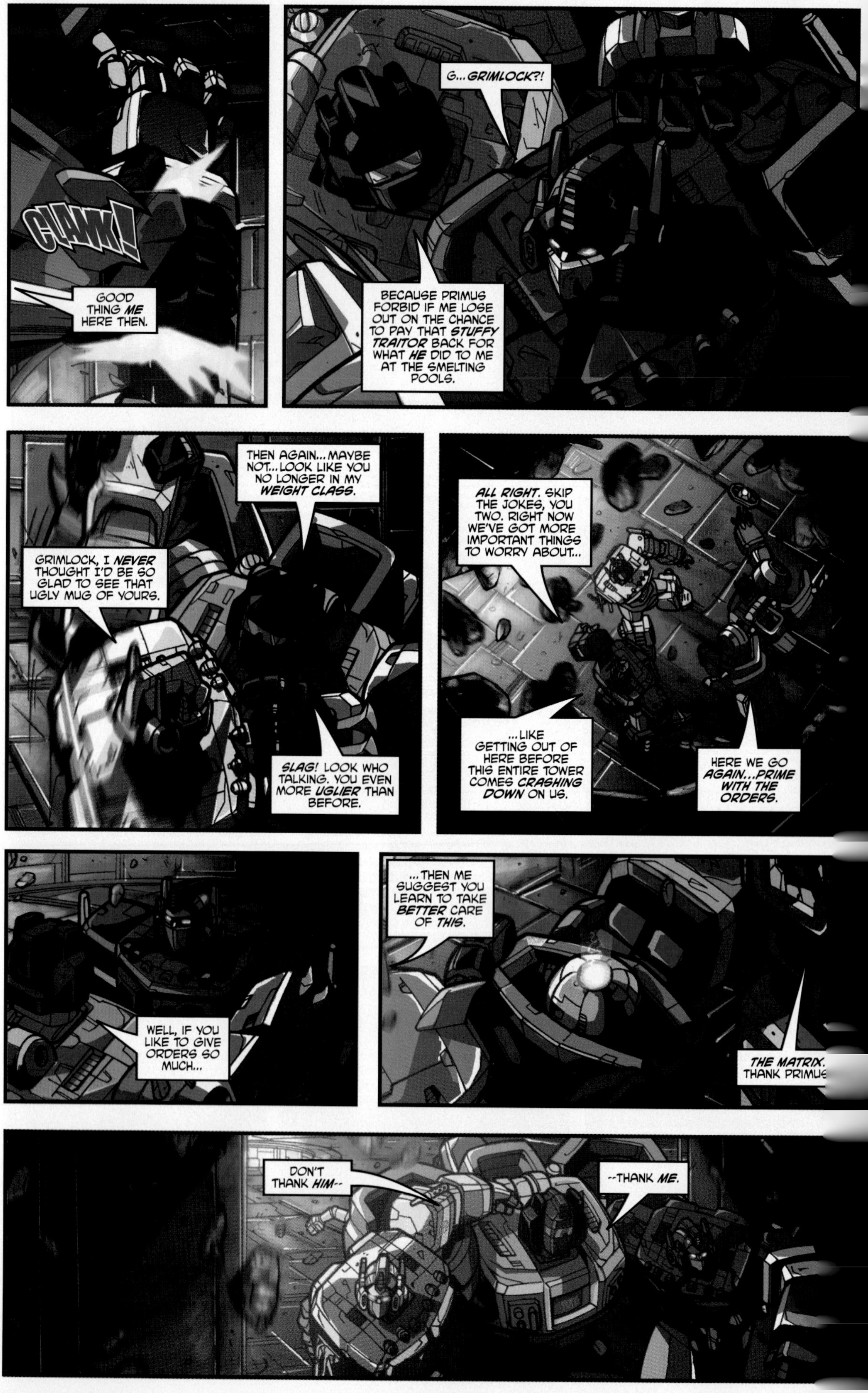
CLANK!
GOOD THING ME HERE THEN.
G...GRIMLOCK?!
BECAUSE PRIMUS FORBID IF ME LOSE OUT ON THE CHANCE TO PAY THAT STUFFY TRAITOR BACK FOR WHAT HE DID TO ME AT THE SMELTING POOLS.
GRIMLOCK, I NEVER THOUGHT I'D BE SO GLAD TO SEE THAT UGLY MUG OF YOURS.
SLAG! LOOK WHO TALKING. YOU EVEN MORE UGLIER THAN BEFORE.
THEN AGAIN... MAYBE NOT... LOOK LIKE YOU NO LONGER IN MY WEIGHT CLASS.
ALL RIGHT. SKIP THE JOKES, YOU TWO. RIGHT NOW WE'VE GOT MORE IMPORTANT THINGS TO WORRY ABOUT...
...LIKE GETTING OUT OF HERE BEFORE THIS ENTIRE TOWER COMES CRASHING DOWN ON US.
HERE WE GO AGAIN... PRIME WITH THE ORDERS.
WELL, IF YOU LIKE TO GIVE ORDERS SO MUCH...
...THEN ME SUGGEST YOU LEARN TO TAKE BETTER CARE OF THIS.
THE MATRIX. THANK PRIMUS
DON'T THANK HIM--
--THANK ME.

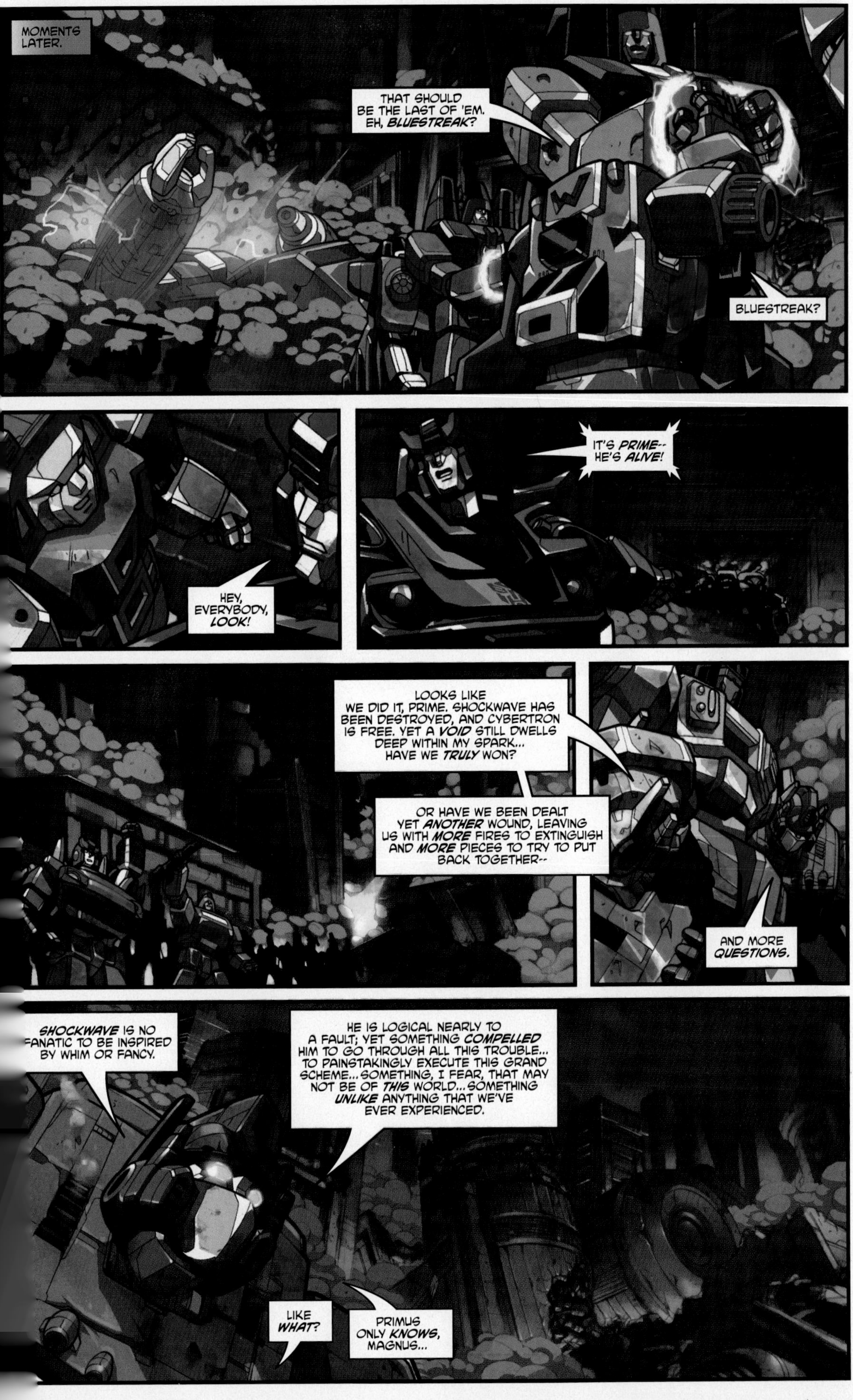
MOMENTS LATER.
THAT SHOULD BE THE LAST OF 'EM. EH, *BLUESTREAK?*
BLUESTREAK?
HEY, EVERYBODY, *LOOK!*
IT'S *PRIME*-- HE'S *ALIVE!*
LOOKS LIKE WE DID IT, PRIME. SHOCKWAVE HAS BEEN DESTROYED, AND CYBERTRON IS FREE. YET A *VOID* STILL DWELLS DEEP WITHIN MY SPARK... HAVE WE *TRULY* WON?
OR HAVE WE BEEN DEALT YET *ANOTHER* WOUND, LEAVING US WITH *MORE* FIRES TO EXTINGUISH AND *MORE* PIECES TO TRY TO PUT BACK TOGETHER--
AND MORE *QUESTIONS.*
SHOCKWAVE IS NO FANATIC TO BE INSPIRED BY WHIM OR FANCY.
HE IS LOGICAL NEARLY TO A FAULT; YET SOMETHING *COMPELLED* HIM TO GO THROUGH ALL THIS TROUBLE... TO PAINSTAKINGLY EXECUTE THIS GRAND SCHEME... SOMETHING, I FEAR, THAT MAY NOT BE OF *THIS* WORLD... SOMETHING *UNLIKE* ANYTHING THAT WE'VE EVER EXPERIENCED.
LIKE *WHAT?*
PRIMUS ONLY *KNOWS,* MAGNUS...

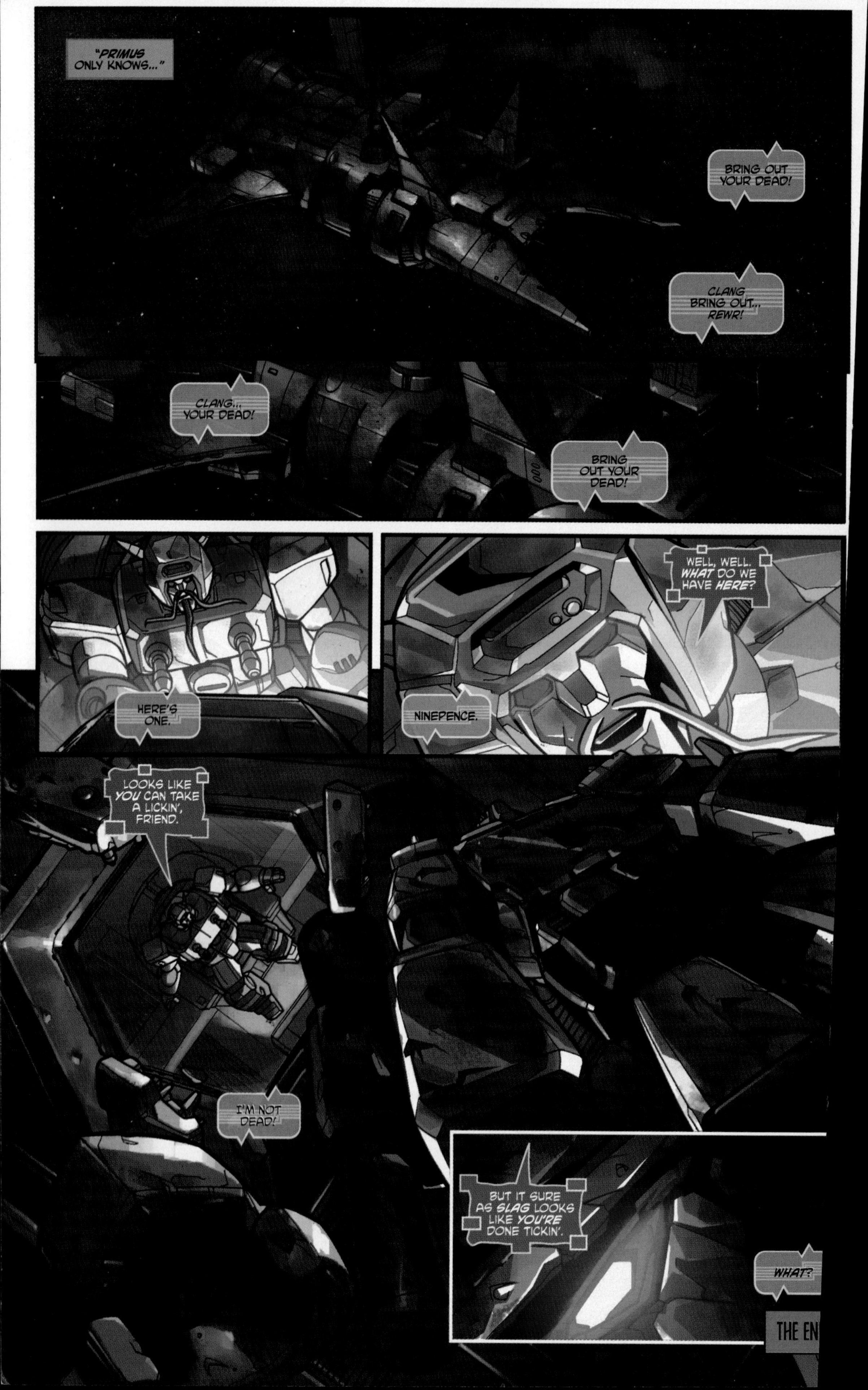
"PRIMUS ONLY KNOWS..."
BRING OUT YOUR DEAD!
CLANG BRING OUT... REWR!
CLANG... YOUR DEAD!
BRING OUT YOUR DEAD!
HERE'S ONE.
WELL, WELL. WHAT DO WE HAVE HERE?
NINEPENCE.
LOOKS LIKE YOU CAN TAKE A LICKIN', FRIEND.
I'M NOT DEAD!
BUT IT SURE AS SLAG LOOKS LIKE YOU'RE DONE TICKIN'.
WHAT?
THE EN

PAT LEE RETURNS

TRANS FORMERS ™

ENHANCED>> 46.7%

TARGET LOCKED
TARGET>> MEGATRON

SPECIAL FEATURES

INTERLOCKING COVERS: ISSUE ONE

The first issue of "*War and Peace*" featured interlocking variant covers, which could be combined to form not just one, but three different *Transformers* battle scenes:

1) Autobots VS Decepticons

2) Autobots/Decepticons VS The Cybertronians

3) Autobots/Decepticons VS Shockwave & The Cybertronians

#1 DECEPTICONS CVR

#1 AUTOBOTS CVR

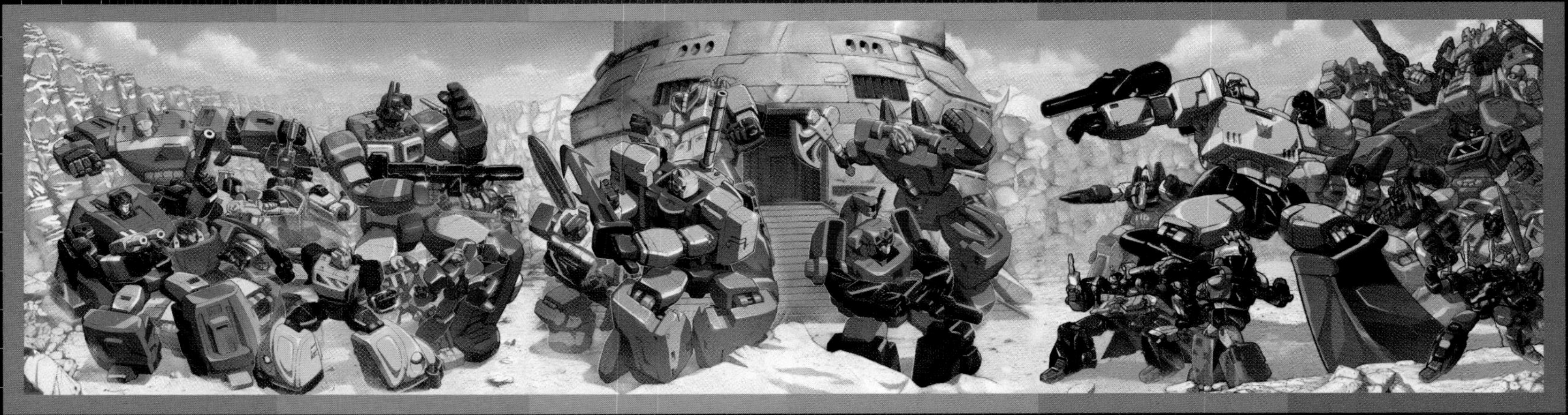

#1 AUTOBOTS CVR (UNFOLDED)

#1 DECEPTICONS CVR (UNFOLDED)

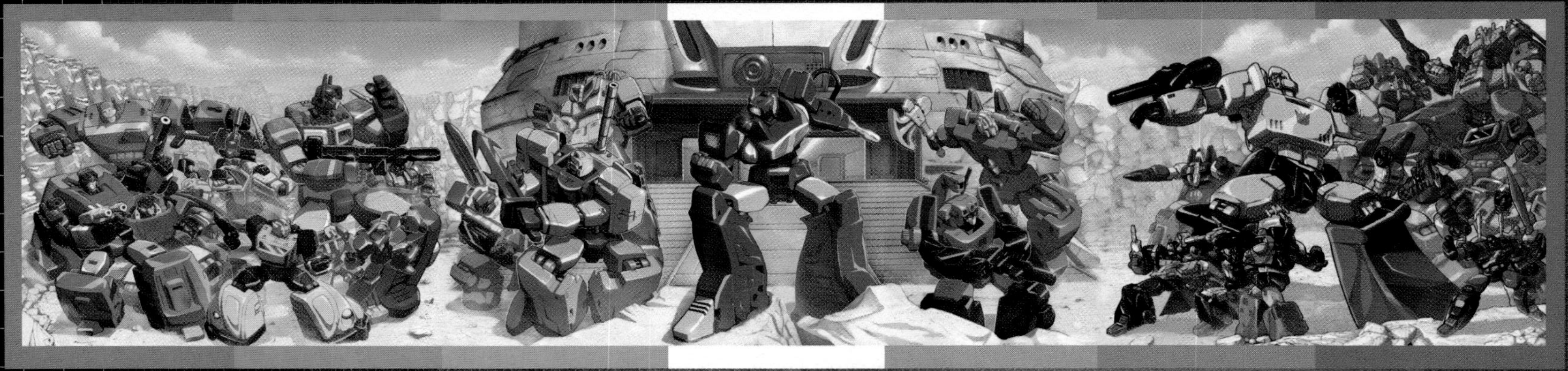

#1 AUTOBOTS CVR (UNFOLDED)

#1 INCENTIVE CVR

#1 DECEPTICONS CVR (UNFOLDED)

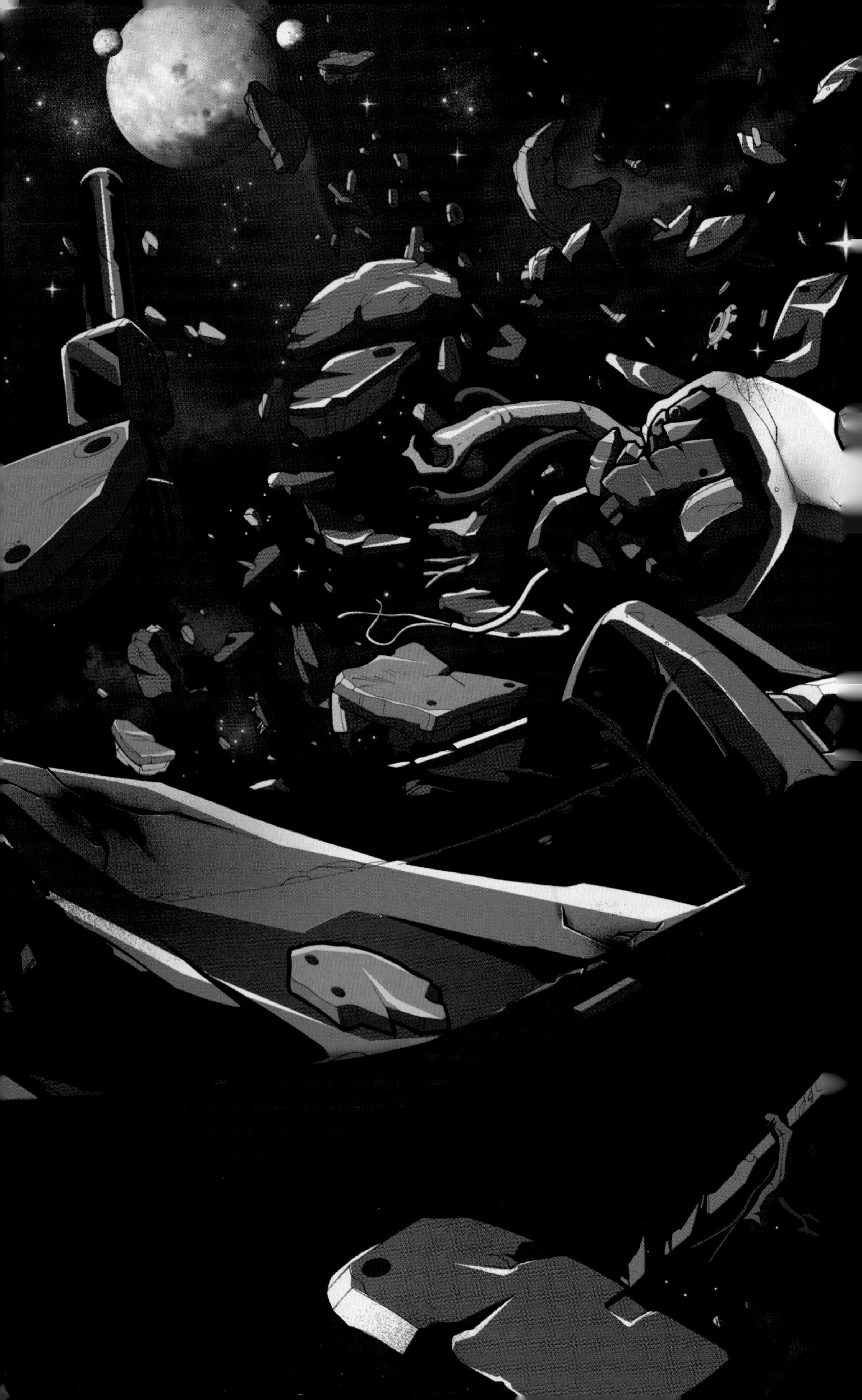

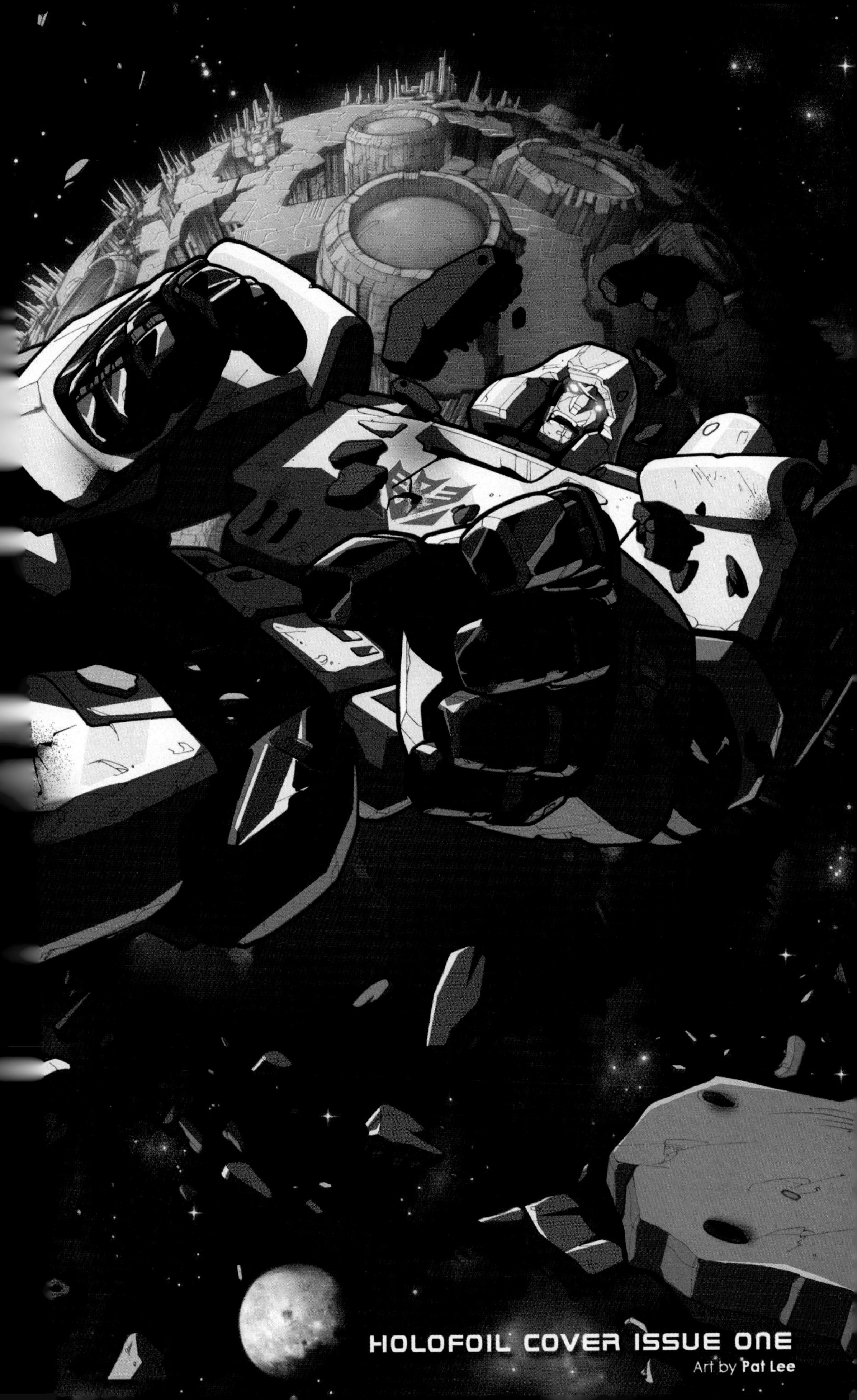

HOLOFOIL COVER ISSUE ONE
Art by **Pat Lee**

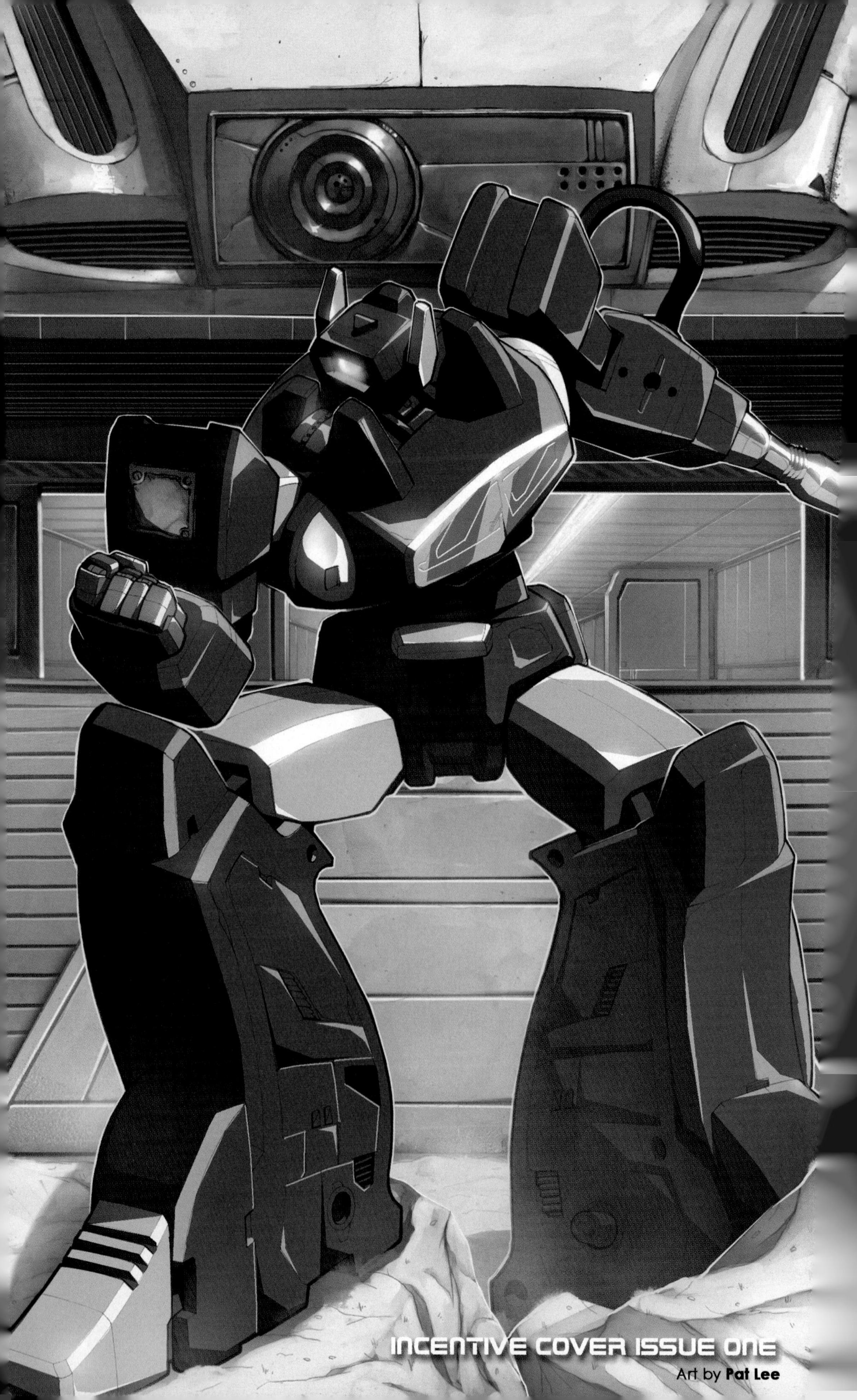

INCENTIVE COVER ISSUE ONE

Art by **Pat Lee**

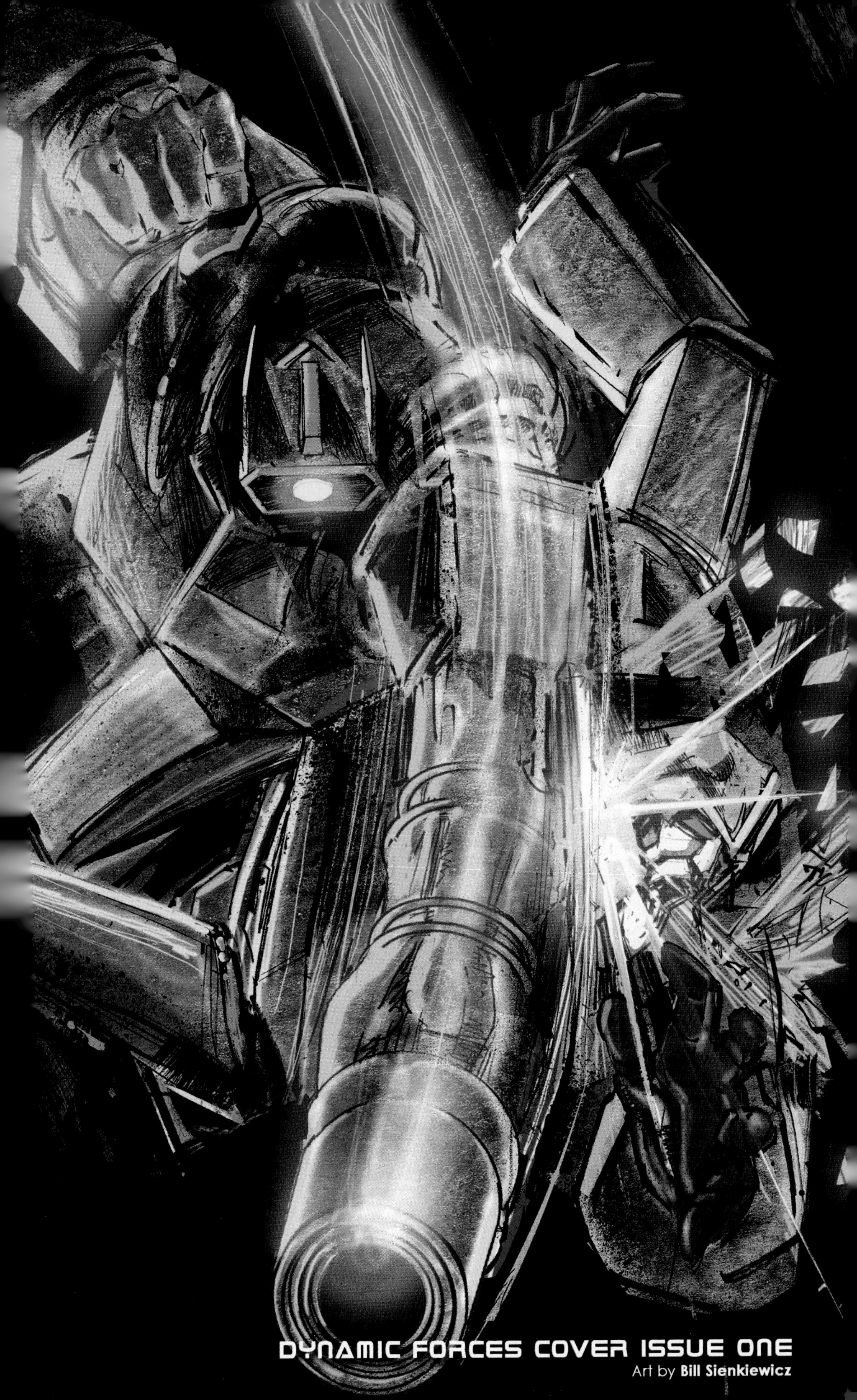

DYNAMIC FORCES COVER ISSUE ONE
Art by **Bill Sienkiewicz**

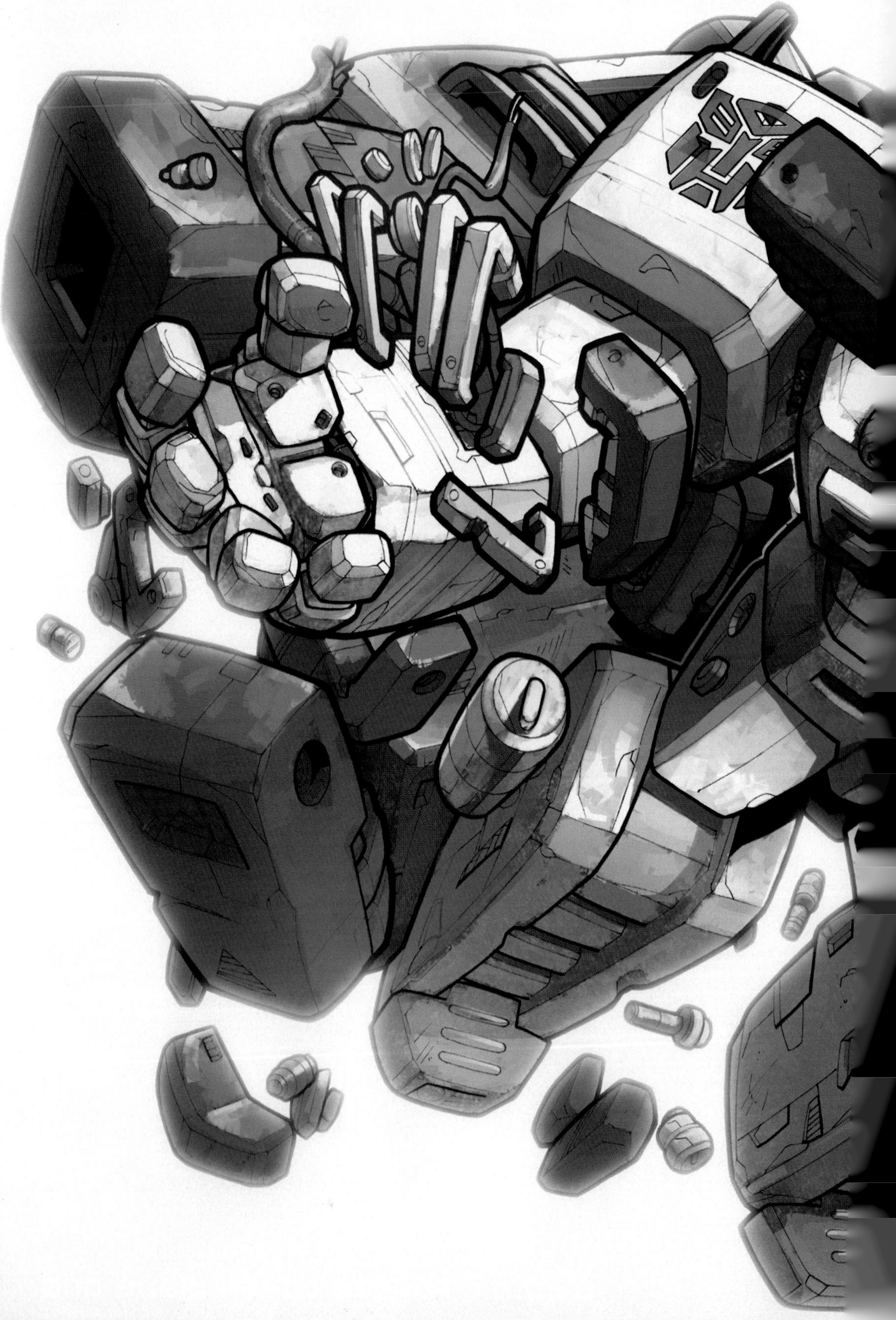

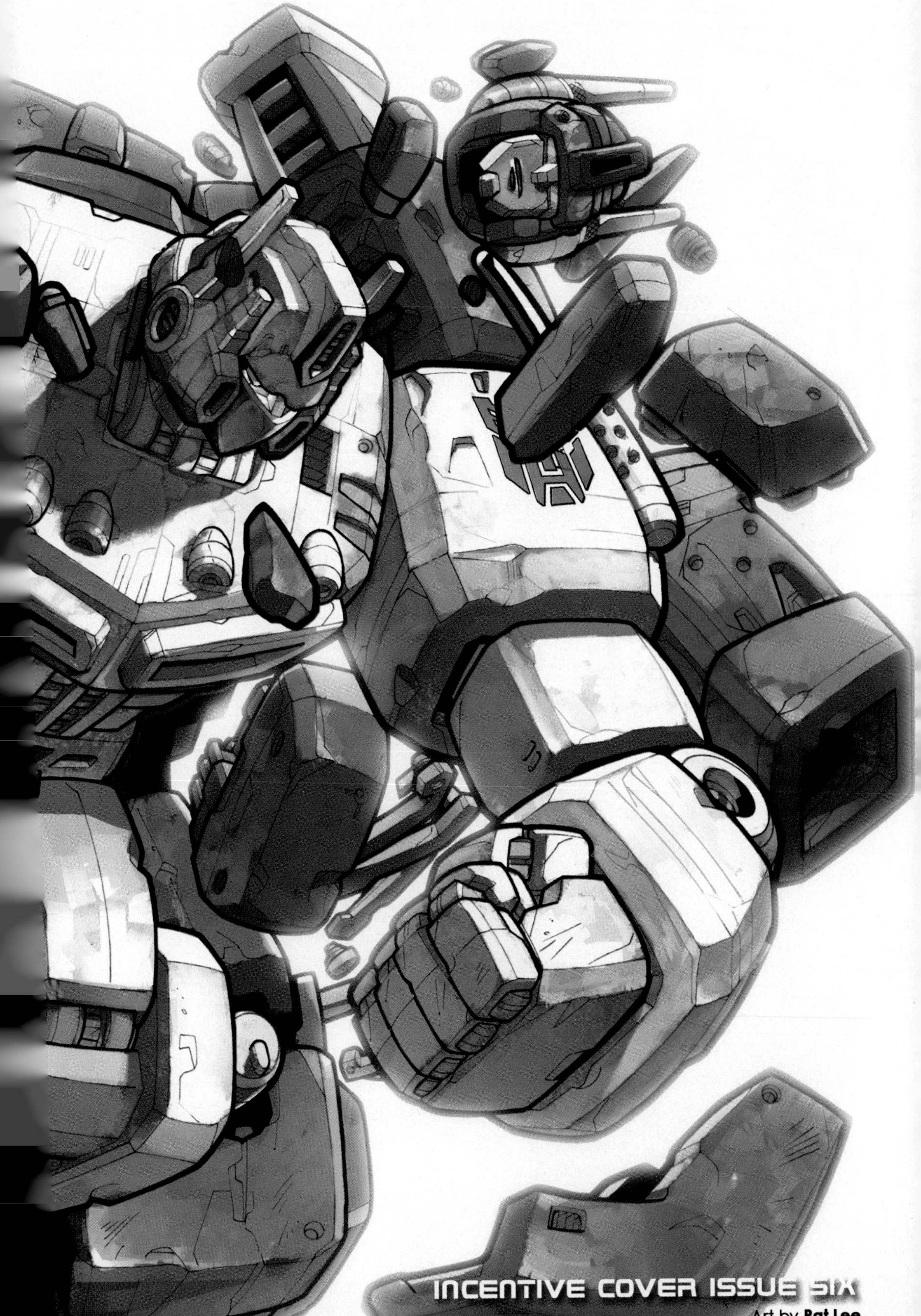

INCENTIVE COVER ISSUE SIX

Art by **Pat Lee**

EASTER EGGS

SUBLIMINAL TRANSMISSIONS

My goal with *War and Peace* was to create an epic Transformers tale that would not only stand the test of time, but also capture the essence of the Generation One experience—you know…the toys, comics, and cartoons…even all those silly gimmicks. Since there are countless nods to all the classic material that came before me throughout this series, I'd like to take this opportunity to present for you my top 10 favorite "Easter eggs" from *War and Peace*.

10 THE MINI-SPIES

Cheesy Transformers toys…or a great form of cheap manual labor? You decide.

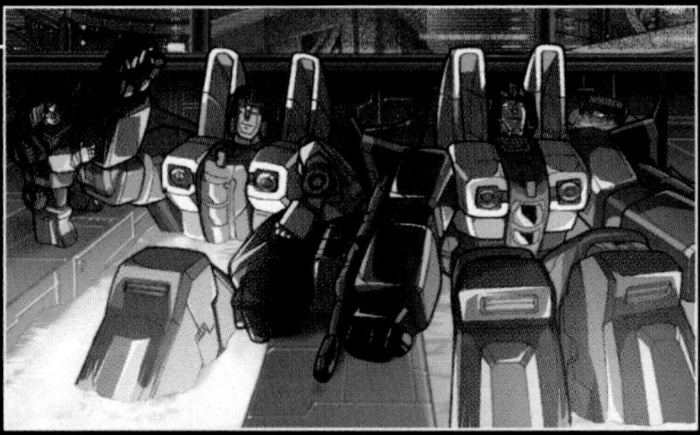

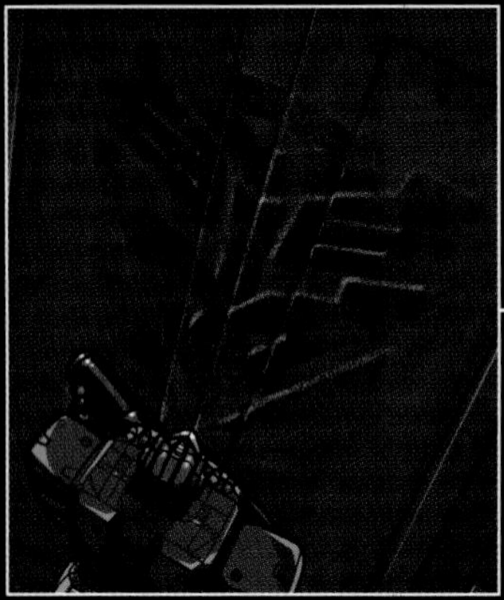

9 'TIL ALL WERE ONE

While perusing the incredible *Transfomers Generations* book, I came across this interesting image…but is this ancient rune a symbol of a more peaceful time…or a much darker era?

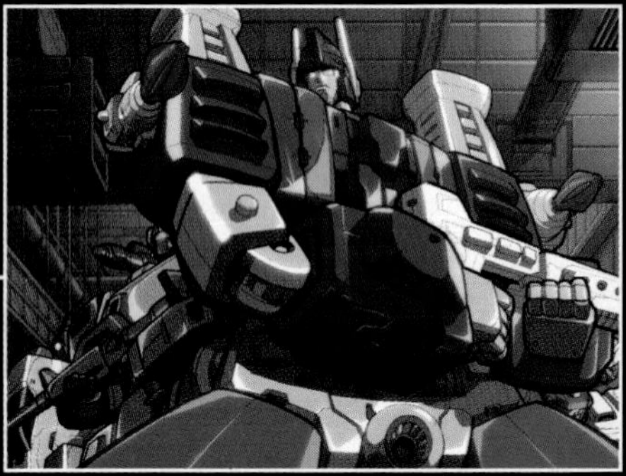

8 WRECKERS REUNITED

A tip of the proverbial hat to Simon's classic *Target: 2006* storyline…my first run-in with the elite commando unit, the Wreckers.

7 DON'T I KNOW YOU FROM SOMEWHERE?

Not exactly a classic, but the episode "The Gambler" did feature the kick-ass Autobot bounty hunter Def-Con (who appears to be a bit down on his luck in *Vol. 2*) teaming up with Smokescreen on the casino planet, Monacus. Note: Smokescreen's comment regarding a "safe bet."

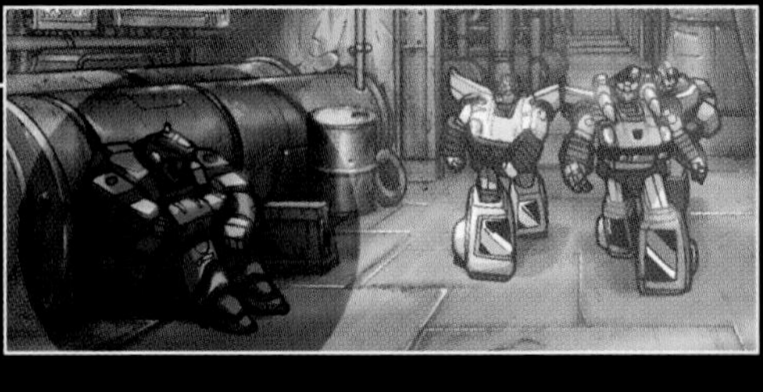

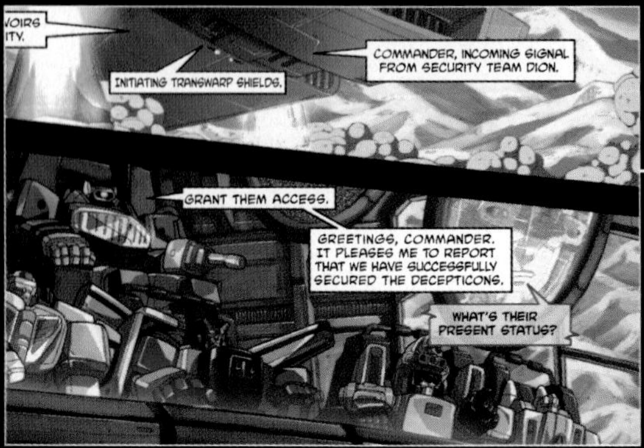

INITIATING TRANSWARP SHIELDS.
COMMANDER, INCOMING SIGNAL FROM SECURITY TEAM DION.
GRANT THEM ACCESS.
GREETINGS, COMMANDER. IT PLEASES ME TO REPORT THAT WE HAVE SUCCESSFULLY SECURED THE DECEPTICONS.
WHAT'S THEIR PRESENT STATUS?

6 PRE-ULTRA MAGNUS

Another nod to the original cartoon series, specifically the episode "War Dawn." It is widely speculated that Dion was the name used by a young Ultra Magnus during his days rolling with a robot by the name of Orion Pax—the Autobot who would someday be rebuilt as the indomitable Optimus Prime.

5 OCD

Okay, I'll admit that my unhealthy obsession with detail can be a bit much, and it has definitely led to some of the jam-packed panels that are primarily responsible for Pat's increasing mental instability! Case in point: notice that while Prime and Megatron duke it out in the foreground, their respective loyal and scheming seconds-in-command (Prowl and Starscream) go toe-to-toe in the background. Also, sneak a peek at Thundercracker and Mirage (two warriors not completely sold on their commanders' causes) battling as well. Within these smaller battles we see the conflict between loyalty and betrayal physically played out, a theme that would be the driving force of the entire series.

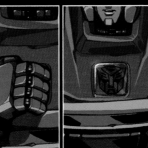

4 CHALLENGE OF THE GOBOTS

Do my eyes deceive me, or could that be the GoBots (fellow transforming robots and former Transformer toy rivals) Leader-1 and Cy-Kill headed for that big junkyard in the sky?

3 RUBSIGN REVELATION

What better explanation for those goofy old rub-sign decals than being a means for hiding allegiances…right?

LOOKS LIKE YOU CAN TAKE A LICKIN', FRIEND.
I'M NOT DEAD!
BUT IT SURE AS SLAG LOOKS LIKE YOU'RE DONE TICKIN'.
WHAT?

2 BRING OUT YOUR DEAD

The opportunity to pay homage to both the great Eric Idle (the voice of Wreck-Gar from *Transformers: The Movie*) and the hilarious *Monty Python and the Holy Grail* (where Idle played the Dead Collector, Sir Robin, and many others) was just too enticing to pass up.

#1 MAGNUS TRANSFORMED

Ever since I was a little kid, I always wondered why Magnus looked like a "white Optimus" underneath. Well, now I know and so do you …sort of. Stay tuned to the upcoming *Transformers: Generation One* ongoing series for more details behind Magnus' relationship with Prime and the origin of that big, shiny suit of armor of his. Shameless plug!

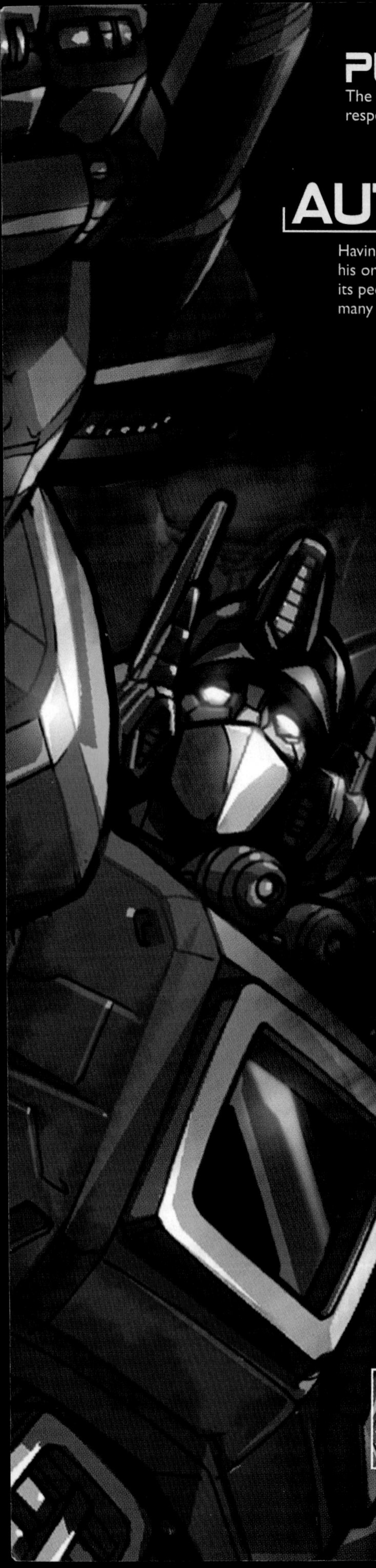

PLEDGING ALLEGIANCE

The following is a virtual scorecard of the various Transformers and their respective allegiances during the events of War and Peace.

AUTOBOTS [EARTH]

Having inhabited and defended the Earth for years, Optimus Prime and his original crew of Autobots grew to accept this organic world and its people as their own...until the arrival of Shockwave's forces forced many of them to return to Cybertron as prisoners.

PRISONERS OF WAR

Fearing for the safety of Earth and intrigued by the events unfolding on Cybertron, Prime surrenders. He agreed to return to Cybertron along with the majority of his crew, some of whom were already captured by Magnus (thanks to Mirage's "betrayal").

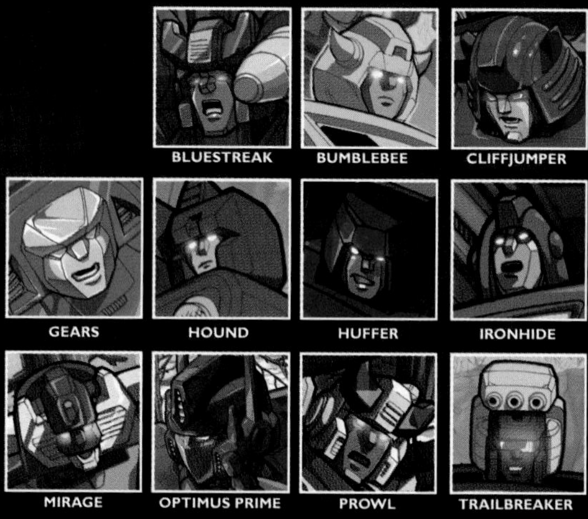
BLUESTREAK
BUMBLEBEE
CLIFFJUMPER
GEARS
HOUND
HUFFER
IRONHIDE
MIRAGE
OPTIMUS PRIME
PROWL
TRAILBREAKER

EARTH'S PROTECTORS

Optimus Prime surrendering without a plan? No way. Prime divided his ranks (and hedged his bets) by ordering a small unit to remain on Earth under the guidance of his third-in-command, Jazz.

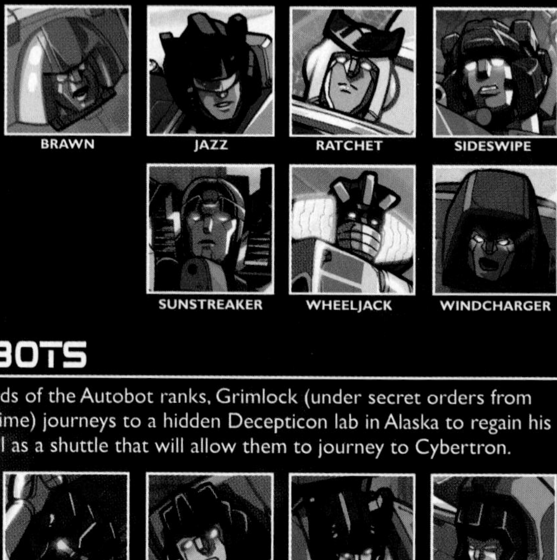
BRAWN
JAZZ
RATCHET
SIDESWIPE
SUNSTREAKER
WHEELJACK
WINDCHARGER

DINOBOTS

The wildcards of the Autobot ranks, Grimlock (under secret orders from Optimus Prime) journeys to a hidden Decepticon lab in Alaska to regain his crew, as well as a shuttle that will allow them to journey to Cybertron.

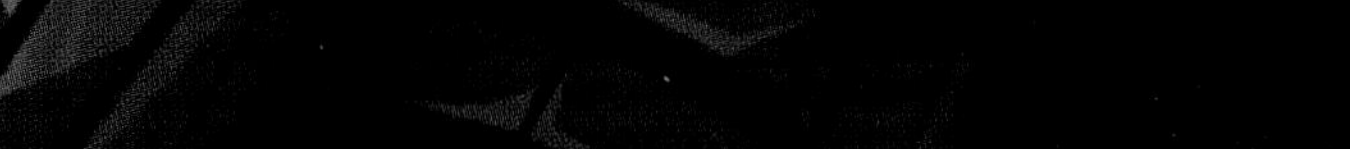
GRIMLOCK
SLAG
SLUDGE
SNARL
SWOOP

AUTOBOTS [CYBERTRON]

Having inhabited and defended the Earth for years, Optimus Prime and his original crew of Autobots grew to accept this organic world and its people as their own…until the arrival of Shockwave's forces forced many of them to return to Cybertron as prisoners.

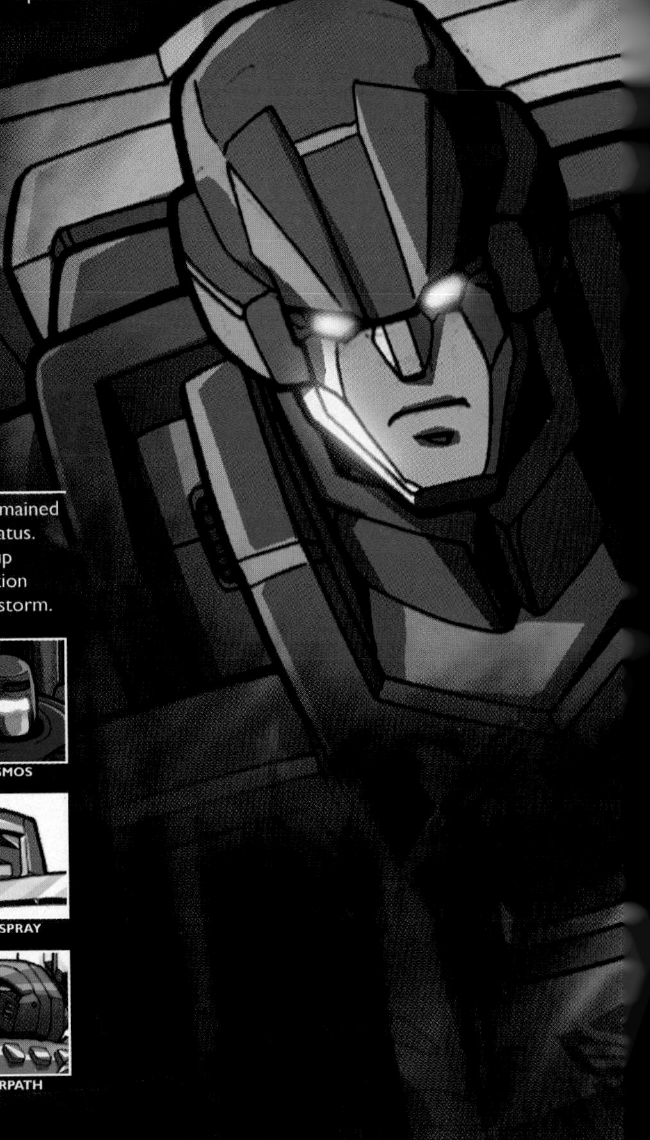

S IN DISGUISE

ub-signs," several veteran Autobots remained
ybertron under the guise of civilian status.
litically minded Smokescreen, the group
their time, covertly analyzing information
neir secret agents, Broadside and Sandstorm.

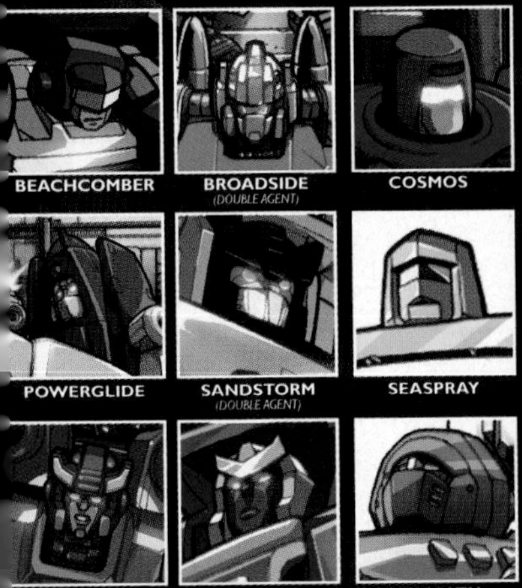

BEACHCOMBER — BROADSIDE (DOUBLE AGENT) — COSMOS

POWERGLIDE — SANDSTORM (DOUBLE AGENT) — SEASPRAY

SMOKESCREEN — TRACKS — WARPATH

RESISTANCE

d that other
nizers were
d resting on
charismatic
ed his own
. Guided by
varrior Kup,
best known
actions and
nark graffiti.

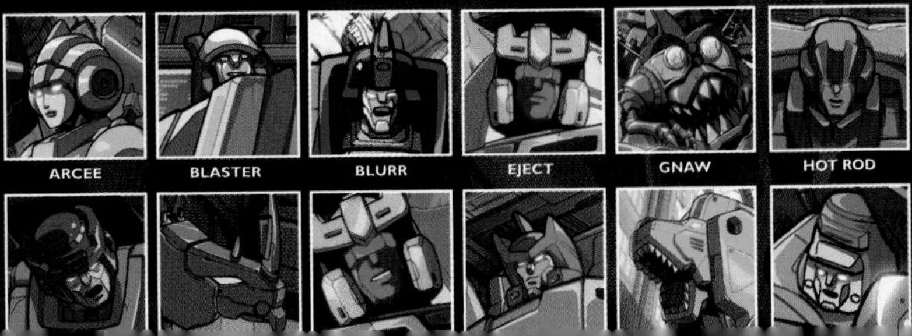

ARCEE — BLASTER — BLURR — EJECT — GNAW — HOT ROD

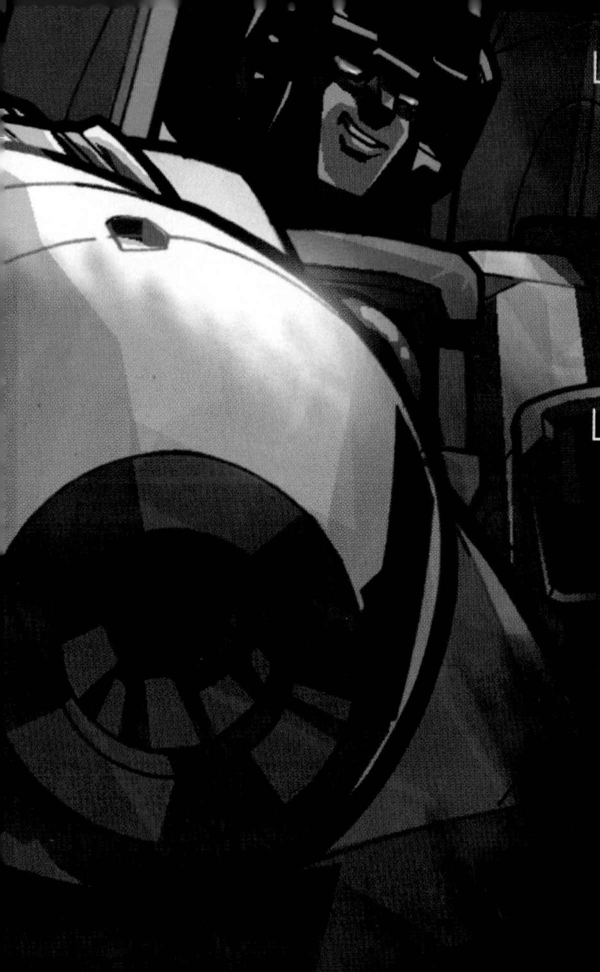

DECEPTICO

Having also been caught off-guard by Shock
machinations, many of the Decepticons fro
and Cybertron were left with no other cho
pledge their allegiance to Shockwave's new

DECEPTICONS

Desiring their assimilation into his growing empire, Shockwave's offer to Megatron's former crew was simple: join him or die.

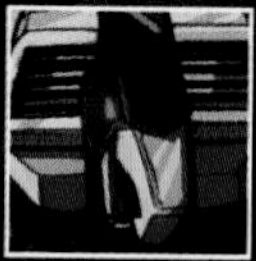
BUZZSAW

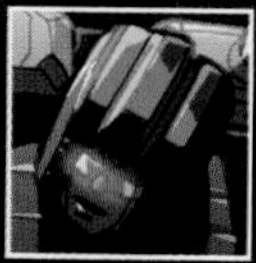
FRENZY

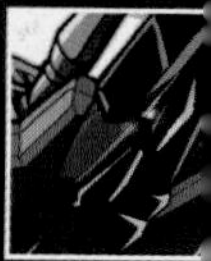
LASERBEAK

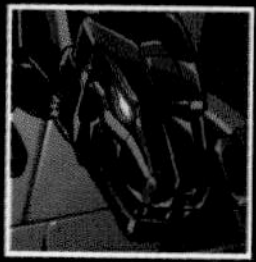
RAVAGE

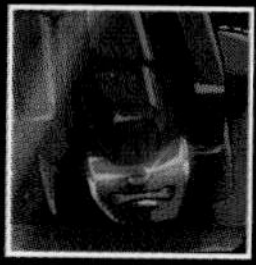
RUMBLE

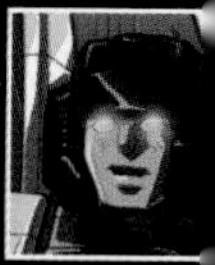
SKYWARP

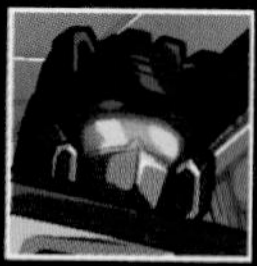
SOUNDWAVE

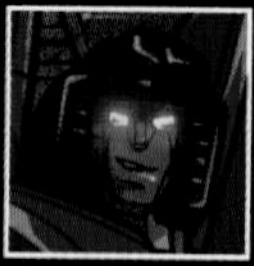
STARSREAM

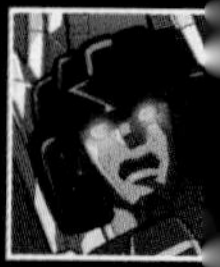
THUNDERCRAC

WAR CRIMINALS

In another empty display of compromise, Shockwave was responsible for the capture and confinement of many of the most feared Decepticon warriors, i.e. any who refused to pledge their allegiance to him.

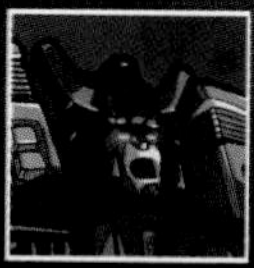
MENASOR

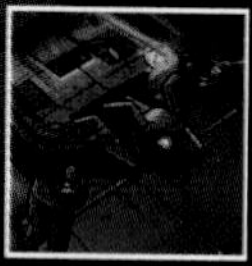
RATBAT

ROGUE OPERATIVES

Secretly taking advantage of their nefarious abilities, Shockwave kept several rogue Deceptions on unofficial retainer, employing them as bounty hunters and enforcers.

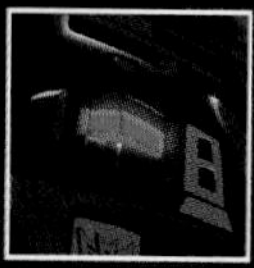
RUNABOUT

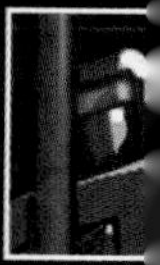
RUNAM

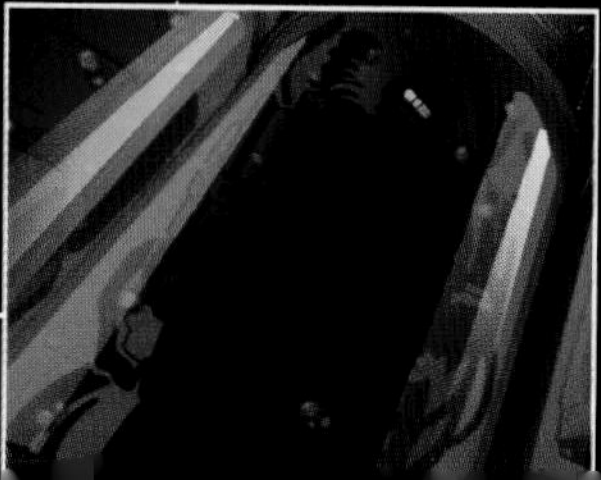

STARSCREAM'S BRIGADE

Ever the opportunist, Starscream found the ideal subordinates for his own militia when he ambushed Rumble and

IN SERVICE OF IACON

Preying upon their physical weaknesses, as well as their desire for a unified Cybertron, Shockwave was able to persuade the majority of Cybertronians to set aside their differences in the name of peace.

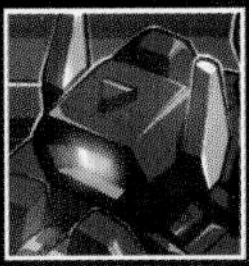
SHOCKWAVE

TRIPLE CHANGERS

Engineered by Shockwave, this next evolution of Transformer technology served as his elite strike force.

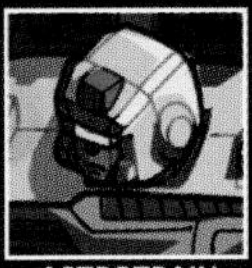
ASTROTRAIN

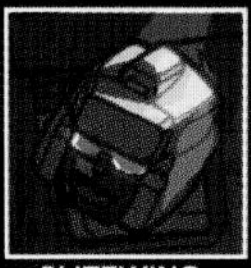
BLITZWING

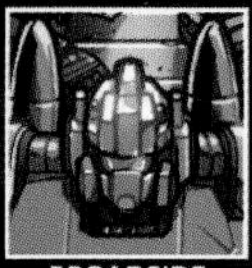
BROADSIDE (DOUBLE AGENT)

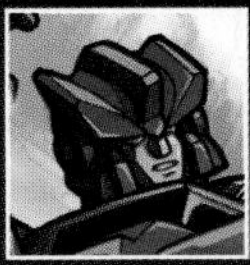
OCTANE

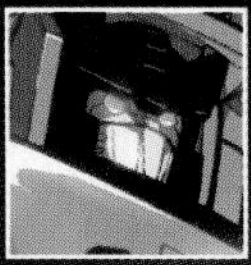
SANDSTORM (DOUBLE AGENT)

SECURITY TEAM DION

Part of Magnus' deal with Shockwave ensured that he would be able to protect Iacon and its inhabitants using his own handpicked unit.

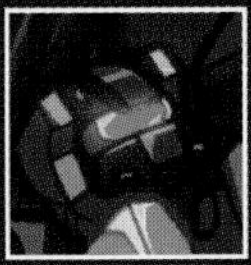
ROADBUSTER

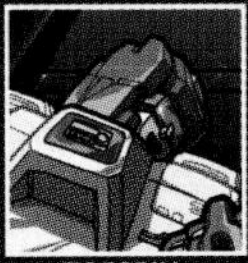
TOPSPIN

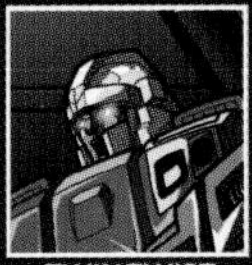
TWIN TWIST

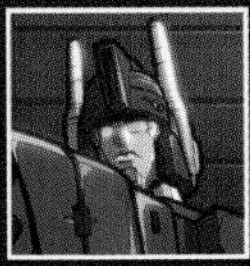
ULTRA MAGNUS

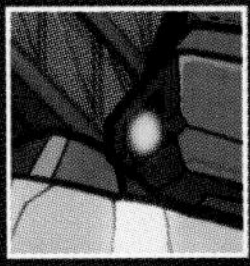
WHIRL

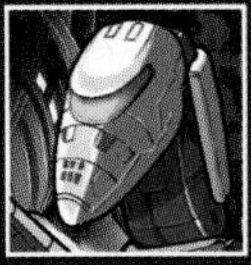
SKY LYNX

HIGH COUNCIL

Placing this specially selected (read: easily manipulated) group of Autobots in power was Shockwave's ultimate gesture of "peace." This figurehead group was primarily responsible for the rebuilding of Iacon, allowing Shockwave to focus on his other pursuits.

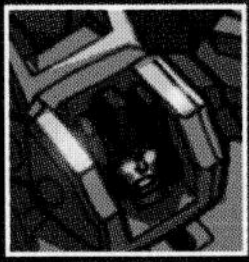
GRAPPLE

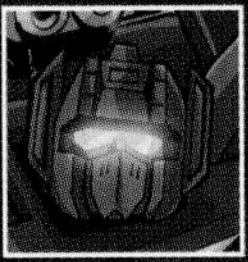
HOIST

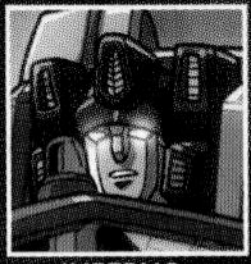
INFERNO

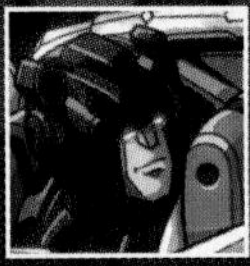
RED ALERT

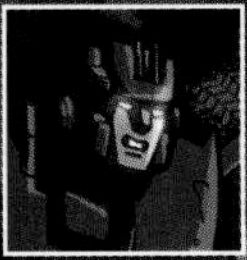
SKIDS

OTHER

Many other Autobots and Decepticons found themselves in the employ of Iacon performing various civilian and military functions.

WARRIORS

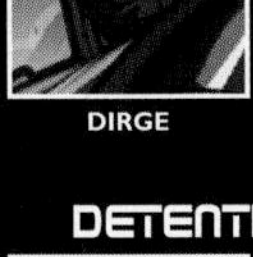
DIRGE

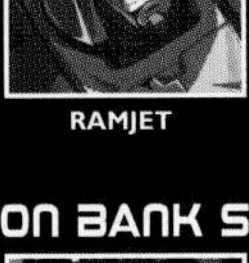
RAMJET

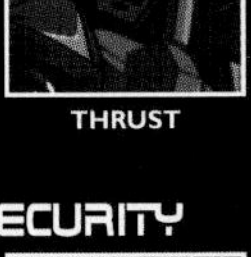
THRUST

CHIEF SCIENCE OFFICER (FORMER COUNCIL MEMBER)

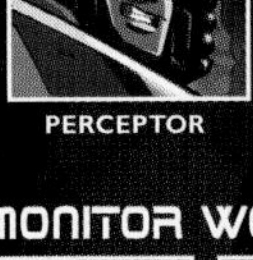
PERCEPTOR

MOBILE POLICE UNIT

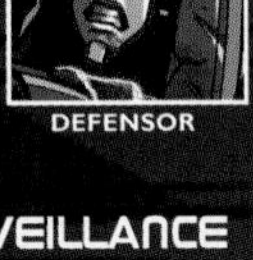
DEFENSOR

DETENTION BANK SECURITY

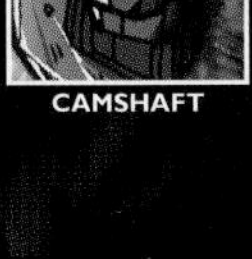
CAMSHAFT

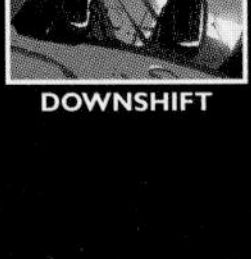
DOWNSHIFT

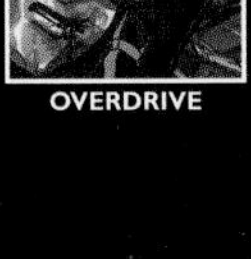
OVERDRIVE

MONITOR WOMB/SURVEILLANCE

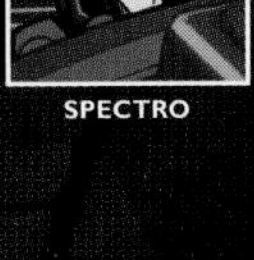
SPECTRO

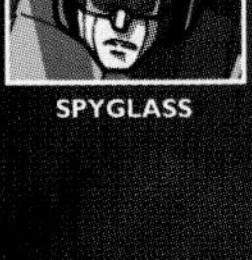
SPYGLASS

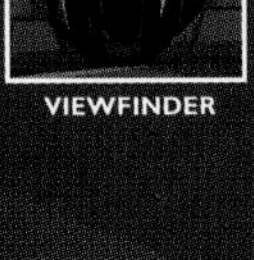
VIEWFINDER

THE TRANSFORMERS GENERATION ONE™

MORE THAN MEETS THE EYE!

THE ONGOING SERIES

Check out the all-new ongoing series based on the timeless TRANSFORMERS: GENERATION ONE franchise. While STARSCREAM and his band of rogue DECEPTICONS make their way towards Earth, PROWL struggles to hold things together as CYBERTRON teeters on the brink of destruction. Plus you'll see the debut of an all-new GENERATION ONE character!

Join fan-favorites creators **Brad Mick & Don Figueroa** as they take the original "Robots in Disguise" to whole new levels of action and excitement!

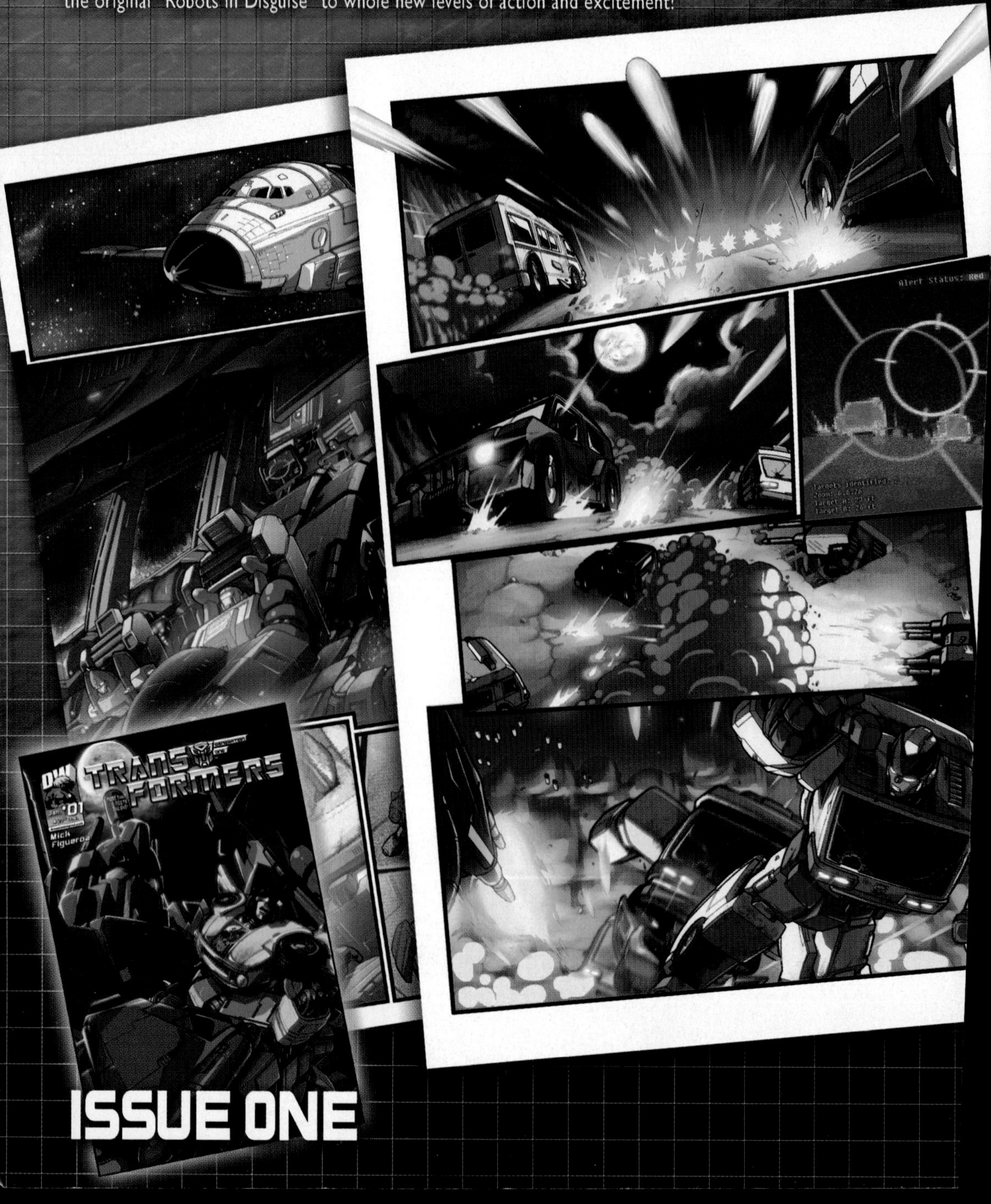
Alert Status: Red
TRANSFORMERS
Mick
Figueroa

ISSUE ONE

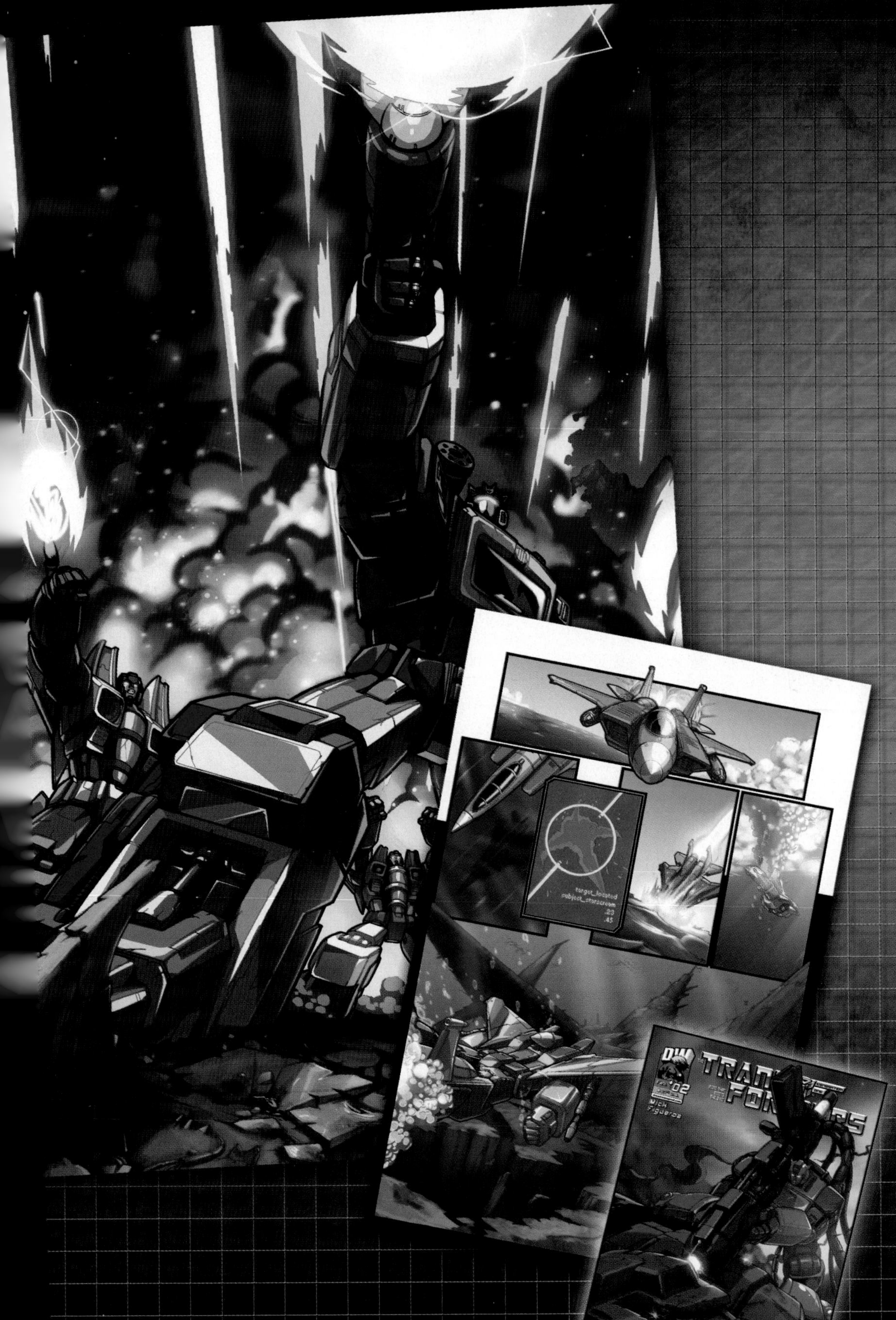

target_located
subject_starscream
.23
.45
DW
02

ISSUE TWO

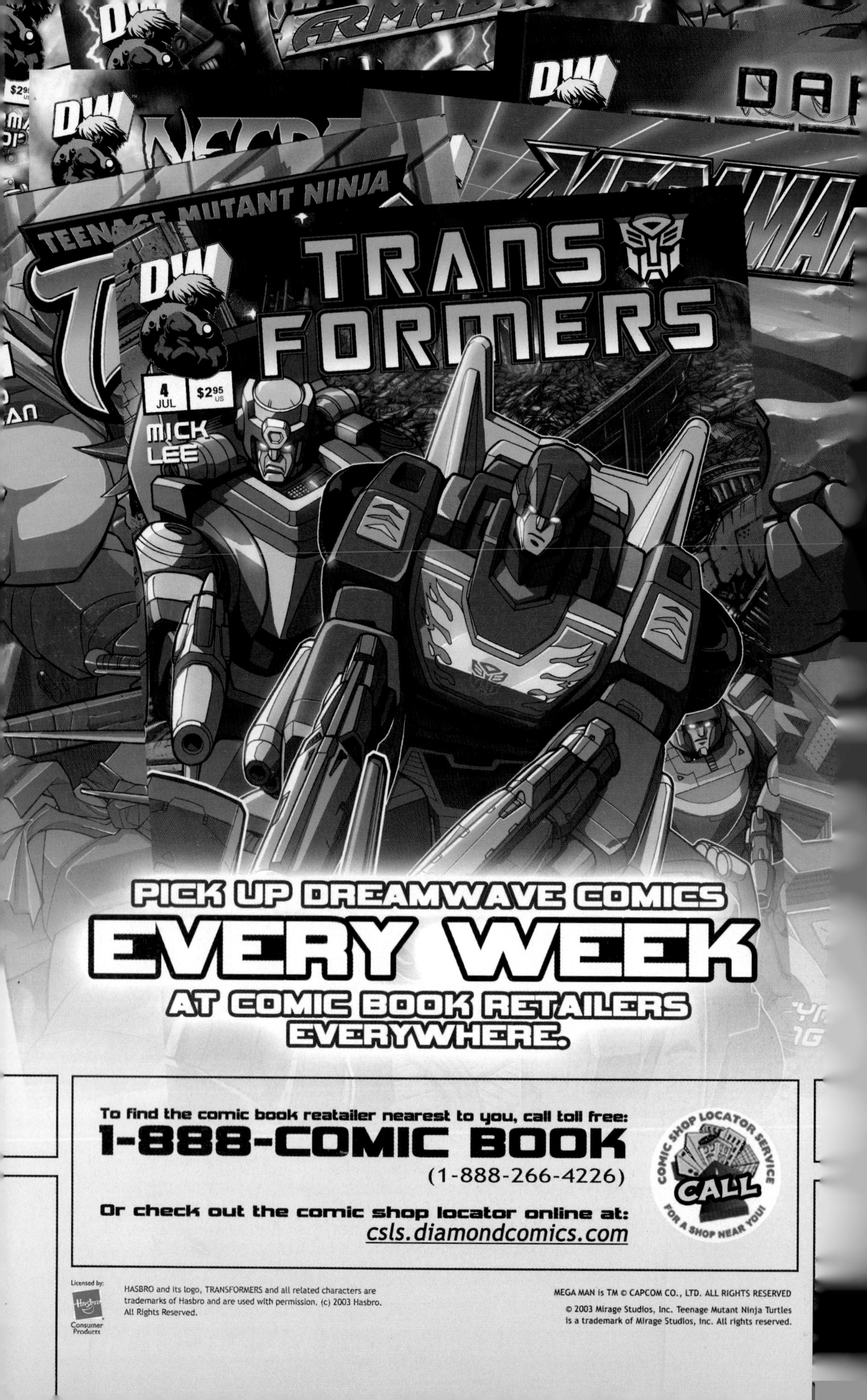
TEENAGE MUTANT NINJA
DW
TRANS FORMERS
4 JUL
$2.95 US
MICK LEE